MODELS OF NATURE

MODELS
OF NATURE

Ecology, Conservation, and
Cultural Revolution in Soviet Russia

DOUGLAS R. WEINER

Indiana University Press

BLOOMINGTON AND INDIANAPOLIS

This book was brought to publication with the assistance of a grant from the Andrew W. Mellon Foundation to the Russian and East European Institute, Indiana University, and the Center for Russian and East European Studies, University of Michigan.

Manufactured in the United States of America

Library of Congress Cataloging-in-Publication Data

Weiner, Douglas R., 1951–
    Models of nature.

    (Indiana-Michigan series in Russian and East European studies)
    Bibliography: p.
    Includes index.
    1. Nature conservation—Soviet Union. 2. Nature conservation—Social aspects—Soviet Union.
    3. Soviet Union—Social conditions—1917–
    4. Communism and Culture—Soviet Union. I. Title.
    II. Series.
    QH77.S626W45   1988   333.95'16'0947   87-45370
    ISBN 0-253-33837-9

1 2 3 4 5 92 91 90 89 88

To My Parents

CONTENTS

Map of Soviet Zapovedniki *circa 1933, page 245*
Photographs and Illustrations follow page 100

PREFACE

During the salad days of the ecology movement in the United States many wondered whether other societies had experienced any greater success than our own in avoiding serious environmental harm. Some speculated, reasonably enough, that the example of the Soviet Union, with its centrally planned economy and proclaimed commitment to community well-being, might be instructive. Recent studies have made clear, however, that guarding the integrity of the natural environment had as low a priority in the USSR as it had in the West.

Understandably, but mistakenly, students of Soviet environmental policy tended to believe that the disappointing record of recent years was simply a continuation of past failings. Claims by Soviet authors that Lenin took an active role in conservation matters were dismissed by American students as hagiographical dross. It is true that a few scholars in this country have shown an awareness of early Russian conservation activity, but they have located the golden age in the decade before the 1917 Revolution and viewed what followed as an uninterruptedly grim Bolshevik wasteland.

Soviet authors, too, by their omissions, have helped to sustain the impression that there was little to investigate in Russian conservation before Khrushchev. To a considerable extent, that is a result of the continuing political difficulties facing Soviet historians who seek to treat events of the late 1920s and 1930s. The paucity of literature on early Soviet conservation has been compounded, unhappily, by the attenuation of this social movement from the mid-1930s through the late 1950s. When I. I. Prezent and T. D. Lysenko cast their shadows over the early Soviet conservation movement and the discipline of ecology, they brought ruin to those enterprises, just as they did to genetics when they wielded unbridled power in that field. While the Lysenko affair in genetics attained worldwide notoriety, the fate of Soviet conservation and ecology languished in relative obscurity.

Although it is impossible to say for certain why that has been so, an unlucky combination of factors seems to have been at work. First, conservation and ecology lacked their Vavilov. No one in those fields enjoyed the degree of international prominence of the plant geneticist (or shared the lurid circumstances of his martyrdom), and Prezent and Lysenko could more easily draw the veil of historical amnesia over their less well-known ecologist adversaries.

A second reason grows out of the divergent histories of the sciences themselves. When the modern evolutionary synthesis—"Mendelism-Morganism," as it was derisively referred to in the late 1940s—was repudiated by Lysenko and his followers in favor of a vague Lamarckism, educated people everywhere recoiled in shock. Through crude political interference, beliefs endorsed by the overwhelming majority of the international biological community had been arbitrarily declared reactionary and in error. Worse still, in their stead, hereditary and evolutionary mechanisms that had been rejected decades earlier were elevated to positions of official approval. The ordeal of Soviet genetics became a vivid parable of legitimate science quashed by politics and ideological dogmatism.

The situation in conservation and community ecology was substantially different. Here, no worldwide consensus existed as to the fundamental tenets of environmental policy or ecological theory. On the contrary, these fields were characterized by controversy and diversity. The suppression of the leading Soviet approaches in conservation and ecology, in this context, was not seen as a devastating blow to legitimate, empirical science—unlike the suppression of genetics. Owing to the same lack of consensus in ecology, the alternative ecological notions favored by Prezent and Lysenko never garnered the flamboyant aura of illegitimacy that surrounded their ideas about heredity and speciation. Perhaps operating here as well were deep-seated cultural assumptions shared by Soviets and Westerners alike. For a long time our cultures have elevated to paramountcy in science those branches, such as physics and chemistry, that have enabled us to predict and manipulate natural phenomena. In biology, the fields that have most approximated this mechanistic ideal are molecular biology and genetics. Ecology, by contrast, particularly until the 1960s, represented a largely descriptive science with little predictive power, "merely" concerned with the messy "loosely ordered systems" of life, to use R. H. Whittaker's apt description. It hardly seems strange that our power-oriented scientific culture took quick note of an assault on genetics but remained blissfully unaware of the subjugation of a gentle, descriptive science.

This book is an attempt to remove the historical veil. What I have found underneath is a rich weave of bureaucratic intrigue, scientific politics, tragedy, and glory. In what will be a surprise to many, through the early 1930s the Soviet Union was on the cutting edge of conservation theory and practice. Russians were first to propose setting aside protected territories for the study of ecological communities, and the Soviet government was first to implement that idea. Furthermore, Russians pioneered the suggestion that regional land use could be planned and degraded landscapes rehabilitated on the basis of those ecological studies. These ideas and strategies now guide not just Soviet policies concerning protected territories but those of many nations. They have even been enshrined internationally in the United Nations' Biosphere Reserves Program, in which our own country has participated.

Russian and early Soviet achievements in the field of community ecology proper—so central to our story—are no less imposing. Suffice it to say that Russians pioneered phytosociology, the individualistic theory of plant distribution, and the trophic-dynamics, or ecological energetics, paradigm.

It is easy to imagine the excitement I felt as I rediscovered Soviet conservation and ecology's dazzling past in a treasure trove of antique journals—some with octavos still uncut. That is the researcher's paydirt. The challenges facing me as a historian, however, were just beginning. W. S. Cooper, the American ecologist, once described ecological succession as a braided stream. Human affairs are often much like ecological phenomena. The interconnected history of Soviet conservation and ecology was just such a dauntingly complex braided stream. What I needed to do was to unravel the strands and examine them, while not losing sight of the fact that they could be truly studied only in the broader context of the stream, and not clinically, in isolation. These are the dilemmas confronting all those who elect to study wholes. Wearing my historian's hat I set about assembling the information I had collected into a coherent, imaginative, and, I hope, convincing reconstruction of the past: a history of that stream—its sources, tributaries, destination, flow rate, hydrology, and denizens.

Finally, I confronted my materials as a thinking and feeling human being. I make no apologies for my sympathy for the early Soviet conservationists and their search for earthly harmony. Nor do I seek to conceal my belief that the severely utilitarian view of nature held by the Stalinists was and remains a confining view of the world. For, as John Rodman tells us in his remarkable essay "Liberation of Nature?" (*Inquiry* 20, Spring 1977, no. 1, pp. 83–131), the moment we remove ourselves from the continuum of life and time we dismember ourselves. By looking into the past and discovering there some pieces of ourselves we never knew, we can begin to regain the fullness of our humanity. I feel privileged that it was possible for me to rescue this fragment of our human heritage.

TERMINOLOGY, TRANSLATION, AND TRANSLITERATION

This book is principally a history of Russian and Soviet conservation. *Conservation* is a term that has become so all-inclusive as to thwart all attempts to define it. Even in its early usage in the United States, it connoted such diverse goals as game protection, preservation of scenery, efficiency, and wise use—exemplified by Gifford Pinchot's famous explication, "the great-est good for the greatest number over the longest time." The meaning of the term has become blurred further by its melding in the public mind with the whole notion of environmental protection, especially with pollution control.

Its Russian equivalent, *okhrana prirody* (literally, protection of nature), which I have translated here as *conservation*, suffers from the same lack of semantic precision. Although *okhrana prirody* has also enlarged its meaning to encompass broader spheres—frequently being used interchangeably with *okhrana okruzhaiushchei sredy*, or environmental pro-tection—its use as *conservation* in this book will be based on how Russians construed the term prior to the mid-1930s: a concern about wildlife, landscape protection, and wise husbandry of resources with only minor emphasis on the dangers of pollutants to human health.

Many other terms that appear in this book may prove unfamiliar to readers who have not devoted their scholarly lives to a study of Russian conservation and ecology. Although I have included potential troublemakers in a glossary, following the appendices, it seems useful to acquaint the reader with the most important of them at the outset.

Four Russian terms designating various types of protected territories appear frequently in the text. They are *zapovednik, okhotnichii zapovednik, zakaznik,* and *pamiatnik prirody.*

Zapovednik presents problems in translation because Russian conservationists them-selves could not agree on what, precisely, it denoted (that is a crucial theme of our story). While I have rendered it as *(nature) reserve,* for many, *zapovednik* had the additional connotation of a protected territory maintained in a state of inviolability and devoted to scientific research. In this connection, *zapovedniki* (the plural form) were regarded by some theorists of conservation as *etalony,* or baseline areas embodying virgin natural communities typical of the surrounding region.

Okhotnichii zapovednik, like *zapovednik,* was a term much in dispute. Introduced by a tsarist economic ministry, and later by Soviet economic commissariats to denote their utilitarian preserves, '*okhotnich'i zapovedniki*' were characterized neither by a regime of inviolability nor by the pursuit of scientific research. Rather, they sought to alter the natural conditions within their borders so as to provide optimal conditions for the propagation of commercial game, both native and introduced. I have translated this term as *game-management preserve.*

Both types of *zapovedniki* could be either state *(gosudarstvennyi)* or local *(mestnyi).* State *zapovedniki* were established by decree of the central government, and were usually (until 1929) funded by the central RSFSR budget. By contrast, local *zapovedniki* were created and funded by organs of local or provincial government. They were frequently under the overall jurisdiction of some national ministry, however.

Zakaznik may be distinguished from both kinds of *zapovedniki* by its impermanence (*zakazniki* were usually established for periods of five to ten years). Functionally, however, they were almost identical with the *okhotnich'i zapovedniki* in their concern for the propaga-tion of particular species of protected wildlife (and not the protection of the entire natural complex). The principle behind the *zakaznik* was the same that guided the farmer's practice of letting his land lie fallow. It was hoped that the game animals, given a respite from hunting and development pressures, would recover so that their exploitation could soon resume. Unlike the *zapovednik,* the *zakaznik* was not the legal master of its own territory; while either certain or all economic activities might be prohibited on its territory, the *zakaznik* continued to belong to its former landholders and did not have its own administration or staff. *Zakaznik* may be translated as *(temporary) game preserve.*

Pamiatnik prirody, the smallest of the protected territories, is literally *monument of nature*. Customarily, these tracts included unique botanical or geological curiosities, such as an erratic glacial boulder or a small grove of relict vegetation.

Another term that may be profitably introduced here is *biocenosis*. Coined by German ecologist Karl Möbius in the late nineteenth century, *biocenosis* has usually come to stand for a relatively self-contained ecological community. Always more popular in Europe than in the United States, the term has largely been superseded by *ecosystem* (although *biogeocenosis* is still widely used in the Soviet Union).

Russian terms commonly used in English works, such as oblast (province), sovkhoz (state farm), and kolkhoz (collective farm), appear unitalicized in the text. Explanations of other foreign terms may be found in the glossary. Sometimes, to avoid undue repetitiveness in passages where the same term appears frequently, I have alternated the use of the Russian original with the English translation.

I have used a modified version of the Library of Congress system for the transliteration of Russian, and have given the plural forms of Russian nouns in the original. Prerevolutionary dates are given in the Old Style (thirteen days behind our calendar).

ACKNOWLEDGMENTS

The history of this study reads like the "Perils of Pauline." Those who snatched me off the tracks in the nick of time include Carly Rogers, Robert S. Hoffmann, and a host of indulgent professors in the Columbia University Department of History. Without the institutional backing of the International Research and Exchanges Board, whose Graduate Student/Young Faculty Fellowship enabled me to pursue dissertation research in the Soviet Union in 1979–1980, this project could not have been successfully completed. I am also inestimably indebted to my Soviet hosts, particularly the Zoological Museum of Moscow State University and its director, Ol'ga Leonidovna Rossolimo, for indispensable and gracious assistance.

Those who have valiantly attempted to broaden my intellectual horizons include Leopold H. Haimson, Jacobus W. Smit, Sheila Fitzpatrick, Stephen F. Cohen, Leonard Zobler, Andrzej Kamiński, Donald Ritchie, and Peter H. Juviler. The person who has most influenced my development as a scholar is Loren R. Graham, my dissertation adviser, who was present at this project's inception and who has remained its inspiration ever since. Loren has been a mentor for me in every sense of the word, for he has provided not only superb intellectual guidance but also an example of a scholar who embodies decency, honesty, and deep personal warmth. To Loren I owe as well a personal note of thanks for his steadfast faith—at times, against the odds—that this project would one day be consummated.

For sharing their expertise with me I am particularly grateful to scholars Feliks Robertovich Shtil'mark, Kendall E. Bailes, Nikolai Fedorovich Reimers, Oleg Izmailovich Semenov-tian-shanskii, Anatolii Georgievich Voronov, and the late Andrei Aleksandrovich Nasimovich. Conversations with the following have enriched my understanding considerably: Mark Kuchment, Mark Popovsky, Mark Boyer Adams, Pavel Mikhailovich Rafes, Evgenii Mikhailovich Lavrenko, Andrei Grigor'evich Bannikov, Iurii Nikolaevich Kurazhkovskii, Valentin Konstantinovich Rakhilin, Tatiana Borisovna Sablina, Nadia Noskova, Sharon Kingsland, Robert E. Cook, Jack Major, and G. Evelyn Hutchinson. To Arran Gare, who has generously shared his profound insights about environment and culture, go special thanks.

It has become predictable for authors to declare in acknowledgments that they assume full responsibility for the content and conclusions of their studies. However, I do not consider my iteration of this declaration to be perfunctory. While I have learned and borrowed much from others, the overall responsibility for this book, especially its interpretations and judgments, must remain mine.

The staffs of the following research facilities all merit special acknowledgment: the Columbia University Libraries, especially the Interlibrary Loan Department; the New York Public Library Slavonic Division; the Lenin Library, Moscow; the Moscow State University Archives; the Library of the All-Union Academy of Sciences in Leningrad; the Moscow State University Biological Faculty Library and Gor'kii Library; the Library of the Moscow Society of Naturalists; the Library of Congress; the Library of the American Museum of Natural History; the USSR Central Archive Administration; and Widener Library, the Museum of Comparative Zoology, and the Russian Research Center Library, all at Harvard. Their virtuosity and kindness remains fixed fondly in my memory.

As I revised the dissertation for publication, I was doubly fortunate to have received support during the academic year 1984–1985 from two sources: an Andrew W. Mellon Foundation fellowship administered by Harvard University's Russian Research Center and a research grant from the National Science Foundation. The supportive environment of the Russian Research Center provided a wonderfully congenial habitat for this student of environmental affairs. Adam Ulam, the center's director, and Mary Towle and the center's staff have my lasting gratitude for easing the way. Also contributing to a sublime year at Harvard was the welcome I received from the History of Science Department there.

To Everett Mendelsohn, Barbara Rosenkrantz, and the staff of the department, who provided an opportunity for me to develop my ideas in the classroom, go enduring thanks. The generous support of the National Science Foundation also significantly contributed to this study, enabling me to explore important new materials relating to the history of ecology in the Soviet Union in the Charles Christopher Adams Archive at Western Michigan University, Kalamazoo. The unfailing good cheer of the WMU archivists kept me going during the final wintry round of "digging."

This is also an appropriate space to express my appreciation to Janet Rabinowitch, my editor, and to Ken Goodall, my copy editor. Their expert and judicious use of the blue pencil has indeed underscored the truth of the saying "Less is more." Nor dare I neglect to thank my loyal typist, DRW, who seemingly tirelessly survived four voluminous drafts of this manuscript.

Finally, I must thank my devoted family and friends, who kept me spiritually alive during the long ordeal. Among those I would like to single out for their support are my parents, Seymour and Sylvia Weiner; Andrew and Ellen Edman Weiner, who helped to propel this book into the age of "high tech"; Ida Silverberg; Richard Mogavero; William Rello; Alan Lipschitz; Irving Silver; Mark and Dory Silverstein; Robert Fradkin; Mabel Thomas; Ari and Fratello; and John Tom Schiavone, to whom I am especially indebted for his efforts to "slenderize" my luxuriant multiloquence. My friend Robert H. Scott has contributed to almost every aspect of this work; I can never hope to repay him for his support. Last but by no means least, among those to whom I offer thanks is my friend Valerii Nikolaevich Soifer, who provided inestimable intellectual stimulation and logistical support while I lived in Moscow. May he soon be allowed to follow his own star.

MODELS OF NATURE

Introduction

The history of humankind . . . has been the road from slavery and blind subjection to the elemental forces of nature to the . . . struggle [and] conquest of her . . . in the broad interests of human society.

The proletarian revolution was the critical moment in this process. . . . In conditions of socialism . . . the natural resource base for the economy is not contracting, but has all of the ingredients for limitless development.

—Kh. S. Veitsman, "Zapovednik budushchego,"
Priroda i sotsialisticheskoe khoziaistvo, 1934, vol. 7, p. 105.

How could a society that prided itself on its scientific underpinnings have enshrined Trofim Denisovich Lysenko as a virtual czar in the biological sciences? Why did a system that made a cult of rationality turn its back on environmental planning? What was the role of distinctly Russian and Soviet cultural and economic factors in shaping an equally distinctive conservation movement?

Behind these questions lies the intricate and neglected story of how some segments of the Russian scientific community confronted the wrenching process of economic modernization and social change. One response central to our study was the desire to protect nature. Whether it was the fear of nature's desecration shared by ethically and aesthetically oriented preservationists, or of ecological destabilization, which unnerved postrevolutionary activists with their unique emphasis on a scientific rationale for nature protection, visions of a crisis in nature's harmony mark a broad range of literature through the 1930s, especially in biology.

On the other side of the coin, modernization had its strong boosters. They, however, did not limit themselves to enthusiastic approbation of the amenities and conveniences we commonly associate with technical progress. Russia's modernizers, specifically those of the revolutionary tradition, saw themselves as people with a mission: to create a new, just society on the basis of a conquered, broken nature ruled by newly transformed *Homo sapiens*—conscious and self-conscious "gods on earth."

To treat the questions raised at the outset of this introduction, it is necessary to examine these two visions. In exploring them, we are drawn, ultimately, to a single nexus: the struggle in Russian and Soviet culture between partisans of the triumph of "consciousness" over the "elemental," and nature's defenders. While this theme has been admirably explored for psychology by Raymond Bauer and for literature by Katerina Clark, it is no better illustrated than through an investigation of Soviet resource policies and views of nature.

1

Building on the work of Loren Graham, David Joravsky, Kendall Bailes, and Ladis K. D. Kristof, among others, this work has sought to understand the roots of Soviet prometheanism, which reached particularly grotesque incarnations in biology, and of its conservationist opposition.

If prometheanism's roots go back to cultural patterns of the revolutionary intelligentsia in the Tsarist period, as Kristof and Clark have argued, as well as to nineteenth-century biological theories, then the pedigree of conservation is no less hoary. Indeed, the histories of conservation and of prometheanism in Russia are parts of an indivisible whole, born in the intelligentsia's groping for a means to transform an outworn social order into a rational, modern, gleaming city on the hill.

For continuity of the narrative line the architecture of this study is basically a chronological one, tracing the intertwined fates of conservation, ecology, and prometheanism from their beginnings in prerevolutionary times through the vicissitudes of 1917, the Civil War, the New Economic Policy (NEP), and the Cultural Revolution. I conclude with the consolidation of the mature Stalinist system in the mid-1930s, by which time the singular experiment in scientific conservation had collapsed before the irrepressible drive to transform nature. Yet, it is hoped, the reader will find in this study's thematic byways more than a descriptive history.

For the historian or political scientist, issues of interest might include interest-group politics, technocratism, the adaptation of the scientific community to changing political conditions, the question of the role Bolshevik leaders accorded science in society, and the nature of the Cultural Revolution.

No longer to anyone's surprise, examining the claims of interest groups has become a highly fruitful way of understanding interagency conflict in the USSR as far back as the 1920s. Even as we no longer assume ideological uniformity among the movers and shakers of Soviet Russia's party and governmental apparatus, we have also come to appreciate the powerful tendency of bureaucracies to frame and assert their own narrowly institutional interests: funding levels, "bureaucratic imperialism," relative ranking within an institutional hierarchy. In the protracted postrevolutionary contest between the RSFSR People's Commissariat of Education (Narkompros) and its ministerial rivals (preeminently, the RSFSR People's Commissariat of Agriculture, Narkomzem), we may see how these two lines of cleavage—ideological and bureaucratic—became articulated in two distinct ministerial *mentalités;* the Education Commissariat and its rivals represented two distinct views of science, socialism, and the social good. With no sensitivity to the ideological dimension, we might easily ascribe to greed and power hunger alone the efforts of the People's Commissariats of Agriculture and of Foreign Trade (Narkomvneshtorg) to wrest control of the Education Commissariat's system of *zapovedniki.* Yet, the pragmatic leaders and scientific staffers of those "economic" commissariats genuinely believed that nature had no utility unless it was subject to active exploitation. The inviolate *zapovedniki* of Narkompros, devoted largely to theoretical ecological research, were regarded by their adversaries as representing "science for science's sake" and therefore were offensive to the ethos of "socialist construction." Conversely, those in and close to Narkompros stressed the importance of the growth of knowledge, precisely through the study of virgin nature, as an indispensable prerequisite for rational "socialist" economic development. They regarded their opponents as simplistic and as cultural vandals. Nevertheless, it would be equally shortsighted to overlook the crassly "imperialistic" aspects of this rivalry, particularly from the late 1920s. Narkompros, under pressure to divest many of its vocational-educational and research responsibilities, in turn sought a monopoly control over conservation affairs, desperately trying to resist becoming a ministerial nonentity. The economic commissariats, meanwhile, were under no less pressure to set and meet reckless target figures for skins, forest, and agricultural products; the Narkompros nature reserves glimmered in the distance as one of the few ways in which the economic commissariats could square *their* circle.

Kendall Bailes's description in *Technology and Society under Lenin and Stalin* (Princeton University Press, 1978) of the technocratic tendencies implicit in the Soviet technical intelligentsia and of the emphatic reaction of the party to these tendencies is especially applicable to the ecologists and conservationists. These groups fairly exemplified technocratic opposition to a Bolshevik monopoly on decision making. Flowing from their convictions that resources could be rationally exploited only on the basis of their expertise, ecologists and conservationists claimed the right to veto economic policies and development strategies. Because nature's balance was so fragile, they argued, and the destructive potential of modern economic forces so great, it was imperative that scientists be consulted at every stage of economic planning. To ignore the need for such consultation was to court environmental disaster and to prejudice the availability of natural resources in the future. Of course, the party could not accept this technocratic challenge with any degree of equanimity. In order to assert its higher-order knowledge over that of the scientists, however, the party now found itself in the science business. And that was a development that had far from exclusively positive consequences, both for science and for the regime.

Another interrelated theme concerns how the profile and agenda of the conservation movement changed in response to the deep shifts in Russia's political culture from the Tsarist period through the mid-1930s. From a gravitation toward aesthetic and moral concerns about nature in the Tsarist period, conservation sported a lustily scientific outlook in the Soviet period. It is not hard to see that the prevailing "materialist" philosophical climate set by the Bolsheviks had much to do with this outcome.

Other changes in the self-presentation of the conservation movement reflected developments in Soviet political culture itself. If conservationists were seen as having mounted an underlying technocratic challenge to what they believed to be ill-conceived economic policies, they simultaneously adopted creative and surprisingly effective strategies to ward off their numerous and powerful critics. The charge of engaging in "science for science's sake," for example, dogged ecologists and conservationists from the late 1920s. While there was no explicit attempt to defend the pursuit of knowledge for its own sake—as a legitimate aesthetic endeavor—a vigorous anthropocentric defense of the utility of basic research *was* made, in terms both of the ultimate applications of such research in the economy and its role in developing a materialist understanding of the world. Another way in which conservationists sought to retain a measure of legitimacy was by employing the grandiloquent rhetoric of "socialist construction." That included renaming their publications and even their very society. In a similar manner, the challenge of scrutiny by Marxist philosophers of science was met by identifying and spotlighting the dialectical facets of ecological and conservation theory, while downplaying or even renouncing the remainder. While it is true that many conservationists and ecologists were sincere in asserting that there was no discrepancy between their doctrines and socialism, as they understood it, it seems certain that these assertions gained the prominence they did as a result of the formidable pressures on those scientists to justify themselves in a society at war with nature. For the sake of convenience, however, I have grouped the variegated adaptive responses of the conservation community—sincere or disingenuous—under the single rubric *protective coloration*.

I have described protective coloration as both creative and, to an extent, successful. Yet, for those who require an unblemished ending to this tale, there is, I fear, discouraging news. As might be expected, the ability of scientists to make increasing concessions to unreason inevitably reached its limits. Although they were aware that the price of resistance was high, some scientists could not bring themselves to concede fundamental scientific beliefs. Their choice, as they saw it, was to remain true to science or to join the growing camp of the opportunists. Ultimately, for many serious ecologists and conservationists, fidelity to their scientific beliefs won out, with tragic consequences both for themselves and for their science. Certainly, Hobson's choices offering professional ruin or moral collapse were a hallmark of the Stalin era. In this respect, sadly, ecology and conservation represent no exception.

That the "monolithic Bolshevik Party" of postwar historiography is more fiction than fact is not news, either. It is new, but not astonishing, to learn that there were a number of Old Bolsheviks who offered their active and, at times, effective patronage to the vernal Soviet conservation movement. Prominent among them were A. V. Lunacharskii, who led the "Commissariat of Enlightenment," and P. G. Smidovich, a former leader of the Moscow Soviet who was closely identified with a variety of humanitarian causes. But this group also included the hard-headed Lenin and even N. V. Krylenko, the procurator-general who sent hundreds of real and imagined political dissidents to the tumbrels of the Revolution.

Much attention has recently been paid to the Cultural Revolution, or, as Stalin dubbed it, the Great Break. This interest is well deserved, for historians increasingly recognize that the Cultural Revolution separates two universes of Soviet history. For conservationists and ecologists, at least, the road from the auspicious days of the New Economic Policy to the bleak thirties was marked by a three-phased assault from the motley minions of the Cultural Revolution. The first phase, vividly described by Sheila Fitzpatrick in her essay "Cultural Revolution as Class War" (in Fitzpatrick, ed., *Cultural Revolution in Russia, 1928–1931,* Indiana University Press, 1984), was essentially a rising of junior against senior. Although the cultural revolutionaries were armed with utopian visions and slogans, their initial attacks on conservationists and ecologists did not focus on these groups' ideas. Rather, the escalades were ad hominem, aimed at the class backgrounds and establishment status of these natural scientists. Additionally, the scientific societies with which conservationists were associated were accused of giving these class enemies undeserved shelter and were derisively likened to *zapovedniki*.

Later, with the triumph of the Deborin faction in the Communist Academy in 1929, conservationists and ecologists came under fire for advancing doctrines that did not accord with a Marxian view of nature. The classics of Marxism, particularly Friedrich Engels's *Dialectics of Nature,* were regarded as embodying absolute scientific truth, with which all other scientific teachings had to agree. Theories and concepts that seemed incompatible with Marxian dogma were denounced as bourgeois science.

The influence of the Deborinites, however, ended by early 1931. Their fall ushered in yet a third period of Cultural Revolution in biology, in which both the ad hominem attacks of the first period—now condemned as a left deviation—and the philosophical pronouncements of the Deborinites gave way to a new form of vigilantism in science. Important now was the compatibility of scientific research and theory not with the Marxian classics but with the specific, evolving social, economic, and political policies of the Soviet state. Compliance with Soviet practice became the determinant of whether a given scientific approach was proletarian (legitimate) or bourgeois (illegitimate).

Various species of Bolshevik arbiters of biology rose and fell in rough correspondence with these phases of the Cultural Revolution. Young, hot-headed, class-conscious vigilantes yielded to Communist Academicians who took their Marx and Engels with the utmost seriousness. These members of the Communist Academy, in turn, were ousted by a last group—which was also the most successful because its leading figures, preeminently Isai Izrailovich Prezent, realized that in Stalin's Russia the policies and pronouncements of the leadership determined scientific truth.

Anyone interested in the history of ecology and conservation should find much to reflect on in this saga. On the theoretical side, the era from the rise of phytosociology (the early study of plant communities) through Stanchinskii's original development of trophic dynamics (patterns of energy flow in food chains) and his subsequent dialectical reconceptualization of the nature of the biocenosis (ecological system) was a time of intensive speculation and creative theorizing. Looking back now at the discussions among early Soviet ecologists about how living nature was put together can only remind us of how unimaginably complicated the problem is and of how little progress we have made toward solving it in the past half-century. Nor has the previously untold story of the development of the *zapovednik,* or ecological reserve, concept lost its relevance in today's environmentally aware international culture. Especially now, when we seek experimentally to determine the minimal natural areas necessary for the preservation of species complexes, the lessons of the Soviet experience are particularly useful.

Perhaps, though, there is an even greater lesson that ecologists and their audiences can draw from this story: that our commitment to a particular view of the organization of nature is intimately bound up with our commitment to a particular vision of human affairs. Especially in light of the incapacity of ecological science, then as now, to tell us much of certainty about the natural systems around us, it is possible to comprehend that whatever model of nature we postulate is the one we ultimately *choose* to see.

ONE

Monuments of Nature

The extinction of life forms has always been a part of natural processes. Vast changes of climate and habitat hastened countless species of prehistoric fauna to their doom. More recently, however, an increasing number of extinctions are attributable to human activity. The extension of settled agriculture and urban civilization have wrought such large-scale changes as desertification, the flooding of large areas, erosion, reclamation, the evaporation of lakes, and a general elimination of primordial areas.

We now have come to realize that the amount of available natural resources is finite. We have also come to recognize as desirable the preservation of biotic and landscape diversity and the wise use—however defined—of nonrenewable resources. The disappearance forever of many types of resources we now regard as irremediable losses to humankind, future as well as present. We now believe that as the chief agents of environmental change and degradation, we humans are capable of halting or even reversing it.

In Russia, individual elements of this kind of conservation sensibility were present as early as the time of Peter the Great. Even before Peter, an awareness of the increasing scarcity of game motivated Muscovite and neighboring monarchs to protect royal hunting grounds.[1]

The reign of Peter (1696–1725), however, marks a significant departure from the previous policies of nature protection. Most notably, Peter was the first tsar to promulgate conservation measures designed to promote the well-being of the whole Russian state and not simply that of the ruler's personal estate. Among the most significant conservation measures of his reign were his forest protection decrees. The first to insist on a sustained-yield basis for logging, he also divided Russian forests into exploitable and protected categories. Foremost among the protected group were the forests that were important for erosion control along navigable waterways and the oak forests that were crucial for naval construction.[2]

Later tsars addressed the concerns of nature protection and resource management only infrequently. While it is true that Empress Catherine the Great in 1763 promulgated the first comprehensive hunting legislation for Russia, introducing closed seasons, conservation was not accorded serious attention from the death of Peter until the late nineteenth century.[3]

In society, the first stirrings of the modern conservation sensibility were discernible in the 1850s, when other areas of Russian intellectual life were also in ferment. These stirrings were particularly evident among zoologists and agronomists associated with Moscow University and the Moscow Agricultural Society. As Westernizers, they were keenly concerned with modernizing Russian agriculture and society. The most prominent leaders of this group included Karl Frantsevich Rul'e, professor of zoology at Moscow University; his students Anatolii Petrovich Bogdanov, Sergei Alekseevich Usov, and Nikolai Alekseevich Severtsov; and Stepan Alekseevich Maslov, secretary of the Moscow Agricultural Society. Having embraced current French doctrines associated with Lamarck and the Geoffroy Saint-Hilaires, they were strong believers in evolution. If belief in evolution spoke to the problem of ideological modernization, then the emphasis of this group on the acclimatization of exotic biota, the creation of new species through hybridization *(sic)*, and the implementation of conservation measures addressed the problem of economic and agricultural modernization. These prescriptions constituted an early Russian gospel of efficiency, if we may borrow Samuel P. Hays's description of American progressive-era conservation.

This gospel was a breakthrough in Russian intellectual life, for it proclaimed the conviction that through science humans could take charge of their fates, emancipating themselves from the status of passive wards of God and tsar. This secularization of the cosmos, not surprisingly, was strongly linked with the rise of political progressivism in Russia.

Although French theories of evolution were important inputs in this reformulation of humanity's place in the universe, Anglo-American influences, particularly in geology, also affected Russian intellectual development.

The idea of human beings as a violent new geological force, first advanced in Charles Lyell's *Principles of Geology,* found forceful exposition in George Perkins Marsh's *Man and Nature.* Tracing the growth of human control over the environment, *Man and Nature,* however, was no paean to the Baconian idea. For the first time, a systematic accounting of the spoliation of nature together with a rudimentary explanation of its causes had been written. By 1866, Russians were able to familiarize themselves with both Lyell and Marsh, whose seminal works appeared in Russian translation that year.[4]

No less important was the emerging notion that human society itself was also a potent evolutionary force. No other idea in the realm of biology held so much fascination for Russian naturalists—particularly the progressive stalwarts of the Moscow evolutionary school—as the prospect of human mastery over the course of natural events. Quoting the English naturalist and theologian Henry Drummond, Nikolai Feofanovich Kashchenko, a student of A. P. Bogdanov's, wrote in 1898:

> From now on man must care for evolution, just as up until now he was in its tutelage. From now on, his selection must replace natural selection; his judgment must take charge of the struggle for existence; his will must determine for each plant on this earth whether it will bloom or wither, and for every animal whether it will be transformed, will flourish, or will become extinct. . . .[5]

Although Kashchenko was concerned that this power of humankind could be exercised unwisely, he was exhilarated nonetheless by the idea of human control over nature. Reflecting the scientistic optimism of the age, he greeted this new challenge as "a task worthy of man" whose framework would be "reason." He saw the exercise of rational human control over nature as a guarantee of the survival of useful endangered species as well as an opportunity for the play of human creativity on an unheard-of scale. We would be species makers and would substitute reason for nature's blind forces.

Others considered the mastery of nature the condition for humanity's own survival. I. D. Lukashevich, the geologist and populist, asked whether man would "be able to master those forces which control the evolution of plants and animals, or will he, like his predecessors, vanish from the historical scene, not having solved the problem of survival?" Much like Kashchenko, Lukashevich saw in this challenge to master nature a glorious opportunity to build his city on the hill:

> if man already in the present occupies an honored place in nature among other geological factors, then in the future unembraceable horizons will open up for his genius. . . . the forces of the people will not be directed toward mutual struggle but toward a reworking of external nature in accordance with the needs of humanity.[6]

Alongside these developments in the second half of the nineteenth century was a growing consciousness of the squander of the natural patrimony of the Russian land. The alarming rate of deforestation began to trouble many Russians by the 1880s.[7] An outraged Anton Chekhov had Khrushchev, the protagonist of *The Wood Demon,* expound:

> Cut forests when it is a matter of urgency, you may, but it is time to stop destroying them. Every Russian forest is cracking under the axe, . . . the abodes of beasts and birds are being ravaged, rivers are becoming shallow and are drying up, wonderful landscapes are disappearing without a trace. . . . One must be a barbarian to . . . destroy what we cannot create.[8]

Another form of biotic impoverishment likewise made an impact on the Russian public beginning in the 1850s. In the journals of the Imperial Russian Society for the Acclimatization of Animals and Plants and of the various hunting societies, an increasing number of authors voiced alarm about the decline in wildlife. By the 1880s a flood of articles bewailed the decimation of game.[9]

Kashchenko, who taught zoology at Tomsk University, was one of the first Russians to extend his concern beyond the decline of game to the phenomenon of the extinction of flora and fauna generally. Among those life forms "obliged to humans for their extermination" he identified the Steller's sea cow, which had been hunted to extinction in a thirty-year orgy following its discovery by Vitus Bering's expedition, and the *tur,** or aurochs, the direct ancestor of the modern cow, which had survived in Russia as late as the seventeenth century. He warned that the same process was occurring now with other species, and on an even larger scale.[10]

By the late 1880s even the government was moved to action. Reviving the

---

*Not to be confused with a genus of wild mountain goats *(Capra severtzovi, C. cylindricornis)* of the same name endemic to the Caucasus and Dagestan. The Latin binomial conferred on the extinct bovine is *Bos primigenius.*

Petrine tradition of protected forests, a Forest Code was enacted in 1888 and supplemented in 1889 and 1901 by special instructions and amendments.[11]

The outworn 1763 hunting regulations were superseded by a new law adopted on 3 February 1892. For the first time, seasonal fees were set and individual seasons were mandated for the three latitudinal zones established by the legislation. Five years later efforts commenced to conserve the dwindling numbers of the Northern Pacific fur seal, culminating in the adoption of a treaty by Russia, Canada, Japan, and the United States in 1911.[12]

Despite these measures Russian biotic resources continued to decline steadily. Early on, the ineffectuality of the Forest Code was evident.[13] Although from 1887 to 1905 in the aggregate European Russian and the Caucasus lost only 4 percent of their remaining woodlands, situations in individual provinces were often catastrophic.[14]

The hunting law, too, was riddled with defects. For one thing, it did not apply to commercial hunting and was in force only in selected provinces of European Russia; huge areas of the Empire were exempted. Moreover, it gave landowners almost unrestricted license to hunt on their own, often considerable, properties. Indicative of the situation were procurement figures for marten and sable, two of the most important fur-bearing animals of Russia. From 1896 to 1913, the sable catch dropped from 100,000 to 35,000, while that for marten fell from 80,000 to 30,000.[15]

THREE TRENDS IN CONSERVATION

By the turn of the century conservation literature no longer simply announced the unfolding crisis in natural resources. Russian conservationists now began to spell out *why* it was important to protect nature. Their reasons can be grouped into three broad categories: utilitarian, cultural-aesthetic-ethical, and scientific.[16]

The utilitarian approach presupposed the division of life forms into "useful" and "harmful" categories. At the apex of the utilitarian economist's great chain of being were those animals that could be directly exploited as objects of hunting or commercial breeding. Under them—still in the "useful" group—were those that conferred such indirect benefits to agriculture as pest control. Lower down still were those whose influence was ambiguous, and at the bottom were animals whose harm to human life, limb, and property was unredeemed by any identifiable economic benefit.[17]

The governmental utilitarian tradition was exemplified by the 1892 hunting law, which allowed "harmful" fauna, such as tigers, leopards, and wolves, to be hunted year-round without restriction,[18] and by V. V. Dits, curator of the Imperial Hunting Grounds, who took the position that the propagation of game is possible only by the elimination of predators.

Perhaps the most notable monument to the governmental utilitarian tradition was the passage in October 1916 by the State Duma of Russia's first law on protected territories, authorizing the Ministry of Agriculture to establish and administer hunting preserves "for the protection and numerical increase" of game on state lands.[19] This law provided the basis for the creation on 29 December 1916 of the Barguzin *okhotnichii zapovednik** along the eastern shores of Lake Baikal. Consisting of a breeding station, 200,000 hectares of land, and a force of eighteen rangers, the reserve was the only prerevolutionary *zapovednik* to be established through the actions of the central government.[20]

Alongside the governmental there was a progressive utilitarian outlook that traced back to the Moscow zoologists of the 1850s and to the Nihilists of subsequent decades. The progressives, wedding scientific doctrine to utopian politics, were far more taken with the idea of creating a paradise on earth through the scientific mastery of nature than were the governmental utilitarians, whose concerns did not transcend revenue matters. The two groups, however, shared important beliefs: that nature had only a narrowly economic, instrumental value; that its components could be divided into "useful" and "harmful" categories; and that it was amenable to successful human management and manipulation guided by the first two beliefs.

From Germany and Switzerland came the example of approaches to conservation that contrasted sharply with the utilitarian view. They focused on the cultural, aesthetic, and ethical aspects of nature protection and were strongly linked to the neo-romantic mood. With their aversion to modernism and industrialism and their yearning for a return to a more pastoral golden age, these impulses also swept Russia.[21]

In addition to a focus on landscape protection *(Landschaftspflege)*, which was its most important contribution to the young Russian movement, German conservationism even provided key terms. Objects of nature meriting protection quickly became known in Russia as monuments of nature *(pamiatniki prirody)*, from the German *Naturdenkmal*.[22]

Important as well were the roles of Germany and Switzerland in providing organizational models for the Russians. These two countries had been among the first in Europe to form both official and nongovernmental conservation organizations. By 1903 Saxony and Thuringia had Committees on Nature Protection, Art, and the Development of the Fatherland, and by 1906 the Prussian government had sanctioned a State Commission on Monuments of Nature, led by the great conservation pioneer, Hugo Conwentz. Swiss zoologist Paul Sarasin, the other towering figure in the early movement, launched Europe's first popular conservation society about the same time.[23]

The German approach was marked by certain philosophically idealist elements. In particular, it was thought that cultivating a love of nature among the young would engender a moral and patriotic sensibility as well. Nature study would instill a respect for all life and a love of beauty. Its harmony was a model for human action. These themes were evident in the conservation work of the Riga Society of Naturalists and the Khortitsa Society of the Defenders of Nature, groups with a considerable ethnic German membership.[24]

---

*This term was used in the sense of "game preserve." During the 1920s, some conservationists questioned whether such utilitarian territories were entitled to use the term *zapovednik,* however modified, since it had by then acquired a more specific meaning as a reserve dedicated to the scientific study of nature and not to the propagation of designated species.

The most influential of the prewar aesthetic-ethical conservationists was the botanist and onetime vice-president of the Imperial Academy of Sciences, Ivan Parfen'evich Borodin. At the Twelfth Congress of Russian Naturalists and Physicians, his address, dryly entitled "On the Preservation of Parcels of Vegetation, Interesting from the Botanico-Geographical Point of View," concealed a powerfully written clarion for the conservation cause.[25]

Borodin exhorted his colleagues to protect nature as "our moral duty," drawing a parallel to the cause of historical preservation. Unlike the Prussia of his friend Conwentz, Borodin's Russia would not have to seek out tiny plots of land for *its* monuments of nature. Its vastness would allow it to create national parks on the grand scale of the American ones, huge temples to nature and to the nation. True to the neo-romantic tradition, Borodin was less interested in the commonality of natural features than in their singularity. Each of his monuments of nature, no matter how large or small, would constitute a national treasure, "just as unique as a painting—a Raphael, for example. To destroy one is simple, but to replace it is impossible."[26]

Much of the practical activity in prerevolutionary Russia embodied the aesthetic approach. It permeated the twenty-year effort of the Ural Society of Naturalists to protect the Sharashskie cliffs from quarrying and the campaign by the Khortitsa Society of the Defenders of Nature, Russia's first, to rescue some picturesque cliffs along the Dnieper.[27]

Alongside the utilitarian and aesthetic-ethical approaches emerged a third: the scientific one. By the early 1890s, the rich practical traditions in agronomy, forestry, and meadow management in Russia had come together into a self-conscious science of phytosociology—the study of vegetational communities. Perhaps conditioned by the traditional Russian value of community feeling *(sobornost')*, the pioneers of plant ecology looked to variegated "virgin" nature as a model of harmony, efficiency, and productivity that the agriculturalist should strive to emulate. To put agriculture on a truly sound basis, the early ecologists stressed, it was first necessary to study pristine natural communities—their origins, development, and spatial and temporal transitions.[28] That could best be done in areas that were specially set aside for this purpose and whose virgin nature could serve as a model *(etalon)* against which cultivated lands could be compared. This approach was explained by botanist Nikolai Ivanovich Kuznetsov in 1890—most likely for the first time in scientific literature.[29]

Not long afterward, following an expedition to the southern steppe regions on behalf of the Forestry Department of the Ministry of Agriculture, soil scientist Vasilii Vasil'evich Dokuchaev and his colleagues made the call for such reserves of virgin nature more explicit. The concerns of the practical world had brought Dokuchaev to the steppe, for the southeastern prairies had just suffered a devastating drought and famine. The Agricultural Ministry turned to him to analyze what, if anything, could be done to make steppe agriculture more viable. Dokuchaev believed that the replacement of virgin steppe by plowed fields had seriously damaged the integrity of the natural system, among other things vastly impairing the soil's capacity to absorb and store water. His prescription was to base agriculture on the possibilities offered by the natural grasslands, protecting as much virgin steppe as now remained and restoring the rest. Protected territories were to serve as the linchpin of this strategy. Such a territory was indeed created at the Veliko-Anadol'skoe parcel by Dokuchaev's colleague G. N. Vysotskii, who summed up their approach:

> . . . since natural vegetation elaborates . . . instructive *forms of adaptation* to local conditions of growth, *the knowledge of natural vegetative formations of various land-scapes may serve therefore* . . . *as a guide to selecting methods* and subjects most rationally suitable for agriculture—in field, forest, and meadow. That is the practical (not to mention purely scientific) significance of the geobotanical research undertaken at the Veliko-Anadol'skoe tract.[30]

In the mid-1890s, however, Russia's educated society was still unprepared for such ventures, and thirteen years elapsed before such an approach was advanced anew by Moscow zoologist Grigorii Aleksandrovich Kozhevnikov.

Kozhevnikov was born in the town of Kozlov (ironically, now Michurinsk) in Tambov Province into the family of a merchant on 15 September 1866. After graduating from the First Moscow Gymnasium, Kozhevnikov enrolled in the Laboratory of Moscow University's Zoological Museum, headed by Bogdanov. By 1905 he had earned his doctorate and had advanced to full professor of invertebrate zoology at Moscow University and director of the Zoological Museum, the construction of whose present quarters he supervised in 1908.[31]

In that year the Imperial Russian Society for the Acclimatization of Animals and Plants celebrated its fiftieth anniversary with a jubilee convention. As president of the society, Kozhevnikov devoted his keynote address to the problem of nature protection. No stranger to the problem of protected territories, Kozhevnikov had acquainted himself with local parks on a trip to the United States, visiting Boston's Blue Hills Reservation. He had also been to Germany in 1907. Despite his admiration for Conwentz's success in bringing the shield of state protection to isolated parcels, Kozhevnikov was struck by one relentlessly disturbing realization: no matter how vigorously conservation was pursued in a place like Germany, certain species were doomed to become extinct. The cause of this extinction he traced, generally, to the encroachment of civilization.[32]

Certainly, Kozhevnikov admitted, every place to which civilization expanded had not been transformed into a wasteland. Frequently, he observed, the density of plants and animals in seminatural or second-growth areas exceeded that of the pristine community they replaced. To illustrate, Kozhevnikov conjured up the vision of a hypothetical well-tended forest on the German model:

> Visualize a forest which was once of primordial character, in which there are now wide clearings and houses. In the clearings are thriving plantations, flowering shrubs, hedgerows, and many trees which were not in the forest originally. All these are growing luxuriantly and provide shelter for many birds. Shooting is prohibited in the forest and this regulation is observed. Many predators remain in the forest. . . . Even herons nest here. There are squirrels, hares, and even badgers and foxes. . . . We obtain a fairly lively picture of animal life. . . .

While to the layman this scene might appear deceptively idyllic, from the scientific point of view, emphasized Kozhevnikov, the forest had been stripped of much of its former complexity and vibrancy. Having witnessed the extent of biotic simplification in densely populated Germany, Kozhevnikov issued this warning for Russia:

> If we do not carry out special measures for preserving virgin nature, it will disappear entirely, and the nature transformed by civilization which will replace it will only deceive us by its one-sided luxuriance, shadowing the image of the vanished past.

To anyone who might wonder why society ought to strive to preserve virgin nature if humanized nature could be just as beautiful and teeming, Kozhevnikov responded by using the arguments of the early phytosociologists: truly rational economic activity was impossible without a prior scientific study of virgin nature. The progress of science itself, apart from its practical applications, also required it. Kozhevnikov spoke of solving crucial problems of biology which would remain forever unsolved "if for (our) study we have first devastated, and then cultivated, nature, with no corner of nature left more or less untouched for comparison." Above all, Kozhevnikov hoped to gain an understanding of "that biological equilibrium that reigns in nature."[33]

In the blueprint Kozhevnikov now presented for *zapovedniki,* the regime of inviolability was the single most important organizational feature. There was to be no shooting, clearing, harvesting, mowing, sowing, or even gathering of fruit in these reserves, "no need to remove anything, to add anything, to improve anything. Nature must be left alone, and we may observe the result."

Zapovedniki, it follows, were not conceived as tourist meccas. Doubtless aware of the downstream effect, Kozhevnikov sought to prevent or minimize the impact of surrounding environments. In particular, he feared contact of human populations or of cultivated areas and their biota with that of the reserves. Accordingly, he recommended that the reserves occupy large areas with wide buffer zones encircling them.

Kozhevnikov's *zapovedniki* contrasted strongly with such already familiar game preserves as the Imperial Hunting Grounds in the Crimea and in the Belovezhskaia Pushcha.[34] He counterposed the managed quality of the game preserves, which distorted the ecological balance in order to maximize the propagation of select species, to the natural equilibrium that he believed prevailed in *zapovedniki,* where "any measures which disturb the natural conditions for the struggle for survival" were inadmissible.[35]

It was, however, precisely the unmanaged character of the *zapovedniki*—the prospect that they might serve as havens for predators, agricultural pests, and other feared life forms—that served as the greatest initial source of controversy surrounding Kozhevnikov's plan. Objections first surfaced in the debate following Kozhevnikov's speech at the Acclimatization Society jubilee. Nikolai Iur'evich Zograf and Nikolai Mikhailovich Kulagin, prominent representatives of the academic-utilitarian tradition, warned that protected territories "might represent a danger for nearby residents since pests might propagate in great numbers and . . . cause a great deal of damage as they spread from the protected areas to croplands."[36] At the Second All-Russian Hunting Congress the matter arose in the course of a heated debate over proposed legislation which sought to continue to permit a long list of predators and other "harmful" animals to be hunted year-round.[37]

Kozhevnikov's response to his critics was an outgrowth of his holistic ecological perception. For him, there was no such thing as a "useful" or "harmful" life form; all were equally needed to maintain "the natural equilibrium (that) is a crucial factor in the life of nature." Ignorance of an ecological and evolutionary framework, he noted, blinded many to the usefulness and even indispensability of predators to game management, "since they serve as instruments of the law of natural selection whose importance . . . has been so vividly demonstrated . . . by Darwin." The "simultaneous flourishing of predators and their prey, of parasites and their hosts," represented for Kozhevnikov "crucial evidence of the existence in nature of a law of equilibrium." The fears of livestock breeders and hunters that predators, unchecked, would decimate their flocks and herds were unfounded. There was "no actual evidence suggesting that any species was driven to extinction *by predators,*" he flatly stated. Indeed, "the only completely documented cause of extinction of species is *people,* who by their interference in the life of nature destroy its equilibrium."[38]

Responding to the related charge that *zapovedniki* might become bases for the propagation of agricultural pests, Kozhevnikov noted ironically that it was croplands, not natural areas, that created propitious conditions for such propagation.[39]

In an unsigned article developing this line of argument further, Kozhevnikov or one of his close associates made the case for virgin nature, with its diversity, as representing healthy nature whereas agricultural monocultures, "planted like so many rows of soldiers," were portrayed as somehow pathological. In monocultures, the author explained, the natural enemies of insect pests often cannot find appropriate niches to support themselves. By contrast, the natural forest, with its rich diversity of shelter and nutritional opportunities, would guarantee a sufficient presence of the pests' natural enemies to keep the pests in check. Viewed from the ecological angle, *zapovedniki* could be regarded as islands of natural pest control rather than as sources of pest outbreaks.[40]

Kozhevnikov's program of creating a network of ecological *zapovedniki* had wider implications both for biology in Russia and for resource management. On the one hand, it was a rebuke to naturalists who had "locked themselves up in their offices" or who had buried themselves in "the study of the microscopic structure and systematics of animals on the basis of laboratory specimens" and who consequently had become "strangers to living nature."[41] On the other, it was a summons to biologists to become involved in land-use and resource planning. The study of virgin nature as "healthy nature" and of economically exploited nature as "pathological" permitted biologists, through the study and comparison of the two, to propose treatment for "sick" nature based on what they deduced about "healthy" nature. *Zapovedniki* would serve as models, or *etalony,* of healthy nature.

"A WARMING RAY OF THE SUN"

By the time Kozhevnikov presented his proposals for the third time, at the Twelfth Congress of Russian Naturalists and Physicians in December 1909, his plans had been embraced by an impressive array of Russian biologists.[42] The desirability of scientifically oriented reserves was even recognized by such exemplars of the aesthetic and ethical viewpoints as I. P. Borodin and Andrei Petrovich Semenov-tian-shanskii.[43]

Both Borodin and Kozhevnikov warned that any delay in creating *zapovedniki* could be fatal in view of the rapid expansion of agriculture and resettlement, spotlighted by the recent Stolypin reforms.[44] First to disappear would be Russia's unique treasure: its virgin steppes. The most urgent task of the conservation movement, consequently, was the creation of steppe *zapovedniki*.[45]

Not surprisingly, the first private initiatives to preserve what remained of original nature focused on the steppe regions. Dokuchaev was instrumental in arranging the transfer of the Derkul'skii Steppe to the jurisdiction of the St. Petersburg Society of Naturalists as a protected parcel. In 1898, pioneering Polish-Russian ecologist Iosif Konradovich Pachoskii successfully persuaded an enlightened landowner, Fridrikh Eduardovich Fal'ts-Fein, to fence off five hundred hectares of virgin steppe on his estate, Askania-Nova, located at the mouth of the Dnepr in Tavrida Province in present-day Khersonskaia (Kherson) Oblast, near the city of Kakhovka, almost 670 miles (1,080 km) south of Moscow. These efforts were soon joined by those of Prince Karamzin, the Countess Panina, and the Polytechnical Institute of the Don.[46]

Within a few years, protected monuments of nature appeared in a wide diversity of geographical settings. With the support of the Academy of Sciences, a rare relict grove in the Caucasus gained protection in 1911. So did picturesque Moritzholm Island in Livonia the following year. Dating from this period also were the private reserves of the Sheremet'evs, of Count Potocki in Volhynia, and of the Solovetskii and other monasteries.[47]

Among the most notable achievements of the prewar epoch was the realization of Borodin's cherished project for a central committee for conservation: the Permanent Conservation Commission under the aegis of the Imperial Russian Geographical Society. Its interagency character was evident by the presence on its board of such institutions as the Mining and Forestry Departments, adjudged among conservation's "natural enemies." Nevertheless, their presence, as well as that of other skeptical bodies, such as the Ministry of Internal Affairs, the Imperial Court Lands Ministry, and the Main Administration for Land Reform and Resettlement, at least assured an exchange of views between the bureaucracy and the conservation movement. Friendly agencies, preeminently the Academy of Sciences and the Geographical Society, were also represented, and Borodin became deputy chair and effective leader.

Aside from the Riga and Khortitsa societies, nongovernmental conservation groups began to emerge across the land. Gatchin, Kazan', Orenburg, Simferopol', Orel, and Congress Poland all had such groups, either as affiliates of existing societies of naturalists or as independent bodies. The most successful was based in Khar'kov, which seemed to pursue everything with special gusto.

In 1911, when Borodin was assembling his Permanent Conservation Commission, one of his most fervent admirers, Professor of Botany Valerii Ivanovich Taliev, founded a Society of Naturalists in Khar'kov. Setting itself apart from the elitist and exclusivist tradition in scientific societies, the Khar'kov group opened its doors to those wishing to become involved in the new cause of conservation. The idea that science belonged in society and not simply within the confines of the ivory tower was a point of special emphasis in Taliev's inaugural speech of 17 October 1911:

> Before scientists . . . looms the necessity . . . of letting the atmosphere of pure knowledge burst beyond the confines of the laboratory, so that the promise of science might be fulfilled. Scientists must show society that the light which is generated by scientific creation is not the cold, passionless light of electricity, but a warming ray of the sun, which even has the power to call the dying back to life. . . .[48]

One of the first official actions of the Taliev group was the publication of a journal devoted to conservation themes, the *Bulletin of the Khar'kov Society of Naturalists*. More than any other conservationist in Russia at the time, Taliev was sensitive to the crucial importance of popularizing the cause among ordinary Russians. This awareness was manifested as well in his organization of Russia's first Conservation Fair, held during the winter of 1913.

Although old Russia was by far no stranger to fairs, this one was like none other before it. For three weeks in the Khar'kov Women's Medical Institute, posters blared the theme of the exhibition: "Protect nature! Preserve Monuments of Nature!" There were hundreds of eye-grabbing curiosities: paintings, photographs, specimens of plants, and dissected, stuffed, and preserved animals. The potpourri of educational materials was distributed among some fifteen exhibits, including ones on "Special forms and results of mankind's destruction of nature," "The life of a forest which is subject to human interference," "Nature's beauty," "The national parks of North America," "Extinct, endangered, and rare animals and plants," and "The biography of a tree, as told by itself."[49]

To assist the visitor, a guidebook, written by Taliev, explained the broadest purpose of the fair as an attempt "to paint a picture of the inner beauty of the majestic temple of nature in which we live, and of its destruction at the hands of humans."[50] Further evidence of the movement's preoccupation in this period with landscape protection and the preservation of natural beauty and of rare and unique life forms, the Khar'kov fair brought to a close a brief but intense chapter in the saga of Russian conservation. In less than seven months, Russia would be plunged into war and social dislocation.

One other event that left its mark on the fledgling conservation movement must be mentioned. On 17 November 1913 the First International Conference for the Protection of Nature, organized by Sarasin, the Swiss zoologist, convened in Bern. Representing Russia were Borodin and Kozhevnikov. Sarasin's speech there had an enormous impact on the two Russians. Kozhevnikov soon reproduced lengthy excerpts from it in his pamphlet *International Conservation,*[51] and fifteen years later, on the occasion of Sarasin's death, he quoted from it again. Others, including Academician D. N. Anuchin, studied the speech secondhand, and it was published in full along with the entire proceedings of the conference by the Permanent Conservation Commission, almost certainly at the urging of the two Russian delegates.[52]

Of particular interest were Sarasin's observations concerning technology and capitalism. He used the plight of the whales to illustrate the lethal consequences of advanced technology in the service of profit. Given unrestricted pursuit of gain combined with the efficiency of the new technology, "the total extermination of whales will be the inevitable result," Sarasin gloomily forecast.[53] Kozhevnikov was particularly affected by Sarasin's conclusion that the fate of the wilderness and of its denizens had been sealed by the proliferation of corporations, "which must necessarily worry about paying high dividends at whatever the cost they are obtained." Paraphrasing Sarasin, Kozhevnikov added in his pamphlet that "only through the agency of capitalist enterprises were such campaigns . . . as the killing off of all the bison [sic] in the United States in the 1870s made possible."[54] While Sarasin's solution to this lethal marriage of technology and the profit motive was extreme— he sought to bar corporations from "exploiting living things"[55]—so was the capitalist challenge to the integrity of nature in the eyes of conservationists. Kozhevnikov and his colleagues knew that from firsthand experience with Russia's rapacious infant capitalism.[56]

Not only the fear of and antipathy toward capitalism of many Russian conservationists but also their perception that the good of the community superseded private property rights led them to view the government as the prime mover in the struggle to save virgin nature. Kozhevnikov had called the establishment of scientific *zapovedniki* a matter of "prime state concern,"[57] while A. P. Semenov-tian-shanskii had even raised the possibility of expropriating privately held lands in the interests of protected territories.[58]

The state, however, failed to fulfill even a fraction of the hopes that the conservationists had placed on it. Despite the last-minute law on game preserves, the ensuing creation of the Barguzin sable preserve, and the limited participation of the government in the Permanent Conservation Commission, the government's conservation record was poor. Kozhevnikov spoke for many of his colleagues when he said: "Unfortunately, at present we do not see any move on the part of (the government) . . . to protect monuments of nature; on the contrary, we see clear examples of their destruction."[59] It should therefore come as no surprise that in March 1917 few conservationists regretted the passing of the old regime.

TWO

Conservation and Revolution

The abdication of Tsar Nicholas II opened the way for a new epoch in Russian history. A Provisional Government was appointed by the Provisional Committee of the State Duma, which, from its inception on 15 March 1917 until its fall on 7 November, would speak in the name of the peoples of Russia.

Among the most enthusiastic celebrants of this sea change were Russia's conservation activists. "Long live the new, free Russia!" proclaimed V. I. Taliev in an editorial of the first issue of the *Bulletin of the Khar'kov Society of Naturalists* for 1917. "From a nation of masked pure oriental despotism, with all of the features of the deep degeneration of the ruling clique," he observed, "we suddenly find ourselves facing the broadest horizons for maximum freedom and full rule by the people." It could not fail to have an effect on the development of science, he believed, because "the fate of science in every nation is organically inseparable from its political conditions." In this instance, the effect of the Revolution on science would be all for the good:

> The spirit of free criticism and of creativity that lies at the base of scientific thought is not compatible with a regime of oppression. . . . Russian science has known this only too well! The people, so full of the potential for creative energies, for centuries simply endured with no possibility of realizing them. And science, a product of [such energies], but faintly glimmered, unable to burst into gleaming flame. Now the externally imposed chains have been removed. . . .[1]

"NIGHTMARISH EXCESSES"

The times, however, were not kind to those scientists who sought to combine liberal democracy with a political culture rooted in rationalism and, especially, in science. Only three months after writing his exuberant editorial, Taliev, in tones of alarm, was speaking of the awesome social dislocation Russia was experiencing and its potential for harm to the interests of science and conservation.[2]

Taliev edgily called attention to those who now questioned the value of "that 'old dame,' European science, and the culture that has been built on it." For Taliev, discarding European culture was a "total absurdity." Nevertheless, from the perspective of the summer and autumn of 1917, the fear in which he and other intellectuals held the Proletkul't, anarchists, and others who sought to mold an explicitly "proletarian" science was quite reasonable. A new organization, the Free

Association for the Propagation of Positive Knowledge, attracted large crowds in Petrograd and Moscow in its defense of traditional science. Even Maksim Gor'kii, "whose position with respect to science," according to Taliev, was "not always altogether clear," lent his support to the association as an orator.[3]

If the danger to Russian science stemmed from popular radicalism, the threat to Russian nature and conservation initiatives grew out of the convulsive, anarchic, and violent social upheaval in the countryside. It was not simply that, "with the furious raging of the agrarian problem out of control, the idea of conservation might well seem superfluous sentimentalism," Taliev stated. Indeed, everything that had been painstakingly achieved by private initiative or through the efforts of the Permanent Conservation Commission was threatened with being swept away. Newspaper accounts "fill the hearts of those who are concerned about monuments of nature with fear," wrote Taliev with great justification.[4]

The pages of the Academy of Sciences' journal *Priroda* (Nature) gave ample testimony to the wanton destruction of parks, gardens, forests, and manor houses together with their owners or superintendents. One of the most "nightmarish excesses" reported by Taliev was the murder of Prince B. L. Viazemskii and the ravaging of his estate in Tambov Province with its parcel of virgin steppe. These lands, Taliev said, the prince had intended to bequeath either to the state or to a scientific society to establish a *zapovednik*.[5] Tracts of virgin steppe, similarly designated for protection, were seized by peasants on the Polibino estate of Prince Karamzin in Samara.[6] Even the world-famous acclimatization park and virgin steppe *zapovednik* Askania-Nova was threatened by escalating social conflict. Evidence of its importance may be seen in a resolution of the Kronshtadt Soviet of Soldiers' and Workers' Deputies—at the other end of the country—calling on the government to dispatch a special commissar to Askania to save the complex.

Another great source of destruction was the World War. The fighting on Russia's western borders decimated the denizens of the Belorussian forests. For the European bison,* "that fragment of the past, our national pride," the war proved catastrophic. "In the din of events," lamented zoologist Nikolai Vasil'evich Sharleman', "we did not even notice the perdition of the largest and rarest of our homeland's mammals."[7] Before the war, the Belovezhskaia Pushcha had been home to seven hundred of the shaggy beasts. In late 1917, despite the appointment by the Germans of a special Military Forest Administration for the Pushcha, a census taken by Conwentz revealed that only two hundred bison were still alive.[8]

Although the last wild bison fell victim not to a soldier's but to a poacher's bullet—on 12 April 1919,[9] after the departure of the Germans—the Kaiser's occupying forces were responsible for the great bulk of the slaughter. *Die Woche* had even published photographs showing Prince Rupert of Bavaria standing atop a mound of bison carcasses.[10] The only mitigating factor in the slaughter was that two of the huge bovines had been taken alive to the Berlin Zoo. (Indeed, a wild population was eventually reconstructed during the 1920s from the breeding stock contained in German and Swedish zoos.)

---

*The European bison *(Bison bonasus)*, sometimes referred to by its German name, *wisent*, is known in Russia as the *zubr*.

One of the most powerful expressions of anguish at the effects of the turmoil came from G. A. Kozhevnikov. Speaking to the founding congress of the Association of Russian Naturalists and Physicians in late summer 1917, he offered the view that "it is difficult to imagine more unfavorable conditions for a discussion of conservation matters than those of the present time in which we meet."[11] He mourned that "the war has ravaged nature as never before. . . . We seek to talk of conservation at a time when . . . not only the old state order has been overturned . . . but when even the principle of law and legality has been temporarily trampled."[12]

Exacerbating the devastating effects of war and revolution were Russia's pitiful backwardness, its lack of technological know-how, its sloppiness, and its lack of any awareness of the duties of citizenship, Kozhevnikov asserted. Such failings created the conditions for appalling waste.

Kozhevnikov outlined three stages in humanity's relationship with nature, and he saw Russia as in transition from the primitive, predatory first phase to the growth-oriented second phase. Even without the war and social turmoil, powerful structural factors would still impede the quick attainment of the conservation-oriented third phase. Motivated by this assessment, Kozhevnikov supported efforts to rationalize and modernize Russia's economy and social structure; this support would translate later into cooperation with the new Soviet regime.

Despite the grisly backdrop, the political events of 1917 nonetheless nourished some hopes of Russia's conservationists. From summer onward, the pace of conservation activities accelerated perceptibly. A series of meetings of the Acclimatization Society devoted themselves exclusively to the question of nature protection, while a new Moscow Society for Conservation was formed on the initiative of F. E. Fal'ts-Fein, the owner of the Askania-Nova estate, who had moved to Moscow some months earlier.[13]

In Petrograd, meanwhile, the Geographical Society's Permanent Conservation Commission also evidenced a renewed burst of activity. A large Conservation Conference organized by the commission was held from 30 October through 2 November 1917. It was truly a reunion of the titans of the cause; I. P. Borodin, Kozhevnikov, Taliev, and Andrei and Veniamin Petrovich Semenov-tian-shanskii all were assembled at the neoclassical headquarters of the Geographical Society. They were never to appear as a group again.[14]

Of prepossessing interest, a draft bill prepared by S. V. Zavadskii was presented, proposing the creation of a central governmental agency for conservation with broad powers to confiscate essential lands for protection.[15] Even more momentous for the future of Russian conservation was the presentation of the first plan for a nationwide network of *zapovedniki*, dramatically conceived by V. P. Semenov-tian-shanskii, "On the Types of Sites Where It Is Necessary to Establish *Zapovedniki* on the Model of the American National Parks."[16] The proposal, which envisioned the creation of forty-six reserves selected from a broad variety of Russia's geographical zones, received no serious official attention for the next five painful years of Civil War and reconstruction. But then it reappeared as the nucleus of a new Soviet network of *zapovedniki*, and by the late 1970s almost 80 percent of the sites listed by Semenov-tian-shanskii had become protected territories.[17]

The Provisional Government seemed more genuinely interested than its tsarist predecessor in protected territories. Representatives of the Agronomic Department of the Ministry of Agriculture's Main Land Administration in attendance at the Petrograd conservation conference expressed "complete sympathy" with the cause of conservation and announced the ministry's readiness to proceed with legislation.[18]

Responding to numerous specific appeals, such as those to aid Askania-Nova, the Ministry of Agriculture did not shirk from taking interim measures. As early as summer 1917, the ministry had dispatched botanist I. K. Pachoskii and then explorer and general Petr Koz'mich Kozlov to Askania as special commissar to ensure its protection.[19] Also during that summer the Provisional Government appointed Simferopol' zoologist V. E. Martino as commissar-director of the Imperial Hunting Preserve in the Crimean uplands near Alushta, empowering him to supervise its conversion to a national park.[20]

There was a sad irony in the flurry of activity among Russia's conservationists in the late autumn of 1917: as the conservationists looked more and more to the state to protect nature from the people, the political positions of the politicians with whom they were dealing became increasingly untenable. Nothing more typified the futility than the elaborate plans for the first meeting of the Moscow Society for Conservation. It was to have been held in the Great Auditorium of the Sheniavskii University in Moscow on 12 November. Public lectures by N. A. Shilov on the American national parks and ecologist V. V. Alekhin on the virgin steppe of the estate of the late Prince B. L. Viazemskii were to have been accompanied by slides and even by that novelty of the day, motion pictures. The meeting, however, was never held. The Bolsheviks came to power in Petrograd on 7 November, and fierce street fighting was continuing in Moscow five days later, forcing the meeting's cancellation.[21] After months of trying to establish a working relationship with the Provisional Government, the conservation movement now had to start again from scratch.

AN UNKNOWN POLITICAL QUANTITY

In early November 1917 not even the shape of the Bolshevik Party's agrarian policies was known, let alone policies toward protected territories or resources, questions which had never been discussed in detail in party literature. Moreover, not one of the leading conservationists was a member of the party. Hence, the Bolshevik attitude toward conservation was a puzzle. Indeed, the very notion that there existed a single Bolshevik position on conservation was profoundly delusory.

If one voice was *primus inter pares,* however, it was Lenin's. But documentation providing insights into Lenin's views on the relationship of nature and humanity is scanty. Not given to speculative philosophy generally, Lenin touched on the problem of the human place in nature during discussions of a practical nature, frequently only by inference. One salient feature of his thinking, however, that is recognized by Soviet and Western researchers is his striving for rationality.[22] While Lenin's slogan, "Socialism equals nationalization plus electrification," was doubtless an oversimplification of his views at the time, it nonetheless sheds light on what he viewed as the essence of socialism: planning, state ownership and control, and modernization. For Lenin, socialism's foremost virtue was its efficiency. Evidence of that may be seen in his warm words of encouragement for the introduction of Taylorism and for the Scientific Organization of Labor campaign, and in his admiration for German wartime state capitalism.

Although Lenin's emphasis was on increasing Russia's productive power, it was to be accomplished within observance of the laws of nature. "To replace the forces of nature with human labor, generally speaking, would be just as impossible as replacing the *arshin* with the *pud*,"* he had written in *The Agrarian Question and the "Critics of Marx."*[23] "Both in industry and in agriculture man may merely avail himself of the actions of nature's forces, if he knew these actions," Lenin continued, ". . . enlisting machines and tools to make this process easier."[24]

Lenin's remark about the *arshin* and the *pud* seemed to imply that there were certain irreducible qualities in the organization of nature which could not be replaced or adequately simulated by human technology. The goal then would be to operate as efficiently as possible within the framework of nature's laws by making our knowledge of those laws as complete as possible.

To this end science had to be enlisted as an ally in economic planning: pure science to expand our knowledge of the workings of nature and applied science to translate this knowledge into enhanced productive capacity. Governed by these considerations, Lenin eagerly seized upon a peace offering from the Academy of Sciences in April 1918. Offers of cooperation from conservationists were accepted just as eagerly.

Although Lenin did not venture into any discussions on the biological organization of nature, contemporaries claim that he evinced a healthy interest in biology, having been influenced by his older brother Aleksandr, who studied zoology.[25] In hiding after the "July Days," Lenin read M. N. Bogdanov's *From the Life of Russian Nature,* one of the books in the extensive collection on agronomy, biology, and agriculture owned by his host and future secretary, M. V. Fofanova. More interesting for us is another book of the same collection that Lenin was said to have read thoroughly: V. N. Sukachev's *Swamps, Their Formation, Development and Properties.*[26] While Lenin is reported to have exclaimed his amazement to Fofanova upon learning from this book how much of Russia was under swamp and to have become excited at the prospect of such a huge source of cheap fuel for electrification, we might speculate that Lenin also was affected by the holistic, ecological spirit of Sukachev's pioneering text in community ecology.

Finally, it seems useful to take brief account of Lenin's recreational interests, so rarely mentioned in his voluminous works. Despite his silence on the subject, Lenin appears genuinely to have loved nature and felt comfortable in the wild. From early life, he was an inveterate participant in *pokhody*—long hikes and overnights in the wilderness. He reportedly began to develop his lifelong interest in hunting and fishing during summer vacations with his father along the Sviiaga River near

---

Arshin: a traditional measure of length, equal to twenty-eight inches; *pud:* a Russian unit of weight of about thirty-six pounds.

Simbirsk. Later, in 1890, with six or seven young revolutionaries, he took a trip down the Volga to the cliffs at Zhiguli (which were declared a *zapovednik* in the 1920s through the efforts of Sukachev); even the normally uneffusive Lenin was charmed by the beauty of the place, and he would later fondly reminisce about it, wishing he could return. And during his sojourn with Krupskaia in Western Europe, Lenin made frequent trips to the Alps, the Jura, and, later, the Tatras. When the Bolshevik exiles made decisions about how to spend their free time, Lenin invariably fell into the "party" of the *Progulisty*—those who used their free time to go to nature—shunning the opposition "party" of the *Kinemasty* (moviegoers). These habits would continue after Lenin's return to Russia, and he would frequently slip away on hunting trips to relax from his grueling regimen. None of this, of course, conclusively makes the case for Lenin as a lay expert in biology or as a conservationist. It does provide, however, a background for understanding later decisions and actions he undertook while in power.[27]

ON FORESTS

Two days after taking power Lenin's government issued the decree "On Land."[28] It declared all forests, waters, and subsoil minerals to be the property of the state and arrogated these resources to the state's exclusive use, thereby fulfilling one of the hopes of conservationists. Nationalization, however, was only a prerequisite for more rational policies of resource use, and the conservationists soon found out that in the chaotic conditions of the Civil War, state timber procurement could be just as plunderous as under the former system. Early in 1918 the journal *Lesa respubliki* (Forests of the Republic) protested:

> The forests are being reduced . . . by order of the . . . authorities. There is no plan, no system. Whosoever desires and is able can take his share from the commons. In fact, "forestry" does not exist any more anywhere.[29]

Responding to the chaos, the government enacted a basic law "On Forests" whose final draft was approved at a 14 May 1918 meeting of the RSFSR Council of People's Commissars (SNK RSFSR) chaired by Lenin.[30] Seeking to introduce a modicum of statewide planning and control over a vast resource, "On Forests" provided for the creation of a Central Administration of Forests of the Republic to manage the forests on the basis of planned reforestation and sustained yield. The forests were divided into an exploitable sector and a protected one; the purposes of the latter included erosion control, protection of water basins, and, significantly, "the preservation of monuments of nature."[31]

The decree on forests was issued under conditions of relative peace, but with the eruption of full-scale civil war the survival requirements of the Soviet state quickly came into conflict with the high-minded legislation. Vital sources of fuel, such as the coal deposits of the Donets Basin, drifted out of secure regime control, and the approach of winter 1918–1919 augured a serious fuel crisis. The operational authority of the Central Administration was soon abrogated, first by a troika with dictatorial powers, and then by the Supreme Council of the National Economy (VSNKh).[32]

Unquestionably, the emergency arrangements enabled the Soviet regime to cling to power. However, with the end of the Civil War and the general dismantling of war communism, it was agreed that these arrangements had outlived their usefulness. In accordance with the new spirit of the New Economic Policy (NEP), the state sought to encourage the preeminence of the most productive and efficient producers through the workings of the market. In place of centralized allotment of forest resources, competitive bidding for exploitation rights was introduced. Each logger now operated as a free agent in the market, bidding to acquire medium-term lots from the local or provincial forest organs of the People's Commissariat of Agriculture of the RSFSR (Narkomzem RSFSR), which now had overall authority in this area.

The state, though, had no intention of abandoning the commanding heights to anarchic market forces; forest users needed to be monitored, as Lenin had noted, even as they pursued their economic self-interest under NEP. Accordingly, the Forest Administration* of Narkomzem RSFSR exercised a watchdog role. Crowning the NEP edifice of forest policy was the new Forest Code, adopted on 7 July 1923.[33] Like the 1918 decree it supplanted, it was informed by the spirit of rational use on the basis of sustained yield and reforestation; it, too, provided for a category of protected forests, including those to be preserved for monuments of nature and *zapovedniki*.

There were other safeguards built into the code. In districts and provinces where woodlands comprised less than 8 percent of the total area, no clearing of forests was permitted. Provincial Land Administrations could authorize clearing of land in districts where the area under forest was greater than 35 percent of the total, and then for clearings no greater than fifty hectares. In all other cases, the central Forest Administration would have to issue the permits. That was of signal importance, because it was precisely in the south-central provinces, with their already alarmingly depleted woodlands, that rural overpopulation and land hunger was creating the greatest pressure for conversion of forest to other uses.

Until 1928 and a new flurry of changes linked with the First Five-Year Plan, Russian forestry practice now rested on the provisions of the 1923 code. All considered, and in light of the previous chaos, it was not the worst of all possible worlds from the standpoint of conservationists.

ON HUNTING

A more emotional question for Russian conservationists was the issue of hunting, an activity which continued to occupy an important place in national life. That was especially true for commercial hunting, which represented a measurable share of Russians' real annual income, and which was far more developed than in any other

---

*Successor to the Central Forest Administration of the Republic. The agency was briefly called the Central Forest Section.

European country. Hunting traditionally represented for Russia a means of acquiring, through the export of pelts and other animal products, desirable reserves of foreign currency, chronically in such short supply. These factors, combined with the evocative power of animal imagery, drew the energies of activists even more insistently than the fate of the forests. After all, the fighting had wiped out the bison, and the other large ungulates, beginning with the moose, were not far behind.

After an abortive try that foundered on the question of the legitimacy of sport hunting under socialism, efforts were renewed in February 1919 to compose an acceptable draft for Soviet hunting legislation. These efforts were centered in a special commission of VSNKh's Scientific-Technical Department (NTO VSNKh), composed of game specialists Frants Frantsevich Shillinger and Boris Mikhailovich Zhitkov; A. V. Smoliarov, president of the Moscow Society of Hunters; and Kozhevnikov.[34] Showing a better sense of priorities than the previous drafting team, Shillinger and his colleagues detached the issue of saving Russia's moose population from the general body of the legislation, and drafted an emergency measure by early spring. Published as the decree "On Hunting Seasons and the Right to Possess Hunting Weapons," the measure was approved by Lenin on 27 May 1919 and became the first Soviet act to treat the problem of fauna protection.[35]

An interim measure until the commission could prepare a general one, "On Hunting Seasons" contained several important features. Of paramount moment, it proscribed the hunting of moose and wild goats, and brought to an end everywhere in the RSFSR the spring and summer open season, which had been a principal demand of the conservation-oriented hunting societies even before the Revolution. To enforce this provision, no fresh game was allowed to be purveyed until 1 August, the new official opening of the season. Finally, the decree enjoined Narkomzem RSFSR and the Scientific-Technical Department of VSNKh jointly to draft a permanent hunting law, optimistically scheduling it for SNK RSFSR review by 15 July of that year.[36]

Running only slightly behind schedule, an amended version was ready on 1 August 1919. After that, however, the draft mysteriously languished; months went by without any word on its status. The concerned members of the drafting commission delegated Shillinger to investigate the matter. In early December, he was finally able to learn of the draft's fate. The final version had been sent to the Scientific Department of the People's Commissariat of Education (Narkompros RSFSR). The latter, however, would not approve it. The reason for Narkompros's temporizing was not a frivolous one; at its heart were the beginnings of a fourteen-year-long battle with the Commissariat of Agriculture, Narkomzem, for the control and direction of conservation affairs in Soviet Russia.[37]

A FATEFUL MEETING

How Narkompros, the education bureaucracy, came to have veto power over the hunting draft is an eminently reasonable question. To answer it, we must examine some events of January 1919. At mid-month, Kolchak's armies were crossing the

Urals and making their way toward the heartland of Soviet-controlled Russia. Lenin's government was fighting for its life. Yet, on the morning of 16 January, Lenin personally took time out from his other concerns to hear the case for conservation.

The circumstances of Lenin's meeting with Nikolai Nikolaevich Pod"iapol'-skii, an agronomist and deputy commissar of the local Astrakhan' branch of Narkompros, were indicative of the highly personalized structure of the Soviet regime. Pod"iapol'skii, representing the Astrakhan' Territorial Executive Committee *(kraiispolkom)*, had come to Moscow on a multiple mission. One of his requests, for Narkompros to establish a university at Astrakhan', was rather routine. His other request was for approval by the central authorities of the creation of a *zapovednik* in the Volga Delta, the first to be created under Soviet rule.

Pod"iapol'skii had been scheduled to meet only with Anatolii Vasil'evich Lunacharskii, the colorful commissar of education,[38] and Lunacharskii routinely approved the agronomist's petition for a local university. But the imagination of the commissar, whose broad range of interests and humane temperament were well known, was genuinely fired by Pod"iapol'skii's proposal for a *zapovednik*.[39] Then and there Lunacharskii dictated a letter of introduction to Lenin:

> I request that you receive and hear out comrade Pod"iapol'skii, a splendid Soviet worker from Astrakhan'. I think that a conversation with him will prove useful.

Pod"iapol'skii recalled later that, as he set out for his meeting with the Soviet leader, the commissar told him to stress conservation in his talk with Lenin, leaving no doubt about Lunacharskii's own sympathies in the matter.

Ushered through white double doors into Lenin's high-ceilinged Kremlin office, Pod"iapol'skii outlined all of the proposals of the Astrakhan' *kraiispolkom* and then awaited Lenin's response. He remembered it this way:

> Having asked me some questions about the military and political situation in the Astrakhan' region, Vladimir Il'ich expressed his approval of all of our initiatives and in particular the one concerning the project for the *zapovednik*. He stated that the cause of conservation was important not only for the Astrakhan' *krai,* but for the whole republic as well, and that he considered it an urgent priority.

Lenin further proposed that Pod"iapol'skii immediately draw up draft legislation for a general decree on conservation which would apply throughout the RSFSR. The next day, after frenetic efforts to locate lawyers and activists to assist him, Pod"iapol'skii somehow managed to complete the draft and to submit it on time for Lenin's review. Just as astonishingly, he received the examined draft back from Lenin that very day, via the secretary of the SNK RSFSR, Dr. V. D. Bonch-Bruevich.[40]

Exhibiting paternal and, perhaps, slightly selective solicitude for procedural legality in the young state apparatus, Lenin directed that the decree be sent back to the executive committee of Narkompros for final approval. That was a crucial decision, for it was the first indication that Lenin specifically sought to entrust

Narkompros with general responsibility for conservation matters. As Fedor Niko-laevich Petrov, an on-the-scenes participant and leading member of Narkompros, later took pains to stress, Lenin had intentionally done so because the Education Commissariat had completely clean hands. It was in no way directly involved with the exploitation of natural resources or with the land question, and could examine conservation problems with at least economic disinterest.[41]

By a stroke of bad luck, Lunacharskii left Moscow shortly after Pod"iapol'-skii's meeting with Lenin, and the agronomist was forced to work through lesser bureaucrats. While historian M. N. Pokrovskii, Lunacharskii's deputy, received Pod"iapol'skii on the first of February, "the entire matter came to a standstill" after it was referred for further review to the astronomer P. K. Shternberg, who headed the Scientific Department. Only a tart note from Lunacharskii himself in June 1919 revived the project from bureaucratic strangulation.[42]

Nonetheless, Pod"iapol'skii's broad draft, "On State Protection of Parcels of Dry Land, Water, and Subterranean Areas," continued to grow moldy on a series of cluttered desks for almost a year and a half. Only when the nation had put the Civil War behind it did a successor bill to the one Pod"iapol'skii drafted see the light of day. Signed into law by Lenin on 16 September 1921, the new measure was modestly entitled "On the Protection of Monuments of Nature, Gardens, and Parks."[43] The most significant feature of the measure was that it officially conferred overall responsibility for conservation on Narkompros.[44] According to the decree, Narkompros was henceforth empowered, "with the consent, in each instance, of the agencies and institutions affected," to declare "parcels of nature and individual components thereof" having "special scientific or cultural-historical value" to be inviolable monuments of nature, zapovedniki, or national parks.

Furthermore, the decree prohibited any development of any natural resource in zapovedniki and national parks, specifying hunting, fishing, and the collection of eggs as three such examples, without the express approval of the appropriate organs of Narkompros. These provisions seemed to buttress the claims of Narkompros to have a say in overseeing protected territories of other commissariats and agencies, particularly those of Narkomzem, which had also been granted the right (in the decree "On Forests," for one) to establish its own "zapovedniki."

Pod"iapol'skii's lobbying for a Volga Delta reserve was more immediately successful. Unlike his draft legislation, the specific proposal for an Astrakhan' zapovednik sailed through Narkompros's Scientific Department on 1 February 1919,[45] enabling the local Education Department of the Astrakhan' krai suc-cessfully to sponsor such a measure within its Territorial Executive Committee.

A third outcome of the January 1919 meeting was the creation in the spring of that year of a Temporary Commission on Conservation, later variously called the Scientists' Committee or the State Committee for the Protection of Monuments of Nature. The Temporary Commission, which functioned within the Museum Depart-ment (Glavmuzei) of Narkompros's Central Academic Administration (AKAD-TsENTR),* attracted some of the most respected names in the natural sciences.

---

*This agency was soon reorganized as Glavnauka, the Main Administration for Scientific Institutions of Narkompros RSFSR.

Heading the list were Academicians D. N. Anuchin, a geographer and anthropologist, and A. E. Fersman, a mineralogist. Bringing up the ranks were zoologists A. F. Kots and S. I. Ognev, ecologist Sergei Alekseevich Severtsov, Kozhevnikov, and Boris Mikhailovich Zhitkov. The head of the commission was Vagran Tigran Ter-Oganesov, a Bolshevik astronomer who enjoyed great influence in the Education Commissariat.[46]

Within a short time the Temporary Commission had amassed a number of achievements to its credit. Of these, the participation of the commission in the creation of the first republican-level zapovednik in the Miass region of the southern Urals had the most far-reaching consequences.

As was the case with the Astrakhan' reserve, the idea to create the Il'menskii mineralogical zapovednik originated in the years just prior to the outbreak of the World War. Its boosters were three of Russia's most esteemed geologists: Academicians Fersman and V. I. Vernadskii, plus Professor Mikhail Nikolaevich Fedorovskii. They all concurred that the Miass deposits were among the most scientifically interesting in Russia, and with study could reveal much about geological processes.[47] The proposal was fortunate to have as its sponsors men who enjoyed not only great prestige but also the political confidence, however limited, of Lenin. Moreover, their deep involvement in the applied aspects of science probably made them, at that moment, more sympathetic figures than three theoretical ecologists would have been. At any rate, the proposal, doubtless introduced into the calendar of the Temporary Commission by its member, Fersman, had by 25 September 1919 been fashioned into a draft for a decree. On 4 May 1920 the draft was finally reported out to the SNK RSFSR by Deputy Commissar Pokrovskii standing in for Lunacharskii, and was signed by Lenin.

The establishment of the Il'menskii zapovednik looms large, not merely because it marked the creation of the first national zapovednik of Soviet Russia.* It was also the first protected territory anywhere to be created by a government exclusively in the interests of the scientific study of nature.[48] As such, it symbolized Narkompros's increasingly distinctive approach to conservation and protected territories.

As early as January 1919, then, even before the 1921 decree "On Monuments of Nature," Narkompros believed that it had been entrusted by Lenin with special responsibility not only for future zapovedniki but for conservation interests generally. On the basis of this understanding, Narkompros RSFSR sought to quash the hunting measure—which gave responsibility for hunting affairs to Narkomzem RSFSR—until its own proposed State Committee for the Protection of Monuments of Nature, whose purview would also include hunting affairs, was firmly in place.[49]

ENTER NARKOMZEM

What probably salvaged the hunting decree was Shillinger's insistent lobbying. As it happened, he also had been serving as leader of the Scientific Department of Narkompros's Scientific-Expeditionary Unit (such multiple involvements were

*The Astrakhan' zapovednik, established on 11 April 1919, was not a republican but a provincial-level institution.

common), and we may presume that he prevailed on his colleagues in Narkompros to relent in the interests of the larger cause. At any rate, "On Hunting" was signed into law by Lenin on 24 July 1920, encoding the institutional bifurcation of conservation for the next decade and beyond.

According to the decree, Narkomzem RSFSR was vested with full responsibility for hunting. It was to establish a Hunting Administration to supervise the issuance of detailed regulations, the protection of game animals and their breeding in captivity, the supply of firearms, ammunition, work clothes, and other supplies to Russia's hunters, and the operations of cooperatives and other hunting organizations. It was empowered to set seasons, take game censuses, and organize laboratories, experimental breeding stations, *zapovedniki, zakazniki,* and shelters *(pitomniki)* for game animals and birds. Lastly, and highly indicative of the generally utilitarian ethos of Narkomzem, the Hunting Administration was charged with the mission of liquidating pests and predators, foremost among them the wolf.

"On Hunting" provided the basic framework for the conduct of hunting over the next decade.[50] Shortly after the law's adoption, Narkomzem created a Central Administration for Hunting Affairs (Tsentrokhota). In its earliest years, under the leadership of the future prosecutor-general of the USSR, N. V. Krylenko, Tsentrokhota generated much hope and interest among conservation activists. Its Scientific Department was graced with an imposing roster of personalities who had excellent credentials as both biologists and activists. Headed by the dean of conservationists, Kozhevnikov, its members included noted game biologists Shillinger, S. A. Buturlin, V. A. Kaverznev, and B. M. Zhitkov.

By 1922, however, Narkomzem's flawed stewardship of its *zapovedniki* on Lake Baikal[51] and the lackluster dispatch of its other responsibilities were beginning to cause serious disaffection among the scientists in Tsentrokhota.[52] In the eyes of Shillinger and other game biologists, Narkomzem had in a few years compiled a record of betrayals and neglect. It is not surprising, therefore, that Russia's naturalists showed increasing interest in the more vigorous conservation organs of Narkompros. By 1925, Shillinger and Kozhevnikov occupied central places in Narkompros-associated conservation organs and had completely abandoned Tsentrokhota, which, now demoted to the Hunting Subdepartment, had dwindled to a pitiful handful of stalwarts.[53]

THREE

Conservation under the NEP

Between 1920 and 1922 the State Committee for the Protection of Monuments of Nature under Narkompros became the indisputable clearinghouse for conservation affairs, linking the far-flung provincial groups into an information network flowing into Moscow. When reports filtered in about the need to initiate or enhance protection of a site, the State Committee promptly made the appropriate representations, as it did to Narkomzem when that commissariat's Vorskla Forest site was threatened with logging.

When necessary, the State Committee took matters into its own hands, as when it mobilized the defense of the woods belonging to the Kosino Biological Station (a future *zapovednik*) in the spring of 1920 against intruders chopping trees for firewood. Here, of course, the task was easier than at Vorskla because the territory was administered not by the Central Forest Section of Narkomzem but directly by Narkompros's own Main Administration for Scientific Institutions, the Arts, Museums, and Conservation (Glavnauka).

Many of the projects represented attempts to revive prior initiatives that were buried in the years of civil war. The project to establish a conservation museum, advanced in the waning days of the Provisional Government by the Moscow Society for Conservation, was reactivated. Other efforts included protection of a variety of virgin areas. However, these activities were not yet guided by a coordinated plan for a network of reserves, and whatever initiatives were made were those of individuals or ones that originated independently in the provinces.[1]

Within Narkompros, in order to administer the new conservation duties, an official Subdepartment for Conservation was created within Glavnauka's Museum Department (Glavmuzei) in addition to the State Committee. Briefly led at first by Shillinger and then by Ter-Oganesov, the new subdepartment attracted many workers who had been involved in Tsentrokhota or had been on the State Committee: Anuchin, Kozhevnikov, Ognev, Fersman, Zhitkov, and Buturlin, among others.[2]

NEP'S FINANCIAL PINCH

What the New Economic Policy gave by way of social peace, hope in the future, pluralism, and a degree of intellectual freedom, however, it took away with its stringent fiscal constraints. The conservation agencies were feeling the pinch even before the introduction of NEP. Owing to the SNK RSFSR's tardiness in approving a charter, the State Committee could not be included in the 1921 republic-wide budget and was completely dependent on the largesse of the Narkompros Executive Committee, which supported the State Committee by dipping into its discretionary fund.[3] The next year found conservation left out of the RSFSR budget once again. This time, it was on account of the disaffection of Soviet leaders with the pace of organizational activities at Narkomzem's new Baikal *zapovednik*. True, Narkompros should not have been punished for the sins of Narkomzem, but in 1922, when entire industry-wide subsidies were eliminated and factories were told to make it on their own, the central government was looking for any excuse to cut its expenses.

One of the first reactions of movement activists was to draw up a petition calling on the government to provide two million rubles for conservation for 1922. Leading the effort was Kozhevnikov, who, together with Shillinger, tried to rally a "united front" of top scientists, important agencies, and scientific societies—"even the Military in the person of Trotskii"—to support the demands.[4]

The budget cuts stuck, however, and not merely the State Committee and Subdepartment for Conservation but their superordinate agencies, especially Glavmuzei, found themselves eyeball to eyeball with the problem of how to continue with no money. A number of proposals were offered to overcome the hardships imposed by *khozraschet*, the NEP policy of forcing agencies and enterprises to generate their own funding. Indeed, this problem dominated the discussions of the State Committee for the final two months of 1921.

Suggestions came forth about selling natural-historical collections taken in the *zapovedniki*. Nikolai Nikolaevich Smirnov, a geologist closely associated with the Il'menskii mineralogical *zapovednik*, enthusiastically supported the idea of letting the reserves turn a profit, citing the opportunities to sell gem collections or to develop tourism in the Il'menskii reserve.[5] Shillinger went even further. *Zapovedniki*, he contended, could be set up along the lines of the U.S. national parks, with fees for admission, for the use of hotels, and for guided tours. Literature, photos, and small collections would also be on sale. All this, observed Shillinger, was already being done at Yellowstone with no observable injury to nature. Shillinger even advanced the bold idea that—as with other sectors of the economy—the Soviet government could invite foreigners in to manage the "national parks" in the RSFSR on a concession basis, bolstering his proposal with the lame justification that conservation was, after all, an international endeavor.[6]

Shillinger's colleagues on the State Committee, led by the ever-vigilant Kozhevnikov, were not won over by these glowing prospects of foreign-managed Soviet Yellowstones. The hostility of the majority to merchandising the reserves was reflected in a resolution they voted, which noted that it was the government's responsibility to provide funding for the *zapovedniki* and that "their exploitation, like that of some industrial enterprise, contradict(ed) their very essence." Logging, extensive collecting, and even the gathering of deadwood in a wild-growing forest were pronounced "impermissible."[7]

Ultimately, though, the reality principle intruded. Bowing to the intense fiscal pressures, the State Committee decided that gem collections, after all, could be assembled without damage to the Il'menskii mineralogical *zapovednik*, while in zoological *zapovedniki* the skeletons and pelts of fallen animals could be sold, as well as a limited number of live animals to foreign zoos. However, it was noted, the best solution of all was to ensure the presence of buffer zones around each *zapovednik* which the staff could exploit for sustenance, tiding the reserve through.[8]

In May 1923 the situation for conservation got even worse. Early that month, by a decision of the Executive Committee of Narkompros, the "pitiful existence of the Subdepartment (for Conservation) in Glavmuzei was snuffed out." Saving the day was an audit of Narkompros conducted by conservation's old friend, Professor N. M. Fedorovskii. His report demanded that Narkompros immediately reinstate conservation as a full, and not a sub-, department. Also, it supported the findings of an earlier study by Pod"iapol'skii calling for the creation of a supra-administrative organ for conservation attached directly either to SNK RSFSR or to the All-Russian Central Executive Committee (VTsIK), the nominal Soviet parliament.[9]

Conservation was restored to life as a full department under Glavnauka directly, but this triumph threatened to be short-lived. In early 1924, interest in conservation once again took a back seat to fiscal considerations, and eliminated were not only the Department of Conservation but the State Committee for the Protection of Monuments of Nature as well (in March 1924). Only pressure from the State Planning Commission (Gosplan),[10] which also added its voice to the department's defenders (and to those seeking the creation of a supraministerial agency for conservation) pushed Narkompros again onto the defensive.

THE *ZAPOVEDNIKI* STRUGGLE TO SURVIVE

For the *zapovedniki,* too, the first years following the end of the war were ones of tribulation. As was the case with the Crimean *zapovednik,* approval of the Caucasus *zapovednik*'s charter by the Council of People's Commissars by no means solved all of the reserve's problems. Until 1926, the entire eastern portion of the reserve was controlled by bandits. An ill-considered attempt on the part of Professor Isaev to conduct scientific observations there resulted in his murder by outlaws.

At least as nettlesome as the security problem was the persistence of disputes concerning the reserve's boundaries. The most serious of them involved claims by the Adygei Autonomous Oblast to the *zapovednik*'s alpine meadows for use as pasturelands. Although the dispute was at long last resolved in a manner favorable to the *zapovednik* in 1927, the attainment of secure and recognized boundaries did not call forth victory celebrations. In October of the same year, an expedition led by Professor D. P. Filatov confirmed the worst fears of the *zapovednik*'s director and scientific staff: at some point in the dispute-plagued recent past, the Caucasus race of bison had become extinct in the wild, just as had its sister race to the northwest.[11]

Professor Pavel Evgen'evich Vasil'kovskii and other distinguished conservationists were so disenchanted with the delays, the bureaucratic infighting, and the unreliability associated with governmental efforts that they counseled activists to look inward, to themselves. "The success of our cause lies not in decrees," lectured Vasil'kovskii, "but in ourselves. We—society itself—and no one else, must take upon ourselves the cause of protecting our natural wealth." He pointed to the example of Germany, where hundreds of nature protection societies flourished.[12]

Russia, however, was not Germany, and for the vast majority of Soviet conservationists, surveying the human landscape of their republic and seeing only benighted masses, the government overwhelmingly remained the repository of their hopes.

These hopes found at least symbolic expression in the existence by 1924 of four state *zapovedniki* in the Narkompros system (the Il'menskii, Crimean, Kosino, and Caucasus), several local *zapovedniki* also superintended by Narkompros organs (the Astrakhan', Penza, and Galich'ia gora), eighty-two parks and gardens of the same system, one state *zapovednik* (Barguzin) administered by Narkomzem RSFSR, and the Ukrainian reserve and acclimatization park Askania-Nova under Narkomzem of the Ukraine. The Soviet regime also restated its commitment to conservation at the All-Union Agricultural Exhibition held in Moscow in the summer of 1923. As if to respond to the exhibit of the United States, which featured a large placard asserting that the attention a society gave to conservation was the best measure of its level of civilization, the exhibit of Glavnauka featured photos, charts, and paintings graphically depicting "the destructive influence of man upon nature." There were also drawings of endangered species, photos from *zapovedniki,* and lectures on conservation themes.[13]

THE SWAN SONG OF THE AESTHETIC APPROACH

No discussion of the period from 1917 to 1924 would be complete without mentioning the brief flowering and subsequent fading of the aesthetic-ethical tendency within the conservation movement. The World War and the Civil War played inestimable roles in deepening the sense of urgency among Russian biologists and others about the need for strong conservation measures. For some, the ugliness of war (and even of modern society in general) led them to embrace outright preservationist positions.

Conservation's aesthetic side was highlighted in the earliest days of Soviet rule as a consequence of the peculiar institutional situation that existed from 1919 to 1923. For want of any better existing subdivision in which to include Narkompros's fledgling Subdepartment for Conservation, it was relegated to the commissariat's Museum Division. As Glavmuzei was the center for artistic, archaeological, and architectural preservation, it was natural also that its leading personalities would view conservation as the creation of "museums of nature."[14]

One of the most eloquent champions of the aesthetic view was the entomologist Andrei Petrovich Semenov-tian-shanskii. A longtime senior staff member of the Academy of Sciences' Zoological Museum, chairperson of the Geographical Society's Biogeographical Commission, and president of the Russian Entomological Society, he had impeccable scientific credentials. In his field of expertise, the systematics and biogeography of insect forms, Semenov-tian-shanskii made a name for himself by his discovery and description of over 900 new species of insects (and 133 genera) and by an influential commentary he wrote in 1910 concerning the nature of species.[15] His collection of insects, which contained no less than 700,000 specimens and which he bequeathed to the Zoological Museum, was among the largest in the world.

Semenov-tian-shanskii owed his distinction among Russia's men and women of learning, though, as much to his philosophical and cultural interests as to his scientific activities. "A humanist in the best sense of the word," as he was described by zoologist S. I. Ognev, Semenov-tian-shanskii had cultural interests that ranged wide indeed. An expert on the theory of poetics, he was also an accomplished poet and an authority on the work of Pushkin. Steeped in the classical tradition, he was one of the first to translate Horace into Russian. A connoisseur of art and music, he was devoted to opera and counted opera singers among his most intimate friends. Even in his declining years, almost totally blind, he continued to go to the opera, having committed whole libretti to memory.[16]

More than anyone else, he explicitly voiced an aesthetic distaste for modern industrial society, capitalist or socialist. In his desire to return to a lost golden age when the world was untainted by what he called industrial sin, Semenov-tian-shanskii articulated attitudes that must have been shared by others of Russia's former elite, embittered and nostalgic over ties to the land that were severed for them by social developments. Industrial man, he pronounced, was a "geological parvenu" who was "disrupting the harmony of nature's picture, . . . that grand tableau which serves as the inspiration of the arts: music, painting, sculpture, and architecture."[17] He thus placed human *industry* in opposition to human *culture*, which had been nourished by nature until industrial man blighted the land.

Although Semenov-tian-shanskii felt that man's "fall" was made possible by his "predator nature," it came only when this predator nature was given free license to exterminate other life forms "thanks to the appearance of big capital" in the world arena. Epitomizing the marriage between "big capital" and technology, the coming of the airplane was especially ominous for the continued survival of animal species, he warned.[18]

Semenov-tian-shanskii's critique was not reserved exclusively for the depredations of capitalist industrialization, however. During the bloody Civil War he wrote that the aesthetic-ethical critique of modern society was just as applicable to the postrevolutionary order, having concluded that "the socialist idea . . . was, all the same, just [another] striving grounded in base self-interest" and represented therefore no moral advance over capitalism.[19]

In part, the power of his critique derived from the revulsion he felt at the wanton desecration of nature in those years of turmoil. "The raging events overturned everything," he wrote in deep gloom in 1921. "The destruction began as early as the (World) War . . . and continues even now, at times in the most senseless ways." Particularly shocking and "deeply saddening" for him was the wholesale destruction of "a majority of gardens, private parks, monastic and other groves."[20] Paradoxically, these gardens and gentry parks, which were the very symbol of the hated old order to the inflamed masses of peasants, represented to Semenov-tian-shanskii the last vestiges of a nobler, golden age to which Russia, temporarily having blundered into an ill-fated experiment of modernization, should seek to return.

He described, in language unmatched by others of the aesthetic tradition, the degree to which humankind's own proper spiritual development was an outgrowth of nature's own tutelage. "Educated minds," he emphasized in his speech to the Narkompros Museum Conference in Petrograd in February 1919, ". . . cannot but recognize that free nature undefiled in all of its portions by mankind is a *great synthetic museum, indispensable for our further enlightenment and mental development, a museum which, in the event of its destruction, cannot be reconstructed* by the hand of man." This "grand museum," as he called nature, was the source that nourished not only the arts but also the sciences. Of paramount importance, though, was his conviction that nature, "the great book of the existence of all things," was the key to the *moral* development of mankind. Not only did nature provide humans with "irreplaceable aesthetic satisfaction," it also "elevated the soul of mankind." "Nature not only nurtured us," he wrote, "she brought us up, educated us. She feeds us, educates us, and nurtures us yet." Indeed, he continued, "only thanks to the various forces of Nature . . . did man at the dawn of his existence 'become human.' "[21]

In turn, he insisted, society had "a great moral obligation toward Nature." He likened it to "the son's duty to his mother." His views were reminiscent of that of the Greeks who held that all life equally emerged from the bosom of Gaia. Industrial society, with its "extraordinary multiplication of humanity at the expense of other organisms," had introduced a dangerous level of immorality into its relationship with its "mother"—Nature. Like the Greeks, Semenov-tian-shanskii believed that mankind would eventually be punished for this hubris; "in snuffing out the hearth of Nature's life, in plundering and squandering her basic stock, we are digging our own graves," he prophesied, "preparing a miserable future for our progeny."

His prescription called for humans to return to living in harmony with the earth, of which they were, after all, only one component. In order to attain this state of harmonious cooperation with nature, humans would have to surrender their pretensions to ontological superiority over the rest of nature and recognize that living nature had rights in and of itself. "At the present moment," he urged, "as burdensome as it is for all of us, we should strive especially vigorously to realize . . . not only a broad right for human beings to live and develop in all of their spiritual variety, but also the right (upon which humanity now tramples) of all living things to their existence!"[22]

As archaic as Semenov-tian-shanskii's views must have appeared in that revolutionary heyday, there were other expressions of the aesthetic impulse that must have seemed equally subversive to Bolshevik sensibilities. One such was a curious article written by a professor of hydrological engineering, Vsevolod Evgen'evich Timonov. A specialist in port construction and canalization, Timonov had previously given no indication of harboring any sympathies for conservation. If anything, his prior work, especially his plan to bring to life Peter the Great's old dream of connecting the White Sea to Lake Onega by means of a ship canal, lent the impression of an engineer strongly committed to the transformation of nature. Thus, it was all the more surprising that Timonov's article featured a discussion of "nature and the destructive activity of man in general, and of engineers in particular."[23] Was this the engineers' answer to the phenomenon of the repentant nobleman?

The key to Timonov's change of heart was his experience in Germany as a prisoner of war. It had made him sensitive to an entire world of aesthetic needs and considerations. It also reenforced the effects of the speeches of Conwentz and Starbaeck on conservation that he had heard at the Baltic Engineering Congress just prior to the outbreak of hostilities, which had apparently made a deep impression on him in their own right.

Timonov, too, indicted humanity with the charge of "ruining Nature's harmony" in the pursuit of "the most immediate profits." Nothing in nature had been spared. The sordid scene of eco-catastrophe painted by Timonov made the images of George Perkins Marsh seem pallid by comparison. "The air, the soils, and the water became polluted," charged Timonov. "Huge tracts of land, lacking any vegetation cover, reverted to deserts. The climate is being ruined. The conditions for life are deteriorating. Capping his 'victory' over Nature, man places amidst the most attractive scenery disgusting billboards." These discouraging trends were now reaching "especially perverse forms in this age of 'steam and electricity.' " Timonov reserved his strongest words for the polluting effects of factories, which "spew their foul-smelling gases into the atmosphere, greatly impairing the enjoyment of nature." He even made mention of the phenomenon we now call "acid rain," referring to the devastation of 143 hectares of pine forest in the Harz Mountains by a German metallurgical factory's sulfuric acid emissions. While the factories could, and at times did, compensate for such damage, nonetheless "the loss in natural beauty cannot be calculated, let alone replaced," he adjudged.

Timonov indicted the rationalist tradition because "man for a long time did not realize that he must seek beauty in an internal and deep harmony of his works and Nature." Indeed, "the most powerful and fruitful impetus of all for the protection of Nature [was] not the scientific one, but that which is rooted in the love of Nature and of the Homeland."

Here the influence of his German sojourn is most telling; his arguments could have stepped from the pages of *Heimatschutz und Naturschutz* or the literature of the Wandervogel movement. If national culture were to continue to develop and grow, he contended, it had to guard its roots, roots located in primordial nature.

While Timonov's suggestions, involving an extremely cautious approach to further industrial expansion, could hardly have appealed to Soviet leaders of the time, the prescriptions of Semenov-tian-shanskii were even more out of line with the official Bolshevik version of the future. "The tasks of conservation . . . at the present time," he pronounced, "boil down to the immediate fencing off and protection of every spot that has still been spared from the devastating onslaught of mankind." It fell to the conservation movement, he argued, "to serve as a counterweight to the ever greater dispersal and accelerated growth of the human population and to the seizure by humans of a greater and greater percentage of the world's land, . . . land which in mankind's own best interests must remain inviolate."[24]

After 1922 Timonov never wrote another essay concerning the problem of nature protection. Indeed, he continued his work in the Higher Technical Commission of the People's Commissariat of Communications and Transport, work which might well have contributed to the final design of the Belomor (White Sea-Baltic)

Canal. Semenov-tian-shanskii, likewise, for the ensuing decade did not take up the pen for conservation, breaking his silence only after the unveiling of the incipient stages of the Stalin plan for the great transformation of nature. Other leaders of the aesthetic tendency in the conservation movement, particularly Borodin and Taliev, also withdrew from active participation precisely in this period.

The dropping out of an entire current was the outcome of a profound reorientation within the conservation movement beginning in the early 1920s. It appears to have been a response to a whole new set of cultural values which were being actively sponsored by the new Bolshevik regime. One student of Soviet history, Loren R. Graham, observed that "no previous government in history was so openly and energetically in favor of science" as that of Soviet Russia. "The revolutionary leaders of a Soviet government saw the natural sciences as the answer to both the spiritual and physical problems of Russia; science was to them not only the refutation of Russia's age-old mysticism but the key to the great wealth of the Russian land."[25]

Few epitomized this faith in science more than Fedor Nikolaevich Petrov, the head of Glavnauka (which from 1923 had immediate jurisdiction over the Narkompros Conservation Department); V. T. Ter-Oganesov, head of the department in the mid-1920s, and Lunacharskii, the commissar of education. These figures embodied the attitude that a genuinely scientific world view was not only compatible with Marxism but was a sine qua non for the development of socialist consciousness (although, as David Joravsky points out,[26] there was not always agreement as to whether science, or nature, was inherently dialectical or whether they needed to be). Narkompros sought to imbue a materialist outlook in the work of all of its subordinate agencies (although generally not by *diktat*), and all scientific work, whether guided consciously by Marxian philosophical principles or not, whether it represented pure science or applied, was encouraged.

Even to these most open-minded of Bolsheviks, however, the idea of an ethics outside of the instrumentalist ethics of Leninist Marxism, the idea that nature could shape certain spiritual qualities of the national psyche, must have seemed alien. There was no real place for Timonov's or Semenov-tian-shanskii's brand of philosophical idealism even in the relatively tolerant Commissariat of Education. Ter-Oganesov made this point explicit in a short essay written in 1927:

> Many have a misimpression about the goals of conservation. For many, this term signifies the wrong-headed notion of a "saccharine-sentimental" approach to nature, a "tremulously overcautious" attitude toward it—a sort of "Society for the Humane Treatment of Nature." Unfortunately, these kinds of views figure prominently even among a few eminent activists of conservation, who are ready to lump humane treatment of animals and conservation together. It is obvious, however, that no matter how honorable and moral the cause of humane treatment might be, the goals of conservation have nothing in common with it.[27]

Thus, voices of aestheticism began to mute into a long silence, while such scientists as Kozhevnikov, advancing rationales for conservation more compatible with the materialist sensibilities of the new rulers, increasingly emerged as spokespersons for the movement. The favored treatment given the scientific approach to conservation by the authorities in Narkompros played a crucial role in advancing this reorientation in the conservation movement during NEP.

In addition to the fading of the aesthetic wing this period was noteworthy for other developments which, in hindsight, stand out as harbingers of future circumstances. One was the decision to raise funds for the *zapovedniki* by opening them up, in the absence of adequate state subsidies, to exploitation of their resources. Whether it meant the sale of gem collections or of live animals bound for foreign zoos, or the opening of *zapovedniki* to tourism, even on a modest scale, these supposedly temporary responses to NEP austerity conditions suspended the principle of inviolability in the reserves. Worse still, the introduction and persistence of these income-earning economic sectors within the *zapovedniki* ultimately divided the reserves against themselves. Hiding behind the argument that they were expanding their activities to better provide the scientific sectors of the *zapovedniki* with funds for their research, the economic sectors began to usurp their position, claiming a more and more central role in the running of the *zapovednik* as a whole.

Yet, these negative trends eased into the background as a new prosperity brought new opportunities. By late 1924, the growing pains arising from the introduction of NEP were quickly diminishing, and a far more propitious period for conservation was opening up. Happily, the Lenin period had left a solid foundation upon which to build.[28]

FOUR

The Limits to Growth

The years 1925 through 1929 held great hope for the young Soviet conservation movement. The recovery of the economy and the patching together of the rent social fabric made society more receptive to the message of conservation than at any time before. That very economic recovery, however, also represented an increased capacity to despoil nature and to wear down stocks of renewable resources. The condition of the most important biotic resources of the USSR—forests and game— became a matter of debate and concern for resource users and conservationists alike.

THE PROBLEM WITH PROCUREMENT

When the State Planning Commission (Gosplan) and the USSR Council of People's Commissars completed surveys of the Soviet timber industry in 1928, they reached some very sobering conclusions. Almost every aspect of the management of the nation's forests was sadly deficient, and as a result deforestation imperiled not only future timber revenues but agriculture, commercial hunting, and other resources as well.[1] It would seem that the advanced provisions of the 1923 Forest Code should have prevented such excessive exploitation. Yet, as was the case with much Soviet legislation of the period, theory and practice did not always coincide.

Aside from nonobservance, other factors promoting rapid deforestation included the imbalanced exploitation of the USSR's forest wealth; only 33 percent of the republic's annual growth of lumber was accessible, almost all of it west of the Urals.[2] Added to this was the growing pressure for timber as a source of hard currency; in most years during the 1920s forest products ranked first or second among all articles of Russia's exports, accounting for between 8 and 15 percent of the total.[3] The RSFSR People's Commissariat of Agriculture and the Narkomzems of the other union republics, which cut the timber, and the USSR People's Commissariat of Trade (Narkomtorg SSSR), which after 1926 monopolized the export sales of the resource, both adopted a short-term perspective, with the emphasis on output, not conservation.

Game management during NEP was marked by its own crisis over theory and practice. Detailed regulations for commercial hunting were issued by Narkomzem in August 1922 and amended in 1924. At their core was "absolute compliance" with the principle of scientifically based, sustained yield. For the first time, certain hunting methods were outlawed: the use of poisons, bollards, mass killing, snares, and other indiscriminate means of trapping. This was to ensure that only mature animals were taken and that juveniles survived to perpetuate the breeding stock. The regulations also included a list of protected animals, the hunting of which was illegal. In European Russia these animals included the moose, sable, red deer, and wild mountain goats, while throughout the RSFSR the hunting of moose calves, fawns of red deer and wapiti, mountain goat kids, adult beaver, desman, European bison, saiga antelope, sika deer, and maral deer (west of the Enisei River) was proscribed.[4]

Considerable local flexibility was built into the NEP regulations. Local hunting organs attached to the agricultural departments of the local soviets, the soviets' executive committees themselves, and the republican governmental bodies all were empowered to declare closed seasons (zapuski) for any individual species. Violators of any part of the regulations were subject to as much as a five-hundred-ruble fine or up to a year in jail, although these penalties were reduced to three hundred rubles and three months corrective labor, correspondingly, in 1927.[5] Other legislation extended protection to marine mammals, barring Soviet citizens from hunting sea lions and otters north of thirty degrees north latitude in the Pacific Ocean and reaffirming Soviet adherence to the 1911 international convention on fur seals.[6]

In addition to a new body of legislation, other institutional features were designed to contribute to rational game management. Prominent among them was the expansion of the systems of zapovedniki of Narkomzem RSFSR and those of the other union republics. Though Narkomzem RSFSR's first efforts to establish game preserves were marked by half-heartedness and failure, by the late 1920s this dismal record was brightened by some successes, the most noteworthy being the rescue of the beaver from total extinction and its eventual restoration to commercial importance.[7]

From the early 1920s, a legal and institutional framework for conservation-oriented game management was in place. Yet, by the onset of the First Five-Year Plan, the ideal of a continually more productive hunting sector seemed to recede ever farther into the future. Reporting on N. M. Kulagin's speech to the Academy of Sciences' Commission for the Study of the Productive Forces of the USSR (KEPS), the journal Priroda concluded that "this question looks so dismal that we are forced to speak about an immediate, catastrophic danger hanging over the fur economy of the USSR."[8] This dreary assessment was seconded by an editorial in the March 1928 issue of the trade journal Pushnoe delo (The Fur Trade).[9]

All studies, figures, and observations supported these gloomy conclusions. In Belorussia, eight years of protection did not seem to have helped the moose much. There were at most 120 of these animals alive in the entire republic by 1927, according to an estimate by the Minsk zoologist A. V. Fediushin. Sharing the fate of the European bison, which had been wiped out in that republic during the Civil War, were the European red deer, the sable, the wolverine, and the grey-lag goose. The last wildcat had gone down in 1927, and the once plentiful brown bear, pine marten, roe deer, bustard, and capercaillie were now the objects only of rare sightings.[10]

The most valuable fur of the entire USSR, that of the Kamchatka sea otter, had become all but unobtainable, and the hunting journal *Okhotnik* (The Hunter) in 1927 put the annual rate of decline in the numbers of furbearers at 3 to 5 percent. "We have, to this moment, been sawing off the very branch upon which we have been sitting," lamented Kulagin.[11]

The most important factors promoting the decline in game—particularly the rarer species, such as sable, otter, and arctic fox—were the appearance of the affluent American market as the world's primary importer and a great, sustained increase in the price of furs through the 1920s.[12] With the resumption of trade between Soviet Russia and the chief Western nations, the only significant brake on production was removed and the way was cleared for all-out development of fur procurement and export in the Soviet Union. Even the ideal of a rational hunting sector was powerless before the blandishments of such a seller's market.

By the mid-1920s the fur trade had become a major economic force in the USSR. Exports of pelts ranked second, behind forest products, in 1924–1925, and remained high in ranking (in third or fourth place) for the next decade, accounting for more than 10 percent of the value of all exports for the latter half of the 1920s.[13] Russia's share of the international fur market was consistently greater than 15 percent, and furs occupied a central place in Soviet trade with the United States. Thus, in terms of both Soviet Russia's need for consolidating a stable position in world trade and its desire to obtain scarce hard currency with which to purchase machinery for the Five-Year Plan, the export of pelts was hardly negligible.

The conditions afforded by NEP made possible Russia's rapid and successful reentry into the international fur market. Until the late 1920s, the central state trading organs under Narkomtorg had to share the field with a variety of cooperatives, all-Soviet and mixed Soviet-foreign joint-stock companies, and even other state agencies.

These conditions also had their dark side. Procurement practices did not always conform to the letter of the law. The journal *Sovetskaia step'* (The Soviet Steppe) reported in its 18 February 1927 issue that, in the provinces, procurement agents behave "literally, like pillagers. They sneak into regions closed to hunting, buy up illicitly gotten pelts, disregard official price limits. . . ." Many of the agents of Narkomtorg's trading agency Gostorg itself, as a piece in *Sovetskaia Sibir'* (Soviet Siberia) of 28 December 1926 suggests, were formerly independent fur traders and middlemen who brought not only their expertise but their "ethics" as well to their new Soviet positions.[14]

One of the responses to the impending game crisis was the creation by local authorities of *zakazniki,* temporary game preserves. On 1 October 1926 there were five hundred of these in the RSFSR alone, with a combined area of five million hectares. Exactly two years later, their number had already trebled and their area doubled.[15]

Although the central procurement authorities of Gostorg themselves realized that something had to be done to stem the dissipation of the basic breeding stock of profitable commercial species, they were far from pleased by the uncontrolled proliferation of *zakazniki* and hunting bans *(zapuski)* at the provincial and lower levels. How was it possible to coordinate export policy, asked the center, in the face of such peremptory decisions as those by the Kalmyk Oblast to ban the hunting of polecats, for example, or by the Kirgiz ASSR prohibiting the taking of marmots?[16]

Compounding the problem was the almost arbitrary manner in which the bans seemed to originate. In one place, they were at the behest of the local lore society, in another, the local branch of Narkomzem RSFSR, and in yet another, the local hunter's cooperative union. Nowhere, complained Gostorg, were the identical methodological criteria being applied.

To put an end to scattered local-level initiatives, Narkomtorg and Gostorg made their bid for complete control over commercial hunting in the RSFSR. Early in 1928 Narkomtorg advanced the idea that a chief prerequisite for putting hunting on a sound basis was to unify and centralize the existing balkanized structure in the sector. *Pushnoe delo,* noting that "experience has demonstrated that Narkomzem cannot cope with the hunting-related tasks with which it is charged," sought to divest the latter of these responsibilities and nominated Narkomtorg SSSR as the new, unified center for Soviet game management.[17]

Paradoxically, within Narkomtorg and its rival Narkomzem there was a certain convergence of attitudes. Both were more and more inclined to view hunting's salvation in the form of a technological fix. Attention centered most of all on two programs of action: ranch breeding of commercial varieties, and the acclimatization of new species to supplement the indigenous, exhausted ones.

Gostorg had expanded into the game breeding business during the early 1920s, funding research into captive breeding of sable and other furbearers conducted by the pragmatic youths of the K. A. Timiriazev Biological Station of the Young Naturalists' Society in Moscow. Later, Gostorg itself began to organize ranches for pure lines of arctic, blue, and silver fox and for sable. Finally, Gostorg was developing plans for a wholesale introduction of the muskrat, a North American rodent, to the USSR.

Perhaps stung by criticism pointing to its inactivity on the research front, Narkomzem by the latter part of the decade began to look into captive breeding and acclimatization as well. In 1927, the Forest Administration upgraded the Biological Station of the Moscow Suburban Educational Forestry Plantations into a central research base: the Central Experimental Forestry Station of Narkomzem RSFSR.[18] Attached to it was a full-fledged Biological and Commercial Hunting Department led by B. M. Zhitkov.

When in 1921 the forty-nine-year-old Zhitkov was chosen to fill the chair of forest fauna biology at the Moscow Petrovskaia Agricultural Academy (soon to be renamed the Timiriazev Agricultural Academy), he already exhibited those attributes that were to be the hallmarks of the Michurinist biologists of the 1930s and beyond: voluntarism, social-mindedness, a preference for applied over pure science, and a fervent belief in the utility of acclimatization and biotechnics.[19] This was not surprising; Zhitkov had imbibed his zoological theory and his ideas on the role of science in society from the very fount of nineteenth-century transformist biology in Russia, Anatolii Petrovich Bogdanov.

Zhitkov epitomized the pragmatic brand of biologist who drew closer to the Commissariats of Agriculture and Trade during the 1920s even as their conservation-oriented colleagues deserted those agencies. The time was ripe for such a collaboration, for these economic commissariats, under pressure to increase their output of resources for export, embraced those scientists who seemed to offer the promise of a technological fix. In turn, Zhitkov, Petr Aleksandrovich Manteifel',[20] Nikolai Petrovich Lavrov,[21] V. Ia. Generozov, and other scientists sought after the opportunities those commissariats could provide to put into practice their ideas on heredity, adaptation, and acclimatization.

Having developed the State Standards for Peltry Quality for use by Gostorg while simultaneously working within the Narkomzem research system, Zhitkov was the perfect bridge to bring together the two commissariats in the interests of export growth. The basis for united action was a jointly supported program of large-scale acclimatization of furbearers and other commercially valuable fauna, beginning with the muskrat. Zhitkov and his students would try to mobilize the scientific community to provide support and expertise, venturing forth from their initial bases of strength in the Agricultural Academy, the Moscow Zootechnical Institute, the Moscow Zoo, and the Forestry Institute.

Other new faces in Narkomzem also could find a common language with the wheelers and dealers of Narkomtorg. Semen Antonovich Petrushin, the energetic head of the Subdepartment for Hunting from the late 1920s, was such a figure. As president of the Hunters' Cooperative Union (Vsekokhotsoiuz) in the early 1920s, he was centrally involved in an embezzlement scandal but emerged relatively unscathed, ousted from office but retaining his key position in a joint-stock fur procurement company.[22] Now this politically astute, profit-oriented and slightly unprincipled personality was bringing to bear his expertise in a bid to keep Narkomzem RSFSR a major actor in the Soviet fur trade.[23] The utilitarian thrusts of the economic commissariats, however, did not go unchallenged.

Independently of the major scientific societies as well as within them, scientists began to speak out vigorously against what they believed to be the excessively plunderous exploitation of natural resources. Academician Vladimir Ivanovich Vernadskii, for one, sought to temper the euphoria of the planners with some thoughts on the limits to growth. Addressing the All-Union Congress of KEPS on 7 April 1926, he reminded the delegates (as Lenin once had reminded another meeting) that even the most advanced social system could never transcend certain bio-physico-chemical realities:

> Natural productive forces are potential forces. . . . They are independent in their composition and their abundance of all human will and reason, however concentrated or organized. As these forces are not inexhaustible, we know that they have limits and that these limits are real; they are not imaginary and are not theoretical. They may be ascertained by the scientific study of nature and represent for us an insuperable natural limit to our productive capacity.

"We now know," concluded Vernadskii, "that as concerns our country, these limits are quite narrow and do not permit—at the risk of cruel repayment—any wastefulness in our use of resources."[24] That Vernadskii should train his sights on the problem of nonrenewable resources and highlight the need for wise use was fully comprehensible; his entire intellectual development, from his professional training as a mineralogist to his political education as a statist Kadet—attracted him precisely to this aspect of the conservation problem.

It was equally appropriate that a zookeeper should publicize the problem of disappearing species. Soviet Russia's first equivalent of the "Red Data Book"—complete with appealing illustrations—appeared in 1928, the work of the curator of the aquarium at the Moscow Zoo, Semen Aleksandrovich Sidorov.[25] Complementing the statements of such individuals as Vernadskii and Sidorov were collective expressions by groups of scientists and scientific organizations. Virtually every zoological and botanical congress during the 1920s and early 1930s went on record in support of stronger nature protection policies.[26]

THE CENTRAL BUREAU FOR THE STUDY OF LOCAL LORE

Apart from the All-Russian Society for Conservation (VOOP), which came on the scene in 1924, the strongest and most consistent support for conservation came not from a scientific society in the narrow sense, but from a peculiarly Russian organization known as the Central Bureau for the Study of Local Lore (Tsentral'noe Biuro Kraevedeniia, or TsBK), officially launched in January 1922 under the auspices of the Academy of Sciences. Despite the fact that it was incontrovertibly led by scientists,[27] the TsBK was not, strictly speaking, a narrowly scientific organization. Its uniqueness and part of its importance in the 1920s lay in its being the only group led by scientists that could properly be called a mass organization. By the late 1920s, within its 2,270 branches embracing almost 60,000 members[28] was doubtless included not only a hefty slice of Russia's academically based naturalists but a good chunk of the provincial intelligentsia as well. Compared with VOOP, the TsBK was a towering giant. Its 1927–1928 budget of 53,042 rubles[29]—to take a representative year—amounted to no less than 600 percent of the budget of the conservation society for the same year.[30]

From its earliest days, both the central administration of the TsBK and its local affiliates took more than a passing interest in nature protection. This was a natural outgrowth of the character of the organization. Here were united those most interested in learning about their native region in all of its fullness: history, folkways, art, architecture, archaeology, and natural history. In many cases, this love of region was only an aspect of love of homeland. Sometimes, in fact, the society seemed to be one of the last legal havens for the expression of an aesthetically colored patriotic sensibility (at least before the implications of "socialism in one country" became apparent) and as a refuge for preservationists of all stripes. It was the internal answer to *Smena vekh,** combined with the aesthetic ethos of the German Heimatkunde movement and the popular flavor of the American National Geographical Society.

Smena vekh (Change of Boundary-Markers) was a movement of Russians in emigration who gave qualified support to the Soviet regime in the interests of a rebirth of a strong Russia.

To a great extent, the leadership of the Central Bureau and that of the conservation organs formed an interlocking directorate. Meteorologist Aleksei Fedoseevich Vangengeim, editor of *Izvestiia TsBK* (TsBK News) and future deputy president of the society, was a member of the governing council of VOOP and a future president of that organization. Mikhail Petrovich Potemkin, a specialist in methods of teaching biology, wore two hats as well: scholarly secretary of the TsBK and specialist responsible for the management of Narkompros's *zapovedniki* in Glavnauka's Department of Scientific Institutions (later, Scientific Sector).[31]

D. O. Sviatskii, another scholarly secretary of the TsBK, also served as scholarly secretary for the Conservation Section of the Leningrad Conference of Gosplan, while the interest of TsBK Vice-President A. E. Fersman in conservation was well known. Indeed, he held the distinction of being the only speaker at the Fifteenth Congress of the All-Russian Communist Party to even mention Russia's *zapovedniki*.[32] A. P. and V. P. Semenov-tian-shanskii and P. E. Vasil'kovskii (who served as deputy editor of *Izvestiia TsBK* under Vangengeim) were all active in the Leningrad branch of the bureau. Lastly, the president of the TsBK from the mid-1920s, Petr Germogenovich Smidovich, was fast becoming a central figure in conservation politics. Among the TsBK leaders, then, only N. Ia. Marr, Al'bert P. Pinkevich, and a few figures of second rank held themselves aloof from the green crusade.

In the pages of the Moscow-based *Izvestiia TsBK*, Potemkin struck a note of urgency. He stated that current efforts at nature protection were only "a drop in the ocean" and warned:

> We have failed to counterpose as yet a broad-based movement of public opinion in support of conservation to the narrowly interpreted economic interests . . . of the economic organs.[33]

According to Potemkin, this imbalance of forces left Soviet society vulnerable to an "awesome threat of . . . the exhaustion not simply of our natural resources, but the destruction of our scientific and cultural values as well." Only a speedy mobilization could meet the challenge, and the first step was to forge a vigorous "united front" of the TsBK and the All-Russian Society for Conservation.[34]

THE ALL-RUSSIAN SOCIETY FOR CONSERVATION

Despite the fact that in the early 1920s many individuals and organizations were speaking out for conservation, a niche in the movement was still going empty. There was still no *social* organization specifically devoted to creating a public constituency around the issues of conservation. The organizations founded in Moscow and Petrograd during the Civil War were quickly washed away by the tide of events, while the Geographical Society's "Permanent" Conservation Commission failed to live up to its name.

In 1924, after Narkompros's Conservation Department had survived the major threats to its survival, Russia's core group of conservation activists felt free to turn their attention toward building a movement. The centerpiece of their efforts was the creation of a new society, the All-Russian Society for Conservation (VOOP).

The organizers of the society included many familiar faces. Kozhevnikov served as president of the Organizing Committee, although the initiative belonged as much to Shillinger, who had been serving as the head of the Conservation Department. Pod"iapol'skii, now a staff member of Narkompros working on problems of nutrition and hygiene and incorporating conservation into school curricula, served as scholarly secretary, and even V. I. Taliev initially loaned his prestigious name to the endeavor.

Close associates of Kozhevnikov were well represented on the committee. Dmitrii Mikhailovich Rossinskii, professor of sericulture at the Moscow Textile Institute, Kozhevnikov's deputy in the moribund Acclimatization Society, occupied the post of vice-president. Kozhevnikov's former student Ivan Il'ich Mesiatsev, professor (and later *prorektor*) of the Industrial-Pedagogical Institute, director of expeditions at the Oceanographic Institute, and, for a time, head of Glavnauka's Department of Scientific Institutions, sat on the committee. So did Kozhevnikov's colleague Boris Petrovich Ditmar, a geologist and limnologist from Tallinn who was a privatdocent at Moscow University as well as chief bibliographer of the Library of the State Historical Museum.

The founders' list also included zoologist Mikhail Pavlovich Rozanov, Vladimir Petrovich Zylev, professor of mathematics at the Moscow Transport Engineering Institute and an expert on matrix theory, and Evdokiia Grigor'evna Bloshenko, who was to serve as VOOP's permanent secretary for over a decade.

Aside from Shillinger, there were others of more practical inclination among the founders as well. These included the grand old man of Russian hunting science, Sergei Aleksandrovich Buturlin, an accomplished ornithologist who had been active for a while in Narkomzem's Tsentrokhota but who had latterly taken up the cause of the small hunting and trapping peoples as a member of the VTsIK Committee of the North; Karl Iosipovich Pokaliuk of Pinsk, an expert on the practice and economics of forestry and deputy president of VSNKh's Scientific-Technical Council for the Forestry Industry; and Nikolai Mikhailovich Kulagin, professor of zoology at Moscow University.

Rounding out the group was the only politician in that number, the veteran Bolshevik Fedor Nikolaevich Petrov, party member from 1896, former deputy chairman of the Council of Ministers of the Far Eastern Republic, and head of Glavnauka.

According to its first charter, approved by the People's Commissariat for Internal Affairs (NKVD) on 29 November 1924, VOOP's aims were above all educational. The society had a mandate to "promote in every way possible the practical realization of conservation through the transmission of information and by awakening interest in it on the part of society in general." The scope of its activities, however, was not limited to propaganda and significantly included "the scientific investigation of questions of conservation in the RSFSR," a task which the society would regard as pivotal.

To attain these objectives, the society was granted the right to conduct a broad range of activities.[35] To help support its agenda, VOOP was authorized to collect annual dues of fifty kopecks. Its only obligations were to keep accurate accounts of its finances and to submit annually two copies of a list of its members to the NKVD, which took an interest in such matters.

One of the first governmental figures to greet the appearance of the new society was Lunacharskii, the education commissar. Although he was too ill to attend a special inaugural meeting of VOOP on 15 February 1925 at Moscow University, he sent along the text of the address he had intended to give, which was read by Kozhevnikov. One figure who did attend, N. A. Semashko, people's commissar of public health, took the opportunity to decry the deforestation of the Crimean uplands.[36]

VOOP settled down to business in earnest on 3 April 1925, when its first general meeting and election of officers was held. If anything, the election indicated the intention of activists to select spokespersons for their cause who enjoyed the greatest rapport with the country's governing elite. The new president of the society, accordingly, was an Old Bolshevik, N. M. Fedorovskii. The selection of the other executive officers of VOOP was further evidence of a cooperative attitude toward the regime. The forester Pokaliuk was elected vice-president, while the post of scholarly secretary fell to party member Pod''iapol'skii. Another colleague of Fedorovskii's, the mineralogist V. V. Arshinov, rounded out the executive board as treasurer.

The first year of the society's existence was marked by modest yet encouraging progress. With a budget of only 1,013 rubles, of which only 313 rubles were realized through membership dues or from sales of VOOP publications (the remaining 700 rubles being a subsidy from Narkompros),[37] the society's propaganda reach was perforce limited. Nonetheless, five general meetings were held, offering the interested public opportunities to hear prominent members of the society. Kulagin spoke on the biology of the European bison, and Kozhevnikov reported on his trip to Berlin in the fall of 1925 where he represented VOOP and the Narkompros Conservation Department at a meeting of the International Society for the Protection of the European Bison.[38] During the year, the society's governing council (*sovet*) met six times, with organizational and policy questions occupying much of its attention.

Foreign ties blossomed. Cordial relationships were struck up with a number of organizations abroad, including the French Société pour la protection de la nature, the American Bison Society, the Polish Panstwowa Rada Ochrony Przyrody, and Pro Montibus of Italy, and literature was exchanged. Contacts were initiated with such governmental agencies as the National Park Services of the United States and Canada.[39] The most intimate collaboration remained between the Russians and the Germans and Swiss, a continuation of the warm relationships that had existed between Borodin and Conwentz and Kozhevnikov and Sarasin before the World War.[40]

The period through April 1929 was one of continued modest growth in a number of areas. Membership advanced to 1,411 although dues receipts continued to lag at only 365 rubles. Many members were in arrears, while almost 40 percent of the membership consisted of students, who were often unable to pay. Contributions received on the lecture circuit, however, netted 1,616 rubles, proceeds from the sale of publications garnered 1,112 rubles more, and Narkompros's subsidy rose to 5,520 rubles, keeping the society in the black despite expenses of 6,839 rubles.[41]

By 1929 VOOP and the TsBK had solidified a close working relationship. Coordinating their efforts, it was agreed that the bureau's special province was to be the organization of Bird Day, Arbor Day, and the radio lecture series "Local Lore and Conservation." VOOP reserved for itself the task of propagandizing in factories and Red Army and workers' clubs and among Young Pioneers and the peasants.[42]

Unquestionably, though, the society's greatest achievement in this period was the publication of its journal, *Okhrana prirody* (Conservation), which hit the newsstands in early 1928. With its attractive format, its pages generously studded with photographs and illustrations, and its at times daring independence, the new bimonthly with a circulation of 3,000 made many new friends for conservation.

Okhrana prirody introduced Soviet readers to a larger world, where they could be transported to a nature park in Poland, Spain, France, Italy, Germany, Canada, Switzerland, Sweden, or the exotic Congo. America's Yellowstone was there, too, in a Russian translation of excerpts from Teddy Roosevelt's reminiscences about the park. Russia's own conservation scene was covered in even more copious detail. Reports abounded from all corners of the USSR, not merely the RSFSR. Readers were able to identify problem spots from Dzhety-su in Kazakhstan to the Berezina marshes in Belorussia and to familiarize themselves with existing and proposed *zapovedniki*. Recognizing the exigency of keeping conservation's constituents politically informed, the journal chronicled the activities of VOOP and the Narkompros conservation agencies. Expeditions of Glavnauka to expedite the creation of new *zapovedniki* were front-page news.

The journal even had a historical sense. Ditmar contributed an overview, however sketchy, of two hundred years of Russian efforts at nature protection.[43] Closer to the present was Kh. G. Shaposhnikov's remarkable saga of the history of one *zapovednik*—the Caucasus—which was serialized over three issues.[44] *Okhrana prirody* had something for nearly everyone. There were articles for and about children and special profiles on the status of individual endangered animals—red deer, moose, tigers, beavers, musk oxen, mountain goats, roe deer, European bison, and Baikal seals, to name a few—and plants, including the Pitsunda pine, water chestnut, and *Polypodium vulgare*. Even such ideologically questionable material as the positive role of shamanism in ensuring a sustained-yield–based exploitation of game among the peoples of Siberia, albeit gingerly treated by Professor of Ethnology V. P. Nalimov, found a place in *Okhrana prirody*.[45]

As seen by activists at VOOP, one of the journal's most important tasks was to convince the people and the government that conservation was essential. Russian nature seemed so abundant that it was difficult for the average citizen to feel the immediacy of the crisis. Kozhevnikov had seen this in 1908, but the problem still persisted when he wrote in *Okhrana prirody* twenty years later:

For us to talk about conservation is considerably more difficult than abroad. There the laying waste to nature and the perversion of its natural contours happened so long ago that it is easy to sound the alarm. . . . For us, though, where the forested area is about one half billion hectares, . . . where there are places with a population density of 0.4 persons per square kilometer, it is as if it were too early to speak of conservation.[46]

The irony of the situation was that the Russian conservationists had learned the lessons of unplanned growth abroad but were unable to transmit their perceptions to their countrymen. However, there were other impediments to the proselytizing campaign. Divergent conceptions of conservation held by the movement's activists did not help matters, especially in getting serious government attention. A fog of confusion concerning its goals and methods enveloped the movement from its very beginnings.

Part of the reason for this state of affairs was the relative newness of the whole idea, as the very first editorial in *Okhrana prirody* properly observed:

Conservation . . . is a conception still comparatively new for broad strata of our population. And, unwillingly, this term is linked up with a host of questions that have not been sufficiently reflected upon by us. . . . Does nature really *need* protection? Why and from whom is it necessary to protect it? Who *can* protect it, and how?[47]

Precisely around these questions conservationists had failed to reach any definitive agreement thus far, only a mutual toleration. The editorial concluded with an appeal for all conservationists to unite under the aegis of the All-Russian Society for Conservation. This call to unity, however, could not mask the fact that the conservation movement was only a confederation of diverse tendencies united by a word—*conservation*—but differing widely in its interpretation. Soon these differences would take on real importance.

LOCAL CONSERVATION ORGANIZATIONS

By the late 1920s VOOP, although it was the most influential voluntary society devoted to conservation, was by no means the only such organization. Along the banks of the Enisei, in Krasnoiarsk, conservationists waged their battles under the banner of the Conservation Section of the Krasnoiarsk branch of the Geographical Society.[48]

Another organization of regional character was the All-Ukrainian Society for the Defense of Animals and Plants (ZhIVRAS), also called the Union for the Defense of Living Nature. Three years after it was founded on 15 February 1925, almost coterminously with VOOP, it claimed 9,000 members (5,500 of them in Khar'kov), a membership almost seven times that of the Moscow-based society. As contrasted with VOOP, however, which had influence greatly out of proportion to its modest size, ZhIVRAS's considerable membership failed to lift it out of deep obscurity. The reasons for this were the contrasting emphases and styles of the two groups. At the same time that VOOP was trying to couch its arguments for nature protection in the language of science and of "socialist reconstruction," ZhIVRAS was accenting the worthy but arcane-sounding message of the need for the humane treatment of animals, "these mute and unselfish friends and helpmates of mankind."[49]

Although its ethical, sentimentalist message continued to appeal to many, ZhIVRAS's appeal did not extend to the most critical groups of all: the Soviet party and government elite. Nor were the leaders of Narkompros RSFSR and Narkompros of the Ukraine any exception. ZhIVRAS, which, unlike VOOP, did not take special care to package its appeals in politically attractive wrapping, proved to be just another example of late-NEP ephemera.

Much like the party or the church, the conservation movement sought to extend its influence first of all by capturing the minds of the young. Attention was lavished on designing ways to incorporate conservation and nature study into the school curriculum. One of the first important breakthroughs came in April 1924, when the Commissariat of Education issued a series of instructions directly encouraging such efforts.[50]

Conservationist-pedagogues, including Kozhevnikov, sought to replace the antisocial behavior of the vandal with a morality rooted in respect for the human and planetary communities. Long a foe of individualistic exploitation of natural resources, Kozhevnikov from the time of the Revolution sought to underscore the common interest of conservationists and socialists in nourishing the idea of community and respect for the commons. In his conservation guide for teachers, he examined the case of the schoolchildren who took some eggs from a duck's nest during a visit to a local swamp and who justified their act by their belief that the eggs "belonged to no one." It was just this view of the commons as a place open to all comers with which Kozhevnikov took issue. "Those eggs are *the property of the state*," he declared, "just as is all game, along with all the forests and all of the swamps. The more game there is, the more the state, and, consequently, the entire people, will benefit. Destroying future game fowl, in the form of eggs, we are consequently doing injury to the people's property. . . ."[51] Kozhevnikov called this a lesson

> concerning general upbringing which must command the most serious attention of the young citizens of a nation having a socialist system. It is imperative to make clear that there are no things that belong to "no one" and that everything is the property of the workers' and peasants' state.[52]

If conservationists lavished a goodly share of attention on the young, the latter repaid the movement with their energy and enthusiasm. Students were a key group in the NEP conservation movement. They were the bulwark of the annual demonstrations for nature protection held on Arbor Day and the new Soviet holiday, Bird Day, which marked the return of migratory birds from their more southerly wintering areas.[53] By 1927, the latter was celebrated throughout the RSFSR. Forming the core of the celebrants were 45,000 Young Naturalists, who were joined by Pioneers, Komsomols, and adults. Moscow's schoolchildren converged on Izmailovskii Park, where they built birdhouses and tidied up, while thousands demonstrated in the streets of Ivanovo-Voznesensk, complete with banners emblazoned with conservation slogans.[54] Participants there and elsewhere then dispersed to make a spring count of arriving birds. In some places the activities continued for a week. Through the celebration of the Bird Day, Soviet youth for the first time made conservation a visible presence on the streets of Russia's cities and hamlets.

Thus, conservation began to make its mark on Soviet society. In Moscow, Leningrad, and even in remote Siberia people were organizing in defense of the integrity of their natural environment. Their vehicles for action reflected the pluralism of the times. Conservation's banner was hoisted in the meetings of the imposing TsBK and at the tiny gatherings of the Krasnoiarsk branch of the Geographical Society. In the vanguard, slowly gathering its strength, was VOOP, the All-Russian Society for Conservation.

FIVE

The Goskomitet and the
Zapovedniki

Almost one year after the founding of the All-Russian Society for Conservation, a new governmental agency for nature protection made its debut. On 5 October 1925 Mikhail Ivanovich Kalinin, chairman of the All-Russian Central Executive Committee (VTsIK), signed into law a new bill which, while basically updating the 1921 Lenin-era decree on protected territories, also contained some novel features. The most striking directed Glavnauka, Narkompros's Main Administration handling conservation affairs, to organize under its auspices a wholly new agency to "unify and regulate the policies of the various commissariats and governmental agencies involving questions of conservation."[1] This body was to be called the State Interagency Committee for Conservation (Goskomitet).

The decision to place the Goskomitet under the aegis of Glavnauka had its drawbacks for the conservation movement. The Goskomitet occupied a position not only beneath the ministerial level, but also subordinate to that of a *glavk*.* As a result, it could not raise matters directly before the RSFSR Council of People's Commissars, but had to petition through Narkompros, its parent commissariat. That hindered its effectiveness, despite the manifest sympathy for conservation held by Commissar of Education Lunacharskii and many of his advisers. Another deficiency of the Goskomitet's lack of institutional autonomy was that it was viewed as a creature of Narkompros, especially by the economic commissariats. That led in time to diminishing participation on the part of those commissariats, their frequent refusals to go along with the majority recommendations of the Goskomitet, and, ultimately, their frontal attack on the Education Commissariat with the aim of divesting it of all conservation functions.

Despite these drawbacks, however, the decision to vest Glavnauka with responsibility for the Goskomitet was in many ways a happy one. The very fact that the Goskomitet and the Conservation Department were under one roof made for excellent exchange of information, and allowed both agencies to share facilities and even staff. Furthermore, the hands on the purse strings at Glavnauka were more munificent than perhaps anywhere else. Finally, that the Goskomitet was dominated by Glavnauka-sponsored activists enabled the body to pursue its fact-finding activi-

*A main administration, or major department, within a commissariat.

ties and to expand the network of *zapovedniki* far more aggressively than had the organization been more neutral.

Because its membership expanded to include an increasing roster of governmental agencies, unions, and scientific organizations, the composition of the Goskomitet plenum was volatile. By contrast, the presidium, which was the real center of power in the Goskomitet, had a less variable structure. Both bodies, however, were clearly dominated by the influence of Glavnauka.

Within the presidium, Glavnauka nominated the president, the deputy president, and the secretary—all ex-officio members of the Narkompros delegation on the plenum—as well as a fourth member from among the representatives of other agencies or organizations in the plenary body. The fifth member was the ex-officio representative of Narkomzem RSFSR on the plenum. Thus, if they voted en bloc, Narkompros's members on the presidium always had at least a three-to-two majority. Although the presidium was expanded in the late 1920s to include a sixth member, Glavnauka never lost its effective grip on the body.

Glavnauka's influence in the plenum was slightly more dilute. In addition to the three members of Narkompros, Glavnauka was entitled to nominate up to five scientists or conservation specialists, giving it a potential vote of eight. Two of the seven remaining places went to representatives considered friendly to Glavnauka— the Academy of Sciences and the Geographical Society. The remaining five went to Gosplan RSFSR, VSNKh RSFSR, and the People's Commissariats of Finance, Internal Affairs, and Agriculture of the RSFSR. Over the next three years, this roster expanded to include delegates of the Agricultural Laborers' Union, VOOP, the Hunters' Cooperative Union (Vsekokhotsoiuz), the Moscow Forestry and Scientific Technical Society, the Moscow Society of Naturalists (MOIP), and the People's Commissariats of Public Health and of the Workers' and Peasants' Inspectorate of the RSFSR. Representatives of the RSFSR's autonomous republics (ASSRs) were allowed to participate in meetings as members where questions involving them were at issue.

The purview of the Goskomitet was broad, underscoring the committee's importance as a policymaker as well as a regulator. As a policymaker, the Goskomitet was given the responsibility not only of planning the expansion of the network of *zapovedniki, zakazniki,* zoos, gardens, monuments of nature, and other protected territories of the RSFSR, but of determining their staff levels, funding, and research programs as well. This was linked with and flowed from its general responsibilities to determine the general direction of scientific research in the conservation field as a whole: to mobilize Soviet science to explore the structure of nature and to inform economic practice on the basis of its scientific findings.

With respect to the larger economy beyond the boundaries of the protected territories, the Goskomitet enjoyed the power to review the actions or policies of any resource user "from the perspective of conservation interests" and to make recommendations for the modification of offending policies based on its own studies and expertise. Such recommendations could be submitted to the highest levels of Soviet government through Narkompros. Additionally, the Goskomitet was entitled to establish ties with similar agencies in the other union republics to help coordinate conservation policy on an all-Union scale.

Policing and enforcement also occupied a major place among the responsibilities of the Goskomitet. Any measures taken by any state or social organization affecting the protected territories of the RSFSR were subject to Goskomitet's review and regulation. The activities and annual reports of the *zapovedniki* and other protected territories were frequently examined by the agency as well. Routine matters, such as proposals for the creation of new *zapovedniki,* were handled by special commissions of the Goskomitet, which were joined by scientists co-opted from outside the agency.

To carry out its functions, the Goskomitet could enlist the powers, procedures, and privileges conferred upon it by the co-signatories of its instructions.[2] If a quorum of one-third of its members was present, the Goskomitet could officially impose binding decisions on all of its constituent member organizations unless the dissenting agencies raised official objections. In that event, the matter could then be taken to the SNK RSFSR by the dissenting parties for final resolution, with Narkompros representing the Goskomitet majority.[3]

THE LOCAL INTERAGENCY CONSERVATION COMMISSIONS

Another important network of conservation organizations grew out of the same legislation that provided for the Goskomitet; the decree also authorized Narkompros to set up interagency bodies on the model of the Goskomitet to function on levels of government below that of the all-RSFSR.

The structural parallelism between the Goskomitet and its local analogues-in-miniature was almost total. The local interagency conservation commissions were attached to the local branches of Narkompros much as the Goskomitet was subordinate to Glavnauka. Similarly, the president of the local commission was always a member of Narkompros, ideally a local representative of the Conservation Department. (This meant that the post often fell to the representative of the local *zapovednik.*) The composition of the local bodies, too, was somewhat variable. In addition to the seat allotted to the representative of the local branch of the People's Commissariat of Agriculture, the commission included representatives from the local Narkompros, the local soviet's executive committee, the Hunters' Cooperative Union, and the local *zapovednik* (customarily, its director). Moreover, a seat was allotted to a delegate who represented all of the local research institutions and scientific societies *in corpore,* and the membership could be augmented further by presidential invitation.

All official acts of the local commissions were subject to approval by the Conservation Department of Narkompros (and later, by the Goskomitet). Deciding by simple majority vote, the commissions deliberated both questions of a purely local character and those having national ramifications; they also monitored the implementation of national policies on the local level, acting as the eyes, the ears, and the tocsin for the superordinate conservation bodies.

While the Goskomitet was financed directly by Glavnauka and was conveniently located in Moscow, the local interagency conservation commissions had to root themselves in the relatively inhospitable soil of provincial Russia and were dependent on the munificence of the local branches of Narkompros. Local-level resistance or indifference, combined with the natural reluctance of the local branches of the Commissariat of Education to take on an additional financial burden, proved to be serious impediments to establishing the commissions. By 1929, only six of eleven oblasts had established them, in addition to one autonomous oblast (the Khakass AO), six autonomous republics, and nine okrugs, mostly in those administrative units where *zapovedniki* already existed.[4] The sketchy response of the localities first prompted F. N. Petrov in a circular of 12 April 1928 to appeal to the local education branches' sense of social responsibility.[5] Another memorandum sent out on 11 December and signed by Deputy Commissar Iakovleva struck a different note entirely; all local branches were now ordered to initiate the formation of the interagency commissions where this had not yet been done, and were given a scant five weeks to do so.[6]

A DELICATE BALANCE

Serving as chairman of the Goskomitet from its inception until its dissolution in 1933 was Professor N. M. Kulagin. Like Fedorovskii of VOOP, Kulagin was a fortunate compromise choice. As a founder-member of VOOP, he had maintained his conservation credentials in excellent order. A highly respected professor of zoology at Moscow State University and corresponding member of the Academy of Sciences, Kulagin was accepted by the older-line academics in the conservation movement as essentially one of their own. Yet, he was a figure who could find a common language with the representatives of the economic commissariats. For a "bourgeois" professor he was in reasonably good political odor; while he was not a member of the Communist Party, he had cooperated with Soviet authorities from the start. (His participation in the 1911 protest against the policies of Minister of Education L. Kasso was another positive item in his political biography.) Equaling, if not outweighing, the importance of Kulagin's strictly political record was his strongly utilitarian outlook. His emphasis on the practical application of scientific knowledge, on its primacy over pure science, his antipathy to preservationism, his championing of wise use, and his efforts not only to conserve but to expand the resource base of the Soviet Union, together with his special interest in commercial hunting, provided for much common ground between him and the economic commissariats, Narkomzem and Narkomtorg.

Kulagin's deputy was V. T. Ter-Oganesov, who from 1925 headed Narkompros's Conservation Department and who held the Goskomitet vice-chairmanship ex officio. Although he was a nonbiologist, unlike Kulagin Ter-Oganesov was by far a more committed partisan of the view that virgin nature should be preserved in the interests of expanding theoretical scientific knowledge in biology. By 1926 he had become an outspoken foe of what he called the manufacturer's deviation, which he accused of failing to take into account the importance of theoretical scientific knowledge for future economic growth, and he proudly declared that "in Narkompros institutes there are no barriers to choosing as abstract a research theme as can be, because all knowledge is the knowledge of nature's laws and, consequently, may aid us in harnessing its forces."[7] Citing recent speeches by Trotskii and Rykov, he stressed the notion that basic research was the indispensable raw material of technological progress, and that current underfunding of the former could result in slackened growth rates for the latter, no matter how many rubles were pumped directly into applied research.

The scholarly secretary of the Goskomitet presidium was that body's only professional ecologist, Sergei Alekseevich Severtsov,[8] who had filled in as director of the Conservation Department for some months in 1925 between the tenures of Shillinger and Ter-Oganesov. Severtsov was intrigued by the possibility of discovering mathematical laws governing ecological phenomena, particularly population dynamics. Not only would the discovery of such regularities enable society to predict and perhaps control outbreaks of agricultural pests, for example, it would also finally remove the stigma of dilettantism from ecology and give it a place in the sun as an exact science. Achieving this goal was particularly important during this period because of the postrevolutionary bias toward matter-oriented hard sciences. Of all the members of the Goskomitet, Severtsov represented the strongest, clearest, and most insistent voice for a network of *zapovedniki* whose paramount mission would be to support ecological research.

The three remaining members of the committee were drawn from outside Narkompros. Narkomzem RSFSR's delegate on the plenum during the first several years was Vasilii Vasil'evich Perovskii, head of that commissariat's Hunting Subdepartment and an academic specialist in the economics of forestry.[9] He was joined by another forester, Grigorii Romanovich Eitingen.[10] By contrast with Perovskii, Eitingen labored over questions not of economics but of silviculture, and one of his major interests was the study of forest communities. The last member of the presidium was the representative of VSNKh RSFSR, Sergei Stepanovich Perov, a specialist in colloidal chemistry and its applications.[11]

The utilitarian viewpoint had two solid defenders on the presidium: Perovskii and Perov. (The latter, as an academician of the Lenin All-Union Agricultural Academy, or VASKhNIL, became in 1936 a vocal backer of T. D. Lysenko.) *Zapovedniki* as centers for ecological study also had supporters in the persons of Severtsov and Ter-Oganesov. Finally, there were the two swing figures: Eitingen and Kulagin. More sensitive to the general Soviet impatience for practical results than Severtsov and Ter-Oganesov, they were nevertheless more understanding of the importance of basic ecological research for rational planning than were Perov or Perovskii.

Thus balanced, the presidium of the Goskomitet harmonized the interests of its competing factions well during the first three years of its existence.[12] This cooperation, however, was made possible only because the commissariats representing fundamentally divergent approaches to conservation respected the division of labor within the field. By late 1928, the spirit of cooperation had begun to fade. The emerging discord among the members of the Goskomitet revealed itself at first in two unconnected matters: a proposed *zapovednik* in a backwoods area of Smolensk Province,* and the question of harvest quotas for commercial game.

*In 1930, with a major restructuring of the administrative units of the USSR, the *zapovednik* found itself in the Western Oblast.

THE BELYI WOODS

In 1926 the idea arose within the Conservation Department to create a large Central
Forest *zapovednik* for the study of the ecology of woodland game. Several expeditions were organized by Glavnauka to find a suitable location for the reserve.
The prime candidate for the site was a forest massif in Belyi *uezd* (district), for it
was not only highly representative of central Russian flora and fauna but had the
added value of lying astride the watersheds of the Dnieper, the Western Dvina, and
the Volga.

Soon thereafter the Conservation Department transferred the matter to the
Smolensk Provincial Interagency Conservation Commission, entrusting it with organizing a *zapovednik* of local designation as a first step until Glavnauka could persuade the
central authorities to approve it as a centrally funded state *zapovednik*.[13]

In a major coup for the local conservation commission, the Smolensk Provincial Executive Committee agreed to set aside 60,000 hectares of forest land in
Belyi for a local *zapovednik* in the Narkompros system. It was therefore disturbing
to the Goskomitet when it learned that the timber procurement agencies of two of its
members—Narkomzem RSFSR and VSNKh RSFSR—were continuing to log on
the territory of the new reserve.

At its meeting of 16 November 1928 the Goskomitet majority voiced its
concern, hoping that the attention trained on the offending *tresty* (trusts) would
suffice to bring to a halt their now-illegal logging. Narkomzem and VSNKh,
however, did nothing; the trusts continued to chop wood in the Central Forest
zapovednik, and the situation continued to simmer.

Indicative of the pointed lack of concern by representatives close to Narkomzem was a talk presented by Professor N. I. Kibovskii of Narkomzem's
Timiriazev Academy on 27 July 1929 to the trade union club of the town of Belyi.
In the course of his remarks Kibovskii announced that Narkomzem intended to
establish a peat-extracting collective farm on land already approved for inclusion in
the *zapovednik*. Answering a challenge from the audience, Kibovskii asserted that
the *zapovednik* was a dead letter; the lumber for export, the power station, and the
peat-collective farm, which was to supply a proposed region-wide electricity
generating station, had all been earmarked for development prior to the establishment of the reserve and therefore had priority.[14]

A little over a month later, the Belyi local lore society held a general meeting at
the headquarters of the Teachers' Union.[15] The *kraevedy* drafted an urgent appeal to
Narkomzem, VSNKh RSFSR, and the RSFSR Council of People's Commissars to
oust the logging trusts from the *zapovednik* conclusively. At the meeting, too, the
local conservationists looked to the forthcoming All-Russian Congress for Conservation, scheduled for September, to place its prestige behind the demand to save
the reserve. Above all, everyone wondered whether Narkompros would rise to the
defense of one of its *zapovedniki*, particularly one that was still technically under
the jurisdiction of a mere local branch of the commissariat. Also, there was fear that
this test of Narkompros and of the Goskomitet could reveal their actual political
impotence.

The other initial area of contention was the question of harvest quotas for game. Kulagin had addressed the question in a major presentation to the Goskomitet on 15 January 1929. As a result, the Goskomitet resolved to send its own game statistics to the Central Statistical Administration so that the latter's control figures could be more accurately adjusted.[16] Moreover, at a special session of the Goskomitet presidium, Narkompros's delegates insisted that any control figures for commercial hunting would have to wait until essential field censuses were completed. Only a new census, maintained Kulagin and his colleagues of Narkompros, could serve as the basis for a five-year plan for the recovery of commercial game.[17]

Now shattering the facade of harmony in the Goskomitet, the economic commissariats rejected the presidium's counsel of caution. Narkomzem presented its plans for the quinquennium at the 5 April 1929 meeting of the committee. It tried a conciliatory tack, sweetening the bitter pill of higher targets with the promise to establish five new *zapovedniki*: three for sable, one for beaver, and one for the protection of wild reindeer. Narkomtorg took another, less apologetic route, even going so far as to attack Narkomzem's targets as overly timorous.

Dramatically, the Narkompros-allied majority now showed its mettle. Exploding a virtual bombshell in the politics of Soviet conservation, the majority in its 23 April session declared that the harvest of furbearing mammals had already attained its upper limits and that increased trapping, combined with accelerated deforestation, "threatens us with a catastrophic decline [in commercial game] in the immediate future. . . ." *All* of the target figures proposed by the economic commissariats in the previous sessions were rejected flat out. The battle lines were drawn. The contradictions between the government's requirements for foreign exchange and the biological productivity of commercial game "have not been resolved in the Five-Year Plans of Narkomzem, Narkomtorg, or the Hunters' Cooperative Union," stated the resolution of the majority, which vowed to "go to the highest levels of government" to resolve the issue.[18]

THE NEW SOVIET *ZAPOVEDNIKI*

From the time of its emergence as a fully independent unit within Glavnauka, the Conservation Department moved vigorously to fortify the still-precarious situation of Russia's existing *zapovedniki* and attempted to add new ones. In four years, through the efforts of three directors, the combined budget of the department's six centrally funded state *zapovedniki* increased by no less than a factor of ten (table 1). Although this increase was not trivial, by 1927 *zapovedniki* were nevertheless receiving only 2 percent of Glavnauka's budgetary allotment.[19] Nor were the numbers of full-time scientific workers in the *zapovedniki* strikingly impressive either. In 1926 they represented only 72 out of the 5,289 scientific workers of the Glavnauka system as a whole, a bare 1.4 percent of the total.[20]

These figures, however, were a deceptively understated reflection of the amount and quality of scientific work that was conducted in the *zapovedniki*. During the summers the reserves were aswarm with visiting academics and students from higher educational centers doing field work.[21] By 1925 scientific research done in

TABLE 1
Budgets for Narkompros State *Zapovedniki,* 1924 to 1927–1928
(in rubles)

Zapovednik	1924	1925	1926–1927	1927–1928
Astrakhan'	950	1,204	20,058	27,200
Caucasus	2,120	4,424	71,569	74,920
Crimean	13,510	19,163	35,687	41,600
Il'menskii	600	3,409	21,892	25,236
Kosino	430	365	688	600
Penza	1,157	1,127	16,846	19,040
Total	18,767	29,692	166,740	188,596

Source: N. M. Kulagin, "Sovremennoe polozhenie voprosa ob okhrane prirody v RSFSR," p. 111.

the reserves began to find its way into print; of particular note was the appearance in that year of the first two fascicles of the Conservation Department's ten-part series, *Studies of the Zapovedniki.*

From 1926–1927 in the *zapovedniki* there began to coalesce bigger and more solid scientific collectives comprising researchers from a broad range of specialities. Biologists, for example, settled into the Il'menskii mineralogical *zapovednik,* which by this time had outgrown its narrow geological profile and had acquired a more multidisciplinary *(kompleksnyi)* one. In the Astrakhan' reserve, the study of the biology and ecology of nesting waterfowl was pursued by a team led by directors V. A. Khlebnikov and A. G. Diunin and by senior scientific associate K. A. Vorob'ev. This team kept phenological records of natural events and cycles in the *zapovednik* from April 1919. These records were soon incorporated into a nature log *(letopis' prirody),* stored on file cards so that long-range trends in the abundance and occurrence of flora and fauna could be traced and the effect of episodic natural events on them could be evaluated. This method was soon adopted by a growing number of reserves, and became a mandatory part of the research program of all *zapovedniki* later on. The Astrakhan' *zapovednik* also pioneered extensive banding of migratory birds, beginning in 1926 on the initiative of Vorob'ev, the reserve's ornithologist. This too caught on, and contributed to a greater understanding of avian life.[22]

Scientific expeditions geared toward inventorying the biota of the reserves got under way as well during the mid-1920s. One sponsored by the Conservation Department and Glavnauka crossed the Caucasus *zapovednik* in the autumn of 1927. Typical of the prevailing penurious conditions, the guide had to be borrowed from the Crimean reserve for the duration of the expedition.[23] By the end of 1930, though, the Caucasus reserve had played host to eleven more expeditions, better funded and availing themselves of the *zapovednik's* own growing support staff. What was important was that the groundwork for making scientific research institutions out of the *zapovedniki* had been laid, and that subsidies were increasing.[24]

Aside from their specifically scientific function, there was another feature that made the Narkompros *zapovedniki* unique. By contrast with the unsystematic selection of sites for reserves that characterized other park systems—Soviet and foreign—the efforts of the Conservation Department were guided by a master plan. Revising V. P. Semenov-tian-shanskii's 1917 proposal, Kozhevnikov in 1923 asserted the primacy of selecting ecologically (and not just physical-geographically) representative areas for *zapovedniki*.[25] Although the department's budget through the mid-1920s could not support a simultaneous improvement of its existing reserves and a broad expansion of the system besides, the very existence of the master plan gave the Narkompros activists a sense of structure and a buoyant esprit de corps.

In addition to the six state *zapovedniki*[26] that were the flagships of the Narkompros RSFSR system, there were seven *zapovedniki* of local designation.[27] That made a total of thirteen reserves with a total area of almost 378,000 hectares. While the other republics' Commissariats of Education were slow to follow suit, that void was being filled by the activity of the republican Commissariats of Agriculture. Narkomzem systems taken as a whole over the entire USSR in 1925 actually supervised almost twice the protected territory of that administered by Narkompros RSFSR.[28]

Overall for the USSR in 1925 there were nine state *zapovedniki* with a gross area of 984,000 hectares, as well as fifteen local ones comprising 57,045 hectares. This added up to a grand total of 1,041,045 hectares, about a fifth again as large as Yellowstone National Park. The passage of four years revealed a picture that conservationists could view with considerable encouragement. By 1929 the USSR's reserves had grown to sixty-one. Territorially, their combined area had increased by nearly four times, to 3,934,428 hectares.

This substantial increase was partially the result of the striking proliferation of local *zapovedniki* in this period; they increased to forty-six incorporating 1,963,272 hectares.[29] More than anything else, this virtual explosion was the direct outgrowth of the legislation of 1925 and 1926 which provided for the establishment of the local interagency conservation commissions.

From 1926 conservation agencies began to appear in the other union republics under the aegis of the republican Glavnaukas, and along with them came legislation modeled on that of the RSFSR providing for the creation of local interagency conservation commissions. In the Ukraine, the existing local *zapovedniki* of Narkomzem were supplemented by two reserves under the jurisdiction of the republic's Narkompros. In the other republics—of the Caucasus and Central Asia—the expansion of reserves was particularly notable between 1925 and 1929.

Surprisingly, the sudden increase in the number and size of the USSR's reserves between 1925 and 1929 owed itself chiefly to the vigorous expansion of the various systems of the commissariats of agriculture. This was particularly the case in the RSFSR and stood in marked contrast to Narkomzem RSFSR's foot-dragging during the latter part of the Civil War and its lackluster record through the middle of the decade. With the upgrading of the Voronezh beaver and game management *zapovednik* from a local to a state reserve in 1927 and the creation of the giant 800,000-hectare Kondo-Sos'vinskii and 1,500,000-hectare Kronotskii *zapovedniki* in Siberia and Kamchatka, Narkomzem RSFSR was once again a potent force on Russia's conservation scene. Indeed, Narkomzem RSFSR had turned the tables on Narkompros, overshadowing the latter's system by a ratio of better than five to one: 3,056,477 hectares to 598,827 hectares. This territorial superiority of Narkomzem over Narkompros was upheld in the other republics as well.

By the eve of the First Five-Year Plan, therefore, two centers—Narkompros RSFSR (and its allies in the other republican Commissariats of Education), and Narkomzem RSFSR (and its analogues in the other republics)—each could lay claim to speak for the USSR's protected territories. True, Narkomzem had a decided areal advantage,[30] but Narkompros made up in diversity, quality, location, numbers, management, and *concept* what it lacked in size.

Roughly until the spring of 1929 (a time, incidentally, when leaders at the helms of both commissariats were replaced), the Narkompros and Narkomzem systems complemented each other. Although they called their reserves by the same name—*zapovedniki*—the two commissariats' protected territories fulfilled quite different functions. On the one hand, the reserves of Narkompros saw their main function as that of studying the ecological dynamics of baseline areas—*etalony*—to advance knowledge of how nature works and, through that, to align economic practice with the carrying capacities of nature. On the other hand, the reserves of Narkomzem functioned as *rezervaty*—game preserves where severely depleted populations of selected species of fauna (chiefly commercial game and furbearers) could propagate without hindrance.

This division of labor prevailed until the late 1920s. Until then, each system generally recognized the legitimacy of the other. As the last embers of NEP flickered and died, doused by the gale of political and economic change, this arrangement, too, collapsed. In particular, Narkomzem and its allies no longer wished to accord legitimacy to the functions of Narkompros *zapovedniki,* which, in their view, pursued "science for science's sake." Conversely, Narkompros-based activists charged that the Narkomzem-run reserves perverted the meaning of the term *zapovednik.* From 1929, then, the term could no longer serve two masters, and the unstable situation of dual power in conservation was propelled onto the tumultuous path of its ultimate resolution.

Mindful, as educated Russians are, of the power of the word, Kozhevnikov early recognized the wisdom of delineating clearly the various rationales for protecting nature and their corresponding terminology. In particular, he saw the value of distinguishing among the diverse varieties of protected territories according to their objectives and functions. That there was a definite need for a standardized typology of protected territories was widely appreciated. In the words of game biologist Dmitrii Konstantinovich Solov'ev, writing in 1917, "there was an extraordinary confusion of concepts in the statements of the various institutions and organizations concerned with conservation." As an example of this lexical disarray he noted that "the terms *zakaznik* and *zapovednik* are frequently considered to be synonymous."[31]

In preparation for the October 1917 Conservation Conference Solov'ev set out to introduce order into the terminological morass of conservation jargon by devising such a typology. His attempt, however, did little to clarify matters because, unlike that of Kozhevnikov, the criterion he used to distinguish between *zapovednik* and *zakaznik* was based neither on function nor on regime. For Solov'ev, the crucial distinction between the two was that the former was a permanent institution, while the latter was only temporary. Consequently, *zapovednik* could represent such altogether divergent institutions as game preserves and ecological *etalony*.

Despite its rather arbitrary basis, Solov'ev's typology achieved a general recognition at the 1917 conference and beyond. Accordingly, while Narkompros and Narkomzem each established systems with widely different profiles and regimes, each rightfully called their reserves *zapovedniki* so long as they were permanent.

The corpus of legislation did little initially to unravel the definitional tangle. The 16 September 1921 statute spoke of *zapovedniki* as areas having either scientific or cultural-historical importance, which seemed to lean toward the Narkompros view; yet there were also the Civil War–era decrees on forests and hunting that explicitly empowered Narkomzem to establish *zapovedniki*. Only the decree of 5 October 1925, which characterized *zapovedniki* as "parcels of nature . . . possessing primarily scientific importance," came close to endorsing explicitly Kozhevnikov's very specific conception of those institutions.

In 1927 there was further evidence that, within Narkompros, *zapovedniki* were viewed as having essentially a *scientific* character. By then, the Goskomitet had largely taken over many of the important functions of the old Conservation Department. Faced with the need to slash its bureaucracy again as part of a new campaign of "rationalization," the Executive Committee of Narkompros decided once and for all to abolish the unhappy department. However, it still needed to entrust the day-to-day management of the *zapovedniki* (a function the Goskomitet was not equipped to assume) to some other agency within the commissariat. Significantly, it chose not to return this responsibility to the Museum Department of Glavnauka but to Glavnauka's Department for Scientific Institutions. Now, with their status as scientific institutions confirmed, the specifically ecological profile of the Narkompros *zapovedniki* was thrown into high relief. The curtain was rising on the golden age of scientific research in the *zapovedniki*.

SIX

Models of Nature: The *Zapovedniki* and Community Ecology

Ecological studies, especially of ecological communities, had been gaining ground in Russia from well before the beginning of the century.[1] Writing in 1924, V. V. Alekhin could justly claim that a central role in the development of the "brand new twentieth-century science [of] phytosociology" was played by Russians. In his view, this was "entirely understandable, since Russian nature, comparatively unaltered by humans, . . . calls straight out for the study of its communities."[2]

The community-oriented tenets of Linnaeus, whose "economy of nature" was given short shrift in early nineteenth-century Western science,[3] found a vibrant echo among Russian agronomists and foresters. Ivan Komov was already treating the forest as a community in 1788, while by the 1840s Gil'deman had asserted that nature prefers diversity to monocultures and Teploukhov had concluded that all species were equally important in the economy of nature, particularly in the process of the regeneration of the forest as a unit.[4] The path blazed by the phytosociologists of the 1890s—P. N. Krylov, I. K. Pachoskii, A. N. Krasnov, G. N. Vysotskii, and S. I. Korzhinskii—culminated in the full-blown forest system of Georgii Fedorovich Morozov of 1904, shedding Linnaeus's mechanism for an exuberant organicism that was mirrored in the work of an American, Frederick Clements, published the same year.[5] The forest community, wrote Morozov,

> is not a mechanistic aggregation of trees, but a complex organism, all parts of which condition each other, and which lives its own life. . . . We must study these complex organisms as we study any organism: from the perspective of its morphology, properties, origin, transformations over the course of its lifetime, reproduction or regeneration, etc.[6]

Before the First World War, the study of biotic communities in Russia (as in the West) was largely limited to plant communities (hence the term *phytosociology*). These plant communities were seen as the basic social units in nature; the role of fauna in conditioning the vegetation was generally held to be minor. In the eyes of the phytosociologists vegetation was the "tenant" of the abiotic substrate, while animals supported by the greenery occupied the lesser role of "subtenants" in nature.

Influenced by hydrobiology and by such animal ecologists as Daniil Nikolaevich Kashkarov, however, Russian ecologists of the 1920s gained a new appreciation of the role of fauna in shaping the historical development of natural communities. The idea that the community was a complex system of three interacting elements of equal importance—vegetation, fauna, and the abiotic environment—gained increasing acceptance throughout the decade. Soon the expression *plant community (rastitel'noe soobshchestvo)* of the phytosociologists lost ground to *biocenosis,* a term which had the virtue of incorporating at least two (vegetation and fauna) of the three elements of the community system. (Only after 1945 did Sukachev's *biogeocenosis,* a term which incorporated the third element, gain currency.) With relatively few exceptions, the leading figures of Russian field biology of the time embraced the concept of the biocenosis as, in the words of hydrobiologist G. S. Karzinkin, "a community between each of whose members there must exist biotic links."[7]

If this was the bare-bones concept, there was no shortage of embellishments or of points in dispute. At one extreme were the intellectual followers of I. K. Pachoskii, who made extended and highly speculative analogies between what he called plant societies and human society. According to Pachoskii, plant and human societies alike shared an entire series of attributes. This belief led him to conjecture the existence of principles of social organization that pertained to all living things, notably that both plant and human communities were governed by laws; that they were both characterized by a division of labor, being organic complexes of diverse, nonequivalent organisms; that both kinds of societies developed and matured from simpler to more complex forms; and that both plant and human societies were organized on the class principle. In plant communities, the lower stories—which Pachoskii analogized to human "lower classes"—existed to make possible the thriving of trees and other "higher" forms occupying the higher stories.[8]

Pachoskii's readiness to draw conclusions about human society from his studies of plant communities embodied a dangerous political heresy in Soviet Russia. What Pachoskii was implying was nothing other than the total futility of the Marxian experiment, for in his view the existence of class differentiation was the ineluctable sine qua non for any community. If inequality was natural, and if that could be demonstrated by science, a pall would be cast over all of the egalitarian strivings of the Revolution.

Although such blatant sociologization as Pachoskii's, with all its implications about the naturalness of inequality, quickly came to an end by the mid-1920s (Pachoskii himself left for Poland in 1923, while others renounced his views as "sins of our youth"),[9] elements of the phytosociological approach survived. Professor V. N. Sukachev, for one, retained much of Pachoskii's Spencerian flavor in viewing the biocenosis as striving in its development toward as complete a utilization of the productive potential of its habitat as possible (the "principle of plenitude"). Sukachev's community moved toward a structure wherein competition among components was reduced to a minimum, while the productivity of the complex exceeded that of any other combination of available biotic components under the given environmental conditions. Eventually, the community would become an orderly, harmonious, and more or less stable complex.[10]

While others managed to avoid the teleological overtones of Sukachev's position, they also conceived of the biocenosis in supraorganismic terms. Structuralists from V. N. Beklemishev, A. P. Shennikov, and N. Ia. Kats to V. V. Alekhin sought to identify presumed shared structural elements in biocenoses and to create typologies of natural communities on that basis. Alekhin focused on morphological features of the community: stories, permanence of vegetation, and distinctive physiological features of the component plant species. Shennikov and Kats, by contrast, took as their inspiration the Uppsala School of Du Rietz, who sought to type communities according to the presence of dominant and subdominant plant species encountered over a given measured area (quadrat),[11] a floristic-oriented approach.

These attempts to classify presumed natural communities were symptomatic of the generally uncertain and speculative state of biocenology in the 1920s. There were a host of unresolved, fundamental questions:

1. Could the existence of biocenoses be empirically demonstrated?

2. Were the biocenoses closed systems, using all of the available resources of their abiotic environments to best advantage, or were they open, with vacancies available for more tenants?

3. Did they, once established, have the capacity for self-regulation or even self-renewal?

4. Were they inextricably linked with their abiotic environments, or did they encompass only the biota?

5. Were they supraorganismic entities that could be analogized to an organism or even to a human community?

6. Could biocenoses themselves be grouped into still higher taxonomic units, i.e., associations or formations, comprising sets of related types of biocenoses?

7. How could the methodology be developed to answer the preceding questions?

Interest in these central questions rose throughout the decade and was reflected in the growing institutional prominence of ecology in Soviet academic life.[12] Ecology began to find a place in university curricula, with Kashkarov initiating such a course at the Middle Asian State University in Tashkent in 1924. He was soon followed by V. V. Alpatov at Moscow State University, Strel'nikov at Leningrad State University, and V. V. Stanchinskii first at Smolensk and then at Khar'kov State University. Ecological laboratories and expeditions were organized. But expeditions, common during the 1920s, were found to be far less congenial for biocenological studies than stationary observation. Hence, there was a real need on the part of ecologists for suitable field conditions for their observations, a need, as Kozhevnikov tirelessly had propounded, which *zapovedniki* were uniquely well-suited to satisfy.

Characteristically, Kozhevnikov led the way. In the second half of 1923 he consummated his efforts to create a model *zapovednik* as an ecological *etalon*, selecting as his site a triad of glacial lakes located near Moscow, at Kosino. A limnological station had functioned there since 1908, and Kozhevnikov had little difficulty in persuading its director, Professor Leonid Leonidovich Rossolimo, to assume the directorship of the new *zapovednik* as well.

Kozhevnikov looked to ecological research in the reserve to corroborate such presumed properties of pristine biocenoses as succession, self-regulation, and equilibrium. Russia was still fortunate compared with her neighbors to the West, where virgin nature no longer existed, Kozhevnikov observed. Nonetheless, even in Russia, the handwriting was on the wall. Modernization could sound the death knell for virgin nature, and

> by way of compensation, managed game farms *(okhotnich'i khoziaistva)* are established—totally useless for purposes of scientific research—where selected varieties of animals, including both native and exotic species, are artificially bred, while others, such as predators, are killed off. . . .[13]

If game farms were Narkomzem's sole response to the challenge of conservation, that was totally inadequate from the standpoint of science and its needs, held Kozhevnikov. Kosino, as a prototype of an ecologically oriented *zapovednik* of the Narkompros system, would demonstrate what science and conservation truly needed.

Kosino's three lakes were all of comparatively recent origin. Yet, because of their small sizes, they already had some symptoms of approaching senescence. Beloe Lake, in particular, was in the earliest stages of bog formation, and Kozhevnikov was especially enthusiastic about the prospect that the process of lake (hydrarch) succession, so recently postulated among ecologists, could now be followed intensively at the reserve. The first results of these studies in lake history appeared after only two years, in 1925. Three years later, looking back at the Kosino years, Kozhevnikov exulted:

> We know that a lake has a history of its own and that frequently we can predict how this history will end, . . . i.e., we can predict that a lake is being transformed into a bog. The composition of the fauna, of course, changes; part of the population dies out, part is replaced or transformed. To follow the course of this process is something of fantastic interest. . . . Has it ever been done anywhere in the past one hundred years? No! And where may it be done? Only in absolutely inviolable *zapovedniki* . . . over a period of time far surpassing the life of a single person.[14]

Kozhevnikov was conscious of the pioneering nature of Soviet *zapovedniki*. Neither in the great American national parks nor anywhere in the proceedings of the Bern Conference on International Conservation of 1913 "was the notion at all reflected that reserves can and must be centers of scientific research," he noted proudly.[15]

After the appearance of the journal *Okhrana prirody* Kozhevnikov wasted no time before promoting the *etalon* concept. "How Scientific Research Should Be Conducted in *Zapovedniki*," appearing in the journal's second number, heralded *zapovednik* research as that which would "reveal such momentous laws governing the course of organic life as natural selection, the struggle for existence, mutation, and heredity," indeed, no less than knowledge of *"the laws of the evolution of the organic world."* With hindsight, we can see that Kozhevnikov was groping for the nexus of the great twentieth-century revolution in biology: the synthesis of ecology, genetics, and evolutionary theory. As ever, Kozhevnikov stressed the need for a regime of total inviolability in the *zapovedniki*. Another condition of research, growing out of the nature of the evolutionary process itself, was that it be conducted on a long-term basis, with a time horizon of hundreds of years.

The actual work of scientists in the *zapovednik* would be centered at its biological station. Before work on ecological and evolutionary dynamics could be attempted, though, investigators would need to complete a comprehensive description of conditions prevailing in the reserve. This information would serve as the baseline for all future studies. That having been completed, the actual ecological work could begin, using quantitative methods then being developed.

No one could accuse Kozhevnikov's work plan of excessive temerity. He specifically warned against expecting quick results and never claimed that the program would be easy to accomplish. In fact, he was well aware of the immense amount of labor that would be necessary for such ecological studies over the entire breadth of the USSR. Consequently, he suggested that research at first be directed to the most methodologically accessible of biocenoses: lakes. Doubtless that is why he worked to establish the first ecologically oriented *zapovednik* at Kosino.[16]

Ironically, the very grandeur of his project's scope lessened its attraction, especially in the years of Cultural Revolution, supposedly years of grand visions. The new radical czars of science expected instant solutions to even the most complex problems. The true implications of empirical science were often unpalatable to the new breed of ideologue. Such science was too tedious, too theoretical, too long-range, too informed by statistics and not enough by dialectical materialism. And grandeur that took two hundred years was no grandeur at all.

Especially in light of the changing climate in academic politics and biology in the late 1920s, Kozhevnikov took pains to demonstrate that his emphasis on basic research was not science for its own sake but would redound to the ultimate benefit of human society. "The understanding of nature through scientific investigation is one of the grandest undertakings of cultured humanity," he wrote in 1925. "But if we go further," he continued,

> we will realize that an understanding of nature forms the basis for a proper understanding of the world, as well as for the material well-being of individuals and whole peoples. Agriculture, technology, and medicine—all these forms of applied natural science require an understanding of nature.[17]

Kozhevnikov believed that a rational use of nature's resources was indeed possible (and, ultimately, necessary), although far from easy. And while he recognized that "to take the regulation of nature into our hands is an unusually difficult and responsible business,"[18] he was not an environmental Luddite and recognized that development was unavoidable to a degree. He asked only that extreme caution be applied and that society turn to science to assist it in its newfound stewardship over the whole of organic nature, warning that "here, with one unthought-out step, e.g., the acclimatization of a plant or animal in a region unsuited for it, we could drastically wreck the natural conditions and disfigure the face of nature."[19]

Kozhevnikov, Severtsov, Pod"iapol'skii, and others saw merit in addressing themselves to the nation's rulers in addition to the general populace and to the much more limited conservation constituency itself. It was this strange crew of Marxist planners and professional revolutionaries that would have to be won over; the case for conservation, were it to succeed, would have to be made within the framework of new Soviet ways of thinking. Kozhevnikov, in particular, took pains to identify a philosophical common ground shared by both ecologists and Marxists—an abiding belief in a materialist world view—and he emphasized a community of interests based on that.

Laying claim to the mantle of materialism, however, was more and more of a tricky matter by the end of the 1920s. Anticipating state backing for their views, other groups and individuals in Soviet science, notably in the Communist Academy and in the economic commissariats, were pursuing policies inimical to conservation and hostile to community ecology while also acting in the name of materialism. Ecologically informed conservation therefore had to demonstrate that *its* policies and strategies were the ones truly speaking for the materialist world view, and that scientific materialism was not to be equated with mere vulgar imitations. As Kozhevnikov put it,

> To develop a materialist view of nature does not mean to calculate how many cubic meters of firewood can be gotten from a forest or how many dollars squirrel skins will bring this year, but means to imbue the world view of the whole people with the correct understanding of nature, . . . of the law of evolution. In prerevolutionary times this was impossible. . . . Now, for this goal, the ideational foundations have been laid.[20]

Zapovedniki, reiterated Kozhevnikov, were precisely the vehicles by which this correct understanding of the life of nature could be attained. But he warned that "if we do not provide a material base" for this study of nature, "then the whole idea will be stillborn. And it is only nature, preserved in a virgin state, that can provide this for us. Therein lies the great ideational significance of the *zapovedniki.*"[21]

Ecologically inspired conservation also took forms other than an interest in establishing a network of *zapovedniki* as *etalony.* Comparatively early, those who subscribed to biocenology's holistic message came to see nature in a new way. Above all, living nature, organized into subsystems called biocenoses, was seen to be characterized by two salient properties: total interdependence of the constituent parts of the biocenosis, and the tendency of the biocenosis to exhibit a relatively long-term equilibrium. These ideas filtered down into popular parlance as "the web of life" and "the balance of nature." Those who came to see nature as organized into such biocenoses also tended to have serious qualms about the pace at which mankind was tampering with these natural systems. "All interventions, even those which we consider to be improvements, such as . . . crop cultivation or the acclimatization of [exotic] animals," warned Kozhevnikov in a piece written for educators, "destroy the natural conditions of . . . biocenoses."[22] The editors of *Okhrana prirody* endorsed this view, cautioning their readers in the first issue that "from this web of life, which has evolved thousands of years of interactions, one may not, without punishment, rip out individual links."[23]

One of the first scientists to base an appeal for nature protection on the need to avoid rending the skein of life was Avram L'vovich Brodskii, professor of zoology at Middle Asian State University and an activist in the Conservation Department of the Turkestan Commissariat of Education. With a remarkable sense of prophecy he correctly divined the industrialization panache of the five-year plans. Events of such magnitude as the devouring of mountains and forests by hungry mills and factories could not fail to rupture the complex fabric of the web of life and violate the presumed balance of nature, Brodskii prognosticated with apprehension, and this would ultimately injure humanity itself.

For Brodskii and others[24] who subscribed to these premises about nature, humans owed it to themselves to redress the violation of the balance of nature and to practice environmental prophylaxis in still unviolated areas. Brodskii foresaw a time when the degradation of the biosphere might conceivably threaten the routine functioning of modern civilization. To avert this, he advocated the creation of *zapovedniki,* similar to Kozhevnikov's in that they would embrace massive territorial tracts in order to ensure the integrity of entire biological systems, but differing from them in one important regard. For Brodskii, the chief function of the reserves would not be to serve as *etalony* for ecological study but to guarantee enough healthy nature in the right places to ensure environmental, and hence economic, stability.[25]

By the close of the decade, the *zapovedniki* of the Narkompros systems were fast being transformed into centers for the study of ecological communities. They became testing grounds for studies representing one or another biocenological approach. Thus, the Crimean *zapovednik* was the site of research led by V. Bukovskii, who took a structuralist approach to the problem of defining and classifying biocenoses, while Askania-Nova, in the Ukrainian steppes, served as the locus for no less than four of the most important studies of the period.

ASKANIA-NOVA

At Askania, Pachoskii, as the reserve's first scientific director in the early 1920s, sought corroboration for his phytosociological theories. In the middle and late twenties, Natalia Shostenko, the *zapovednik*'s botanist, directed a project to replant former croplands with native steppe grasses, one of the first attempts to use virgin nature in a *zapovednik* as a model, or *etalon,* for the restoration of degraded lands.[26] In 1927 and 1928, the talented young ecologist Mikhail Solomonovich Shalyt and his colleagues succeeded in disproving the Uppsala school's hypothesis that each biocenosis had a minimal area which could be identified by the presence in it of all (or nearly all) of its putative constituent species, particularly dominants and subdominants. By using Du Rietz's method of quadrats, Shalyt demonstrated that the biocenosis had no measurable floristic center—a finding that undermined Du Rietz's own supposition that certain plants sought each other out to form associations as a result of certain affinities. Shalyt thus left a gaping hole in the notion that natural communities could be readily identified by species composition alone. That proved to be of critical importance, because it cleared the path for other ways of conceptualizing the biocenosis. The most significant, also developed at Askania-Nova, was the concept of the brilliant but now nearly forgotten prewar ecologist Vladimir Vladimirovich Stanchinskii, who pioneered the entire field of ecological energetics.

The history of Askania-Nova was a synecdoche, for in that reserve all of the salient problems and most crucial developments of Soviet conservation and ecology were interwoven. From its earliest years, as a 42,345-desiatin land grant from Tsar Nicholas I to the Duke of Anhalt-Cöthen in 1828, the estate was at the cutting edge of agricultural innovation in Russia. By the eve of the First World War, under its last private owner, Fridrikh Eduardovich Fal'ts-Fein, the estate comprised a colossal sheep-breeding operation, a zoo, an acclimatization park, and a small fenced-off area of virgin steppe. Throughout the Russian Empire and beyond, it was renowned as "the oasis of the southern Ukrainian steppes."[27]

The war and the ensuing political upheaval, however, quickly brought an end to Askania's first golden age under Fal'ts-Fein. Unfortunately, Askania was located right at the gates to the Crimea, just north of the Perekop Isthmus, in the direct line of the periodic advances of all contending forces in the Civil War. By 1921, the reserve had been almost totally devastated, and almost three-fourths of the zoo animals had perished.[28]

During the Civil War years, Askania's juridical status remained almost as fluid as the military situation. When the Reds retook Askania for good in October–November 1920, the park and its entire administration were a shambles. Although the 1919 decree placing the reserve under the aegis of the Ukrainian Narkompros was technically still in force, it was apparent that Narkompros UkrSSR was largely out of the picture as concerned Askania. In any event, D. Z. Manuilskii, commissar of agriculture for the Ukraine, boldly moved to assume de facto curatorship of the reserve, a move which was soon ratified by the adoption of a new charter for Askania by the Ukrainian Council of People's Commissars on 8 February 1921.[29]

Although jurisdiction had shifted to Narkomzem, Askania's tasks, according to the decree, were a hybrid of both the Narkomzem and Narkompros approaches to the management of protected territories. This outcome was in great measure historically conditioned by the multifunctional nature of Askania under Fal'ts-Fein. Objectives now included not only preservation and study of the virgin steppe by a scientific steppe station on a fully inviolate tract but also the "acclimatization and study under steppe conditions of the greatest possible number of plant and animal species" and even the "creation and mass propagation"—by means of hybridization, it was thought—"of economically valuable plant and animal species." These utilitarian tasks were assigned to the reserve's zoo, botanical gardens, zootechnical station for selection and husbandry, and other agricultural facilities. To support this elaborate mélange of theoretical and applied scientific directions the reserve also included, as one of the decree's provisions, a Production Sector *(khoziaistvo)*, a direct outgrowth of the austerity conditions which dominated the economic practices of scientific institutions in the early years of NEP.

During these early years the Scientific Sector of the *zapovednik* did not prosper as visibly as the production unit, however. There was just barely enough money to pay for the reconstruction of the ravaged buildings, and scientific work consisted of B. K. Fortunatov's research on the heredity of hybrids; the studies of the resident ornithologist, S. I. Snegirevskii; the phytosociological studies of I. K. Pachoskii; and the field work of visiting scientists and students, all of whom paid their own way.

One significant development, however, held great promise for future scientific work at Askania. In the spring of 1922, Narkomzem UkrSSR officially issued a set of instructions entrusting the leadership of the Scientific Sector of the reserve to a special Askania Commission under the presidency of the commissar of agriculture or his special deputy and including representatives of a wide range of economic and academic organizations. While this did not entirely emancipate the *zapovednik*'s Scientific Sector from the pressures of partisans of narrowly applied lines of research, it certainly made their domination less complete. The arrangement even made likely a continuation of theoretical work in ecology, owing to the heavy representation of Narkompros UkrSSR and its allies on the commission.

After Askania's first director fell ill in January 1923, he was replaced by V. O. Zitte, an agronomist and old Bolshevik party worker who had been serving as director of the Khar'kov Provincial Land Administration. Zitte was able to effect a dramatic expansion of the *zapovednik*'s territory. Three nearby peninsulas were absorbed along with a large slice of the Kinburnskii sandbar, all major resting stops on the migratory flyway from Africa. Thus, added to the rectangular Askania-Uspenka-Dornburg tract created by the 1921 decree were maritime satellites to the southeast and the southwest.[30]

Despite such a promising beginning, however, the administration of Zitte and his deputy, Diumin (another agronomist), collapsed scarcely one year later in utter ignominy. To raise funds for capital construction in the reserve they had sold off wool "futures" one year early. Owing to a catastrophe that killed off all of the sheep, however, they were unable to make good on the promised delivery of wool from the *zapovednik*'s Production Sector. While the ostensible reason behind the fall of Zitte and the suicide of his deputy lay in their accretion of a 119,000-ruble debt, the real cause had its roots in the tension between the economic and the scientific activities of the reserve.

A 24 March 1924 report to high officials of Narkomzem UkrSSR by the director of the reserve's Scientific Sector, zoologist A. A. Brauner, drew a detailed picture of the sorry state of affairs. Suggesting that the administration of the reserve be brought up on criminal charges (after which suggestion Diumin hanged himself), Brauner charged that the advance payments on sheep futures had been squandered on unfinished, extravagant, and pointless projects, including the construction of a theater, while zoo animals starved.[31]

The scientific community was outraged by the usurpation of power by the Production Sector of the reserve, which was, after all, merely supposed to serve as a financial base for the work of the Scientific Sector. Writing at the time, Pachoskii, who had de facto run Askania's scientific affairs until 1923, lamented that the Scientific Sector came to be viewed "as something merely to be tolerated and not as the chief and basic unit of the *zapovednik*. . . . Shepherds knew that the poor condition of their cattle had serious consequences down the line, while herding the cattle over the boundary onto the territory of the [inviolable portion of the] *zapovednik* brought only a slap on the wrist."[32]

Indicative of the depth of concern among scientists was a letter published in the 10 April 1924 issue of *Izvestiia,* signed by Kulagin, Kozhevnikov, Fortunatov, and M. M. Zavadovskii. "The means for a simultaneous maintenance of both a huge economic sector and a *zapovednik* do not exist," the zoologists declared, and they warned that the recognition of that fact by some insiders in Narkomzem UkrSSR had generated a proposal to liquidate the zoo and the *zapovednik* and to turn Askania into a state farm (sovkhoz). This proposal was described by Pachoskii as the reductio ad absurdum of the "sovkhoz tendency" in reserve management.[33]

The four zoologists sought to turn the Narkomzem proposal on its head. They noted that the Scientific Sector had only modest requirements—twenty-five to thirty workers and five thousand puds of grain and twenty thousand puds of hay per year—and appealed to Narkomzem UkrSSR to set matters right. If the economic and scientific sectors could not coexist, then let the Production Sector be eliminated and a modest subsidy from the commissariat's budget be substituted in its place.[34]

Narkomzem UkrSSR sought to defuse the wave of protests and to refute at least some of the accusations made in the embarrassing letter in *Izvestiia.* B. K. Viktorov, the director of the Agricultural Administration of the commissariat, who had traveled to Askania during the thick of the scandal as chairman of an interministerial investigatory commission, in particular rejected the charge that Askania was about to be converted into a sovkhoz.[35]

Viktorov's assertion that Narkomzem UkrSSR stood opposed to the expansion of the sown area on the reserve's territory, however, was belied by the facts: by 1924, sown area had surpassed 4,400 hectares, far above the limit set earlier by the commissariat of 3,000. Withal, Viktorov had failed to calm the deep fears of the conservationists, voiced by Brauner, that "Narkomzem has cast its eyes on the remaining area of virgin steppe, and sees in it only future cropland."[36]

Outraged scientists were joined by politicians. A strong protest was lodged personally by Aleksandr Shumskii, commissar of education of the Ukraine. This more than anything staved off the sovkhoz plan, for, in the interests of avoiding an interministerial row, the Council of People's Commissars of the Ukraine now stepped in, appointing a new commission composed of authoritative scientific figures and sending them off to Askania to devise a new plan.[37]

After about a year, a new compromise plan was agreed upon by the blue-ribbon commission. Its conclusions essentially reduced to the following:

1. Roughly 6,500 hectares were to be set aside for a totally inviolable tract of virgin steppe *zapovednik.*

2. The Production Sector was awarded 11,000 hectares to be sown to crops.

3. Almost 24,000 hectares were to be set aside for the grazing of livestock and zoo animals.[38]

Essentially, though, the ingredients of instability and conflict were still very much in place. The fears of Kozhevnikov and others—that a *zapovednik* could not simultaneously serve two masters—proved increasingly well-founded. Even as the Scientific Sector continued to be starved for funds, the Production Sector expanded its operations daily. The flock of sheep, which had numbered 8,547 at the end of 1922, had grown to 21,500 by 1927.[39] In addition to its responsibilities of supplying the internal needs of the *zapovednik* complex for grain fodder and the upkeep of the Scientific Sector, the Production Sector had taken on the extraneous tasks of supplying the Black Sea coastal areas with seed materials and of aspiring to become a model farm with full mechanization; what profits there were, it turned out, had been invested in the purchase of forty Fordson tractors, presumably with the rationalization that temporarily starving the Scientific Sector in the present would ensure a more than bountiful income stream later on.[40] Indeed, the director of the Production Sector, D. I. Iamkovoi, had become so carried away by the prospect of agricultural expansion that he was already projecting an annual income of from 200,000 to 300,000 rubles for the reserve by 1930–1931, when the reserve would become self-sufficient. Much of the income was to be provided by the projected 3,000-head herd of cattle and the 60,000-head flock of sheep which, he assumed, could be supported by the 24,000 hectares of hayfields and pasturelands.[41]

Another area that prospered was tourism. While niggardly toward the requests of the Scientific Steppe Station, Narkomzem UkrSSR lavished 250,000 rubles in 1927 on the construction of tourist facilities. Apparently, this was only another convergence of pre- and postrevolutionary politics-as-usual; the "steppe oasis" continued to be a popular destination for high government figures on junkets and vacations.[42]

Actually, had the Scientific Sector been united in its goals, the aggrandizing aspirations of the reserve's Production Sector might have been resisted with greater success. Far from being united, however, the Scientific Sector was divided against itself; there were in fact strong constituencies within the sector whose interests aligned far more closely with those of the Production Sector than with those of their fellow scientists. Chief among them were the Phytotechnical and Zootechnical Stations, directed by A. E. Kovarskii and M. F. Ivanov, respectively.

The Phytotechnical Station, founded in 1925, was principally engaged in developing parched-wind–resistant varieties of cotton and wheat and was run by an agronomist. Founded in the same year, the Zootechnical Station concerned itself chiefly with hybridization and "selection" experiments with hogs, cattle, and sheep of the reserve, as well as with zebroids, cattle-bison crosses, and other hybrids.

Although Ivanov was a professor of animal husbandry, having taught for twelve years at the Moscow (Timiriazev) Agricultural Academy and after 1926 at the Moscow Higher Zootechnical Institute, he was a man considerably more at ease with the agronomists and *praktiki* of the Production Sector than with his fellow professors at the Scientific Steppe Station. Ivanov, it seems, still nourished resentment against the old-line "bourgeois" professoriat, ascribing the rejection of his application to study as a youth at the Moscow Agricultural Academy to the professors' bias against a gardener's son.[43] (He was educated at the Khar'kov Veterinary Institute instead.)

Moreover, it seems as though Ivanov early on was a supporter of the theory of the inheritance of acquired characteristics as well as a strong proponent of the acclimatization of exotic fauna. These positions distanced him from the academic biologists associated with the Scientific Steppe Station, many of whom were adherents of Mendelian genetic theory and who were distrustful of acclimatization on ecological grounds.

We may surmise that it was partly out of a desire to aggrandize his Zootechnical Station at the expense of the more theoretical scientific research units at Askania and partly out of his personal feelings of resentment toward the "bourgeois" professors who staffed these units that Ivanov early in 1928 proposed yet another organization of the reserve. In this he made common cause not only with the Production Sector, but with influential circles within the central agencies of Narkomzem UkrSSR as well.

Ivanov sought to paint his proposal as the very picture of moderation, the only possible compromise between those seeking to turn Askania into a "giant grain factory," as he put it, and those who allegedly wanted to drive out all of the sheep to the North Caucasus and the cows to Poltava, and turn the entire 42,000-hectare reserve into a giant, inviolable *zapovednik*.[44]

What Ivanov's proposal entailed, however, was, if not the conversion of the estate into a giant grain factory, then its rebirth as a mammoth livestock-breeding combine. It envisioned large-scale irrigation of the steppe as a result of the completion of canalization projects tied to Dneprostroi, with the formerly arid grasslands blossoming into resplendent fruit orchards; the fruit, stored in huge silos that would now tower over the low buildings of the Askania compound, would supply the fodder needs for a tremendous expansion of the flocks of fine-fleeced sheep and other livestock.[45] Others, including Kovarskii and Professor of Agronomy V. F. Levitskii, embellished the plan by noting the expanded possibilities of acclimatizing exotic subtropical plants and crops once the irrigation system was in place.[46] The Scientific Steppe Station, while it would be permitted to continue its activities according to Ivanov's "compromise plan," would be allotted only 6,500 hectares for its totally inviolable virgin steppe, as before.

Ivanov made it clear, however, that there was no love lost between him and the theoretically oriented scientists, and that under the reorganization the latter would be but barely tolerated. Commenting on the putative plans of the ecologists to turn the entire reserve into a total *zapovednik,* Ivanov wrote that "Instead of a thriving agriculture on this broad expanse, the population will see nothing except a bunch of zoologists and botanists fanning out into the protected virgin steppe." He added, "Naturally, the people will not approve of such virgin steppe *zapovedniki,* and they will present their own demands as to the area's use." Lastly, Ivanov offered his opinion that steppe flora and fauna "have already been sufficiently studied" and he saw no compelling need for further investigations.[47]

As might be expected, Ivanov's article drew bitter fire from the conservationist camp. One of the hardest-hitting responses came in a letter to *Okhrana prirody,* signed jointly by V. G. Averin, then deputy president of the All-Ukrainian Committee for Protection of Monuments of Nature;* E. M. Lavrenko, a prominent botanist and regional inspector for conservation for the Khar'kov Oblast under Narkompros of the Ukraine's Main Administration for Scientific Institutions;** and Professors G. N. Vysotskii, a pioneer ecologist, and D. Vilenskii, N. Belousov, and I. K. Tarnani, biologists.

The authors of the letter were shocked by Ivanov's breach of professional solidarity. They were especially offended that Ivanov had appealed to "the people" against "the botanists and zoologists" and publicly chided that a professor should have better sense and a broader outlook, "the more so in that among these botanists and zoologists 'fanning out (into the steppe)' . . . are great scholars, widely known not only in the USSR but all over the world." The letter's co-signers also took issue with Ivanov's contention that further research into the biota of the steppe was not needed. "On what grounds can he make such an assertion?" they asked with consternation. Even a stockbreeder, they argued, should at least be interested in studies of natural foraging. Lastly, the letter exposed the spurious nature of Ivanov's "middle position," noting that no one had proposed turning all of Askania into a total *zapovednik* and charging that Ivanov had created a straw man to disguise the radical nature of his own proposal.[48]

The latest crisis brought forth yet another plan proposed by Narkomzem UkrSSR, which provided for the creation of a 10,000-hectare *zapovednik* incorporating the zoo, the experimental stations, and the virgin steppe. In addition, it envisaged the transfer of the remaining 32,000 hectares of steppe to various grain-growing state farms.

Narkomzem tried to justify its plan by pointing to the unsatisfactory level of scientific work at Askania. This argument, however, was casuistic, explained Stanchinskii, who had in 1929 seized the reins of the Scientific Sector; the Agricultural Commissariat neglected to point out that it had never lived up to the provisions of the 1925 agreement and for four years had allowed the scientific research stations to go begging for funds and equipment. According to Stanchinskii, nothing had changed since the early 1920s:

> Large-scale economic units (hybridization and domestication of animals and grains) which were included in the *zapovednik* demanded much effort and funds. Suffice it to say that out of a general budget of 2,000,000 rubles, only 200,000 were spent on scientific work.[49]

Despite its apparently more generous allocation of land to the Scientific Sector than Ivanov's plan, the Narkomzem proposal aroused even greater fears. Although Ivanov's plan had set aside 22,000 hectares for pastureland and haymowing, those uses would still leave the steppe largely intact. Were the Narkomzem plan to be implemented, on the other hand, the steppe grasses could vanish irrevocably, replaced by fields of grain.

---

*UKOPP, the Ukraine's equivalent of the Goskomitet.
**Ukrnauka, the Ukrainian equivalent of Glavnauka.

The proposals of Ivanov and of Narkomzem UkrSSR, however, were stopped dead in their tracks. Amazingly, the reorganization of the reserve, again under the auspices of the Ukrainian Council of People's Commissars, took a different course. The Production Sector, with its 11,000 hectares of grain fields, was now seen as a cause of divisiveness and was parceled out to a sovkhoz outright. The Scientific Sector was awarded 25,500 hectares, and the remaining 7,000 hectares were allotted to a grain sovkhoz trust with the proviso that it make an annual contribution of 100,000 rubles to the sector. Ivanov's sheep-breeding operation was limited to no more than 10,000 pedigreed animals so as to limit their impact on the steppe, and 6,000 hectares of the steppe would remain completely off-limits for all uses but purely scientific ones.[50]

Moreover, the Scientific Sector was placed on the Ukrainian central budget with a funding level of 400,000 rubles annually (though Stanchinskii had requested twice that amount), and the fencing off of the larger virgin steppe was begun.[51] Conservationists hailed the reorganization as auguring a bright new period in the history of Askania, where scientific concerns at long last would no longer take a back seat to economic ones.[52]

By any measure, this was a stunning victory for the conservationists over the "sovkhoz tendency" as represented by Narkomzem and the sheep and hog breeder Ivanov. In part, it was a result of the resurgence of the People's Commissariat of Education of the Ukraine in conservation affairs.

Aside from its ephemeral stewardship over Askania during the Civil War (one that was largely a formality), Narkompros of the Ukraine had not involved itself actively in conservation matters for a number of years. True, the commissariat began to take a more active interest in the fate of Askania after the reserve's crisis of 1923–1924 through its representative on the Askania Commission. Nevertheless, until 1927, the only official conservation organ in the Ukraine remained the Conservation Commission of the Scientists' Agricultural Advisory Committee, a group formed in 1919 and tied to Narkomzem UkrSSR, and which was responsible for managing that commissariat's other *zapovedniki*.[53]

During the mid-1920s, though, the situation began to change, paralleling— with a certain time lag—events in the RSFSR. In April 1926 Narkompros of the Ukraine indicated its interest in establishing a formal nature-protection apparatus, and on 16 June the Ukrainian Council of People's Commissars and the All-Ukraine Executive Committee officially vested overall responsibility for conservation with the Education Commissariat, much as did the RSFSR legislation of 1921 and 1925.[54]

Soon, Narkompros's involvement in conservation increased, and by 1927 the commissariat had organized a network of its own conservation organs under the immediate jurisdiction of its Main Scientific Administration.

Again following the lead of the RSFSR, a new interagency body called the Ukrainian Committee for the Protection of Monuments of Nature (UKOPP), modeled after the Goskomitet, emerged in March 1929. A crucial detail was that UKOPP by law was granted the right to stay the implementation of any decision or policy until Narkompros UkrSSR and, if need be, the entire republican Council of People's Commissars could examine the case. It appears that just such a stay had been invoked by UKOPP after Narkomzem unveiled its proposal for reorganizing Askania.

Combining with the rise of UKOPP and Narkompros as forces to be reckoned with in Ukrainian conservation politics, another factor stood in the way of Narkomzem's plans. In the Ukraine, the Union of Hunters and Fishermen, led by the dedicated activist V. G. Averin, was one of the most militant forces for conservation and a strong ally of Narkompros. Thus, in the guise of the Ukraine's organized hunters, ecological research at Askania-Nova had the backing of a solid social force.

Finally, we must add a third reason why the conservationists triumphed in the 1929 battle over Askania: the prestige, brilliance, and skill of the reserve's new scientific director, Stanchinskii, who mobilized the defense of the Scientific Sector under the banner of an audaciously novel and promising research program.

VLADIMIR VLADIMIROVICH STANCHINSKII

Today, Stanchinskii is almost totally forgotten. During the 1920s and 1930s, however, he was known for the depth of his thinking and for his imaginative solutions to important problems of biology. Born on 20 April 1882 into the family of a chemical engineer who made his living as a factory inspector, Stanchinskii spent an itinerant childhood and adolescence. By the time he graduated from Smolensk Men's Gymnasium in 1901, he had studied in no fewer than five high schools.

Stanchinskii continued to be dogged by interrupted studies. He enrolled at Moscow University in the Physical-Mathematical Faculty's Natural Science Department to study under Menzbir, only to leave after one year to study with Otto Butschli at Heidelberg University. Although he received his doctorate in 1906 from Heidelberg, Stanchinskii found that it was not honored at Moscow University, and so he had to re-enroll as an extern. Quickly passing his exams, he began teaching, at first private women's courses in Moscow and later in the Zoology Department (*kafedra*) at the Moscow (Timiriazev) Agricultural Academy.

During the Civil War, Stanchinskii headed the local El'ninsk district (*uezd*) branch of Narkompros RSFSR in Smolensk Oblast, and was one of the organizers of the new Smolensk University. In Smolensk, where he had attended gymnasium, Stanchinskii soon became a major figure in intellectual life, becoming full professor at Smolensk University and the head of its Department of Zoology (to 1929), while also serving as the president of the Smolensk Society of Physicians and Naturalists, which he founded.[55]

Stanchinskii was not content to carve out a little niche in taxonomy or to spend his days in a laboratory studying *Aves* morphology. A field biologist by temperament as well as a scientist of exceptionally broad vision, he soon gravitated to a consideration of one of the leading theoretical problems in biology: the mechanism of speciation. "There is an insistent need to unite the data of genetics with those of systematics and ecology," he declared in a study of the problem published in 1927, "with the aim of providing a conception of the evolutionary process in nature consistent with contemporary levels of scientific knowledge and capable of resolving those contradictions which have arisen between the two basic tendencies in contemporary biology—Darwinism and Neo-Lamarckism."[56]

On the whole, Stanchinskii was a supporter of the idea that the stuff of heredity was contained in the chromosomal apparatus of the living organism, and that it conformed to the laws of Mendelian segregation. Indeed, he stated, the only explanation for heritable transformations in organisms lies in a mutation or change in the organism's genotype. Stanchinskii took issue, however, with other aspects of classical genetic theory, specifically as they applied to the problem of evolution and speciation. In particular, he questioned the notion that individual mutations were the basis for the emergence of new populations and, ultimately, new species, and he developed his own synthesis.[57]

Although Stanchinskii's solution to the riddle of speciation has been rejected by modern science in favor of "the great synthesis," the questions he raised have not yet found entirely satisfactory answers. The publication of Stanchinskii's 1927 study is important for us, however, in that, believing that he had answered the problem of speciation, Stanchinskii now took on that other great theoretical issue of the day: the nature of the biological community. His work on this problem made his greatest mark on twentieth-century biology.

Even in his 1927 work there were indications that his attention was already turning to this great problem in ecology. Above all, he was fascinated by the ever-changing nature of living matter. "Being in a continual state of matter- and energy-exchange with their environment," he wrote, "organisms are themselves continually changing, destroying and synthesizing substances within themselves." These exchanges, he averred, were governed by regularities that shaped the life cycle of the organism and that differed from species to species. Each species consequently had a very specific biochemical and physico-chemical role in the "economy of nature."[58]

During the summer of 1926 Stanchinskii traveled to Askania as a member of the Askania Commission. Though his stay there was brief, he came away convinced that Askania-Nova was an ideal spot to relocate his biocenological investigations. The research scientists there were also taken with the idea of a systematic program of biocenological study and, at Stanchinskii's suggestion, they began preliminary studies during the growing season of 1927. The most important of these studies were censuses of insects, conducted by the staff entomologist, Sergei Ivanovich Medvedev, in conjunction with samples, also by dry weight, of the biomass of the steppe vegetation. In the spring of 1929 Stanchinskii, taking some of his best students with him, followed through with his intention to relocate his research to Askania, and assumed the posts of deputy director of the reserve and director of its Scientific Sector. After successfully leading the Scientific Sector through its crisis and gaining an appointment nearby as the head of the Department of Vertebrate Zoology at Khar'kov University, Stanchinskii was ready to put his program into high gear.

Before Stanchinskii, ecological communities were defined either by their floristic composition, by certain structural features, or, in the case of the Swiss school, by a certain visual homogeneity. No one had thought to look closely at food webs as a way of identifying the boundaries of communities in nature, tracing the production of the primary biological producers (vegetation and other autotrophs) of a given area through their myriad biotic pathways until all of their energy potential was exhausted. Charles Elton had taken some of the first steps in this direction, and so had American investigators Nelson Transeau and Chancey Juday; but none had really followed through in a comprehensive way to study productivity beyond the level of primary producers on a system-wide basis. This highly ambitious task formed the core of Stanchinskii's program for Askania-Nova.

Organisms' abilities "to transform energy into matter" and "to carry on exchanges of matter which they themselves have synthesized" engrossed Stanchinskii. As he readily admitted, this preoccupation with the ubiquitous processes of chemical cycling and energy flow—the transformation back and forth of matter and energy between living and nonliving nature—had been inspired by V. I. Vernadskii. It was Vernadskii who had originally pointed out the unique role of each species in the dynamic processes of mineral cycling and energy flow and who posited individual species as performers of unique biogeochemical tasks in the economy of nature. Conditioning the role of a species in this economy, theorized Vernadskii, were the unique biochemical and energy requirements of its members. These requirements, in turn, were determined by the unique "stuff" (biochemical makeup) of these species' tissues.[59]

Intrigued by the possibilities of what Vernadskii had so sketchily outlined, Stanchinskii aimed ultimately to construct a picture of the dynamics of a natural community, with its multitudes of species, that was reducible to a set of mathematically expressed regularities.

Stanchinskii wrote in 1931 that he was confident that "ecology was becoming an exact science . . . with a need to apply quantitative methods."[60] In striving to make it more empirical, he was far from alone. Severtsov and Gauze in Russia, Alfred Lotka in the United States, Vito Volterra in Italy, and Vladimir Kostitzin in France had been trying to reduce predator-prey and parasite-host relationships, i.e., population dynamics, to laws drawn from physics and physical chemistry.[61] Although Stanchinskii's reductionism was far less pronounced than that of some of his colleagues, his work, at least initially, represented an attempt to reduce biological phenomena to a common physical denominator: energy. That would render those phenomena accessible and, thereby, predictable, through mathematical modeling. Ecology had thus far demonstrated no such possibilities, particularly at a time when an increasing premium was being put on applied science in Russia. This was a state of affairs that Stanchinskii now hoped to redress.

The premise that "the quantity of living matter in the biosphere is directly dependent on the amount of [solar] energy that is transformed by autotrophic plants" was Stanchinskii's starting point;[62] autotrophs were no less than "the economic base of the living world."[63] The biosphere itself consisted of subsystems—biocenoses—each of which had its own "economic base" and an equally individual "superstructure" which gained its sustenance from the primary producers at the bottom of the trophic ladder.

One of the chief properties of the biocenosis, he asserted, was that it was marked by relative stability, a "dynamic equilibrium."[64] Relative numbers of the various component species of the biocenosis remained surprisingly constant over long periods of time, he noted, despite their theoretical ability to propagate exponentially.[65] The key to this picture was the existence "between the autotrophic and heterotrophic components of the biocenosis, between herbivores and carnivores, hosts and parasites, etc., . . . of definite relationships, proportionalities," which had "up to now gone unstudied by anyone."[66]

Placing the various organisms on a "trophic ladder," from primary producer to decomposer, Stanchinskii ingeniously invoked the Second Law of Thermodynamics to explain what he described as a decreasing aggregate of biomass for each successive group on the ladder. The law held that energy is lost each time it is transferred because some of it is dissipated as heat from the work performed to make the transfer possible. Applying this law to energy availability in a biocenosis, Stanchinskii concluded that each successive rung on the ladder would have less energy in the form of food than the next lower level, since each successive level was dependent on the previous one for its energy supply yet could not appropriate it all; work had to be performed in capturing and digesting the food, as well as in carrying on a whole universe of other life functions. The riddle of "Elton's pyramid," which concerned the question of why there were relatively so few of the larger predators, was now solved. According to Stanchinskii's theory, these predators were at the very pinnacles of their biocenoses' trophic ladders, and their energy supply was therefore most restricted of all, preventing an unsupportable expansion of their numbers.

To study this complex problem Stanchinskii set as his first task the mathematical determination of the energetics role of each species. For a simple theoretical biocenosis, consisting only of green plants and a generalized heterotrophic sector, Stanchinskii gave different mathematical symbols to the various pathways of energy production, use, and flow. Perhaps his crowning achievement was then to synthesize these symbols into a mathematical paradigm to describe the annual energy budget of the theoretical biocenosis; it was the first time such a formulation had been attempted.[67]

Stanchinskii believed that, by studying the energy flows in a whole range of biocenoses, humans eventually would be able to calculate with a fair degree of accuracy the productive capacities of these natural communities and would be able to structure their own economic activity in conformity with them. Of particular value, he noted, would be an understanding, through a study of the trophic dynamics of biocenoses, of those "optimal conditions" under which various organisms are able to transform the greatest amount of energy into biomass. Needless to say, such a program had particularly important implications for agriculture and for the economy in general.[68]

Such a program of biocenotic research also could aid in such areas as the biotic protection of cultivated croplands, obviating "the use of pesticides, which often contain toxic substances . . . that not only kill the pests but cause injury to humans and to useful organisms."[69] Here, a profound knowledge of the ecology of insects could allow scientists to harness other, natural mechanisms of population control that would not be nearly as disruptive to the human and natural communities.

Medvedev had already begun taking censuses of the vegetation and principal heterotrophic consumers living in the low saucer-like depressions of the Askania steppe in 1927. Arriving in 1929, Stanchinskii took personal charge of the project. Even in his first summer there, his research was rewarded with interesting and significant results. He found that the periods of maximum biomass of a preceding and successive trophic level do not coincide, but that the first peaked considerably before the latter. Explaining this variance as a result of adaptive evolution, Stanchinskii speculated that it allowed the plants to be pollinated and to disperse their seeds before they were eaten by herbivores and so ensured undiminished propagation during the next growing season. Accordingly, the cycle continued in a state of relative equilibrium.[70]

That same year, Stanchinskii also developed a methodology and an instrumentation for measuring the biomass of the various component species inhabiting the fescue-feathergrass steppe. Of these, we must particularly mention his use of experimental sampling areas of varying sizes and his introduction of special traps for capturing and measuring the insect, arachnid, and other small fauna populations of the sampling areas. He called these instruments biocenometers.[71]

The determination of the primary production of vegetation and of the secondary production of animals was only the first step in Stanchinskii's program. Physiologists were invited to Askania to assay the energy requirements of individual species, and other specialists were welcomed as well. It was even planned to make a comparative study of various types of cultivated croplands and the virgin steppe, comparing productivity, stability, and other attributes of the communities.[72]

Stanchinskii's program was the first of its kind anywhere. While it took as its point of departure some new ways of viewing nature inspired by Vernadskii, it went beyond them to introduce a kind of mathematically based systems analysis into the study of natural communities. Stanchinskii's reduction of natural communities to a series of formal relationships between trophic levels based on energy transformation constituted a central new paradigm in twentieth-century biology.

THE *ZAPOVEDNIKI* OF NARKOMZEM

By contrast with the ecological direction of the *zapovedniki* of Narkompros and of that special case, Askania-Nova, in the reserves of Narkomzem RSFSR and its republican analogues theoretical scientific work was totally absent. What little scientific work existed was concentrated in the Voronezh game-management beaver *zapovednik*, where studies on beaver biology, captive breeding, and acclimatization were initiated.

The Narkomzem reserve saw its function first and foremost as that of a *rezervat:* an area for the replenishment of depleted game stocks. Typically, there were one or two commercially important species of game animals for which the reserve was brought into being: beaver in the Voronezh *zapovednik,* sable in the Barguzin *zapovednik,* and wild reindeer in the Chuna-Tundra *zapovednik* in Lapland. In some of these reserves, it appeared that only those commercially important species were under true protection and that the reserves' administrations turned a blind eye to such activities as logging, fishing, and grazing. These lapses often proved injurious even to the *zapovednik*'s objects of special protection.[73]

Some, including Severtsov, tried to pretend that there was no substantive difference between the *zapovedniki* of Narkomzem and those of Narkompros—nor should there be. Comparing the decrees chartering the various reserves of each commissariat, Severtsov failed to find "any essential differences in their juridical character." All were supposed to be "total *zapovedniki,* protecting the natural complex as a whole and not game animals exclusively," he noted. All were likewise remanded to pursue the scientific study of their natural conditions.[74]

Perhaps hopeful that his words would become a self-fulfilling prophecy, Severtsov maintained that the epithet *okhotnichii* (pertaining to game management or hunting), which Narkomzem persisted in using to describe its *zapovedniki,* represented merely "a previous attitude toward *zapovedniki* as simply 'hunting preserves' " and was now only a "historical curiosity."[75]

Looking back, it seems that Severtsov's attempt to paper over the divergent views of Narkompros and Narkomzem about protected territories was a deliberate gambit and not an act of Panglossian self-delusion. Could he have so quickly forgotten how, in April 1927, the Goskomitet, which he represented as scholarly secretary, had threatened to withhold its approval of the proposed upgrading of the local Voronezh beaver reserve to a state *zapovednik* on account of just such a narrow interpretation of *zapovednik* functions on the part of Narkomzem?[76] In that case, the Goskomitet made it clear that its approval was contingent on Narkomzem's acceptance of three conditions that went to the heart of the question "What is a *zapovednik?*" These conditions were:

1. That scientific work in Narkomzem's reserve be coordinated with that of other interested parties represented in the Goskomitet.

2. That income derived from the exploitation of resources of the reserve's buffer zone go toward support of scientific research in the *zapovednik,* instead of flowing into the coffers of Narkomzem's Forest Administration.

3. That the question of the exact designation of the reserve be left up to the Scientific-Methodological Commission of the Goskomitet.

By contrast with the utilitarian gestalt of the Voronezh reserve, the objectives of Narkompros's Astrakhan' *zapovednik,* upgraded to a state *zapovednik* only seven months later, were colored by the needs of science, namely "the preservation of the Volga River Delta with its characteristic fauna and flora for the scientific study of its virgin nature. . . ."[77] Whatever identity of mission the two reserves eventually shared was the result of conditions imposed by Narkompros on a less-than-enthusiastic Narkomzem.

In the Voronezh reserve affair, Narkompros successfully insisted on its right to set minimum standards for the activities of *zapovedniki* of any system. It was moved to do so by two factors. First, it believed that previous legislation conferred upon it overarching responsibility for *zapovednik* affairs in the RSFSR, not only within its own system, but for all agencies. What impelled the commissariat to act in the name of this presumed responsibility, however, was a growing belief among its conservation activists that any reserve claiming the designation *zapovednik* needed to pursue the scientific study of the entirety of the reserve's natural complex in addition to any other goals. What conservationists minded was not that Narkomzem was creating a network of unvarnished game preserves, but that it persisted in calling them *zapovedniki* or, worse yet, *okhotnich'i zapovedniki*. To Narkompros activists, the latter term was an absurdity, because to them a true *zapovednik* would never be created for the sake of protecting one or a few select species but for the protection of the entire natural complex.

Both sides, though, were hardly to be blamed in this semantic debacle, for no really suitable taxonomy of protected territories based on function or regimen had been generally agreed upon. Each commissariat was loath to cede exclusive use of the popular term *zapovednik* to the other, nor did either break through the impasse by devising new terms to describe their distinctive reserves. Accordingly, conservation limped along with Solov'ev's ineffectual schema, while the two commissariats geared up to do battle over the soul of Soviet *zapovedniki*.

SEVEN

The Conservation Congress of 1929

In September 1929 a long-planned congress convened in Moscow to chart the future course for the conservation movement. Originally, it had been set by Glavnauka to meet in the spring and was projected to be not much more than a round table of the leading activists of the RSFSR. Word of the forthcoming meeting spread, however, generating such a groundswell of enthusiasm, particularly in the provinces, that the original plans were scrapped and a full-blown congress was scheduled for the fall.[1] It was a tumultuous time; the First Five-Year Plan, a comprehensive economic strategy to industrialize the Soviet Union, was under way, while pioneer brigades of workers and young urban party members were sweeping through the villages, organizing the peasants into collective farms.

While the 1929 Congress was not an exact mirror image of the conservation movement as a whole, it provided at least a sociological profile of the leading activists. Despite the disproportionate representation of Moscow and Leningrad, just over half of the delegates with voting privileges (64 of 124) hailed from the provinces. This high level of provincial participation was highly correlated with involvement in the local lore movement; fully two-thirds of all delegates reported such involvement, as contrasted with only 44 percent who claimed membership in VOOP, the Moscow-based All-Russian Society for Conservation.

Although age was a category that betrayed no striking pattern, there were characteristics that clearly distinguished this gathering: level of education, party affiliation, and gender. The 1929 congress was unreservedly dominated by the intelligentsia. A good three-quarters of the delegates had completed higher education, while only 15 percent had gymnasium schooling or less. There was an even more complete domination by nonparty people; only 13 percent of the delegates professed membership in the All-Russian Communist Party, in its other republican permutations, or in its subsidiary organizations. Finally, the domination by members of the male gender was almost total; a mere 8 percent of the delegates were women, reflecting the persistence of old structures of power even in the NEP academe.[2]

On the morning of 23 September 1929 the First All-Russian Congress for Conservation gathered at the Moscow House of Scholars on Kropotkin Street. The delegates represented a real ethnic potpourri. Even representatives from the Transcaucasus, Ukrainian, and Belorussian union republics were accredited, although the congress, strictly speaking, was limited to "All-Russian" matters.

The delegates also represented a wide range of occupations. Zookeepers, museum workers, and artists were present; *zapovednik* staff members and directors were, too. A physician was in attendance, as were a member of the presidium of VTsIK, quite a few students, and numerous members of official Soviet bureaucracies. The largest single contingent was academics; there were at least a score of professors, of whom fifteen were specialists in some area of biology, plus a respectable number of docents and instructors. From the perspective of institutional affiliation, too, the congress was highly diverse. Almost all of the major protagonists were assembled: Narkompros RSFSR, Narkomzem RSFSR, Narkomtorg of the USSR, Gostorg RSFSR, VSNKh RSFSR, VOOP, the TsBK, the Goskomitet, the Hunters' Cooperative Union, the Academy of Sciences, plus yet other agencies, *zapovedniki,* museums, zoos, universities, and botanical gardens.

Calling the delegates to order was the tall, bearded, bespectacled chairman of the congress, the Old Bolshevik Petr Germogenovich Smidovich.[3] Best known in the West as the mystery man in the white fedora standing next to Lenin and Sverdlov on Red Square in a Civil War-vintage photo, or, perhaps, as the spouse of Sof'ia Nikolaevna Smidovich, leader of the party's Women's Section (Zhenotdel), Smidovich was a fascinating personality. For over a decade after the Revolution he occupied positions of considerable prestige and delicacy in the party and the government. Speaking with the authority of a senior government official and trusted party member (as well as from his own deep commitment to the cause), Smidovich offered the congress the government's blessing; "Soviet power," he announced, "cannot but strive to create favorable conditions for the growth of the conservation cause."[4]

Smidovich, however, did not simply present a message of good tidings, for along with his reassuring greeting came a portentous note. The conservation movement, he intimated, might have to undergo an essential alteration if it was to survive in conditions of "socialist construction." It could no longer limit itself to "the protection of nature" but had to shift its emphasis to "the study of factors that raise [nature's] . . . productive capacity . . . in the interests of the nation's economic development." No longer, either, could conservationists permit themselves to remain isolated from the world of society and of politics, noted Smidovich, who called upon the activists to reach out to "the widest circles of Soviet public opinion."[5]

Until the convocation of the congress, the conservation movement appeared to have been largely exempted from official scrutiny. This, however, was a mixed blessing, for although the sciences were being politicized to an extent unknown even during the Civil War, safe obscurity condemned the movement to marginal status at a time when nature was threatened as never before. The stakes had been raised, it is true, but if the movement did not enter the whirlwind and gain the ear of the regime and of society, it would certainly become irrelevant and its cause doomed.

The dangers of visibility, though, were not inconsequential. Much like the

Soviet intelligentsia as a whole, delegates to the congress could not fail to be aware of the gathering storm of Cultural Revolution outside. For any activity that betokened even the most remote political content, there was danger in staking out *any* identifiable position. This was all the more true for conservation, an area veritably fraught with political overtones. Many were already cognizant of the perils of outspokenness (or were soon to find out) and the prudent weighed their words. Accordingly, no speaker at the congress was so foolhardy as to openly dispute the notion that conservation ought to be put at the service of the construction of the new socialist society. Many, however, regarded their loyalty oaths to socialist construction as empty sloganeering. Broad differences lurked behind the apparent consensus.

At one extreme stood the delegate of the Young Naturalists, Petr Petrovich Smolin,[6] the outspoken voice of youth. Aesthetics, the joy of wilderness, the desire to preserve biological diversity—all of these things played little part in Smolin's conception of conservation. He could not or did not wish to see the inherent opposition between rampant industrialization and conservation:

> We must dissociate ourselves from that understanding of conservation in which the productive . . . activity of the human collectivity is placed in opposition to the play of elemental forces, and where (conservation) work reduces to shielding off this elemental play as much as possible from the planned, productive intervention of humans. Such "conservation" cannot find a place in the work plan of Soviet youth. . . . The naked idea of preservationism is organically alien to active youth and in particular to Soviet youth, seized . . . with the enthusiasm of socialist construction and reconstruction.[7]

Smolin's one-sidedness was countered by A. F. Vangengeim, president of VOOP, deputy director of Glavnauka, and one of the organizers of the congress. "It is extremely important to link up the cause of conservation with the entire Five-Year Plan," declared the meteorologist-turned-administrator. "However," he warned, "we must recognize as extremist that interpretation of conservation that views it exclusively as the rationalization of production and of the exploitation of natural resources; we should not shunt out of view the purely cultural or scientific interests which are associated with this cause."[8]

At the other pole were those whom Smolin derisively alluded to as upholders of "the naked idea of preservationism," that is, those who harbored the proclivities to venerate primordial nature on aesthetic or even ethical grounds. To attack these approaches to conservation in 1929, however, was much like beating a dead horse, for by the mid-1920s adherents of those tendencies had largely adapted their views or had fallen silent.

Nevertheless, a certain residue of the aesthetic tendency remained in VOOP. A small number cloaked themselves in the rhetoric of economics and of socialist aesthetics even as they continued to advocate the creation of American-style national parks. One rather interesting permutation of the aesthetic approach was the claim advanced by some conservationists that the love of nature was an integral part of the new socialist aesthetic. This line of argument implied that the essence of socialist man transcended mere *Homo oeconomicus* and that the new man required a return to the natural simplicity of primitive life. Proponents of this socialist aesthetic argued that socialist society required a democratization of leisure besides. Both of these goals were ideally satisfied through the cultivation of an interest in nature among the workers and by promoting recreation in the wild.[9]

At the congress, though, the issue of aesthetically founded preservation was muted. Only S. G. Grigor'ev, professor of geology at Moscow State University, openly complained that the congress had little to say about the need to preserve general landscape formations and nothing at all about the protection of geological "monuments," but even here it was unclear whether Grigor'ev was speaking out of an aesthetic sensibility or on behalf of scientific concerns. At any rate, the majority of the delegates evidently reasoned that pure landscape protection smacked of preservationism—now out of favor—and appreciated that under current conditions it would be virtually impossible to take such large territories out of immediate exploitation without providing a direct or indirect economic justification. Even conservationists were capable of making *some* compromises with realities.

One fundamental issue facing the congress was game procurement targets. The dispute between the Goskomitet and the economic commissariats had simmered during the summer after the sharp clash in late April, and nothing had been resolved. From the very first, it was evident that the fur was going to fly. M. P. Potemkin, who had succeeded V. T. Ter-Oganesov as deputy president of the Goskomitet in October 1927,[10] forcefully defended the conclusions of the committee's majority that the First Five-Year Plan targets of the economic agencies had far exceeded the bounds of good sense. Going into details, region by region and species by species, Potemkin painted a picture of the plan's targets as an orgy of irrationality. In the Murmansk-White Sea region, for example, the plan called for an increase in the annual catch of seals from 117,000 adults and 4,735 pups to an aggregate harvest of 350,000.[11] As it was, the Norwegians were already taking an additional 200,000 annually, for a current annual depletion of 320,000 of a herd that now numbered only one million.[12] The Norwegians could not be expected unilaterally to lower their catch out of concern for the seals at the same time that the Soviets were trebling theirs, and so the plan's targets were simply a prescription for quick catastrophe.

Potemkin likewise wondered how the Five-Year Plan's annual projected take of 350 sea otters in the Far East and the Pacific could be attained when the entire population numbered only about 450. Again, it was a recipe for extinction. Nor had Potemkin anything encouraging to report about whaling or commercial fishing in Lake Baikal.[13]

The economy could hardly tolerate overinflated targets, warned Potemkin, particularly when stocks of fish were already imperiled by a growing water pollution problem and by massive hydroelectric projects on the major watercourses.[14] Of particular urgency was the need to correlate the procurement norms for the various species with their natural rates of reproduction, as well as to eliminate the anarchy resulting from uncoordinated harvesting in waters shared by more than one union republic. Concluding his remarks about the procurement targets, Potemkin pronounced that "there are good grounds to assert that the prerevolutionary tradition of plunderous exploitation still has not been overcome. . . ."[15] Observations in the same vein were offered by Kulagin and by Severtsov, who used the game question to make a case for support for the science of ecology and for *zapovedniki* as leading centers of this work.[16]

Replying to the critical onslaught, a gallant few tried to defend the record of the procurement agencies. Gostorg's Kudriavtsev, for one, denied Kulagin's assertion of a catastrophic depletion of game, and maintained that violations of conservation regulations by official agencies were merely "individual distortions" and not a consistent policy. With continued planning of targets combined with the expansion of ranch breeding and of acclimatization efforts, he cheerfully predicted, much of the pressure now on wildlife would be eased.[17]

Kudriavtsev's optimistic assessment, however, was not generally embraced. With Narkompros supporters in the wide majority at the congress, the delegates approved a resolution that hewed closely to Potemkin and Kulagin's criticism and recommendations. Even as it noted "certain achievements" of Narkomzem and other agencies, the resolution underscored the crisis nature of the "progressive decline in game" and backed the call for a game census, a game biology institute, and stronger Goskomitet powers to veto output quotas. Similarly, the congress issued a strongly worded resolution on marine mammal protection and warned that the agencies responsible for the "new, grandiose forms of Soviet economic life—hydroelectric projects, irrigation works, log floating," and other activities—could ill afford to disregard the interests of the fishing industry. To do so would risk incurring serious losses.[18]

Although the resolutions of the congress had no real power to change anything, they were indicative of a growing mood of frustration among conservationists. Attempts to educate and compromise with the economic bureaucrats were now yielding to a readiness for confrontation.

The debate over logging and the clearing of the remaining virgin steppe also heated up during the congress. Again, Potemkin struck the first blow against the economic commissariats, particularly Narkomzem. Forest renewal was a fiction, he charged, and to make matters worse, the control figures for the Five-Year Plan envisioned 100 percent increase in the annual output of timber over the course of the plan. Even *zapovednik* lands, actual and potential, were in danger, Potemkin warned ominously.[19]

Until late 1929, most conservationists, while deploring the lax regime of the Narkomzem *zapovedniki,* did not view the situation as urgent. True, Glavnauka had attempted to impose its own preconceived notions regarding the regime and function of *zapovedniki* on Narkomzem RSFSR at the time of the chartering of the Voronezh state *zapovednik*. That struggle, however, was for possession of the rights to the use of the term *zapovednik*. On 20 June 1929, though, at the start of the two-month summer recess for official Moscow, Narkompros this time found itself on the receiving end of a conservation bombshell. Through behind-the-scenes maneuvering, doubtless made easier by the imminent replacement of Lunacharskii by A. S. Bubnov at the head of the commissariat and by multiple leadership changes in Glavnauka itself,[20] Narkomzem RSFSR effected a veritable *coup de main*.

Seemingly out of the blue, the RSFSR Economic and Social Council, a decree-issuing arm of the Council of People's Commissars, decided to transfer three of the most important Narkompros *zapovedniki*—the Caucasus, the Crimean, and the Astrakhan'—to the jurisdiction of Narkomzem RSFSR.[21]

Voicing the distress of many, Potemkin feared that the forests of the Caucasus *zapovednik* were already in jeopardy. Even more alarming was the prospect that yet other *zapovedniki* might fall into the clutches of Narkomzem as well. Narkomzem had tasted the first, sweet fruits of triumph, and the bounds of the Agriculture Commissariat's appetite were anybody's guess.

Reaction was bitter. Professors S. S. Ganeshin, S. G. Grigor'ev, and P. E. Vasil'kovskii immediately proposed a resolution that the *zapovedniki* be returned forthwith to the Narkompros system. V. G. Averin of the Ukraine went even further, calling for a resolution explicitly requiring all *zapovedniki* to be placed under Narkompros administration; game reserves, which would be clearly desig-nated as such *(okhotnich'i rezervaty)*, would constitute the lone exception, and would fall under the jurisdiction of Narkomzem, fittingly.

At the outset of the debate, Potemkin tried to prevent the matter from escalat-ing into a fracas between the majority of the delegates and the representatives of Narkomzem RSFSR by proposing that a special commission look into the matter; the congress would defer any declarations pending the commission's report. Events, however, overtook his efforts at bureaucratic diplomacy; bowing to the outraged majority, he was obliged to agree to draft a strong letter of protest to the SNK RSFSR in the name of the congress.

Aside from the shocking raid on the three Narkompros reserves, the single other most disturbing development in this *zapovedniki* war was Narkomzem's continuing, effective campaign to thwart the establishment of the Central Forest *zapovednik*. Grigorii Leonidovich Grave, senior lecturer in zoology at Smolensk State University and leader of the Glavnauka expedition that had selected the site in the Belyi woods for the *zapovednik*, informed the delegates that Narkomzem RSFSR had already openly announced its opposition to the creation of the reserve. Challenged at a conference called by Narkompros in May 1929, Narkomzem was forced to abandon its policy of verbally assenting to repeated Goskomitet resolu-tions in favor of the *zapovednik* while surreptitiously continuing to log on the proposed site. Now, Narkomzem finally had put to rest any uncertainty concerning its true intentions in the area. But that was not all. Grave had gotten wind—from Petrushin, Narkomzem's representative at the congress, it turned out—of even bigger things afoot. Not simply the *zapovednik* lands but all of the forests of the entire Western Oblast, including the Belyi woods, were scheduled to be clear-cut to make way for cropland. A wave of shock overwhelmed the audience as the implications of Grave's revelation sunk in.

Many delegates could not believe that an entire province's forests were to be cleanly wiped off the face of the planet according to "plan." The issue turned out to be far, far bigger than the fate of the Central Forest *zapovednik*. Passions were running high, and the congress was urged by three of its most respected figures—Kozhevnikov, Averin, and Stanchinskii—to at least take a decisive stand on the fate of the *zapovednik,* making sure that Narkompros took the matter to the Council of People's Commissars at once. As Grave had observed, "while years go by trying to resolve this matter, whole forests are being cut down."[22]

Conservationists close to Glavnauka and those of Narkomzem diverged no less sharply on the issue of protecting the last remaining parcels of virgin steppe in the RSFSR, particularly in European Russia. Potemkin reminded the congress that time was quickly running out, and no less an authority than botanist Boris Aleksandrovich Keller put the total number of discrete remaining steppe parcels at eight, with an aggregate area of a scant five thousand hectares.[23]

Although beginning in 1928 the Goskomitet had funded expeditions to identify virgin steppe parcels for protection, those efforts had been stalled by the obstructionism of Narkomzem and its subsidiary agencies. The lone parcel of feathergrass steppe remaining in the Central Black Earth Region, for instance, had the bad fortune to be located within the boundaries of the sovkhoz Panika, which refused to alienate the territory for a *zapovednik.* Likewise the designation of the Khrenovskii bor Steppe *zapovednik* was delayed after the Kursk Oblast Forest Department of Narkomzem "lost" the relevant correspondence not once, but twice. The true feelings of the director of the department finally emerged in one letter, in which he wrote that "there is no need to establish a *zapovednik* that nobody needs."[24]

As ecologist Severtsov had tried to do with respect to the hunting sector, Moscow ecologist V. V. Alekhin labored to show that ecological studies in steppe *zapovedniki,* far from being the "useless" removal of valuable agricultural land from the economy, would in fact enhance agricultural productivity in the Black Earth Region and could contribute to reversing the worrying decline of soil fertility there. "The introduction of new grasses into agriculture, the identification and planting of new, arid-tolerant varieties, the selection of new mixes of grasses," he stressed, "can only be accomplished'after studying the virgin steppe, . . . *etalony* of the natural productive forces of a given area. . . ."

Again, the beleaguered operatives of the economic commissariats rose to reply. Responding to the parade of hostile speakers Petrushin of Narkomzem decried "irresponsible declarations to the congress." While conceding that steppe *zapovedniki* were an important question, he derided the atmosphere of hysteria, declaring that "there was no need to cause panic."[25]

To no one's surprise, however, the congress failed to share Petrushin's languid assessment of the peril to the steppes, and it went on record in support of the basic Narkompros program for an entire network of steppe *zapovedniki.* Their organization had to be done with the "utmost haste," the resolution said, with expeditions ready to set out within the year.[26]

Whether the discussion concerned game, forest, or steppe protection, two general recommendations kept resurfacing. First, there needed to be a general census of all natural resources, for only on the basis of such an inventory could scientifically based decisions regarding their exploitation be made. Second, Glavnauka and the Goskomitet had to enjoy full authority both to review all targets of the plan and to monitor fulfillment and compliance. One of the most widespread convictions among the mass of delegates was that, somehow, something had to stand between the juggernaut of the Five-Year Plan and Russia's natural resources and that "something" was the Goskomitet.

Although some of the blame for the "completely unsatisfactory performance" of the "central conservation organs" in the area of plan monitoring, as Vangengeim put it, could be laid at their own door, a great deal of their ineffectiveness was built in. The Goskomitet's powers needed to be enhanced. It was time, resolved the delegates, legally to ensure that "not one decision of the government should be implemented" until hearings on controversial actions affecting the environment were held by the Goskomitet. Moreover, it was essential that the committee enjoy the full right to subpoena "reports, materials, and an accounting on all matters touching the question of conservation" from all agencies, institutions, and individual enterprises alike. Finally, commensurate with its national watchdog role, the Goskomitet needed to be included directly in the RSFSR republican budget on a separate line from Narkompros. While exaggerated claims of Soviet "firsts" in other fields strain credulity, it is not too far-fetched to propose that the idea of an environmental impact statement was born in these earnest sessions at the Moscow House of Scholars in late September 1929.

The top priority for conservationists was to make the need for protected territories intelligible to both officials and the population at large. Viktor Averin underscored the need for such a strategy:

> It is very difficult to persuade the population or the local authorities of the necessity of a particular *zapovednik*. Occasionally, if we can point out how it serves the interests of the economy, we may meet with success. The matter becomes more difficult when we speak of public health and other considerations. Generally speaking, we compromise ourselves by using delusive arguments. We must find a broad, principled basis for keeping nature inviolable. The task of the congress is to formulate it. . . .[27]

In a sense, Averin was arguing against the position of such speakers as Daniil Nikolaevich Kashkarov, who advocated "selling" the idea of protected territories to the people as essentially a recreational program. The scientific functions of *zapovedniki*—considered by ecologist Kashkarov to be hopelessly unintelligible to the general populace—would have to sneak through on the coattails of a popular, tourism-oriented national parks program; in addition to an extensive zone for camping and other recreational activities, Kashkarov's proposed multizone national park would include an educational zone and an inviolable zone for scientific research. Conservation had to appeal to the masses' self-interest in readily understandable terms, argued Kashkarov. "If we continue to stress the interests of pure science," he cautioned, "then we will not attract any broad-based support."[28]

One delegate who seized on Kashkarov's suggestion with enthusiasm was A. F. Skorobogatyi, a forester and acclimatizer who represented the Forest Administration of the Ukrainian Narkomzem. Indeed, argued he, it was insufficient merely to proclaim the *zapovednik* open to tourism. Roads and facilities were needed. With a proper infrastructure, the Caucasus *zapovednik* could become no less a tourist mecca than any of the American national parks, and could generate an income of foreign exchange besides.[29]

What Skorobogatyi cleverly failed to divulge was that such a program of road construction would make the exploitation of the resources of the *zapovedniki,* particularly their forests, much more expeditious. That was not a moot point because the Caucasus *zapovednik,* to use Skorobogatyi's example, had just been transferred to the jurisdiction of the Forest Administration of Narkomzem RSFSR, prompting fears of logging. Already the tourist trails were being laid down, commercial logging operations had begun in the surrounding buffer zone, and Narkomzem had ordered the reserve to give up four thousand hectares of grazing land to three settlements nearby (reversing the 1927 decision of the SNK RSFSR). While this last order had been successfully resisted by A. G. Diunin, the *zapovednik's* director, it was clearly a bad omen.[30]

Skorobogatyi's endorsement confirmed the deep misgivings of many delegates concerning Kashkarov's approach. Kashkarov's friend and fellow ecologist Stanchinskii spoke for most when he reaffirmed as a "given" that *zapovedniki* were first of all institutions devoted to scientific research. "If *zapovedniki* were to be converted to spas," he warned, "that would be a great mistake."[31]

Before the delegates could agree on how to market conservation, however, they had to agree on what kind of product they were selling. That amounted to reaching a consensus on the nature and function of *zapovedniki,* which were the instruments as well the embodiments par excellence of Soviet conservation, about which there were serious differences of opinion. The most serious of these, as we have seen, involved the growing rift between the Commissariats of Agriculture and Education.

The debate over the whole thrust of *zapovednik* activity erupted in earnest during the morning session on 25 September 1929. Leading off, Severtsov at last was prepared to admit that there *was* a real difference between the *zapovedniki* of Narkompros and those of Narkomzem, a fact that he had sought to deny a few short months before. When asked by a questioner whether it was "possible to eliminate the dual jurisdiction of Narkompros and Narkomzem over the *zapovedniki,*" Severtsov now had to recognize this as *the* pivotal problem. "It is true," Severtsov concluded; "Narkomzem is claiming that *all zapovedniki* come under *its* jurisdiction."[32] Needless to say, such a resolution of the problem was little shy of anathema to the overwhelming majority of the delegates.

Since the takeover of the three Narkompros reserves three months earlier, Narkomzem in unconcealed haste had taken steps to parcel out a large chunk of territory from the Caucasus *zapovednik* to surrounding agricultural interests. Respected informants, including Potemkin, believed that the commissariat was preparing to mount large-scale timbering operations within those reserves as well. Now there was also talk that Narkomzem was seeking to use the *zapovedniki* as staging areas for the acclimatization of all kinds of exotic fauna and flora, many from overseas. All this spelled irreversible damage to the existing pristine ecological communities, it was thought; such damage would make these areas worthless as *etalony* and could even imperil some rare endemic species. It was clear to the delegates that ecologically oriented *zapovedniki* could not serve *this* master.

Frightened by Narkomzem's predatory intentions, Severtsov struck a pose of compromise. In effect, he suggested that Narkompros was prepared to abandon its claim to the sole use of the term *zapovednik* and that each system could continue to go its own way without interference from the other (on the unstated condition that Narkomzem return the three raided *zapovedniki*).

Narkomzem's Petrushin appeared to grasp at the olive branch. Astounding everyone, Petrushin went even further than the status ante bellum proposed by Severtsov and proposed to clear up the terminological confusion once and for all, ceding to Narkompros the exclusive use of the term *zapovednik*. "Narkomzem is prepared to come to terms with Narkompros," he announced, and was disposed "to accept any new term for its *zapovedniki* that expresses their essence as game preserves *(rezervaty)*." "Let Narkompros carry on its scientific research itself," concluded Petrushin, not without a small dollop of condescension. "We shall carry on other work."[33]

The spirit of compromise, however, proved too fragile. As a matter of fact, Petrushin's overture was undermined by the very next speaker, K. A. Kiselev of the Narkomzem-run Voronezh *zapovednik,* who took it upon himself to lecture Narkompros on how to organize work in a *zapovednik*.

Kiselev made three central points. The first was that pure research, so-called, was an unaffordable luxury. "In our day, under our economic conditions," he announced, "science for science's sake just won't do." The second point addressed the question of funding for the applied work that would replace basic research in the *zapovedniki*. Here he embraced the controversial approach that had been tried at Askania; funds would be generated by *zapovednik* production sectors *(zapovednye khoziaistva)* through the sale of resources exploited on *zapovednik* territory. The third point took on the belief that *zapovedniki* should be inviolable. Conservationists had no right to regard the reserves as a sanctuary for birds and animals; on the contrary, it was right and desirable "to reacclimatize [sic] all valuable animals and birds which the changed conditions permit." All of this sent a shudder through the Glavnauka benches.[34]

Kiselev's proposals, reflecting the predominant style of thinking in Narkomzem circles, spotlighted an important problem of semantics. Many delegates now realized that it was no longer sufficient to define *zapovedniki* as reserves having prominent scientific research programs; *research* could mean acclimatization or other deliberate alterations of natural conditions. *Zapovedniki* must also be inviolate. As mineralogist D. I. Rudenko, director of the Il'menskii *zapovednik,* remonstrated, any economic activity in a *zapovednik* (let alone *zapovednik* production sectors) was a contradiction in terms, for a *zapovednik* was nothing if it was not a place where *zapovednost'*—inviolability—was scrupulously observed.[35] The function of the *zapovednik*—scientific and, especially, ecological research—had to be accompanied by the appropriate regime: inviolability. Kozhevnikov's old preachment had finally sunk in.

Kiselev's talk unleashed a torrent of protests; the atmosphere of compromise had broken down. Rebutting Kiselev in the strongest terms, entomologist and ecologist Shalyt drew upon the experiences of his home *zapovednik,* Askania-Nova, and warned:

> Economic activity in a *zapovednik* is impermissible! If we set economic goals for *zapovedniki,* we must then view them as industrial enterprises. . . . The experience of Askania-Nova leads us necessarily to reject flat out any type of economic activity. This experience *must* be taken into account.[36]

That exclamation summed up the almost unanimous mood of the delegates, who did not wish to permit direct, undisguised economic activity in the reserves. Even so, there was far from complete unanimity among this group concerning the finer points of *zapovednik* management. Some of these divergences were revealed during the long-awaited discussion concerning the role of the *zapovednik* as a scientific research institution, which began on the afternoon of 26 September 1929.

The stage had been set for a full-dress debate on the *zapovedniki* by the confrontations over Askania-Nova, the Narkomzem RSFSR takeover of the three reserves, and the question of how to market the *zapovedniki,* all of which had taken place over the previous days' sessions. Now, as Stanchinskii delivered the keynote address of the session, "The *zapovednik* as a Scientific Research Institution," the emphasis shifted to the scientific and even technical aspects of the problem, an arena where there were no definitive answers.

In his address, Stanchinskii moved to cover his "left," economic flank, observing that while the *zapovednik* was a scientific institution its "rationale is, at base, economic." Accordingly, he advised the selection for *zapovedniki* of "the most typical territories which will have the greatest economic significance as natural *etalony.* . . . The network of *zapovedniki* must be linked with the Five-Year Plan."[37]

Following Stanchinskii's presentation, the question and answer exchange revealed some serious theoretical problems inherent in the *etalon* concept; the major, unresolved gaps in ecologists' knowledge about the nature of ecological systems did not permit easy answers. A number of queries put to Stanchinskii questioned the possibility of viewing the *zapovedniki* as self-contained, isolated parcels. One delegate's query, "Where can we find inviolate nature, since all of it has been so strongly altered by people?" borrowed more than a leaf from the "web of life" notion that no place in our interdependent biosphere had evaded direct or indirect human influence. Another wanted to know whether it was permissible to introduce exotic species into the reserves, while a third wondered about the advisability of eliminating predators or exotic species that had accidentally found their way into the *zapovednik.* Finally, there were those who sought to know whether there was a place for rehabilitated or even second-growth areas to be included into *zapovedniki,* or whether the reserves had to consist exclusively of "virgin" territory.

Responding to this battery of challenging questions, Stanchinskii retreated to a posture of relativism. Prefacing his replies, he conceded that no *zapovednik* could be absolutely isolable, "since nothing in the world is absolute, anyway."[38] Having established that the reserves could enjoy only a relative inviolability, he granted that humans could at times justifiably intervene in the life of the reserve, eliminating or controlling native and in-migrating species that seemed to threaten the equilibrium of the *zapovednik's* natural complex. Finally, Stanchinskii allowed that *zapovedniki* should be permitted to introduce such exotic species as promising varieties of wheat grains (presumably in experimental plots isolated from the main, inviolate *etalon*) in order to establish their suitability for commercial introduction in the surrounding area for which the *zapovednik* served as a prototype. (Interestingly, the example he used was of a sessile plant, and not an animal.)[39] All these concessions and allowances, however, turned Stanchinskii's *etalon* into a rather murky standard indeed.

Tending to share Stanchinskii's flexible attitude was Severtsov. As an ecologist intimately familiar with the problems of Russia's *zapovedniki*, Severtsov was particularly aware that, in many instances, economic and political considerations did not allow for the creation of reserves whose territories were set large enough to encompass what he believed to be a truly viable, self-regulating parcel of nature. All too often, *zapovedniki* turned out to be too small or unhappily sited to be considered self-regulating in any sense. The tiny Kosino and Penza *zapovedniki* were excellent examples of that. Even the fairly large Astrakhan' *zapovednik* proved a hapless victim of the downstream effects of Caspian Sea fishing practices, pollution, and hydroelectric construction on the Volga River.

With these factors in mind Severtsov recommended a sliding scale of human intervention in the natural life of the *zapovedniki*, with minimal or even no intervention in the larger reserves, where pest outbreaks, for example, would pose no lasting threat to the stability of the community, rising to active pest control when needed and even the prophylactic removal of deadwood in small reserves, where the natural community was perhaps truncated and did not have the resiliency to recover on its own. Nonetheless, Severtsov emphasized that the Goskomitet held up the principle of inviolability as its guiding ideal and "countenanced variances in individual cases only with the most extreme reluctance." In such cases, we may assume, the Goskomitet felt that it was better to preserve a truncated portion of virgin nature and to sacrifice principle than to preserve the latter and to sacrifice what was left of the original biocenosis.[40]

There was, however, a second factor at work behind the readiness of some delegates to intervene in the natural life of reserves seemingly menaced by mass outbreaks of insects, invasions of wolves, or other disruptions. From their inception the *zapovedniki* began to be burdened with another task in addition to serving as inviolable *etalony*: the protection of rare and endangered species of plants and animals. Thus, the Caucasus *zapovednik* (dubbed *zubrovyi*, or bison, by some) had also been a sanctuary for the Caucasus race of European bison (until local poachers killed the last of them in the mid-1920s) as well as for the tur, a Caucasian mountain goat. Similarly, the Astrakhan' *zapovednik*, in addition to serving as an *etalon* for the entire delta zone of the Volga, functioned as a refuge for numerous species of waterfowl, including flamingo and about a half-dozen species of heron. *Zapovedniki* likewise served as refuges for rare flora.

If the two functions of *etalon* and refuge were not seen as conflicting at the time by Narkompros conservationists, this was not entirely the result of self-delusion or of a crucial lack of reflection on this problem. In many cases, in the early 1920s there were still areas outside the *zapovedniki* where these rare, endangered, or simply endemic species could be found. As the decade wore on, however, and the pace of economic development accelerated, many of those wild areas that sheltered wildlife disappeared. Frequently, *zapovedniki* became the only remaining patches of the original virgin nature that once covered the entire region. Correspondingly, they also became the last refuges for the region's vanishing endemic flora and fauna.

Experience soon exposed the drawbacks of saddling the *zapovedniki* with the dual responsibility of ecological research and preserving vanishing wildlife. The two goals, while compatible over the short term, were mutually antagonistic over the long haul, it now appeared.

A program of ecological research mandated that a regime of total inviolability be maintained so that natural successional dynamics—the "evolutionary play"—would proceed unimpeded. However, with time this natural process of the slow evolution of the biocenosis eventually would result in the elimination of many of the original species of the community. At some point, even the rare, protected endemics would also be slated for natural extinction as the community matured into new seres (successional stages).

At this juncture, with all other natural habitats of the rare species having been eliminated by economic development, the *zapovednik* administration would be faced with the Hobson's choice of "freezing" the successional dynamics of the biocenosis to save the endangered species (and thereby interfering with the presumed self-regulatory activities of the system) or allowing the natural processes to run their course and sustaining a loss to the world's genetic diversity. Either way, it was an unenviable dilemma. However, with the exception of Kozhevnikov and a few others, conservationists refused to recognize that the *zapovednik* could survive either as an *etalon* or as a refuge *(rezervat)* but not as both.

This thorny issue had become poignant only shortly before the congress. A. G. Diunin, then director of the Astrakhan' *zapovednik,* reportedly had approached Kozhevnikov with such a problem, citing the need to eliminate the cormorants and ravens from the reserve because they threatened the continued survival of the Volga Delta's last remaining colonies of herons, also in the reserve. True to his principles, Kozhevnikov reportedly replied that the ecological dynamic of the competition between the avian groups should proceed to its conclusion with no interference from the *zapovednik* administration.[41]

With the reluctant approval of the Goskomitet and against Kozhevnikov's advice, Diunin and K. A. Vorob'ev, the *zapovednik's* ornithologist, initiated their campaign to rid the reserves of the ravens and the cormorants. Soon, the director of the Aksu-Dzhebagly *zapovednik* in Kazakhstan ASSR was posing the question of "the extermination of the wolves" inside his reserve.[42] It was almost as if adherents of the policy of active management in *zapovedniki* sought to save nature from itself.

Yet, for thoroughly consistent partisans of the ecological-*etalon* approach, all species of the biocenosis had equal standing. The long-range task of observing and analyzing the ecological dynamics of the community, a drama that was itself part of the larger "evolutionary play," required the ecologist to watch impassively as new biotic actors entered and old, familiar ones exited the stage. He or she could not play favorites; even the most seemingly inconsequential organism had its unique role in nature's economy.

This view of scientific research in *zapovedniki,* however, was not shared by all. Like their counterparts in Narkomzem who envisioned the reserve as a place for the propagation of select species, voices in the Narkompros camp held that the highest priority for *zapovedniki* ought to be ensuring the protection of rare and endangered natural objects. Professor Nikolai Shul'zhenko of the Dagestan Institute of Culture stated the case for this approach, seeking to liberate preservationist values from behind the screen of ecological justification.[43]

Doubtless aware of the political unacceptability of Shul'zhenko's position and keen to defend his ecological program, Stanchinskii protested against this old-fashioned conception. In any case, he retorted, "one cannot view the *zapovednik* as an absolutely inviolable museum of nature."[44] There was a profound irony to this last comment, however, for the ecological-*etalon* approach as represented by Stanchinskii was the one that truly had need of keeping the *zapovednik* inviolable (though not a museum, of course), while it was the preservationists who were behind attempts to introduce more active "management" to maintain, restore, or promote more propitious habitat conditions for endangered life forms.

Unlike many of his colleagues, Stanchinskii was a dynamic man who did not fear change; he did not seek to use ecological *zapovedniki* to isolate pockets of natural diversity and beauty from the onrushing leveler of Stalinist culture. Rather, he emphasized in his defense of ecologically oriented *zapovedniki* that the goal of a truly planned economy that functioned within the sustainable limits of productivity provided by nature could come about only with the active participation of conservationists in socialist construction, rather than by the adoption of a confrontational stance vis-à-vis the authorities and society.[45]

Although many delegates agreed about the need for *zapovedniki* to serve and to be seen as serving the ultimate needs of the economy, some felt that Stanchinskii had been unnecessarily lax concerning the reserves' inviolability. One delegate who quickly spotted the self-contradiction of the flexible *etalon* was the representative of the Crimean *zapovednik,* B. K. Fortunatov. The door should not be opened even a crack in the direction of human interference, he protested, lest the scientific value of the research be contaminated: "the standard must be inviolate, or else it ceases to be a standard." Even Smolin, who could hardly contain his enthusiasm for socialist construction otherwise, supported this rigorous understanding of the *etalon.* "The boundaries of the *zapovednik* must be fixed," he added, "so that the biological balance is not violated, so as to preserve the entire biological complex."[46]

Clearly, what was desired was some way to ensure that all newly established *zapovedniki* were designed to include entire, putatively self-regulating biocenoses; this was the crux of the matter. Yet precisely here ecological theory demonstrated its continued impotence. On one hand, not enough was known about the structure of ecological systems to determine the minimal areas needed to preserve those systems viably intact.[47] Such knowledge, paradoxically, could only result from the intensive, long-term ecological investigations of such systems as were pursued in *zapovedniki*. On the other hand, for such studies to bear fruit, they would have to be conducted not on remnants of fragmented biocenoses but on integral communities, which alone could provide a picture of the manifold interrelationships among their myriad components. But—and herein again the paradox—ecology thus far had not been able to furnish a method to identify the boundaries (or even the conclusive existence) of such natural communities to begin with.

Past practice of the Goskomitet was, as Kozhevnikov explained, to determine the territory of a proposed *zapovednik* by means of a formula based on the population densities of selected fauna and flora within the general area of the sites under consideration for protection.[48] This method, however, was little better than thinly disguised guesswork, and was challenged by Fortunatov, who charged that the inclusion of the entire biological complex could be assured only through field study.[49] Vasil'kovskii tried to strike a compromise, suggesting that field studies could be used to revise the provisional frontiers of the reserves after they were established, but that their original size had to be set by the relationship between wildlife and territory.[50]

Those familiar with the actual situation, though, could not help but be struck by the air of unreality of this discussion. More often than not, unstated economic and political factors outweighed ecological considerations—however interpreted—in the site selection process. European Russian and Ukrainian *zapovedniki,* with their constricted areas determined at least as much by the presence of nearby settlements and collective farms as by the intentions of ecologists, were already compromised in the chief aspect of their activity: ecological research.

Despite these conundrums, paradoxes, and impediments, the delegates bravely upheld their faith in the ecological *etalon* as *the* organizing principle for *zapovedniki*. This view carried the day in a resolution fashioned by a committee of nine—Stanchinskii, Shalyt, Severtsov, Rudenko, K. A. Zabelin, I. I. Puzanov, A. A. Umnov, V. P. Semenov-tian-shanskii, and Diunin. However, the resolution's framers now felt obliged to justify *zapovedniki* in economic terms, as "a vital link in socialist construction."[51] *Zapovedniki* could no longer legitimate themselves merely by their potential to increase the fund of human knowledge; they now had to point to the economic benefits their research could confer. That marked a significant shift from the heyday of NEP, when pure science was defended without apology, even by Bolsheviks. A great danger also resided in this new turn; in the future, conservation and ecology would be measured against the practical, economic benefits they had promised to deliver. Nevertheless, the practical expression of conservation work still officially remained the ecological research of the *zapovedniki*, which, despite the lip service to socialist construction, still tried to retain its scientific integrity.[52]

Despite its failure to resolve any of the practical or theoretical problems facing conservation, the congress did perform some very useful functions for the movement. It permitted some of the central, perplexing problems to be ventilated, initiating a much-needed debate. For another, it achieved its purpose in providing a forum where activists from all over the Soviet Union could meet, compare their experiences, and, in many cases, establish enduring ties. Finally, it was an effective show of strength for the conservation lobby, one which, perhaps, saved the Narkompros network of reserves from utter liquidation—and just in the nick of time. These were not minor accomplishments. The problems confronting the conservation movement were mounting at a frightening tempo, and the failure of the congress to settle some of the most fundamental issues—particularly those concerning the Narkompros-Narkomzem rivalry—would exact a high price in the months and years ahead.

1. Zoologist Nikolai Feofanovich Kashchenko (1855–1935): "Man must now care
for evolution."

2. Hugo Conwentz (1855–1922), Prussian
apostle of neoromantic conservation.

3. Botanist Ivan Parfen'evich Borodin
(1847–1930), moving spirit of prerevolutionary nature protection.

4. Grigorii Aleksandrovich Kozhevnikov (1866–1933), standard-bearer of the *etalon*.

5. Nikolai Nikolaevich Pod"iapol'skii (1883–1934), whose unexpected meeting with Lenin was a turning point for conservation.

ОХРАНА ПРИРОДЫ

Орган Всероссийского Общества
охраны природы при ГЛАВНАУКЕ НКП

ОХРАНА
И
ПРИРОДЫ!

ЗЕМЛЕДЕЛИЕ.
ОХОТА.
НАРОДНОЕ ЗДОРОВЬЕ.
КРАЕВЕДЕНИЕ.
ХУДОЖЕСТВЕННЫЕ ЦЕННОСТИ.
ДЕТИ. ЮНОШЕСТВО, ШКОЛА
КРАСНАЯ АРМИЯ.
ПУТИ СООБЩЕНИЯ.
ТУРИЗМ.

N 1   1928

Москва-центр, Чистые Пруды, 6.

Так были истреблены зубры!

6. Cover of first issue of conservation journal *Okhrana prirody*, 1928:
"And that is how the bison were exterminated. . . ."

„День птиц", проведенный Отделением О-ва в Юрьеве-Польском Иваново-Вознесенской губ.

7. *Okhrana prirody*, 1929, no. 3. Bird Day celebrated by thousands in Iur'ev-Pol'skii, Ivanovo-Voznesensk province.

8. Daniil Nikolaevich Kashkarov (1878–1941), pioneer in Soviet animal ecology.

9. Kashkarov, circa 1931, with first Uzbek students of zoology, Central Asian State University, Tashkent.

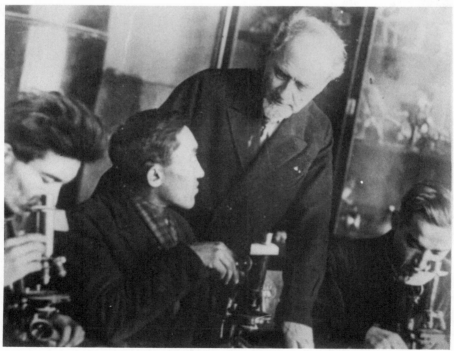

10. Kashkarov, second from left, leading expedition to study ecology of the Betpak-Dala desert, Kazakhstan, 1927.

11. Kashkarov, co-founder (with V. V. Stanchinskii) of USSR's first journal of ecology.

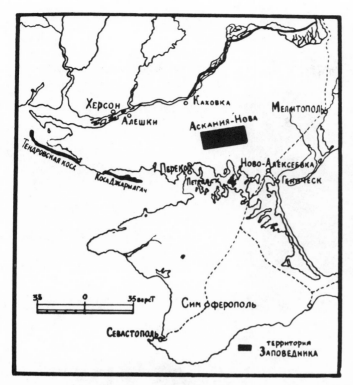

12. Map of Askania-Nova, 1932, showing branches of the
zapovednik along the Black Sea littoral.

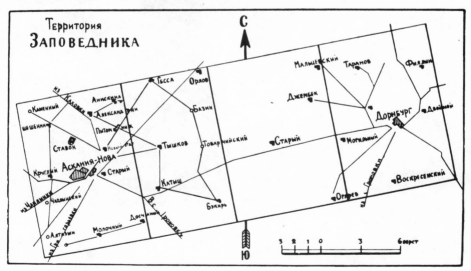

13. Askania-Nova, including Dornburg, with surrounding villages.

14. Fridrikh Eduardovich Fal'ts-Fein (1863–1920), landowner who established the Askania-Nova *zapovednik* on his estate.

15. Vladimir Vladimirovich Stanchinskii (1882–1942), forgotten giant of Soviet ecology.

16. Stanchinskii's student Nina Trofimovna Nechaeva with biocenometer at Askania-Nova, circa 1930.

17. View of pond at Askania with flamingos.

18. The last *tabun* (herd) of Przewalski horses, Askania.

19. Acclimatized zebras at Askania.

20. A zebroid (zebra-horse cross) at Askania, product of early attempts (circa 1932) to create new species through hybridization.

21. An unlikely mixture of zebras, zebu, and caribou, brought to Askania from different continents.

22. through 25. Askania idyll. Views of prerevolutionary "oasis of the steppe" as captured on postcards.

22. Rhea, the African ostrich's cousin, brought to Askania from South America.

23. The pond teems with waterfowl.

АСКАНІЯ-НОВА — Зоологическій садъ, Ф. Э. Фальцъ-Фейнъ.
ASKANIA-NOVA — Zoologischer Garten von F. E. Falz-Fein.

24. Sika deer from Manchuria pause along the water's edge.

АСКАНІЯ-НОВА — Зоологическій садъ.
ASKANIA-NOVA — Zoologischer Garten.

25. Swans, geese, and ducks practice peaceful coexistence.

«год издания
Цена 35 к.

ОХРАНА ПРИРОДЫ
Орган Всероссийского Общества
охраны природы при ГЛАВНАУКЕ НКП

ОХРАНА
ПРИРОДЫ!
И

ЗЕМЛЕДЕЛИЕ.
ОХОТА.
НАРОДНОЕ ЗДОРОВЬЕ.
КРАЕВЕДЕНИЕ.
ХУДОЖЕСТВЕННЫЕ ЦЕННОСТИ.
ДЕТИ, ЮНОШЕСТВО, ШКОЛА.
КРАСНАЯ АРМИЯ.
ПУТИ СООБЩЕНИЯ.
ТУРИЗМ.

№ 6   1929

Москва-центр, Чистые пруды, 6.

Участники Печорско-Илычской экспедиции.—X—Руководитель экспедиции Ф. Ф. Шиллингер.

26. Frants Frantsevich Shillinger led a Glavnauka expedition to establish a
zapovednik in the basins of the Pechora and Ilych rivers.

27. Delegates to the First All-Russian Conservation Congress, September 1929, pose in Moscow House of Scholars.

28. Petr Germogenovich Smidovich (1874–1935), veteran Bolshevik leader and patron of the conservation cause.

29. Isai Izrailovich Prezent (1902–1967), arbiter of biology and close ally of T. D. Lysenko; played a central role in suppression of ecological conservation.

30. Vasilii Nikitovich Makarov (1887–1953), conservation's leader during its darkest hour.

ОХРАНА ПРИРОДЫ

Орган Всероссийского Общества Охраны Природы при ГЛАВНАУКЕ НКП

ОХРАНА **И** ПРИРОДЫ!

ЗЕМЛЕДЕЛИЕ.
ОХОТА.
НАРОДНОЕ ЗДОРОВЬЕ.
КРАЕВЕДЕНИЕ.
ХУДОЖЕСТВЕННЫЕ ЦЕННОСТИ.
ДЕТИ И ЮНОШЕСТВО, ШКОЛА.
КРАСНАЯ АРМИЯ.
ПУТИ СООБЩЕНИЯ.
ТУРИЗМ.

№ 5   1930

Москва, Софийская набережная, 38.

Фридрих Энгельс и Владимир Ильич Ленин об охране природы (См. след. стр.)

31. Conservationists, seeking a "Marxist benediction," featured Engels and Lenin on cover of *Okhrana prirody*.

IV ГОД ИЗДАНИЯ

ЦЕНА 40 КОП.

ПРИРОДА И СОЦИАЛИСТИЧЕСКОЕ ХОЗЯЙСТВО

ОРГАН ВСЕРОССИЙСКОГО ОБЩЕСТВА ОХРАНЫ ПРИРОДЫ И МЕЖДУ
ВЕДОМСТВЕННОГО КОМИТЕТА СОДЕЙСТВИЯ РАЗВИТИЮ ПРИРОДНЫХ
БОГАТСТВ РСФСР

№ 9—10   1931

МОСКВА, СОФИЙСКАЯ НАБЕРЕЖНАЯ, 38

СОДЕРЖАНИЕ:

Молодые колпики в гнезде. См. текст Астраханский заповедник

32. *Priroda i sotsialisticheskoe khoziaistvo* (Nature and the Socialist Economy), new title and new look for *Okhrana prirody*.

33. Building the Belomor (White Sea–
Baltic) Canal, one of the gigantic, heroic
projects ardently opposed by Soviet conservationists.

34. Vladimir Leont'evich Komarov (1869–
1945), president of VOOP, the conservation society, from 1938.

35. Desmans, or aquatic shrews *(vykhukholi)*, an endangered species, from Sidorov's *Animals Near Extinction* (1928).

Sources of Photographs

From *Okhrana prirody* or *Priroda i sotsialisticheskoe khoziaistvo:* nos. 5, 6, 7, 31, 32; from the personal collection of Inna Danilovna Kashkarova: nos. 8, 9, 10, 11, 27; from *VSSOP, Trudy:* no. 28; postcards of Askania—nos. 22, 23, 24, 25—a gift from Academician Evgenii Mikhailovich Lavrenko; from *Estestvoznanie i geografiia,* 1911: nos. 18, 20, 21; from *Okhrana prirody i zapovednoe delo v SSSR,* 1958, no. 3: no. 30; from B. M. Fortunatov and M. M. Zavadovskii, *Askania-Nova:* nos. 12, 13, 14, 17, 19; from *Khar'kovskoe obshchestvo liubitelei prirody, Biulleten'* (BKhOLP), 1913, no. 4: no. 2; from *Zhurnal ekologii i biotsenologii,* 1931, no. 1: no. 16; from *Vestnik Leningradskogo gosudarstvennogo universiteta,* 1948, no. 10: no. 29; from B. N. Mazurmovich, *Vydaiushchiesia otechestvennye zoologi:* no. 15; from M. Gorky et al., *Belomor: The Construction of the Great White Sea–Baltic Canal* (New York and London: Smith and Haas, 1935): no. 33; from S. A. Sidorov, *Vymiraiushchie zhivotnye* (Moscow, 1928): no. 35; from B. G. Ioganzen, "K stoletiiu so dnia rozhdeniia N. F. Kashchenko," *Trudy Tomskogo universiteta,* 1956, vol. 142: no. 1; from N. Bush, "I. P. Borodin," *Izvestiia Russkogo geograficheskogo obshchestva,* 1917, vol. 53: no. 3; courtesy, Moscow University Archives, D. M. Viazhlinskii, photographer: no. 4; courtesy, New York Public Library: nos. 6, 7, 26, 27, 31 32.

EIGHT

The Cultural Revolution Comes to Biology

Although the conservationists strove during the 1929 congress to project an image of themselves as supporters of socialist construction, the congress had scarcely ended when events overtook their efforts to reconcile their positions with the new economic direction. Of particular concern to conservationists was the breakneck pace of the collectivization campaign. Stalin, Iakovlev,* and, later, the All-Union Central Executive Committee called upon Soviet agriculture to increase the grain harvest over the period of the Five-Year Plan by 35 percent.[1] Much of the official rationale for collectivization, it seemed, was to meet this target.

Writing in the preface to a short pamphlet, *Conservation and Increasing the Harvest,* Professor S. V. Pokrovskii of Moscow State University seemed to argue that almost the entire goal of raising the harvest by 35 percent could be met by a successful campaign to eliminate vermin and pests from the fields.[2] Pokrovskii's focus on pest control was an implicit argument against collectivization. It seemed to contend that the drastic, even draconian collectivization campaign was not the exclusive means to increase agricultural productivity; conservation measures, promoting natural pest control, could be equally effective and, presumably, far less socially disruptive.

Others took a riskier stand, aiming their fire directly at the hasty pace of collectivization itself and cloaking their arguments in the rhetoric of environmentalism. The very first issue of *Okhrana prirody* for 1930 bravely sounded the alarm about the ecological dangers of full-scale collectivization in a column by activist A. A. Teodorovich. "From one end of our unembraceable Union to the other," he wrote, "an incessant war cry is blaring about the Four-Year Plan** . . . with its increase of the harvest by 35 percent." However, he warned in the bluntest language possible, "without conservation, without rational . . . use of natural resources, there cannot be *any* talk about increasing the harvest."[3]

Adding even greater weight to his warnings about "the destruction of the

---

*Ia. A. Iakovlev, the USSR people's commissar of agriculture.
**At the time, there was a great campaign to complete the First Five-Year Plan in four years, hence the usage of Four-Year Plan.

121

equilibrium in the animal, vegetable, and mineral kingdoms," Teodorovich brought to bear the words of Friedrich Engels from "The Part Played by Labor in the Transition from Ape to Man," a work incorporated into *The Dialectics of Nature.*[4] This served as a kind of Marxist benediction for his perilous critique.

Following Teodorovich's article in that same issue of *Okhrana prirody* appeared a questionnaire designed by the Kraeved Society to identify the biotic casualties of the Five-Year Plan in the RSFSR, noting that a "comparison of [current] lists of wildlife for any region with those compiled a few years ago often records the disappearance of many species." The questionnaire proceeded to ask specifically which animals, birds, or vegetation had become rare or extinct, or whether the respondents had noticed any instances of the unusual proliferation of individual species and to what causes they attributed these developments. It sought to know, too, what measures the respondents recommended to halt these processes and directed readers to send all replies to the chairman of the TsBK's Conservation Commission, A. I. Grishin.[5]

Not long afterward, in the March 1930 issue of *Okhrana prirody,* another voice was raised against the tempo of collectivization, making it appear as if this opposition were the journal's deliberate policy. This time, it was Pod"iapol'skii who aired deep misgivings. The agronomist's argument centered on the contention that the increasing mechanization of agriculture in the wake of collectivization would lead to the homogenization of the landscape over large areas of the Russian plain. This result was embedded in the internal logic of the new agriculture:

> The tractor . . . and, even more, the combine . . . can be effective only so long as they are applied on great expanses of uniformly sown land. Before their advance fade forever the cross-strips, fields dissected by ravines and dotted with copses. Those modest patches of virgin land and virgin nature—completely untouched as yet by the plow— will be eliminated, lands which up until now have served as refuges for wild fauna . . . of which a significant percentage constitute the . . . natural allies [of the farmer], guaranteeing his harvest either by fertilizing and pollinating the flowers . . . or by protecting the harvest from pests.[6]

With the unchecked advance of the new agriculture, warned Pod"iapol'skii, Russia faced "the prospect of the elimination of whole species of steppe vegetation and the great devastation of the avian kingdom and of the . . . hunting sector."[7] He knew that to try to halt the juggernaut of collectivization would be politically futile. "It is clear that the progress of agriculture as a whole and of mechanization in particular shall and must come to pass," he acknowledged. "However," he insisted, "it is essential that we take the appropriate measures in time to prevent the attending undesirable side effects, which otherwise will be inevitable."[8]

"Given the tempo of agricultural industrialization now gripping the country we must not continue to defer the resolution of this problem," Pod"iapol'skii pointed out in conclusion, "for the failure to take timely measures of conservation may prove excessively costly to our young republic." For him, as for Alekhin at the 1929 congress, such measures preeminently consisted of the establishment of inviolate *zapovedniki* over all the remaining areas of virgin steppe.

In addition to the collectivization problem, the All-Russian Conservation Society (VOOP) continued to be preoccupied with the unsatisfactory situation in Smolensk,[9] and with its conflict with Narkomzem's policies regarding *zapovedniki* generally. Finally, the forced march of industrialization brought to the fore a problem that had heretofore occupied only a peripheral place among conservationists' concerns: pollution. In mid-1930 A. I. Grishin reported that on the Kud'ma River, a tributary of the Volga, hundreds of tons of fish—mainly bream and pike—had perished. As described by Grishin, the incident "occurred as a result of the criminal negligence on the part of the administration of the tanning factories of the town of Bogorodsk, which allowed their industrial effluents to be dumped into the Kud'ma."[10]

By 1930 *Okhrana prirody* had become the environmental gadfly of the Five-Year Plan. If the conservation society had struck out on a more aggressive road after the 1929 congress, though, it did so at increasing risk. As early as the beginning of 1930, the not entirely benign attention of certain meddlesome actual and would-be majordomos in the Soviet administration of science had been drawn to the affairs of the young society. This interest in VOOP, it turned out, was by no means a chance development, but was part of a larger process taking place in the Soviet academic world.

A MARXIST BIOLOGY?

Natural science does not strike one as a likely arena of raging conflict between the heralds of the Cultural Revolution and the Old Guard professoriat, especially in the earliest hours of the Great Break. Yet, in many ways, the life sciences—whose core concerns included an assessment of the role of science in Soviet life, the question of how nature works, and an exploration of the relationship between nature and humanity—embodied some of the most central issues of ideology. Any group seeking to transform society along utopian lines, as did many Bolsheviks (and, certainly, cultural revolutionaries), had to come to grips with certain possibilities seemingly adverse to their utopian programs that were suggested by recent scientific investigation.

For the Bolsheviks, these disturbing possibilities were manifold. They included the possibility that all people were not biologically identical in all respects and social equality might therefore be unattainable;[11] that productivity in nature might be limited by a number of immutable factors; that no utopian program could yet speak in the name of all human needs; that the human species-essence, as Marx put it, was still a matter of conjecture; and finally, that human nature, whatever it may be, might constitute a fundamental roadblock to the type of utopian egalitarianism and collectivism espoused by the cultural revolutionaries. These important questions were beginning to be addressed by Russia's most thoughtful scientists—geneticists and ecologists, in particular.

As a number of students of Soviet science have shown, the teaching of natural science flourished impressively during NEP. We might even speak of the 1920s as a golden age for the teaching of biology in Russia. Freed from the shackles of the obscurantist Romanov censors, biology was free to introduce the most advanced notions into the classrooms. An entire generation of geneticists, ecologists, and experimental biologists of world rank was in formation. This enviable state of affairs persisted until the late 1920s.

Storm clouds began to gather in early 1928, when the first attacks on Professor Boris Evgen'evich Raikov, Russia's foremost authority on the teaching of biology, were lofted by radicals in the Young Biologists Society.[12] Soon, waves of Cultural Revolution began to wash over other institutions of Russian biology. Thus it happened that at the very time that Kozhevnikov was elected to the honorary presidium at the First All-Russian Congress for Conservation in September 1929, his position in his bailiwick at Moscow University was becoming daily less secure.

In the autumn of 1929, a general meeting of graduate students and student organizations of the Physical-Mathematical, Medical, and Chemical Faculties of the university was held. After they had elected bureaus for the individual sciences and a joint steering committee, the students launched a critical examination of their home faculties. The judgments made by the zoology graduate students on the state of their *kafedra*[13] and of the university's Zoological Scientific Research Institute were particularly severe. Among the students' most serious accusations was "the almost total absence within the institute of scientists who stand on positions of dialectical materialism." On the contrary, asserted the students, "we have a whole group of workers who are alienated from Soviet society both ideologically and politically." The scientific work of the institute was run along narrow "caste" lines, they charged, with an almost complete absence of criticism and self-criticism and with the domination of "vulgar empiricism along with the absence of Marxist methodology."[14]

The only way to redress this state of affairs, concluded the student assembly, was "to reorganize the presidium of the institute, as it has shown no interest in linking its work with the economic needs of the nation."[15]

Kozhevnikov, who was simultaneously head of the chair of vertebrate zoology, deputy director of the Zoological Scientific Research Institute, and director of the university's Zoological Museum, was evidently an important target of this resentment. What may have sealed his downfall irrevocably was his association with Raikov.[16] Within weeks his academic career was a shambles, despite his quarter-century of distinguished service. The loss was not Kozhevnikov's alone. The conservation movement lost an important power base within Moscow University, particularly the Zoological Museum, which, significantly, passed to Professor L. A. Zenkevich, a warm supporter of acclimatization of exotic fauna.

Soon, the Zoological Institute of the USSR Academy of Sciences came under fire as well. The case against the institute was made by Professor Anton Vital'evich Nemilov, a specialist in zootechnics associated with Narkomzem's State Institute for Experimental Agronomy. Writing in the journal *Varnitso,** which had earlier

---

*Varnitso is an acronym for Vsesoiuznaia assotsiatsiia rabotnikov nauki i tekhniki dlia sodeistvii sotsialisticheskoi konstruktsii (the All-Union Association of Workers in Science and Technology for Promotion of Socialist Construction).

spearheaded the defamation of Professor Raikov, Nemilov lavished particular scorn on the academy's journal, *Priroda,* which he labeled "a relict of the past." "Apolitical and neutral in the extreme," charged Nemilov, ". . . it is the only journal where you can turn one thousand pages and not once come across the name of Lenin, never meet up with the words *socialism, communism, dictatorship of the proletariat,* etc."[17]

Nemilov ridiculed the "Nikolaevan-era style" of the journal, which had not changed a whit after the Revolution, finding particular fault with the overly supplicating attitudes toward nature that he alleged characterized *Priroda*'s pre-Soviet mentality. His prescription, like that of the students, was the reorganization of the editorial board of the journal and the transfer of its management to a cell of the militant Society of Materialist-Biologists within the academy.[18]

The attacks on Raikov, on the old bourgeois professors, and on *Priroda* were signs of the times. They were part of a common process, a shared impulse among those who regarded NEP as a retreat from the revolutionary promise of a radical restructuring of society, including the replacement of tsarist-era holdovers by a new Communist intelligentsia. These largely emotional critiques were also supplemented by those of Bolshevik philosophers of science.

A DIALECTICAL BIOLOGY?

In his history of science in Russia, Alexander Vucinich informs us that "science for science's sake" had also been repudiated by the social thinkers of the 1860s.[19] Science to them was more than a simple technique of identifying apparent regularities in nature. They saw it as the key to all knowledge, including moral and political knowledge. Most crucially, science was regarded as the agent of the old regime's destruction, the antidote capable of counteracting the mystifying ideology of "Tsar, Nation, Orthodoxy."[20]

By contrast, the newer crop of radicals in the late 1920s had a rather different conception of the role of science. They stripped natural science of its revolutionary role as the key to *all* knowledge. That role was now securely tenanted by what they called the science of Marxism. Nonetheless, the Bolsheviks did retain something out of the tradition of the 1860s: the idea that science should serve the social agenda. There was, however, a great difference in the significance of this for the two groups of social transformers. The men of the 1860s wanted science to expand *beyond* the boundaries of the study of nature to draw conclusions about the larger social and political world. In stark contrast to this, theoreticians of the Cultural Revolution wanted science to contract to the narrow limits of handmaiden to technology, eschewing broader social or political questions. These were now the exclusive province of Marxism, hailed as a science with its a priori tenet of "the dialectical organization of nature" and its methodology of "dialectical materialism."

The question of the role of science in shaping the new social order arose with full force during the 1920s. At mid-decade the debate still revolved in great measure around the antinomy of pure versus applied science, but by the late 1920s a new question had displaced it as the central problem involving the social implications of science. That question was the role of dialectics in science.

Dialectics transposed by Engels from social theory to the understanding of nature in general was a seemingly extraneous addition to the body of Marxian theory.[21] Yet, during the 1920s for many Soviet Marxists the corpus of Marx's and Engels's writings ceased to serve merely as a guiding basis for the creative elaboration of social theory but as unchallengeable dogma whose only proper treatment was exegesis. Included were Engels's teachings about the dialectical essence of nature. These theories were even more firmly ensconced after the publication of a number of Engels's writings on natural science in 1925 *(The Dialectics of Nature)* by David Borisovich Riazanov, director of the Marx-Engels-Lenin Institute.

Although Bolsheviks agreed publicly that nature and its regularities were inherently dialectical, there was less uniformity regarding two related questions: What was the specific nature of the dialectical essence of nature, and did the methods employed by science need to be dialectical as well? Within the Communist Academy, the center of this debate during much of the late 1920s, two identifiable factions emerged: the Mechanists and the Deborinites. Each had a different set of answers to the two questions.

Both the Mechanists and the Deborinites professed that a dialectical structure inhered in nature and in natural processes. The Mechanists diverged from their rivals, however, in asserting that traditional empirical science was entirely capable of ascertaining nature's dialectical regularities; dialectical materialist philosophical and methodological guidance did not need to be consciously imposed on science.[22] The Mechanists were also characterized by a certain reductionism, which the Deborinites denounced as a repudiation of the dialectical structure of nature. At their most extreme, some Mechanists espoused the belief that one day all biological and social phenomena would be reducible to particular instances of the law of the conservation and transformation of matter and energy, an idea once held by Wilhelm Ostwald.[23]

By 1926 the Mechanists had been painted as the faction intent on undermining dialectics altogether in the natural sciences. They had also received the kiss of death in the support they enjoyed among the "bourgeois" professoriat, who viewed the Mechanists as by far the lesser of the two Bolshevik evils.[24]

In April 1929 the Deborinites routed the Mechanists and gained control of the Communist Academy and other institutions. Entire fields of science were now scrutinized to determine whether or not they were guided by dialectical thinking. If science was a part of the ideological superstructure, as Marx and Engels seemed to assert, and could reflect the interests of various classes, then the dialectical approach became the crucial criterion distinguishing legitimate, Marxian proletarian science; approaches where this criterion was found to be absent were deprecated as bourgeois.[25]

Not surprisingly, those who sought thus to bifurcate science also claimed for themselves authority to decide which scientific theories and approaches corresponded to which ideological camp. Each field of science seemed to generate its own arbiters of ideological purity. In biology, guardians of the faith appeared among the Young Naturalists, the Young Biologists Club of the Moscow Zoo, the Timiriazev Agricultural Academy, the Timiriazev Institute for the Study and the Propagation of the Natural-Science Bases of Dialectical Materialism, the Sverdlov Communist University, the All-Russian Association of Workers of Science and Technology for the Promotion of Socialist Construction (Varnitso), and, most prominent of all, the Communist Academy.

In 1926, within the Section for the Natural and Exact Sciences of the Communist Academy, a Society of Materialist-Biologists made its appearance, and a Ukrainian counterpart was formed in May 1929 in Khar'kov.[26] Many important professionals who genuinely believed that science could be enriched by a dialectical perspective were attracted to these societies in their earliest days. Despite the impressive contributions of many of these scientists,[27] the materialist-biologists also played a role in getting the Marxian inquisition in science under way.

Ecology came under the scrutiny of the materialist-biologists for the first time in 1928–1929, while the Deborinites were still riding high. What attracted the society's attention was the tendency of some ecologists to analogize natural communities with human societies, with all of the philosophical implications of such an approach. The materialist-biologists were Marxists first. They accepted Marxism's social theory as scientific truth. Scientific facts or theories that seemed to cast doubt on the validity or attainability of Marxian precepts or prescriptions were viewed by them, quite simply, as bourgeois science and, hence, bad science.

One of the strongest potential challenges to the Marxian social vision came from the ranks of the phytosociologists. Pachoskii's theory, for example, held that inequality was indelibly embedded in the very structure of nature, and that it was precisely this inequality that made the existence of both natural and human communities possible. In a similar vein, others, including botanist V. N. Liubimenko, emphasized that since humans, too, were products of nature, the principles uncovered in the study of natural communities applied to human societies as well.[28]

Militant Marxists found these attempts to "prove" the inevitability of inequality in nature and to extend them to human society as general biological principles particularly repugnant and subversive.[29] Phytosociological views were first challenged at the January 1928 All-Union Botanical Congress by P. N. Ovchinnikov.[30] By the following January, phytosociology had been delivered a mortal blow. Writing in *Natural Science and Marxism,* the journal of the Communist Academy's Section for the Natural and Exact Sciences (and published in collaboration with the Society of Materialist-Biologists), I. I. Bugaev forcefully refuted the positions of the phytosociological school. One consequence of the article and the entire campaign against phytosociology was the renunciation of that term in favor of *phytocenology.*[31]

Bugaev agreed that there existed "general biological laws which animals, plants, and humans follow." However, he noted, in human society the expression of these laws is colored by higher, social laws intrinsic to human society alone. "What sort of 'biology' lies at the basis of the class structure of society?" he challenged. "Could it be eugenics?"[32] (That was an allusion to the biological doctrine, then repudiated in the Soviet Union, that social classes were determined by heredity and not by the economic organization of society.) He made it clear that the phytosociological view of life that equated ecological and human communities was reductionist and therefore in conflict with the laws of the dialectic. Finally, Bugaev observed that Pachoskii's brand of phytosociology had become too wedded to an ideal of the biocenosis and had failed to take into account the frequent divergence of actual communities from the abstract model.[33]

Bugaev's intention was not to demolish the young science of community ecology but to identify and eliminate those tendencies within it that came into conflict with Marxian method or theory. As a measure of his sincerity, Bugaev was quick to point out that phytosociology was far from guilty of all that was being done in its name.[34] Indeed, the recent inclination of ecologists themselves to retire the unfortunate term *phytosociology* he considered to be heartening. More important from the philosophical standpoint was that there was much in ecology that confirmed the dialectical view of nature and that was therefore especially worthy of the attention of Marxist biologists. In particular, he observed that the notion of the biocenosis as continually creating its own changing environment and thus making for its own continuous evolution was profoundly dialectical. With its general application of feedback processes, ecology was a most congenial "Marxist" science. Bugaev also recognized that Pachoskii's successors, including V. N. Sukachev, had not only moved away from sociological analogies but had rejected Pachoskii's fondness for abstract models as well.[35]

Bugaev took Sukachev's decision to proceed inductively from the study of *actual* vegetation to the community-as-an-abstraction as a great step forward for ecology. Ironically, Bugaev did not see that by insisting that science be guided by the dialectical method he was committing the same vice for which he denounced Pachoskii; he was, in fact, imposing an arbitrary method on science, forcing it to proceed from the abstract to the concrete. Apparently, what was good for the subject matter was poison for method. For the future, ecologists now had to incorporate dialectical methods into every aspect of their science, summoning extra vigilance in light of their shadowy, Mechanist philosophical roots.[36]

The style of discourse exemplified by Bugaev soon gave way to one far coarser and philosophically less literate as the Deborinites suddenly fell from favor in October 1930 and were supplanted in the Communist Academy and elsewhere by a new breed of academic politician. Those who supplanted the Deborinites represented little more than undiluted political opportunism. They had cudgeled their way to the apex of the Soviet philosophy of science apparatus by attacking the Deborinites not for their ideas but for the ties that some of them had maintained with the Trotskii opposition. For these latest arbiters of ideological purity in science, considerations of a truly philosophical nature meant little. They did not much care whether a particular science was philosophically compatible with the principles of the dialectic. Their criteria for distinguishing proletarian science from bourgeois science was more mundane: Did that science possess a political or material utility? Did it fit in with the spirit and goals of the Five-Year Plan? About the only "philosophical" criterion in operation was a pervasive, uncompromising rejection of the application of mathematical methods to biology. In biology, perhaps the most notorious of this new breed was the shadowy figure Isai Izrailovich Prezent.

I. I. PREZENT

Historians remember Prezent chiefly as the man who provided Trofim Denisovich Lysenko with the rudiments of Marxist education. Loren Graham has written that by "systematically formulating Lysenko's [biological] views . . . and attempting to integrate them with dialectical materialism," Prezent must reap a good share of the credit for facilitating Lysenko's phenomenal rise to domination in Soviet biology.[37] Despite his importance in the Lysenko affair, however, he has remained for us a drab, gray figure, reluctant to move out of history's shadows.

Prezent's association with Lysenko was one of Soviet science's most fateful partnerships, but it remains one of the least understood. Prezent is often depicted as having hitched his star to Lysenko's already rising one, of having persuaded Lysenko to retain him as a behind-the-scenes ideological tutor while Lysenko fashioned his stardom in genetics. The evidence increasingly seems to suggest, though, that Prezent was actually a key figure in his own right in guiding Soviet biology into a thirty-year excursion into the realm of the absurd. What may come as an even greater revelation is that ecology, and not genetics, was Prezent's first target in his campaign for a proletarian biology, and that he had already created for himself a formidable reputation as a leading arbiter in biology fully four years before the first skirmishes between Lysenko and N. I. Vavilov took place.

Highly intelligent and clever, Prezent became a figure of unusual influence during the high Stalin period. In the late 1940s and after, he simultaneously chaired the departments of Darwinism at Leningrad and Moscow State Universities and additionally served as the dean of the latter's Biological Faculty. After July 1948 he flaunted his title of academician, having been named in that month a full member of the Lenin All-Union Academy of Agricultural Sciences, just in time to participate in its notorious August 1948 session. Despite his undisputed importance, however, there is an extreme paucity of biographical material.

We must make do with a lone, eulogizing thumbnail biography which appeared in the *Leningrad State University Newsletter* in 1948, hardly the most complete or critical source. Yet, the account manages to shed at least some light on Prezent's mysterious career. What strikes us first is the ample scope of his ambition. Having graduated from Leningrad University in 1926, we are told, Prezent rejected the path of "lock[ing] himself up in a laboratory and devot[ing] himself to the study of just any problem of limited importance. Biological science, infiltrated by idealist concepts, always had been an arena of ideological struggle. He took up a central place in this struggle."[38]

Although his biographer implied that Prezent was formally trained as a biologist, that seems not to have been the case.[39] Rather, Prezent was a graduate of the three-year program of the Faculty of Social Sciences of the university. At some point either during his studies or soon after graduation, though, he decided to specialize in the philosophy of the life sciences. His first step was to organize a seminar on the study of the dialectics of nature, which attracted the participation of students and colleagues alike from the biology, philosophy, philology, and mathematics departments of the university and from those of other institutions of higher learning.[40]

At this time, Prezent apparently had cast his lot with the Deborinites and, following their lead, had become a partisan of the Mendelian and Morganist theories of heredity and speciation. He joined the Deborinites' attacks on neo-Lamarckism and, in his search for a patron among genuine biologists, first approached classical geneticist Nikolai Ivanovich Vavilov. Vavilov took Prezent into his All-Union Institute of Plant Breeding, unaware that this was the beginning of a relationship that would end in tragedy for himself. Most likely owing to Prezent's unsuitability for productive work, he and Vavilov soon had a falling out and Prezent left the institute to resume his search for a suitable patron. Evidently, he also began to nourish a consuming resentment of the geneticist.[41]

This experience demonstrated to Prezent that it was expedient to create his own power base in addition to finding an established patron. This he accomplished with remarkable rapidity, doubtless profiting from the opportunities presented by the triumph of the Deborin faction in the Communist Academy. By 1930 he was already a senior staff member and effective leader of the Leningrad Branch of the Communist Academy, the president of the Society of Materialist-Biologists, and a docent at the A. I. Gertsen (Herzen) Pedagogical Institute. By 1931, he had founded and assumed the leadership of the *kafedra* of the Dialectics of Nature and Evolution-ary Science at Leningrad State University, the first such department anywhere.[42]

Having climbed so high so quickly, Prezent proved uniquely adept at reading the political straws in the wind. Along with other politically agile Deborinites as well as some politically supple ex-Mechanists, Prezent sometime during 1930 managed to jump ship, surviving the wreck of the Deborinites in October of that year.

The program of the successors to the Deborinites called for a vaguely defined Bolshevization of philosophy and science and for the primacy of practice over theory, with the relegation of major matters of theory to Stalin. Stalin himself had pointed the way toward this Bolshevization in a pair of speeches in late 1929. Not willing to accept establishment biology's limited ability to know, predict, and control events and unable to live with the limitations of acting in a statistical, probabilistic middle ground, Stalin turned to the forces of home-grown practical science to give him the manipulative powers he craved. Embedded in this was a deep paradox, since in his desperate quest for the elimination of chance and spontaneity in human and natural affairs, i.e., for security and mastery, Stalin had recourse to a treacherous gamble *(avos')* on outsiders' claims of new agricultural miracles.[43] Reminiscent of the ancient faith in wonder-workers *(chudotvortsy)*, Stalin's response was nowhere more evident than in his remarks, made on the twelfth anniversary of the November seizure of power, about the "truly miraculous" forthcoming gains in agricultural productivity:

> All the objections raised by "science" against the possibility and expediency of organiz-ing great grain factories of forty to fifty thousand hectares have collapsed and crumbled

to dust. Practice has refuted the objections of "science," and has once again shown that not only has practice to learn from "science," but that "science" also would do well to learn from practice.[44]

Linked with the new faith in grass-roots invention was Stalin's denigration of theoretical science, which he—along with many cultural revolutionaries and utilitarians of the economic commissariats—seemed to view as a barren self-indulgence. "While we have reason to be proud of the practical successes achieved in socialist construction," Stalin told the All-Union Conference of Marxist Students of Agrarian Questions, meeting at the Communist Academy on 27 December 1929, "the same cannot be said with regard to theoretical work . . . in agriculture in particular." Ominously, Stalin indicted theoretical work further for "not keeping pace with our practical successes." This implied that there were new agronomic achievements that defied conventional theoretical scientific wisdom, for which new scientific explanations needed to be found. Indeed, socialism had already generated such "achievements": vernalization, acclimatization, and, on the social side, collectivization itself. In a passage that seemed perilously applicable to the conservationists' misgivings about collectivization, Stalin lauded the expansion of agriculture to virgin areas as a triumph over the timorous objections of old-line science:

The question of cultivating neglected land and virgin soil is of tremendous importance for our agriculture. You know that . . . in the old days . . . there were many who thought that this shortage of land was absolute. . . . Now it is quite clear that scores of millions of hectares of free land were and are still available in the USSR. . . .[45]

Everything hinged, of course, on acceptance of the regime's premise that these policies constituted practical successes. At first, such acceptance was far from universal in the scientific community. Conveniently, however, the Stalin government was developing the capability of ensuring just such universal acceptance.

As David Joravsky had observed, this new means of distinguishing proletarian from bourgeois science deleted intellectual content from philosophy and science. Stalin had now arrogated to himself the right to pass final judgment on all matters of Marxian theory and science, a right that was willingly conceded by fawning figures in Soviet science. (Stalin was lauded as a genius, a coryphaeus of science.) Yet even Stalin could not review all developments in all fields. In each field of learning, a need therefore arose for "little Stalins," trusted vicegerents of the supreme leader who could guide and censor developments both intellectual and practical, interpreting Stalin's will as the need arose.[46] It was to this position of viceroy of the biological sciences that Prezent ultimately aspired, a position uniquely suited to his intellectual disposition and political gifts. In his pursuit of it, Prezent never lost sight of the new criteria distinguishing proletarian science, in particular the need for theory to accord with the new practical "successes" celebrated in print and on screen.

With an impressive degree of political acumen, Prezent immediately identified ecology and conservation as areas that were abundantly vulnerable to criticism on the basis of the new criteria for scientific legitimacy. Less than six months after

Stalin's Communist Academy speech, at the Fourth All-Union Congress of Zoologists, Anatomists, and Histologists in Kiev in May 1930, Prezent made his first move.

Although he had not yet published anything on philosophical or theoretical problems of biology (let alone ecology),[47] Prezent was nonetheless allotted two opportunities during the opening plenary sessions of the huge congress to deliver full-length critiques of the talks of the featured speakers. This alone was evidence enough of his rise to influence in Soviet biology, and a probable indication that as early as 1930 he had gained the ear of well-placed political patrons.

Opportunity first came knocking for Prezent in the guise of Stanchinskii's landmark, speculative talk on trophic dynamics. In his extemporaneous comments following Stanchinskii's presentation Prezent first emerged as a "critic" of biocenology.[48] According to Stanchinskii's close associate S. I. Medvedev, who was at the congress during the exchange, Prezent even "expressed doubts about ecology's right to call itself a science."[49] Medvedev reported that "Stanchinskii answered the uninformed outburst of Prezent with dignity." Regrettably, this failed to deter Prezent's campaign.

Prezent pressed his claim to become ecology's ideological arbiter. This he did through his leading role in the organization of the Academy of Sciences' First All-Union Conference of Geobotanists and Floristics Experts—as the representative of the Leningrad Branch of the Communist Academy. Although the conference had been sponsored officially by the Botanical Institute of the academy and was held at its Botanical Gardens in late February 1931, a report of its activities published soon afterward recorded that the Communist Academy had "assumed methodological leadership."[50]

Having now reduced the plant ecologists, who were already cowed by the campaign against the phytosociologists, Prezent had yet to subjugate the most vital center of biocenology in the USSR: the zoologically oriented ecologists associated with Glavnauka, the conservation societies, and the zapovedniki in particular.

However, Prezent did not march on that citadel immediately. That he aimed to do later, at the All-Union Faunistics Conference, scheduled for December 1931 in Moscow, again ostensibly organized by the Academy of Sciences (its Zoological Institute) but actually planned with the intimate collaboration of the Communist Academy in the person of Prezent. In the meantime, he turned his fire to an unfinished matter: the case of Professor Raikov.

As early as 1930, according to Zhores Medvedev, Prezent was attracted to the spectacle of "unmasking" Raikov, that epitome of bourgeois professordom. Prezent's animus toward Raikov was almost certainly exacerbated by whatever personal contact they had while teaching at the Gertsen Institute. Rather than allow such potential rivals for the post of ideological vicegerent in biology as the Young Naturalists' leaders to take all of the credit for the uprooting of Raikovism, Prezent speedily took charge of the campaign. In a special address to Leningrad educators, he vilified Raikov in terms that went beyond even the previous attacks. Raikov was denounced as an "agent of the world bourgeoisie" and the author of a "wrecking theory" that taught "a passive 'love of nature.' " "What does Raikov and his whole group represent?" asked Prezent rhetorically. "You know, comrades, he was exposed by an organ of the proletarian dictatorship—the GPU."[51] Prezent's address, *Class Struggle on the Natural Science Front,* was soon published (1932) in an edition of 20,000. The hapless Raikov and the remnants of his Society for the Propagation of Natural-Science Education were speedily arrested and thrown into prison or exile to the Far North, where they languished for many years.[52]

Prezent's shadow was moving rapidly across Soviet biology. Natural-science education had already been darkened by it, and now it was poised to eclipse the young and vital field of community ecology. However, before proceeding to an examination of Prezent's incursion into the affairs of Soviet conservation and ecology, we shall examine how the ongoing turmoil of the Cultural Revolution affected the Soviet conservation movement.

NINE

Protective Coloration

Pressure on Soviet conservationists, and especially on the old "bourgeois" professors who made up such a large proportion of conservation's cadre, continued to mount through 1930. After the Shakhty Trial of 1928 and that of the Promparty group two years later,* the goateed figure of the professor with his pince-nez and homburg was considered fair game for the most unrestrained vilification. While this situation eased somewhat after Stalin's famous speech of February 1931 and particularly after his pronouncements in the summer of that year,[1] "bourgeois" professors continued to participate in academic life only at the sufferance of university, government, and party officialdom, themselves awash in a sea of insecurity.

Attacks on the professoriat reached their zenith in 1930, after Stalin's speeches of late 1929. One consequence of the wave of anti-intellectualism legitimized by Stalin was the convocation of a conference on the work of Russia's scientific societies by Varnitso, the all-Union association that had recently been formed to mobilize scientific and technical workers for the Five-Year Plan. Led by the pliant pro-party Academician A. N. Bakh, a biochemist, and with a Central Bureau and core of activists that boasted some of the most uncompromising Bolshevizers of science (and future supporters of Lysenko),[2] Varnitso in 1930 and 1931 put in its bid to become an ideological arbiter of the natural sciences. This objective was well illustrated by the conduct of the conference, which, we are told in Varnitso's journal, "in essence turned into a trial . . . of the leadership of the scientific societies in which Varnitso, the Scientific Workers' Section of the Educational Workers' Union, and [the Soviet publishing agency] Sovpechat' leveled the accusations and where the assembled secret defenders of unwholesome academism tried to justify themselves."[3]

Speaking for Varnitso, Professor Boris Mikhailovich Zavadovskii[4] assumed the mantle of prosecutor. He noted that the scientific societies betrayed "a *total* absence of good faith in transforming themselves from citadels of the reactionary professoriat—which they are today—into Soviet collectives." He cited their "total inability and frequently willful refusal to redesign their work and bring science closer to practice." "Why are the scientific societies unable to involve themselves in

*Two widely publicized trials of technical engineers for alleged sabotage of production processes.

questions of nutrition, physical culture, and agronomy?" he asked, pointing to the need to create a new, official organizational center for the societies that would henceforth answer for their work.[5]

In Varnitso's journal, an entire series of articles mercilessly pummeled away at the scientific societies. One contributor, likening them to "*zapovedniki* where, protected in their virgin forests, great-maned bisons roam, ..." painted a picture of the societies as the last undisturbed refuge of the bourgeois professoriat. Just as *zapovedniki* tried to shield nature from the improving hand of humankind, their academic counterparts—the scientific societies—sought to shield out the influence of postrevolutionary ideas and values.[6]

The *zapovednik* analogy evidently was a popular one, in part reflecting the widely held view that the *zapovedniki* were not only a waste of good land but a breeding ground for agricultural pests and dangerous wild animals. Professor E. K. Sepp, a member of Varnitso's Central Bureau, used the *zapovednik* analogy as a vehicle for ridicule:

> During the twelve years of revolution, the scholars of the [Soviet] Union lived as if in a fastidiously protected *zapovednik*. In this All-Union *zapovednik* for the Endangered Species of Bourgeois Scientists, they found cozy corners for themselves . . . far out of sight of Soviet public opinion.[7]

The litany of charges against the societies was long and damning. The societies had cut themselves off from Soviet youth by "etching membership limitations into their charters," while at the same time allowing counterrevolutionary elements to participate actively. When new cadres were admitted to membership, they were exposed to undiluted bourgeois ideology, Sepp charged. He even tried to paint a picture of "White terror" in the societies, using as evidence a 1929 balloting episode in the Academy of Sciences[8] and the more recent rejection of Communist candidates to leadership positions in the Moscow Microbiological Society. (There, even members of Varnitso were "forced" to vote with the "reactionary" majority, Sepp alleged.) "We see this phenomenon everywhere that scientific societies are protected like *zapovedniki* from the influence of the Soviet environment," Sepp observed. "It is clear," he concluded, "that the system of *zapovedniki* for scientific cadres has outgrown its usefulness."[9]

At the Varnitso conference, a number of natural-science societies were attacked by name. The Moscow Society of Naturalists (MOIP)—the oldest scientific society in Russia[10]—the Endocrinological Society, and the Botanical and Mathematical Societies were all upbraided for a variety of sins, all of which boiled down to the charge that they combined " 'pure' science with impure politics."[11] Unfortunately for Russia's conservationists, two of the societies that proved the targets of the most intense scrutiny at the conference were the All-Russian Society for Conservation (VOOP) and its closest ally, the Central Bureau for The Study of Local Lore (TsBK). The *zapovednik* analogy, it seems, had more to it than had at first appeared.

About the time that the Raikov affair first got under way, which was also about the time that the first arrests at Shakhty were disclosed, the world of *kraevedenie,* or local-lore study, was also jolted out of its complacency by awakening political stirrings. As early as March 1928, the First All-Union Conference of Marxist-Leninist Scientific Research Institutions, dominated by the Communist Academy, resolved that the academy itself assume "the task of directing all scientific local-lore and natural resource prospecting and expeditionary work in the USSR."[12]

After the takeover of the Communist Academy by the more aggressive Deborinite faction in April 1929, a Kraeved Section was promptly created by the Academy's Presidium. Work got under way seriously by the following February, and the first meeting of the Society of Marxist-Kraevedy was held in January 1931.[13]

The slow pace of organizing the new society, however, did not deter individual activists from launching their own critiques of old-line *kraevedenie.* As identified by these Marxist-*kraevedy,* the leading danger was "right opportunism," which was characterized by "an academic orientation, indifference to the requirements of socialist construction, a permissive attitude toward the struggle with ideologically alien tendencies in Soviet *kraevedenie,* and the turning of a blind eye toward apoliticism in *kraeved* work."[14]

The opening shot in the campaign against the "right deviation" in the local-lore movement was fired on 17 January 1930 by Al'bert Petrovich Pinkevich,[15] a deputy president of the TsBK, in a speech to the Kraeved Section of the Communist Academy.[16] Pinkevich particularly dwelt on the notions regarding the scope of *kraevedenie* embodied in the work and writings of Professors Ivan Mikhailovich Grevs[17] and Sergei Sergeevich Ganeshin.[18] Grevs, who had written on the importance for the local-lore movement of identifying and preserving monuments of antiquity, art, architecture, and culture generally, was tarred by Pinkevich with the brush of German *Heimatskunde.* To follow Grevs, asserted Pinkevich, would mean giving Soviet *kraevedenie* entirely over to German-style "nationalism and chauvinism."[19] Ganeshin's infraction, which consisted of appealing to *kraevedy* to help save rare and unique flora, also harkened to an unwanted German-style romanticism. Pinkevich evidently was making a strong case that the whole endeavor of preservation was a diversion which threatened to deflect the Soviet "soul" of the *kraeved* movement from its true tasks.[20]

When in late March 1930 the Fourth All-Russian Conference on Kraevedenie assembled in Moscow the delegates were informed by Gleb Maksimilianovich Krzhizhanovskii that the atmosphere in the factories was one of "quasi-wartime mobilization." People, he reported, were even talking about a "new October."[21] Even so, the TsBK, piloted by the enlightened, staid Smidovich, moved only tepidly to meet the utopian tide, offering only verbal concessions to socialist construction. Significantly, no overt rejection of traditional *kraevedenie*—including its conservation concerns—was voiced in the resolutions.[22]

This continuity of policy was amply demonstrated by the activities of the TsBK's Conservation Commission over the following months. Far from retreating to the security of a low profile, the commission actually stepped up the pace of its activities, in particular by consolidating its ties with VOOP and the Goskomitet.[23]

By autumn, conservation-minded *kraevedy* went on the counterattack. V. N. Balandin, writing in *Sovetskoe kraevedenie* (Soviet Local-Lore Studies), made an impassioned plea for continued *kraeved* support for conservation. Although he conceded the need for socialist construction, he rejected that view of development that would "ultimately plow the steppe under to the last plot of land, chop down the woods to the last tree, and exterminate all the animals. . . ." Yet, he warned, "we now stand on the verge of exterminating a great array of life forms."[24]

Balandin called upon all local-lore organizations not to look the other way but "to engage immediately in propaganda among the broad masses of toilers for the rational use of natural productive forces, for a sensitive, protective attitude toward beneficial animals and plants and for the conservation of monuments of nature." Moreover, in view of the rapid changes in the natural landscape wrought by the pace of human development, *kraevedy* must hasten to support the struggle to create both national parks for tourism and *zapovedniki* as *etalony,* endowed with adequate areas to do their job.[25]

Balandin's response to Pinkevich was quite restrained and avoided polemicizing the issue. The velvet gloves were taken off, however, in a rebuttal to Pinkevich published in *Okhrana prirody.* The author of the piece, V. Luchnik, noted that although Pinkevich "does not reject the need for conservation of monuments of nature, [he] at the same time incites a boycott of that cause by the multitudinous legions of our *kraevedy.* . . ." He pledged: "There is no way that we will consent to that!"[26]

The pressures of the Cultural Revolution, however, were not to be deflected so easily. By late October 1930, after an investigation by the RSFSR People's Commissariat of the Workers' and Peasants' Inspectorate (Rabkrin RSFSR), the TsBK was finally forced to make some changes. Heading the list of recommendations by the investigatory commission were that the TsBK undertake a purge of its numerous "class-alien elements," that it introduce shock-work and "socialist competition," that it add Marxists to its national and provincial leadership, and that it liquidate its Conservation Commission.[27]

As a result of the Rabkrin RSFSR commission's charges of a persistent "apoliticism," the TsBK reluctantly undertook a limited purge. Nikolai Aleksandrovich Geinike, a docent at Moscow State University and specialist in the methodology of natural-science field trips (he was the TsBK's official delegate to the First All-Russian Congress on Conservation), lost his post as scholarly secretary of the TsBK, while historian B. B. Veselovskii was dropped as a deputy president of the organization. Numerous local leaders were swept from their posts as well.

With the election of new leaders in Moscow and other branches, the TsBK took its first steps to implement the "mass line." In Moscow Oblast, there was heavy recruitment of Communist university students, and the oblast bureau now also included two factory workers, reflecting the addition of eighty new branches in factories and collective farms.[28] As a final concession, the TsBK even eliminated its Conservation Commission.

These measures caused sharp conflicts throughout the society's network of branches, however. In Tver', for example, *kraevedy* who had been stalwarts of the society for years flatly refused to hand over the branch's materials to the new leadership. Aside from the *kraevedy* purged, others left in disgust, "unable to comprehend the tasks of the new, Soviet *kraevedenie*." The society languished "in the throes of a very profound crisis" whose basic cause was "the massive exodus of the old-time *kraevedy*."[29]

Even Smidovich, at the Tenth Plenum of the TsBK, tried to resign the presidency of the society out of disgust for the purging and the infighting.[30] This potential disaster for the movement was averted only after the plenum implored the Old Bolshevik to stay on during the period of crisis, declaring that "the future of the TsBK is unthinkable without P. G. Smidovich at the helm. . . ."[31]

Although forced to purge some of their old colleagues, the conservation-oriented NEP-era *kraeved* leaders nevertheless held their own. In particular, their continued control of the renamed (but largely unreconstructed) journal, *Sovetskoe kraevedenie,* was a source of bitter complaints from their more militant challengers.[32]

"MONUMENTAL IMMOBILITY"

Despite the slight measure of restraint produced by Stalin's condemnation of specialist baiting, depredations on the TsBK continued from a number of quarters. The TsBK's strategy failed to deceive more than disgruntled members of the Society of Marxist-Kraevedy. At the Varnitso "trial" of the scientific societies, B. M. Zavadovskii, for one, keenly noted that "the turnabouts experienced recently in the work of some scientific societies can in no wise satisfy us, since they doubtless were effected not out of principle but for opportunistic motives, as a result of which these societies continue to wallow in the swamp of 'pure academism.' "[33]

The TsBK, in particular, was singled out for having masked its "unswerving academism" and its "monumental immobility" in a welter of "fashionable slogans about socialist construction."[34] One article in Varnitso's house organ even went so far as to describe the TsBK as "an exemplar of that type of organization in which un-Soviet elements, having barricaded themselves against Soviet youth, conducted . . . frankly treasonous work."[35]

Emboldened, perhaps, by what they perceived to be a shifting of the winds in 1931, the leaders of the TsBK refused to cringe before this latest barrage; instead, they mounted a counteroffensive. Bravely, in an official resolution, the Presidium of the society not only expressed its "deep dismay at the libelous, unprincipled nature" of the author's characterization of the TsBK but described his article as "a vicious distortion, . . . made in bad faith" and itself constituting "genuine wrecking."[36]

Apparently, the show of backbone worked. Now bereft of active political support from the party leadership, the critics from Varnitso folded. Nevertheless, the leadership of the TsBK was increasingly baited by the self-appointed arbiters of Marxian *kraevedenie* of the Communist Academy. Frustrated at not yet having stormed the bourgeois citadel of old-line *kraevedenie,* the Marxist-*kraevedy* in their attacks betrayed an increasing desperation. They no longer exuded the confidence of 1930 and early 1931. Typical was one hysterical outburst of V. F. Karpych, secretary of the Society of Marxist-Kraevedy (OKRAM), directed at preservation-oriented *kraevedy:*

> The entire work of these wreckers . . . [is] aimed at . . . narrowing the circle of *kraevedy* to a tiny group of experts, admirers and appraisers of Russian antiquities and 'eternal sacral objects.' This is in order to deflect the masses . . . from the problems of the present and the future, to turn *kraevedenie*'s face to the past, to turn *kraeved* organizations into some kind of 'Society for the Preservation of Antiquity,' . . . i.e., . . . [for] Protection *from* the Revolution.[37]

As was the case in many other areas of intellectual life, more pragmatic and opportunistic Bolshevizers soon saw their opportunity to displace the fractious and often hysterical utopians, who were quickly pigeonholed as "the left deviation." Among the *kraeved* leadership, I. G. Klabunovskii—one pragmatist who survived this difficult period—lambasted the "left deviation" for its "pretentious assertion . . . that Marxist-*kraevedy* . . . are the 'salt' of the Soviet earth (and that) our party had entrusted *them* to create Marxist-Leninist theory."[38] As Klabunovskii's account makes amply clear, the utopians made the serious error of persisting in the delusion that as political activists (and, especially, as members of the Communist Academy) they still enjoyed the prerogative of interpreting Marxist theory creatively on their own. That prerogative, however, was no longer theirs; by 1931, it had passed exclusively into the hands of the party, i.e., Stalin.

The leftists, however, did not go down without a fight. In a desperate move, Karpych, the leader of the leftist faction of OKRAM, took the dispute to the party at-large, publishing an acerbic piece in the 17 September 1931 issue of *Pravda.* Karpych's fiercest ridicule was reserved for conservation. Citing two (un-representatively) bathetic pieces purportedly drawn from recent issues of *Okhrana prirody,*[39] Karpych clearly aimed to create a fatal representation of the nature of the conservation movement. Totally dismissing the overwhelmingly scientific and materialist rationale for conservation officially emphasized by the journal, Karpych declared instead that those who wrote in *Okhrana prirody* "view nature in the main not as a base for developing [the nation's] productive forces, but rather as a subject of aesthetic satisfaction. . . . The general conclusion that forces itself upon us after reading . . . *Okhrana prirody* is that this journal, under the slogan of the un-conditional protection of nature, is striving to save this nature . . . from the Five-Year Plan!"[40]

In addition to lashing the old professors, Karpych's article was a vehicle by which he implicitly sought to impugn their Bolshevik patrons, in particular P. G. Smidovich and N. V. Krylenko. Smidovich was culpable owing to his permissive stewardship of *kraevedenie* and conservation. Krylenko was answerable for his less-than-militant pilotage of the Society of Marxist-Kraevedy and the Society for Proletarian Tourism and Excursions.[41] To rectify matters, he proposed a crusade by

"Marxist forces" under "the methodological leadership of the Communist Academy" to unite *kraevedenie,* ethnography, proletarian tourism, and conservation under new, politically correct leadership.[42]

This time, though, Karpych had gone too far. The Smidovich-Krylenko forces rallied, not simply to parry this latest leftist thrust but to drive that faction out of the *kraeved* movement altogether. Potemkin, writing in the year-end issue of *Sovetskoe kraevedenie,* called on the forthcoming Eleventh Plenum of the TsBK to expel Karpych and his allies from the movement.[43]

At a special session of OKRAM held at the Communist Academy on 3 March 1932, three weeks earlier than the convocation of the plenum, the conflict had already come to a boil. For his part, Karpych had enlisted the formidable support of M. A. Savel'ev, a former editor of *Pravda* and the Communist Academy's deputy president (ironically, Savel'ev once had worked closely with Smidovich in the Bolshevik underground).[44] Addressing the session, Savel'ev emphasized his belief that the struggle needed to be redirected away from an alleged leftist danger as identified by Potemkin, Krylenko, and others, and refocused against the "danger of right opportunism" instead.[45]

For some months, though, leftist challenges no longer enjoyed their erstwhile support from the party high command; the Central Committee displayed a telling indifference to the cultural revolutionaries' recriminations against *kraevedenie,* and the outcome of the dispute hinged on the political clout each side could muster. Here, Savel'ev found himself clearly outgunned by Smidovich and Krylenko. Karpych lost his post as secretary of OKRAM and was then formally expelled by the Eleventh Plenum from the TsBK for his lack of constructive participation and for his "left deviation."[46]

Coldly examined, this political hullabaloo, while disruptive in a general sense, affected the actual policies of the TsBK surprisingly little. This was particularly true in the area of conservation, despite the liquidation of the TsBK's Conservation Commission, an early concession to the inquisitors.[47] Strong institutional ties were nevertheless maintained with VOOP and grass-roots collaboration flourished.[48] Significantly, these conservation activities continued to be reported in *Sovetskoe kraevedenie.* Perhaps of greatest importance, the TsBK and VOOP continued to be united in the person of M. P. Potemkin, who, in addition to holding a leading position on the editorial board of *Sovetskoe kraevedenie* and serving as the TsBK's representative on the Goskomitet, simultaneously occupied the presidency of VOOP. Indeed, in a major address to the Goskomitet on 28 December 1931 Potemkin strongly reaffirmed the *kraeved* movement's commitment to conservation, dispelling all doubts raised by the clamorous attacks of the Marxist-*kraevedy.*[49]

Believing that they had left the dangerous rapids of cultural revolution behind, the leaders of the TsBK in mid-1932 now turned their energies to rebuilding the decimated ranks of their society, the most distressing casualty of the turmoil.[50] At the same time, they continued to ply their old familiar path, liberally garnishing the articles in *Sovetskoe kraevedenie* with the fashionable rhetoric of socialist construction.

"UNDISGUISED APOLITICISM"

The tempestuous Cultural Revolution also buffeted VOOP, the All-Russian Society for Conservation. Shortly after the installation of A. S. Bubnov as commissar of education and of Ivan Kapitonovich Luppol as head of Glavnauka in late 1929, the new Narkompros leaders were faced with the prospect of an investigation and purge of their commissariat conducted under the aegis of Rabkrin RSFSR. A special commission was assembled to investigate Narkompros's rich assortment of scientific societies, among them VOOP.

The commission was led by Varnitso activist Natalia Viacheslavna Kirillova, a forty-seven-year-old docent at the Sverdlov Communist University who served as the deputy chairperson of the Biology Department there. Serving under her on the commission were the production manager of the Moskvoshvei clothing factory, plus assorted activists of the Narkompros local of the Educational Workers' Union's Scientific Workers' Section and of Varnitso.

Commencing in early January 1930, the investigation proceeded speedily. During the inquest, brochures, protocols, and publications of VOOP were reviewed and the commission's members even sat in on sessions of the society's Governing Council and Presidium.[51]

According to one of Kirillova's later accounts of the inquest, VOOP's situation at the time was decidedly precarious. The commission had seriously considered disbanding the society—along with several other scientific societies under investigation—because of its reputation for "undisguised apoliticism." This grim prospect, however, was ultimately averted. As Kirillova explained, VOOP was saved owing only to its "mass" character, notably the presence of large numbers of students in the membership. VOOP, in fact, was praised for its willingness, alone among the scientific societies, to accept students as members whether they were in first grade or in an institution of higher learning. The commission also applauded VOOP's links with planning and economic organs and even its active ties with like-minded foreign organizations.[52]

Despite the praise, though, the fact remained that in the eyes of the commission the society suffered from serious shortcomings all the same. True, VOOP had transcended the "caste" principle in its recruitment, but it still did not let itself be guided by the masses it now inducted. "Instead," reported Kirillova to the 1931 "trial" of the scientific societies, "it was led by its most backward strata and continued to display a lack of integrity, while its work was suffused with amateurism."[53] To make matters worse, VOOP enjoyed "a sad notoriety as the publisher of *Okhrana prirody*," added Kirillova. (The journal was "severely criticized for its alarmism in addition to its lack of integrity" at the Varnitso conference.)[54]

There were other shortcomings identified by the Kirillova commission as well. The tiny percentage of Communists in VOOP (only 75 of a membership of 2,500 at the time of the investigation) was decried, as was the society's failure to keep accurate records of the social composition of its members. This last failing allowed the penetration into the society by all manner of "class alien" elements, it was alleged, particularly by the *lishentsy:* those who had been deprived of the right to participate in the political life of the nation after the Revolution. Kirillova's commission presented VOOP with a long list of recommendations, the most important of which included attracting more party members and increasing their role within the leadership of the society, attracting workers and peasants, and conducting a precise census of its membership to identify unwanted "class aliens."[55]

While the Governing Council of VOOP conceded some shortcomings in its work and pledged to overcome them,[56] it could also point to substantial sociological changes in the society's membership since its founding in 1924, changes which would continue and intensify during the course of the First Five-Year Plan. Few would dispute the contention that, from the moment of its inception through the first years of its existence, the All-Russian Society for Conservation was not only a creature of academics but had a strikingly high percentage of learned members as well.[57] Five years after its establishment, however, the entire social complexion of the society was different. Students—40 percent of the membership—were now the preponderant group, overshadowing educators and even the white-collar and civil servant group.[58] If Kirillova's reminiscences accurately reflected the state of affairs in January 1930, then we may credit this mass influx of students with staving off the society's liquidation.

Students were easy to enroll in the society (certainly, with the efforts of sympathetic teachers), but getting workers and peasants to join was another matter. One of the most vexing problems that faced VOOP was its continuing failure to broaden its social base among adults and become a truly mass organization. In great measure, this failure was the result of the awesome apathy toward, if not active hostility to, many of the policies of conservation on the part of Russia's vast peasantry. Too many of conservation's causes seemed to involve material sacrifices on the part of the already overly burdened rural population, be it the forfeiture of the use of a local forest, the prohibition of the spring hunt, or the confiscation of convenient pasturelands owing to the establishment of a *zapovednik*. While VOOP took great pains to publicize any gains among the peasantry, these gains were puny by comparison with those that were needed in order to make an impact on rural attitudes and practices.[59]

VOOP's efforts to recruit members among urban workers similarly lagged, although there were a few hopeful signs of heightened interest, as VOOP activist Adol'f Adol'fovich Teodorovich reported in a dispatch to *Okhrana prirody*.[60] By mid-1930 an extensive lecture campaign in Moscow-area factories was under way, with talks presented at the Serp i Molot, Dzhut, and Krasnyi Tekstil'shchik plants, some of Moscow's largest.[61] This attempt to reach out to workers, already considerable in view of the society's modest resources and membership, intensified still further as cultural revolutionaries continued their harassment of VOOP to broaden its social base. Accordingly, between 1 January and 22 February 1931 twenty-six talks were presented by VOOP in schools, factories, plants, and the dormitories of seasonal workers and Red Army soldiers. This drive resulted in the enrollment of two thousand new members.[62] This was, in fact, the high-water mark of the campaign for social integration of the society.[63] Soon, the ideal of social mobility, as expressed in *vydvizhenstvo*,* faded before the regime's realization that it still needed the services of the generally more competent "bourgeois" specialists. These, however, were brought back into the fold not as "bourgeois" experts but as reformed, loyal members of the new "Soviet intelligentsia." By 1932, mass recruitment to VOOP, as with other Soviet institutions and societies, was at an end.[64]

Despite its failure to take Russia's factories and collective farms by storm, VOOP continued to wield considerable influence not only within academic circles but inside Narkompros as well. Narkompros's subsidies to VOOP roughly doubled for each successive accounting period: 700 rubles were allotted for the period 1924–1926; 1,480 rubles for 1926–1927; 5,520 rubles for October 1927–April 1929; and 11,100 for April 1929–October 1930 (after which no financial data are available).[65]

Although VOOP lost an important battle within Narkompros when the Main Administration for Socialist Upbringing rejected the society's petition to make mandatory the establishment of VOOP cells in schools, the introduction of basic conservation lessons, and school participation in Arbor Day and Bird Day,[66] this was counterbalanced by the commissariat's blessing for the first university courses specifically on nature protection.[67] At any rate, the Main Administration's decision evidently had no dampening effect on VOOP's recruitment of students; there was no shortage of volunteers from among the 5,620 student members of VOOP (as of October 1930)[68] for a vigilante force to patrol Moscow's railroad stations on the lookout for illegally gotten pelts and trophies.[69] Also in 1930 students continued to bring conservation into the public eye through their demonstrations on Bird Day.[70]

Despite this progress in expanding its social profile, VOOP continued to lag in its recruitment of Communists.[71] Equally little seems to have been done to drive the "class aliens" from the ranks of the society. Even those who were elsewhere under a cloud, such as Kozhevnikov, were still very much in evidence in VOOP affairs.

As for enhancing the role of party members in the leadership of the society, there was already ample representation both on staff and in the highest councils. By April 1929, Komsomols and party members represented one staff member in six.[72] Moreover, the presidency of the society had long ago fallen irrevocably into the hands of veteran party members. Perhaps the real problem, from the point of view of the "party-minded," should have been identified as follows: the views of VOOP Communists were practically indistinguishable from those of the old-line "bourgeois" professors for whom the Communists ought to have served as a vanguard.

Ironically, a nonparty person, Manteifel', was closer in spirit to the mood of the Five-Year Plan era than were the nominal Bolsheviks on the VOOP Governing Council, Segal'[73] and Potemkin, or the society's president in early 1930, Vangengeim, a man of the same mold as his predecessor, Fedorovskii. As for the VOOP Bolsheviks' central roles, together with Smidovich and Krylenko, in assuming leadership of the Communist Academy's Society of Marxist-Kraevedy, these

---

*The promotion of persons of a proletarian or poor-peasant background to positions of authority in industry, education, and the party to replace those of "bourgeois" backgrounds.

were in fact attempts to keep the lid on a potential hotbed of cultural revolutionary mischief.

Perhaps the feature of VOOP that changed least during this period of the Kirillova commission and the Cultural Revolution was, interestingly enough, its militancy. Through *Okhrana prirody* the society launched a plucky and perilous campaign to prevent the further encroachment of collectivized agriculture on the remaining virgin steppes. It successfully pressured the Moscow City Soviet to issue an edict prohibiting the felling of fir and birch trees for the Christmas and New Year holidays, and played an important watchdog role in campaigns to protect parks, gardens, and groves of all description, particularly in the increasingly grimy cities.[74]

Of particular significance were VOOP's efforts to mobilize public opinion and official support for the establishment of new *zapovedniki* and the defense of existing ones. Such campaigns were launched to bring an end to the precarious situation of the Central Forest *zapovednik*,[75] to consummate the creation of the Kyzyl-Agach *zapovednik* in Azerbaidzhan,[76] and to promote the creation of *zapovedniki* near Lake Borovoe in Kazakhstan and in the northern Urals in the basin of the Pechora and Ilych rivers.[77] With respect to the last two *zapovedniki,* VOOP even took the initiative in putting together expeditions, complete with moving picture cameras, to reconnoiter the prospective sites for the reserves and to draw up blueprints. This was yet another indication of the considerable effect that a voluntary society could have on conservation policy. Nor did VOOP let matters rest with the provisions of an expedition and the compilation of a blueprint; it then drummed up support for these proposals from all quarters, filling *Okhrana prirody* with pages and pages of letters and memoranda of endorsement.[78]

Perhaps the one concession made to the sensibilities of the partisans of the Five-Year Plan was the creation within the society of a new Section for Assisting the Growth of Livestock Breeding and for the Protection of Domestic Animals. This section, known by its acronym SOZh, was created chiefly to persuade the collective-farm peasantry to stop slaughtering their livestock in the name of "humane treatment." It had little effect, however, on the peasants' only means of registering their emphatic opposition to "the revolution in the countryside," and seems to have been disregarded by the bulk of conservationists as well.[79]

Thus, as of early summer 1930, the All-Russian Society for Conservation remained almost completely unaffected by the buffeting winds of the Cultural Revolution. Bearing out to a great degree the analogy offered by B. M. Zavadovskii and others at the Varnitso "trial," VOOP, like the reserves it sought to protect, had become a sort of sociological *zapovednik*. The implication here was that under the cover of its titular Communist leaders, the society had become a haven for "bourgeois" professors in their efforts to restrain the pace of economic development in the Soviet Union.

By the next general election of officers on 1 October 1930, however, the society's business-as-usual had been disrupted by two developments: an attack from within the society, and an investigation from without. Sensing the radical tide of cultural revolution running in their favor, some "Young Turks" in VOOP took the offensive against the hitherto dominant "bourgeois" professors. When, in the August–October issue of *Okhrana prirody* for 1930, the journal published a belligerent letter of Vladimir Vladimirovich Karpov's[80] attacking the "university professors" who led VOOP, it could be said that the Cultural Revolution had finally come to conservation.

Although the leaders of VOOP dismissed Karpov's letter with a withering rebuttal, they had to be more circumspect in responding to the recommendations of the Rabkrin RSFSR investigation of the society and of the TsBK released on 26 September. Meeting less than one week later the society's plenum now finally agreed to "conduct a review of the membership . . . with an aim of eliminating *lishentsy* and all other elements unfit for membership. . . ."[81]

The election of new officers also provided an opportunity for VOOP to make a conciliatory gesture to its critics. To the Governing Council were elected two factory workers, the first representation for that group on VOOP's ruling body. In addition, one seat apiece was assigned to representatives of the Young Naturalists, the Young Pioneers, and the Komsomol. The top post stayed in the hands of a respected party member, the amiable and outspoken Potemkin.

Some old faces were gone from the Governing Council, including Buturlin, Vangengeim, and Rossinskii, but Shillinger, Manteifel', and others stayed on. Evdokiia Bloshenko, the recording secretary of the Goskomitet, was promoted from candidate to full membership and, in a gesture of defiance at the extreme demands of Karpov and other cultural revolutionaries, G. A. Kozhevnikov was returned to the Governing Council along with S. A. Severtsov after an absence of one and one-half years. Other new faces included the VOOP Moscow provincial leaders A. I. Grishin and K. V. Anan'ev; VOOP recording secretary Suzanna Fridman; and V. K. Diablo, active in the protection of whales and other marine mammals.

Perhaps the most important result of the election was the elevation of a very dark horse, Vasilii Nikitovich Makarov, to the second spot in the society. Much as Kozhevnikov had dominated the first twenty years of Russian conservation, Makarov would dominate the next twenty. Within months of his election Makarov, though nominally subordinate to Potemkin, moved visibly onto center stage. Soon, in the Goskomitet as well, Makarov rose to preeminence, although there too he was juridically only deputy chairperson, subordinate to M. N. Kulagin. Never in the history of the movement had one person become so representative of conservation as Makarov did now, yet here was a figure who had not even been elected to the Governing Council of the society before his sudden elevation to deputy president in October 1930. Until Soviet archives become more accessible, the reasons for Makarov's rise are likely to remain unknown. Nevertheless, Soviet biographers[82] have brought to light a combination of work history and expertise—a long association with Narkompros plus a specialization in natural-science teaching—similar to the career of his immediate superior, Potemkin.[83]

One of the first challenges to face him and Potemkin after their election was how to respond to the continuing pressures of the Cultural Revolution on the conservation movement. Karpov's letter, though rebutted in *Okhrana prirody,* was symptomatic of a growing impatience—within Varnitso, within Rabkrin RSFSR, and among the Young Naturalists and the Marxist-*kraevedy*—with the conservationists as a group that was somehow dedicated to impeding the progress of socialist construction and that was committed to "the protection of nature for the sake of nature itself."

A DRAMATIC GESTURE

Potemkin and Makarov realized that their greatest hope of deflecting a fatal attack on VOOP from the "left" was a dramatic gesture. By a glance at the cover of the January 1931 issue of the VOOP journal, startled readers learned that their publication was no longer called *Okhrana prirody* (Conservation). Instead, in keeping with the times, it had been renamed *Priroda i sotsialisticheskoe khoziaistvo*, or *Nature and the Socialist Economy*. Turning the page to the lead editorial, an even greater shock awaited the reader. No more was there an All-Russian Society for Conservation. Its new avatar was the All-Russian Society for Conservation and the Promotion of the Growth of Natural Resources. And, reading the editorial through, readers might well have concluded that the change in orientation that Smidovich had forecast for the movement was already a fait accompli.

The editorial, signed by Makarov, echoed many of the concerns of Karpov's letter. "Our Tasks," as the piece was titled, pronounced the final excommunication of "the old tendencies of 'conservation of nature' for the sake of nature itself." Moreover, it announced that VOOP now had to foreswear ventures whose relevance to socialist construction could not be demonstrated; "from now on," the editorial pledged, "the society will not give a thought to, let alone involve itself in, any activity lying outside the general tasks of socialist construction."[84]

The limitations now enunciated by the editorial meant that the conservation movement would have to revise its conception of its own importance and its special mission. No longer would it be permitted to set *its* goals above those of others. Makarov outlined new tasks for the conservation movement, which included assisting the creation of an industrial concentration around the coal- and ore-rich Ural-Kuzbas region, increasing exports, wholehearted support for the mechanization of agriculture and for the extension of collective farm agriculture, and, in general, "the many-sided development of the resource base."[85]

The apparent rejection of so many distinctive positions of the conservation movement was the most striking feature of this list of new goals. No longer was the movement to seek aggressively to restrain procurement quotas of biotic resources. Now it was to promote the opposite: the speed-up of exports. No longer could it sound the last note of opposition to agricultural mechanization under conditions of collectivization and monoculture. Now it was instructed to join the cheering section for those developments. No longer could it unconditionally raise the banner of the preservation of the steppes and other natural pasturelands, together with their populations of wild grazers and other fauna. The movement was now committed to abet the rivals for those resources: the Russian livestock-breeding industry. Makarov's remarks could not fail to create the impression that the conservation society had become reduced to little more than a transmission belt by which elements of the population could be drawn to the real goal: socialist construction. Conservation was being asked to relinquish its uniquely critical character and to survive simply as a shadow of its former self.

Happily for VOOP, however, Makarov's bark was far worse than his bite. Much of the sound and fury of the editorial was for outside consumption, and when Makarov observed that "wrecking in science and technology does not always come cloaked in reactionary theories and in overt guise"[86] he was cleverly setting up a line of defense against conservation's "leftist" critics. Indeed, with a good deal of historical hindsight, one could state that Makarov was employing precisely the tactic used by the hypothetical "wreckers" about whom he warned. He was using the rhetoric of socialist construction to defend as much of the old conservation program as he could. At the Varnitso "trial" of the scientific societies, that much was suspected, despite the bombastic rhetoric of the VOOP editorial and the renaming of the journal and of the society itself. "Even now," charged Kirillova, "the society has still failed to take [our] criticisms into account."[87] Another participant at the Varnitso gathering said it plainer:

> The protective coloration in which the scientific societies have bedecked themselves, employing to this end Marxist terminology and certain changes within their leadership, has been completely exposed here. It remains only for us to put the question to the Materialist societies[88] attached to the Communist Academy: Why haven't they shown any desire thus far to take the matter in hand and to reorganize the [scientific] societies in the necessary manner?[89]

The Varnitso critics, for the most part, were right. The change spoken of by Smidovich had turned out to be more of a face-lift than a more profound volte-face in the conservation movement's direction. Nevertheless, despite having been "unmasked" by Varnitso activists and Marxist-*kraevedy* such as Karpych, Makarov's policy of "protective coloration" effectively spirited the conservation movement safely through the difficult years of 1931 and 1932. With the possible exception of Kozhevnikov,[90] none of the conservationists seems to have been arrested during this period, and many doggedly pursued the same dangerous opposition to the rapacious policies of the economic agencies, though with more subtlety. One of the less subtle, more highly publicized actions taken by VOOP during this period was the exposure of widespread violations of the conservation laws by Pushsindikat, the fur procurement and export arm of the People's Commissariat of Foreign Trade of the USSR. After reports of the discovery of pelts of protected animals, including beavers, saiga, and moose calves, in the Leningrad refrigerators of Pushsindikat, not only did the president of the Leningrad branch of VOOP conduct an inquest, but a brigade was organized by the Governing Council in Moscow as well, including official representatives of the Goskomitet. Inspections were then held in the Moscow warehouse of the Foreign Trade Commissariat (in July 1932), and the incriminating evidence was duly passed along to Rabkrin for further action.[91]

The involvement of VOOP in the promotion of new *zapovedniki* and in the defense of old ones did not slacken either,[92] nor did the society's vigorous efforts to encourage the protection of urban green belts and the creation of large urban parks.[93] Finally, in our attempt to demonstrate the essential continuity between conservation's "old course" and the "new," we cannot neglect to mention the continued efforts of VOOP members to halt the turning over of "Red virgin soil."[94]

For the scientific societies of the Soviet Union and, of particular interest to us, for VOOP and the TsBK, the period from 1929 to 1932 was a time of testing. But by 1932 the battle over the scientific societies had been joined and decided. The result was a defeat for those who sought the societies' dissolution or total reconstruction under the auspices of the Communist Academy. VOOP and TsBK were able to continue unchanged to a surprising extent.

TEN

Conservation and the Five-Year Plan

As the Five-Year Plan stormed into its third year, its "planned" aspect increasingly yielded to over-optimistic, impromptu upward revisions of plan targets. Resources were exploited with an intensity never before seen in Russia.

Troubled as the conservationists had been about the state of Russia's forests, a 25 February 1930 decree of the RSFSR Council of People's Commissars (SNK) gave them even more cause for concern: all aspects of forest administration and exploitation were officially transferred from the People's Commissariat of Agriculture (Narkomzem RSFSR) to the Supreme Council of the National Economy (VSNKh RSFSR).[1] This decree was soon followed by a similar one of the USSR Council of People's Commissars of 3 September, concentrating executive responsibility for forestry and the forest industry in the Soviet Union overall in the hands of the All-Union VSNKh, the engine of the industrialization drive.[2]

Industry was experiencing a sharply increased demand for wood, both for itself and for export (so that it might obtain needed machinery and parts from abroad). The Five-Year Plan figures published as a decree on 27 August 1929 foresaw an increase in logged area over the entire USSR from 157.4 million hectares in 1928–1929 to 200 million hectares in 1932–1933. Over that period, output was to rise to 280 million cubic meters from 178 million.[3] The leaders of the party believed that the required shock-pace production of forest products could only be assured by the direct control by the All-Union VSNKh over the entire timber industry.

The transfer of forest administration to VSNKh of the USSR was yet another example of that organization's rise to preeminence among the various economic commissariats in the period 1929–1930. This rise was also reflected in the transfer of vocational and technical education to VSNKh from the People's Commissariat for Education (Narkompros RSFSR). Behind these developments lay the exigencies of the Five-Year Plan.

THE PROBLEM WITH PROCUREMENTS

During the VSNKh tenure, the original target figures for timber procurement were revised sharply upward, partly in response to VSNKh's initial successes.[4] While comprehensive figures showing rates of deforestation by region for the Soviet period have not yet been made public, there is at least some evidence that the stewardship of VSNKh (RSFSR and USSR) in 1930–1931 was a particularly unhappy one, quite reminiscent of its prior stewardship during the years of the Civil War.[5]

One region that elicited great concern on the part of conservationists was the Western Oblast,* where Narkomzem's plans to convert the province into a giant granary were now being assiduously pursued by VSNKh. "At present," wrote one agitated observer in *Okhrana prirody,* "Smolensk Oblast is literally living through a catastrophe. In the opinion of qualified experts, . . . in 1929–1930 the extraordinary timber procurements proceeded at such an incredible rate that if they continue through the winter of 1931–1932 the oblast will be completely deforested."[6]

Leading the campaign against VSNKh's logging activities was VOOP, the All-Russian Society for Conservation, which had loudly raised the issue of deforestation at a 14 May 1930 conference in Smolensk and which had successfully persuaded the Oblast Central Executive Committee to stand up to VSNKh.[7] Under the circumstances, the campaign to save the forests of the Western Oblast was surprisingly successful. VSNKh was pressured to transfer responsibility for forest protection back to the local governmental authorities. Now, with control over the oblast's forests restored, the Presidium of the Oblast Central Executive Committee moved speedily to enact appropriate conservation measures. Apart from the continuing wrangling over the boundaries of the Central Forest *zapovednik,* conflict between conservationists and VSNKh over the forests of the Western Oblast seems to have subsided after this turn of events, suggesting that the intervention of the Oblast Central Executive Committee did in fact promote a more restrained attitude on the part of the procurement agencies.

As the disastrous implications of VSNKh's policy of wholesale clear-cutting became evident, the USSR Council of People's Commissars reconsidered VSNKh's carte blanche. This led to the promulgation of a decree on 31 July 1931, "On the Organization of the Forest Industry," signed by V. M. Molotov, the council's chairman.[8] Importantly, the chief problems addressed by the decree were those of conservation: procurement norms, forest regeneration, and forest protection, particularly in arid regions.

The return of the semiprotected forests—reinstated as per the decree—to Narkomzem, was a major turnabout from the policies of one year earlier. However, it would be erroneous to ascribe this solely to the entreaties of conservationists or to a dawning sense of wise use among Soviet leaders. The new solicitude for vulnerable woodlands only became possible after the collapse of the international market for timber in 1930–1931. With lumber mills idle everywhere in the West, some of the edge was taken off the Soviet drive to intensify logging indiscriminately.

Politics also played a role in the divestiture of much of VSNKh's forests. By mid-1931, VSNKh's days as a superministry were numbered, and Stalin must have already been considering the creation of the ministerial system for industry that we

---

*Smolensk Province was the major territorial component of the newly created Western Oblast, in an administrative reorganization of 1929 which was based on economic-geographical divisions rather than on historical ones.

associate with the latter portion of his rule. Thus, the forests having the most importance for agriculture were returned to the Narkomzem system, while those having industrial importance were retained for the time being by VSNKh, even as the latter's division into the Commissariats of Heavy, Light, and Forest Industries was being contemplated.

Despite the indisputably positive aspects of the decree, however, the reversion of forests to Narkomzem did not always mean a return to the status quo ante. The Crimea, for example, by contrast with the pre-1930 situation, was now officially open to lumbering, albeit within the strictures applying to the new semiprotected silvicultural category, i.e., that procurement not exceed annual growth. Lack of agreement regarding the calculation of annual growth rates, however, permitted Narkomzem to continue vigorous logging efforts under the banner of "sustained yield," to the anguished protestations of conservation activists.[9]

The issue of game procurement also remained a sore point for conservationists during the years of the Five-Year Plan. On 10 February 1930, the SNK RSFSR promulgated a new decree on hunting to replace the statute that had been in effect since 1923.[10] Apparently, this measure had been drafted with little or no foreknowledge of the impending decree of 25 February transferring Narkomzem RSFSR's Forest Administration to the jurisdiction of VSNKh RSFSR. It was therefore ironic that the decree conferred a victory of sorts on Narkomzem, placing its stamp of approval on the use of the term *game-management zapovednik (okhotnichii zapovednik)* to describe the Agriculture Commissariat's preserves—a usage Narkompros-backed conservationists strongly opposed—just at the moment that the SNK RSFSR was poised to divest Narkomzem RSFSR of its control over hunting matters and the *game-management zapovednik* as well as forestry matters.

Barely two weeks later, however, the status of hunting in the RSFSR was marked by uncertainty. The decree of 25 February took all areas of forest administration out of the hands of Narkomzem RSFSR and placed them under the jurisdiction of VSNKh RSFSR. Typically, though, no specific provision was made for the institutional future of hunting, which had been administered by the Forest Administration's Subdepartment for Hunting Affairs. Deprived of the Narkomzem corps of forest rangers to enforce the hunting laws and no longer having a clear institutional home base, hunting became a virtual orphan among the areas of Soviet economic life. For the time being, VSNKh's Syndicate of the Forest Industry filled the vacuum.[11]

The leadership had another fate in mind for hunting, however, than incorporation into the industrial ministry VSNKh. The divestiture of Narkomzem's far-flung forest, fishing, and wildlife empire also served to bulk up another ministry: the USSR People's Commissariat of Trade (Narkomtorg). In May 1930, responsibility for poultry-raising and wildfowl procurement was taken from Narkomzem and transferred to Narkomtorg USSR.[12] In August, it was the turn of the fishing industry.[13] By mid-September, hunting, too, had been included in the purview of Narkomtorg.[14]

Hunting's bureaucratic odyssey did not end there, however. Narkomtorg USSR and its republican analogues were divided anew on 22 November into two commissariat systems, one for foreign trade (Narkomvneshtorg USSR) and one for supplies (Narkomsnab USSR, RSFSR, and for the other republics). Hunting, including responsibility for the game-management *zapovedniki,* was entrusted to the latter.[15]

In its efforts to consolidate its hold over the fur trade, the People's Commissariat of Supplies of the RSFSR moved quickly to undercut the authority of the State Interagency Committee for Conservation (Goskomitet) in hunting matters. As a counterweight to the Goskomitet, which had traditionally reviewed pelt procurement plans harshly (especially those of Narkomtorg), Narkomsnab RSFSR created a more pliant organ, which it christened the Committee on Hunting Affairs. It, too, was an interagency body, but with a difference. Chaired by an official of Narkomsnab RSFSR, the committee was heavily weighted toward production-oriented organizations.[16]

The range of responsibilities of the new committee was impressively broad. It was to review plans for hunting, game breeding, investments, and procurement quotas; to supervise predator control; to determine which species would be protected; to organize the research of biology institutions along lines relevant to hunting; and to pass judgment on "all other questions that concern hunting." The committee arrogated to itself also the final say on questions of administrative jurisdiction relative to hunting.[17]

The Goskomitet reacted with understandable apprehension to this challenge to its authority. It promptly requested a copy of the charter of the new committee and arranged an inquest to determine whether Narkomsnab had encroached on its own sphere of competence. By May 1931, the Goskomitet's Presidium had thrown out an open challenge to Narkomsnab, initiating a new campaign to ban spring and summer hunting throughout the USSR, and by June relations between the two bodies had soured to the point that Narkomsnab's representative pointedly failed to show up at a Goskomitet hearing called to review gamefowl quotas.[18]

Before the conflict between the Goskomitet and Narkomsnab's Committee on Hunting Affairs could be resolved, however, yet another bureaucratic reorganization gave hunting a new master. On 16 May 1931 the USSR Council of People's Commissars decided to turn over hunting matters to the new People's Commissariat of Foreign Trade (Narkomvneshtorg) of the USSR.[19] This new development was not viewed by conservationists as an improvement, however. Narkomvneshtorg of the USSR, if anything, was regarded as being even less congenial to the aims of conservation than was Narkomsnab, if only because of Narkomvneshtorg's *direct* interest in the export of pelts.

With the advent of Narkomvneshtorg control over hunting came a new, enhanced role for the fur-marketing conglomerate Pushsindikat, which was soon transformed into the All-Union Peltry Association (Soiuzpushnina).[20] This new superagency, under the jurisdiction of Narkomvneshtorg but having its own "juridical personality" and operating on a self-financing basis, represented a wholly new threat to the established patterns of hunting.

Soiuzpushnina meant to close the gap that existed between the requirements of the export market and the procurement performance and marketing patterns of the hunters and their organizations. The association was empowered to procure pelts by means of its own network of purchasers, and to organize and administer all breeding operations in the USSR. Its tasks also included establishing sovkhoz-style hunting-production collectives (which aimed to supplant individual and cooperative hunting, extend hunting to unexploited areas and encourage regular collective and state farms to take up a greater share of procurement in their off-season); organizing and administering the entire fur-dressing industry in the USSR; collecting and sorting skins and furs provided by all other organizations; managing the export of peltry and of live animals; and, finally, developing a program for the acclimatization of exotic animals, which had commenced with the introduction of the muskrat from North America in 1928.[21] The new superagency soon delivered a rude shock to the conservationists; pelt procurements, it announced, would be increased to 145 percent of current levels by 1932.[22]

Soiuzpushnina had every intention of making good on its plan. Enormous areas were set aside for pelt procurement; 200 million hectares alone were allotted to the hunters' cooperative, and an additional 100 million hectares were set aside for hunters contracting directly with Soiuzpushnina. These included collective and state farms, which contracted with Soiuzpushnina for agreed-upon deliveries of pelts in exchange for scarce consumer goods disbursed at the agency's procurement stations.

Despite undoubtedly great efforts, though, it seems unlikely that the procurement of pelts ever increased by 145 percent. Reviewing the weekly bulletin of Narkomvneshtorg USSR, *Our Foreign Trade,* we are struck by the endless reports of shortfalls and failures to meet procurement targets.[23]

The shortfalls were caused by a number of factors. The late arrival of consumer goods and food shipped to the procurement stations defeated their purpose as inducements to go out and hunt, particularly when they appeared toward the end of the season.[24] The institutional in-fighting and confusion between Narkomsnab and Narkomvneshtorg also had cut into the efficacy of the hunting sector; Narkomvneshtorg could not extend its network of agents into the periphery in time to save the season, and in many cases this led to the absence of any institutional presence for hunting in remote areas.[25]

Chairmen of state and collective farms as well as party secretaries in rural cells, reluctant to allow the peasants to leave the farms for the hunt, often actively debarred them from the procurement campaigns. Local editors maintained a curtain of silence about the entire procurement effort in collusion with the collective farm managers.[26]

Yet another factor that impeded procurement was a basic lack of coordination between Soiuzpushnina and other economic organizations. In the North Caucasus *krai,* for example, fulfillment of Narkomvneshtorg's plan targets reached only 48 percent, despite the fact that five million ground squirrels, hamsters, and voles had been destroyed by brigades of the Society for Pest Control and the Society for the Promotion of Military Applications of Aviation and Chemistry (Osoaviakhim). Because of poor coordination between these voluntary organizations and Soiuzpushnina, only 400,000 of the rodents' skins were turned in at the association's procurement stations.[27]

Still another reason explains the poor showing of the procurement agency: the exhaustion of the reserves of furbearing animals. In almost every region, for one variety of animal or another, there was a reported population crash. In Iakutiia, foxes and hares had disappeared;[28] in Nizhnyi Novgorod, squirrel.[29] Even in such normally lush regions as the Far East, biotic impoverishment began to cast a pall. At a session of the Goskomitet of 25 November 1932, Bilibin, a *kraeved* and conservation activist from the Far Eastern *krai*, pleaded for support for a *zapovednik* on the Sea of Okhotsk, emphasizing just how "devastated the natural resources of that . . . region had become after the region's sovietization."[30]

Bilibin was especially critical of the attempt to impose a settled, collectivized way of life on aboriginal groups that had attained an apparent sustainable balance with the natural resources that supported them. Aside from mindless efforts indiscriminately to impose "Soviet" mores on local cultures, a desperately short-term mentality came to characterize Soviet procurement efforts. Of a thousand sea lions taken off one island not far offshore from Kamchatka, for example, 950 were reportedly pups, and it was claimed that this was not an isolated instance.[31]

Not all the news was negative. Important new game conservation measures made their appearance in the midst of all the other gloomy developments. One such measure was a migratory wildfowl protection decree, in which the SNK RSFSR directed the establishment of three temporary wildfowl preserves *(okhotnich' i zakazniki)* in important wintering and nesting areas (the Crimea, the Kuban' Delta, and near the mouths of the Terek and Sulak rivers in Dagestan); these were to enjoy adequate security to be funded by the procurement agencies.[32]

Even the procurement organs themselves occasionally acquiesced in conservation measures. An excellent example of this was the agreement by Uralgostorg in April 1930 to set aside 12 percent of the territory of its proposed Verkhnekamskii hunting sovkhoz as a *zapovednik*. There was cooperation even between Narkomvneshtorg and the Goskomitet on rare occasions. Thus, the agencies mounted a joint campaign of opposition to the Karelian ASSR's lifting of the ban on the hunting of moose in 1931.[33]

These bright spots, however, should be viewed as exceptions to the grim game procurement situation. The adversarial relationship that had existed between the Goskomitet and Narkomvneshtorg (and the other economic commissariats, too) if anything, deepened.[34] The rift between the two camps would soon be emphatically highlighted at the First All-Union Congress for Conservation in January 1933 as the reconciling of short-term and longer-range economic considerations became more difficult.

THE GOSKOMITET AND THE *ZAPOVEDNIKI*

In the Goskomitet, too, Makarov pursued the policy of protective coloration that marked his pilotage of VOOP (see chapter 9), rhetorically endorsing socialist construction while spiritedly defending the conservation agenda. The central Goskomitet (and, later, its local interagency conservation commissions) was renamed, becoming the Goskomitet not for Conservation but for the Promotion of the Growth of the Natural Resources of the RSFSR,[35] much as VOOP had been renamed. But the "new" Goskomitet, just like the "new" VOOP, tried to hold to its previous path as much as possible.

Nowhere was this more evident than in the Goskomitet's continued vigorous support for the consolidation and extension of the network of *zapovedniki*. Indeed, some of the sharpest exchanges between the Goskomitet and the economic commissariats occurred not over procurement targets but over the repeated attempts by the economic commissariats to impede the establishment of *zapovedniki* or to dismantle them.[36]

One important unresolved dispute turned on the opposition by a succession of economic organs to the creation of the Central Forest *zapovednik*. In its time, Narkomzem RSFSR had rebuffed all attempts at accommodation, and its policies of obstinate stonewalling were faithfully continued by its successor in forest administration, VSNKh. Even after a decree of 4 May 1930 approving the creation of the Central Forest *zapovednik,* issued by the SNK RSFSR, VSNKh's All-Union Forest Industry Association (Soiuzlesprom) and its subsidiary trusts continued their operations within the *zapovednik*'s territory.

Much the same situation arose in connection with the establishment of the giant Pechoro-Ilych *zapovednik* in the northern Urals (Komi Oblast), incorporating one million hectares of boreal forest. Although VSNKh had voiced no objection in the Goskomitet to sending the proposal to the SNK RSFSR for approval[37] (which was granted in the decree of 4 May 1930), the obstructionism of its Soiuzlesprom prevented the actual setting of boundaries for the reserve for over a year.[38] This was also the case with the Altai *zapovednik,* an equally impressive reserve (one million hectares) approved by the same measure. Perhaps the most serious cases of hindrance were to be found in the Kazakh Autonomous Republic in the RSFSR.[39]

Other instances concerned *zapovedniki* that were already in place and functioning. The Mid-Volga *zapovednik,* a conglomerate of the former Penza and Zhiguli reserves, was the victim of a variety of depredations by economic organs. VSNKh's All-Union Peat Association insistently advanced its demand to extract peat in areas of the *zapovednik* where the topography was largely sphagnum mire, while sovkhozes cast longing gazes at the tiny remaining parcels of virgin steppe in another portion of the reserve.[40] To the southwest, the venerable Caucasus *zapovednik* again found itself the target of local economic interests seeking the reserve's liquidation,[41] while the shadowy hand of Soiuzlesprom lurked in the background.[42] Finally, and this list is by no means exhaustive, a case involving a bid by Soiuzpushnina's Karakul-Export Sovkhoz to seize territory of the Chernomorskie *zapovedniki* became so embittered that it landed on the desk of the prosecutor-general of the Ukraine, who agreed with the *zapovednik*'s administration on the need "to make an example" of the economic organs in this case.[43]

Although the decree of 4 May 1930 had conferred the approval of the SNK RSFSR on the establishment of six new *zapovedniki,* the measure set only the maximum area for each reserve. Actual determination of the final boundaries was left to Narkompros RSFSR in consultation with other interested parties. After agreement was secured, the final boundaries would be resubmitted to the SNK for final confirmation. Consequently, Narkompros, acting through the Presidium of the

Goskomitet, was forced to seek out compromise with its adversaries, who continued to challenge the original boundary proposals proposed by the commissariat.

Faced with this impediment to its plans, the Goskomitet in May 1931 decided formally to invite VSNKh's Soiuzlesprom to talk over their differences. Beleaguered by cultural revolutionaries and others, the conservation establishment recognized that the times were not running in their favor. Rather than face the prospect of interminable litigation and conflict over the setting of boundaries for the reserves, therefore, the Goskomitet reluctantly agreed to revisions proposed by the timber association.[44]

From the territorial point of view, the settlements reached in the summer of 1931 were not particularly disastrous; the Pechoro-Ilych *zapovednik* retained all of its territory, while the Central Forest *zapovednik* was able to preserve 35,000 of its original 50,000 hectares as a zone of absolute inviolability, with the remaining 15,000 hectares set over as a buffer zone.[45] On the other hand, the Mid-Volga *zapovednik* was forced to liquidate two of its small, dispersed parcels of steppe; not every battle was worth fighting.

The price paid by the Goskomitet in these compromises was not one of territory so much as one of principle. That principle was the inviolability *(zapovednost')* of the reserves. In the Mid-Volga *zapovednik,* for example, the Goskomitet bought peace by allowing the All-Union Peat Association (Soiuztorf) to extract peat from the sphagnum mires in the reserve.[46] To permit the Central Forest *zapovednik* finally to commence operations, the Goskomitet had to consent to the presence of the timber association's logging camps in the reserve's buffer zone.[47] Similarly, the decree that confirmed the final boundaries of the Pechoro-Ilych *zapovednik* also left the door open to future logging there by VSNKh USSR (to be planned, of course, "in consultation" with Narkompros RSFSR and the local authorities).[48]

Perhaps we may never learn the precipitating cause that impelled Makarov to publish the editorial "Our Tasks," which first sanctioned the new policy of human intervention in the *zapovedniki,* but we can identify a number of factors that certainly contributed to that outcome, undermining the principle of inviolability in the Narkompros reserves. One development that surely played a part in recasting the *zapovedniki* as appropriate arenas for economic activity was the promulgation of the new decree on hunting in February 1930. For the first time, Soviet legislation made specific reference to a type of *zapovednik (okhotnichii zapovednik)* in which active game management was not only tolerated but openly encouraged. Mentioned specifically were the need to cull game animals for captive breeding, the need to thin herds, and the need to eliminate "harmful animals and birds."[49]

Although Narkomzem RSFSR was soon thereafter divested of its network of game-management *zapovedniki* (also having to return to Narkompros the three *zapovedniki* it had raided one year earlier), thus dropping out of the *zapovednik* war a loser,[50] it had won the semantic skirmish over the use of the term *zapovednik.* In going down to institutional defeat, Narkomzem succeeded in destroying the efforts of the Narkompros-based conservationists to build the concept of inviolability into the official definition of the *zapovednik.*

After the divestiture of Narkomzem, the commissariat's former *zapovedniki* experienced a period of institutional "homelessness," in the words of a group of Soviet historians. The fates of the Barguzin, Kronotskii, Kondo-Sos'vinskii, and Lapland (Chuna-Tundra) *zapovedniki* were typical, passing after a relatively short period of time first to VSNKh, then to Narkomsnab RSFSR, and finally to Narkomvneshtorg USSR.[51] Little time passed before this new, last overlord of the game-management *zapovedniki*—like Narkomzem before it—began to look covetously at Narkompros's rapidly growing network of reserves. Indeed, by mid-1932, an official directive of Narkomvneshtorg was instructing its local plenipotentiaries "to identify for purposes of their economic utilization stocks of game animals that currently find protection within the *zapovedniki* of Narkompros."[52]

Not only was Narkompros under pressure to relax the standard of inviolability from economic organs such as Soiuzlesprom, the timber association, which threatened to veto the creation of new *zapovedniki* or to disrupt the orderly functioning of existing ones if easements and variances to exploit resources within them were not granted; it was also under continuing pressure to prove that its reserves were as useful and productive as those of Narkomvneshtorg, which measured *its* system's productivity in readily understandable terms: tons of meat procured, kilograms of pelts exported, and increases in the numbers of game animals.

This pressure for relevance and usefulness—more a by-product of the heroic optimism of Stalinist economic voluntarism than of the ideologizing by cultural revolutionaries—slowly but assuredly began to affect the system of *zapovedniki* belonging to Narkompros RSFSR. A general decree on *zapovedniki* of 20 June 1930 governing the administration of the reserves of the Narkompros system (superseding the legislation of 1925) subtly indicated a greater willingness to permit human intervention in the reserves.[53]

Yet another factor was at work corroding the principle of *zapovednost'*: the growing attack on the science of the study of ecological communities. Where biocenologists saw holism, cohesion, and a dynamic equilibrium in natural communities, their critics, led by I. I. Prezent, saw only limitless plasticity. Insofar as the inviolability of the *zapovedniki* was inextricably linked to the biocenological program of research conducted in them, any successful attack on biocenology was bound to have deleterious consequences for the *zapovedniki* as well.

These factors, acting synergistically, created a climate of opinion that was increasingly hostile to what was labeled a contemplative approach to nature. Less than one year after assuming de facto leadership of VOOP and the Goskomitet, Makarov was already identifying two contrastive periods of *zapovednik* history: before and after 1930 (his accession). The period to 1930, he wrote in notes prepared for a conference of representatives of the various republics' Scientific Sectors,* had been characterized by "a false, politically harmful orientation, both on the part of the scientists working in the field of conservation and on the part of

---

*In 1930, the *glavki* were replaced by sectors in a structural reorganization of the various republican Commissariats of Education. Accordingly, Glavnauka was superseded by the Scientific Sector in Narkompros RSFSR; an analogous process occurred in the other republics.

zapovednik workers, which emphasized the inviolability of the *zapovedniki*. Any link with the concrete goals of socialist construction was rejected."[54]

Contrasting sharply with this picture of old-line "science for its own sake" was the one presented by Makarov of the most recent period, following his election; now, he claimed, "the idea of a *zapovednik* as a natural scientific laboratory where one may not only observe nature but also perform experiments has already ceased to sound heretical and does not elicit furious protests, as had been the case in the past."[55]

Whether he was forced to take such a public posture, as the Soviet historian Feliks Robertovich Shtil'mark suggests,[56] or whether, as is argued here, his endorsement of "interventionism" represented a gambit designed to preserve as many of conservation's gains as possible (protective coloration), Makarov's pronouncements were soon reflected in more entrenched ventures than a one-time culling of cormorants and ravens in the Volga Delta reserve. In the Caucasus *zapovednik* in 1931 there appeared the very first production plan for a Narkompros *zapovednik,* downplaying inventorying and theoretical studies and featuring organization of an experimental forestry station, a survey of the hunting potential of surrounding areas, and research on six species of plants thought capable of supplying rubber. All of these, obviously, were expressions of the growing desire among Soviet *zapovednik* administrators to make their reserves appear "useful." For the Caucasus reserve, the production plan for the following year (1932) included an experimental game-breeding farm on the *zapovednik* (reminiscent of Narkomzem's and, later, Narkomvneshtorg's *zapovedniki*) and even a unit involved in prospecting for minerals and deposits of fuels.[57] Just as illustrative of the new trend was the 1931 charter of the just-created Pechoro-Ilych *zapovednik*.[58]

Yet, even in his public statements Makarov could never suppress his lifelong ambivalence over his strategic decision to renounce publicly the principle of absolute inviolability. Nowhere is this better reflected than in the very speech to the Goskomitet in which he repudiated the "pre-1930 view." The preponderant portion of his address was devoted to a defense of the *zapovednik* as a center for ecological research—as an inviolate *etalon*.[59] Sounding not much different from Kozhevnikov or Stanchinskii, Makarov emphasized that the studies of the "holistic parcels of nature" of the *zapovedniki* were "essential for the calculation and understanding of those alterations that result from the active human intervention in the course of natural events; . . . [they] allow us to comprehend both the short-term and the longer-range consequences of our active intervention, . . ." ultimately enabling society to establish "that direction in which human activity must be pursued so as to master the forces of nature for planned purposes."[60]

Viewed in such a light, argued Makarov,

> the basic, leading theoretical problems in *zapovednik* work must be problems of ecology . . . although they must also be linked with concrete tasks in the areas of livestock breeding, hunting, plant breeding, agriculture, forestry, and the study of natural productive forces. *Zapovedniki* by their very nature are ecological scientific-research institutions. . . .[61]

Central to Makarov's strategy of saving the *zapovedniki* as centers of ecological research was his insistence that such research be seen as directed toward the solution of real-life economic problems. He quickly took the lead in proposing a list of such concrete themes and problems, which included animal reproduction and fertility studies, development of accurate censusing methods, study of species composition and distribution in natural communities, migration and overwintering patterns, the relationship between the organism and its environment, and the study of changes in fauna (presumably abundance, distribution, and species composition) and its causes. All of them were highly ecological in nature and some were highly statistical. Yet, they were all themes aimed not at "science for science's sake" but at providing a scientific basis for rational game management.

Other tasks, excluding the patently utilitarian ones of acclimatization and reacclimatization of commercially valuable animals and plants, had more obvious economic applications: introducing hitherto commercially unexploited natural products into the economy, assisting the economic agencies in developing plans for the rational exploitation of resources, and protecting the normal hydrological and climatic regimes of broad regions.

Finally, alongside all of these sensibly pragmatic objectives Makarov also included the goal of preserving rare or endangered animals and plants as well as other objects of nature "having not only scientific or economic value, but cultural and aesthetic significance as well."[62] Here was an anomalous clause that a better politician, perhaps, would have left out, but which suggested that Makarov himself might have harbored a personal, aesthetically motivated attraction to nature.

On the face of it there is no way to fashion a consistent whole from Makarov's self-contradicting pronouncements on *zapovednik* function and regime. However, this does not mean that his position was bereft of all logic. Indeed, its paradoxical quality was at the very heart of its logic, for Makarov believed that he could at once assuage the would-be arbiters of biology and other enemies of conservation with rhetorical condemnation of the principle of inviolability while pressing forward sotto voce with the ecological programs that he genuinely supported. Reckoning that he could keep the impact of human "intervention" in *zapovedniki* to a minimum, Makarov bet on outlasting the transformers of nature. Having gone on record as one who rejected "science for science's sake," Makarov nevertheless made it known to his conservation constituency that it could discreetly continue basic research—so long as it was properly justified.

Rhetoric aside, the first years of Makarov's leadership of Soviet conservation were marked by continued innovation in ecological research in the *zapovedniki*. Funding for the Narkompros *zapovedniki* showed a generally upward curve, and was particularly impressive when compared with that for the reserves of the economic organs.[63] A most encouraging sign was Makarov's serious rededication of the Goskomitet to realizing its longtime goal of establishing *zapovedniki* in every biogeographical zone of the USSR.[64]

Even before Makarov's accession there had been the beginnings of a renewed, vigorous push to expand the Narkompros network. These efforts bore their first fruit on 4 May 1930, when the SNK RSFSR gave its stamp of approval to the creation, in principle, of six new *zapovedniki,* including the Central Forest *zapovednik* in the Western Oblast, with an area of up to 50,000 hectares.[65]

When Makarov assumed leadership he found the conservation movement's bargaining power severely eroded by the national mood and by Narkompros's declining stature among the governmental ministries, and he reluctantly made concessions. By allowing the procurement organs of the economic ministries to log and extract peat in the *zapovedniki,* however, Makarov struck a fateful bargain; he traded away the principle of inviolability of the Narkompros *zapovedniki* for the possibility that the reserve network might survive and expand. What Makarov received in return at first seemed impressive. After reaching agreement with the economic agencies, only the long-harassed Central Forest *zapovednik* actually lost territory. The already enormous Altai reserve even augmented its territory.

After bringing the six new *zapovedniki* to life in 1930, the Goskomitet, together with the Narkompros RSFSR Scientific Sector, energetically proceeded with the establishment of six more in 1931 and 1932,[66] and an audacious plan was drafted to double the territory of the reserve network by the end of the Second Five-Year Plan.[67]

As may be seen in appendix 1, the three-year period from 1930 through 1932 was another one of considerable territorial gains for the *zapovedniki* of the Soviet Union. In contrast to the growth from 1924 to 1929, however, this spurt was almost exclusively the result of the remarkable expansion of the reserve systems of the various republican Commissariats of Education, with Narkompros RSFSR in the lead.

The manifold bureaucratic vicissitudes in the administration of forestry and hunting during the period of the First Five-Year Plan had taken its toll on the dynamism of the systems of utilitarian reserves. Some had been left to fend as best they could under local control. Others probably withered on the vine. By the time that the remaining former reserves of Narkomzem RSFSR finally had found their way to the fold of Narkomvneshtorg USSR in 1931–1932, Narkompros's burgeoning network had just about wiped out the huge territorial advantage that had been held by the game-management *zapovedniki.*

Conservationists long had looked on Narkompros with affection. It was their institutional haven and had long defended their interests forcefully and with no small degree of skill. By 1931, however, elements of disenchantment began to intrude into the relationship. This was particularly the case following Lunacharskii's resignation as Narkompros's commissar in September 1929, an event which reflected the political repudiation of the Commissariat of Education's more humanistic vision of communism and its political eclipse by the economic commissariats. Narkompros's inadequate funding of the Goskomitet, always a sore point, was the spark that set off open grumbling at the committee's plenary session in January 1931. The plenum first noted that "the attention paid to [the Goskomitet] by the Scientific Sector is totally inadequate"; that the committee had, absurdly, been "expected to function in the absence of its own budget or of any allocation of funds (as has been the case)"; and that "a far-off, drawn-out resolution of this situation would be intolerable." It then "categorically insist[ed] on the approval in full of the budget that had been duly presented to the director of the Scientific Sector for operations of the Goskomitet for 1931 in the sum of 41,047 rubles and 55 kopecks."[68]

At the very same plenum, the Goskomitet unsuccessfully advanced a bold bid to exercise overall leadership over the work of the various biological research institutes of the Narkompros system "in order to avoid parallelism" in research and "to exploit more productively the experience and knowledge embodied in these institutions."[69] Clearly, the Goskomitet was chafing in its restricted role subordinate to the Scientific Sector of a not-very-influential ministry.[70]

Yet, there were even more compelling reasons why the Goskomitet now sought to break out of its parochial official status. Not least among them was that by 1932 the decisions of the Goskomitet were routinely ignored by the most powerful economic agencies. Things had come to such a low point that representatives of Narkomvneshtorg, VSNKh, and other agencies even failed to attend those meetings of the Goskomitet Presidium at which they were to have presented their annual procurement plans.[71]

While the need to enhance the authority and power of the Goskomitet seemed to dictate that it emerge from out of the shadow of the Education Commissariat, a different need likewise behooved it to enlarge its geographical scope, up to now juridically limited to the Russian Republic. Kulagin and Kozhevnikov had highlighted the need for an all-Union organ as early as 1930. They noted that the good of conservation measures in one republic could easily be undone when animals unwittingly migrated to the less hospitable territory of another. Additionally, the Goskomitet, while already assuming de facto leadership in the planning and administration of *zapovedniki* across the Soviet Union, particularly those of the various republican Narkompros systems,[72] lacked legal authority outside the RSFSR, however, and could only organize and advise, but not truly supervise. Many conservationists recognized the value of coordinating *zapovednik* research, both thematically and methodologically, as well as the urgent need to coordinate procurement plans among the republics. Taken together, these arguments made a powerful case for upgrading the Goskomitet.[73]

Even the Narkompros Executive Council was constrained to acknowledge that "the Goskomitet has not become truly interagency in character" and that its effectiveness, influence, and relative standing among other agencies was "not commensurate with its serious mission . . . as an interagency organ for planning and developing measures for *all* agencies and economic organs aimed at the . . . development, rational use, and conservation of the natural resources of the nation."[74]

The response of the Executive Council and of the republican Narkompros Scientific Sectors was to urge the Goskomitet to broaden use of its power to subpoena information and to hold inquests on the activities of the economic agencies and review their production plans and annual reports. Likewise, urged the Narkompros officials, in carrying on its "decisive struggle with . . . the rapacious

use of the nation's resources" the Goskomitet should be more vigorous in publiciz-
ing its case in the national press and, if need be, in "calling the guilty to account
through the organs of the Workers'-Peasants' Inspectorate and the prosecutor's
office." The Education Commissariat even indicated its willingness to petition the
Presidium of the All-Russian Central Executive Committee to provide a permanent
staff for the conservation agency, with an adequate subsidy to cover salaries,
scientific reports, the cost of operations, travel, and a network of inspectors.
Ultimately, the Narkompros report resolved to gain a pledge from the commissariat's bursar-expediter that the Goskomitet would now enjoy "normal conditions for its current operations," presumably including the timely and adequate
disbursement of funds—a sore point of the recent past.[75]

Narkompros's professions of renewed interest in the Goskomitet, however,
came too late. The conservation lobby's calculation of its own self-interest had
already propelled a search for a change in the committee's juridical status and for a
more powerful institutional patron. By 1932, these sentiments had come out into the
open. At the conclusion of two extraordinary expanded sessions of its plenum, the
Goskomitet adopted a resolution urging that it be placed under the jurisdiction of the
USSR Central Executive Committee, with the *zapovedniki* under the Goskomitet's
direct administration.[76] Additionally, it was decided to request the upgrading of
VOOP, the All-Russian Society for Conservation, to an all-Union organization.[77]

When Kulagin and Kozhevnikov first identified the need to upgrade the status
of the Goskomitet in 1930, they sought the speedy convocation of an all-Union
conservation congress as proposed by the 1929 all-Russian congress in order to
discuss and implement their suggestion. Although an organizational committee for
the all-Union congress, chaired by Smidovich, had been named by the 1929
congress, the committee apparently had done very little. By early 1931, the
Goskomitet took matters into its own hands and began preparatory work for the
proposed all-Union gathering. After two organizational meetings in the late spring,
5 September 1931 was set as the opening day of the congress, whose 130 invited
delegates would be hosted by V. V. Stanchinskii's research base at Askania-Nova.
A new organizational bureau consisting of members of the Scientific Sector of
Narkompros of the Ukrainian SSR was entrusted with the actual arrangements, with
an initial meeting scheduled for 10 July 1931 at Khar'kov.[78]

Despite its energetic beginnings, however, this effort, too, proved barren. The
fifth of September came and went, but at Askania no gavel called the conservation
congress to order. Access to those Soviet archives that might shed some light on the
reasons for the cancellation is restricted, so it is only possible to conjecture. There
is, however, one suggestive piece of evidence. A few months after the proposed
convocation of the congress at Askania, the Faunistics Conference of the Academy
of Sciences' Zoological Institute convened in Leningrad on 3 February 1932, some
365 delegates strong. Almost all of the USSR's leading conservation biologists
were in attendance. While nominally under the aegis of the Zoological Institute, the
conference was actually organized under the guiding hand of I. I. Prezent and the
Leningrad branch of the Communist Academy. Prezent, whose vast ambition and

whose animus toward Stanchinskii are now clear, must have played an important behind-the-scenes role in the cancellation of the Askania event. It was, after all, obviously to his advantage to assemble the biologists in Leningrad, on his own turf, where he, and not Stanchinskii, would control the conference and where he now hoped to appear before the doyens of Soviet biology as its new, undisputed theoretician.

ELEVEN

The Great Transformation of Nature

By a cruel coincidence theoretical ecology in the Soviet Union was making its greatest strides precisely at the time that the social and philosophical climate became increasingly unpropitious for its further development.[1] As early as the Third All-Russian Congress of Zoologists in 1928 scientists were aware of the importance of that frontier of biology, and even voted to organize a commission to standardize "biosociological nomenclature" to report back to the next congress.[2]

Although the commission was never constituted, the matter was raised again at the Fourth Congress of Zoologists (now All-Union) meeting in Kiev in May 1930. Recognizing V. V. Stanchinskii's growing leadership in the young field, the delegates conferred responsibility for organizing the commission—now set to report to the Fifth Congress—jointly on him and hydrobiologist S. A. Zernov.[3] Moreover, the congress, pronouncing the "extraordinary importance" of ecology "not simply from the applied but also from the theoretical point of view" sought to ensure ecology "its rightful place in the curriculum of higher pedagogical and agricultural schools."[4]

ECOLOGY AT APOGEE

In early 1931, Daniil Nikolaevich Kashkarov completed the Soviet Union's first great survey textbook of community ecology, *Environment and Community,* which was later published in English under the auspices of the New York State Museum at the initiative of the museum's director, ecologist Charles Christopher Adams, who knew Kashkarov.[5] Conceived as a manual designed to disseminate ecological principles among a large readership in the life sciences, Kashkarov's work was pioneering, treating such essential themes as the dynamics of ecological communities over time, ecological succession, the evolution of communities, paleoecology, methods of synecological fieldwork, and the problem of ecological terminology. *Environment and Community* also included one of the first comprehensive treatments of the history of ecology and represented, consequently, an invaluable bibliographical guide to the field. Finally, Kashkarov's book took note of the new and important studies in the "biology of production"—that ecological direction that sought "to explain as fully as possible, in concrete figures, the individual steps in the economy of nature of the cycling of organic matter and the quantitative calculation of the value of each of those steps"—citing in particular two recent seminal articles on trophic dynamics by Stanchinskii.[6]

Quantification and symbolic expression of ecological relationships, however, was not being pursued by Stanchinskii exclusively. Increasingly, other researchers, particularly in the *zapovedniki* but also at the large universities, were caught up in the analytical quantification of ecology. V. Bukovskii, an ecologist who studied the oak forest communities of the Crimean *zapovednik* and who had been influenced by the sociological-structuralist school of V. A. Dogel' and V. N. Beklemishev,[7] was an early convert to Stanchinskii's paradigm as well as to the application of statistics to community ecology. In *Okhrana prirody* early in 1931, Bukovskii called not only for the application of the "quantitative method" to the study of biocenoses, but also for special emphasis on the study of energy requirements and specific nutritional needs of individual species. "In particular," he noted, "a knowledge of the theory of probability is absolutely necessary for every ecologist and biocenologist." This was a point which needed an aggressive defense, for, as Bukovskii percipiently observed, "many biologists harbor[ed] feelings of revulsion toward mathematics."[8] Such negative attitudes toward the application of mathematics to biology were especially characteristic of the younger, party-minded biologists, and would soon become a hallmark of Prezent and Lysenko's critiques of various fields within biology.

Aside from trophic dynamics, perhaps the most exciting work being done in the USSR in ecology involved the study of population dynamics. At the Moscow State University Zoological Museum, which Kozhevnikov had led until so recently,[9] the brilliant young ecologist Georgii Frantsevich Gauze set up shop in Vladimir Vladimirovich Alpatov's ecological laboratory. Working at first with natural populations of insects under field conditions in the North Caucasus and then with yeast and *Paramecium* in his laboratory, Gauze sought to identify those natural mechanisms that regulate the populations of organisms, given their theoretical ability to multiply exponentially. While he hypothesized that the limitation of the number of species in such biocenoses "is apparently connected with the limited number of 'ecological niches' which can be realized by different species without expelling one another" from the community, he saw the limits to the numbers of individuals for each member-species of the biocenosis as imposed by a natural feedback mechanism: the population's own density. While Gauze did not originate the notion of density-dependence as key to the self-regulation of animal populations and willingly acknowledged his debt to Raymond Pearl of Johns Hopkins University (whose ideas were brought to the USSR by V. V. Alpatov),[10] his genius lay in designing elegant laboratory experiments to illustrate the effects of density, refuge, and predation in simple biocenotic systems. These experiments immediately attained worldwide renown, adding to the luster of Soviet biocenology.

Pioneering the study of population dynamics in the field was Sergei Alekseevich Severtsov, who based his work on continuing observations made in the recently established Bashkir *zapovednik*. Severtsov also shared Gauze's view that the biocenosis, as a closed system, was marked by a stability of numbers among its

constituent species enforced by regulatory mechanisms. "Although species theoretically may multiply exponentially," he wrote, "in practice no species may expand its
numbers beyond a certain limit determined by what we shall call the differential
biological carrying capacity (ëmkost') of the biocenosis." This carrying capacity
was specifically determined by a variety of environmental limiting factors, for
instance the availability of specific sources of food or shelter or by predation and
parasitism. Perhaps the most important limiting factor, Severtsov said, concurring
with Pearl, Gauze, and Alpatov, was the population density of the species itself.
Excessively great population densities would lead to diminished food per capita,
which in turn would make more likely the spread of infectious diseases among the
weakened individuals. This factor of epidemics in population control was not the
least important, especially in the regulation of rodent pest populations.[11]

Complementary with his study of the role of density in the regulation of the
population size of species, Severtsov sought to determine, for each species, a
quantitative quotient of reproduction that represented the theoretically highest rate
of increase for a given species. This quotient would take into account such factors as
the average number of offspring per mating pair per year, the age at which females
became reproductively mature, the interval between two successive pregnancies,
and the ratio of males to females in the population. This quotient, however,
represented only a "biotic potential" of the species, emphasized Severtsov. In actual
natural conditions, each species' increase was strongly dampened by high juvenile
mortality, the death of reproductively mature individuals, and the density-
dependent factors just discussed. The real rate of increase for a species' population
in a stable biocenosis over the medium term was, it was thought, zero.

Severtsov pointedly reminded his readers that the very science of game management and of pest control could never hope to be effective without "a clear notion
of the processes of natural population growth and mortality of these animals in their
natural habitats." German zoologist Karl Friedrichs, recounted Severtsov, once
observed that the practical man could not wait for science's lengthy method to solve
immediate agricultural problems, and that scientists must sometimes offer palliatives. Exactly such a situation had materialized in the Soviet Union, where from the
late 1920s scientists were under great pressure to abandon "science for science's
sake" and to place their expertise at the immediate service of the practical goals of
socialist construction. Nevertheless, Severtsov bravely counseled his colleagues to
resist the temptation to purvey agronomic "snake oil" for the profound agricultural
problems of the day, noting that in agriculture, "just as in medicine, palliatives
rarely provide the needed results" and that an effective "cure" could come "only
after a full scientific study of the problem." True utility, founded on true knowledge, allowed for no short cuts.

Population dynamics research, he argued, could contribute vastly more to the
economy than could zapovedniki converted into game farms (a policy he regarded as
one brand of snake oil). Severtsov cited two examples. Had it been known ahead of
time that hares would have three consecutive fecund years followed by a massive
die-back in 1928–1929, then the population could have been thinned in 1926–1927
to maintain population stability, thereby assuring an undisrupted flow of pelts under

sound, human management. Conversely, the unusually severe winter of 1929–1930 left 57 percent of the female capercaillie in the Urals without broods. In that case, it was necessary to have declared a closed season. The *zapovednik,* declared Severtsov, should be the key to monitoring these developments in nature, and its observations and recommendations should serve as bases for game policy over the entire region for which the reserve served as an *etalon.* In this regard, he outlined a specific research program for each of the major Soviet *zapovedniki* in the area of population dynamics.[12]

Another example of community ecology at the service of the economic needs of the country was the research conducted by Professor N. A. Troitskii in the Caucasus *zapovednik.* In that reserve, despite its "production plans" (perhaps another exercise in protective coloration), a particularly valuable study was undertaken to determine how best to manage alpine pasturelands by means of an examination of the natural alpine meadows of the reserve and of patterns of natural foraging. On the basis of his research Troitskii recommended that ranges more suited to cattle grazing not be given over to sheep and goats, that overgrazing be eliminated, and that a proper crop rotation be followed. Significantly, these conclusions were endorsed by Professor A. M. Dmitriev, director of the Institute of Meadows of the Lenin All-Union Academy of Agricultural Sciences (VASKhNIL).[13]

Stanchinskii, Bukovskii, Sukachev, Beklemishev, Alekhin, Troitskii, Severtsov, Kashkarov, Zernov, Shalyt—these were only the most prominent members of a growing confraternity of Soviet ecologists involved with the study of natural communities in both their theoretical and practical aspects. Additionally, a younger group of talented ecologists, trained primarily in the *zapovedniki* by the more senior pioneers,[14] was preparing to add its contribution to the development of the new science. As late as 1931 things still looked so promising that the editors of the new *Journal of Ecology and Biocenology** boldly declared that the "natural economic and political conditions of our Union" permit those in ecology and biocenology "to state with the greatest assurance that . . . 'We shall catch up to and overtake our neighbors!' " With respect to ecology and biocenology, the editors perhaps too rashly concluded, "the USSR is a country of truly boundless possibilities!"[15]

It was not long, though, before the truly boundless possibilities of biocenology came into deep conflict with other truly boundless possibilities promised by the First Five-Year Plan. Obstacles to the further development of community ecology along the lines it had recently pursued emerged from the closing years of the 1920s. One main group of critics faulted some currents in biocenology for their apparent lack of concordance with dialectical principles. Singled out in particular was the reductionist phytosociological school of Pachoskii. Another group of critics trained their fire not on the content of ecological science as such but on the suspect "class-alien" backgrounds of many of that science's practitioners. However, these attacks were either limited to ecological theories that seemed to challenge central principles of

---

*Stanchinskii was editor-in-chief. His co-editors were Dr. Maks Liudovikovich Levin and Academician Boris Aleksandrovich Keller.

Marxian dogma or to individual ecologists as representatives of bourgeois academia and not as ecologists. Ecology and biocenology as sciences remained unassailed as legitimate new directions in biology, and even profited (although Sukachev disagreed) from the well-taken objections to the various teleological and overly speculative theories that had been popular during the 1920s. By 1931, though, the prospects for ecology as a whole were increasingly clouded by two related developments: the rise of a heroic mood in the land, and the coalescing of "Soviet" biology along the lines pointed to in Stalin's speeches of late 1929.

"MAN, IN CHANGING NATURE, CHANGES HIMSELF"

With the advent of the First Five-Year Plan the national imagination of Soviet Russia was stirred to dizzying heights, to borrow Stalin's notorious phrase. There were "no fortresses that Bolsheviks could not storm," the people incessantly were told, no projects that were too difficult for the will, talents, and strength of the Soviet people led by the party. At first, the people were told that the mastery of technology was the key to solving all of the economic tasks of socialist construction. Later, it was announced that cadres, not technology per se, would decide the whole issue. One element in these announcements, however, remained unchanging: the abiding conviction of the party that, through whatever instrumentality, everything would in fact be decided, resolved, accomplished.

This ebullient optimism was combined in the early 1930s with a great fear that if Soviet Russia failed to accomplish its economic miracle it would be overcome by the dark forces that had kept Russia in backwardness for so many centuries: rural primitiveness, the remnants of the old ruling classes, and hostile, spontaneous nature—all led now by international capitalism. This fear was quintessentially expressed in another of Stalin's aphorisms: "We are fifty to one hundred years behind the most advanced countries. We must close this gap in the span of ten years. Either we do that or they will sweep us away."[16]

No small portion of this fear was directed at elemental nature. Populist geologist L. Lukashevich once offered the thought that unless humans mastered an essentially hostile nature, they would remain passive victims of its caprice and mere playthings of its passions. Ultimately, nature would sweep us away as it did the dinosaurs. Russians, more so perhaps than most other peoples, were receptive to this way of looking at nature. After all, what other nation had experienced a greater sampling of the vast cruelty of elemental nature than the land of the *sukhovei* (parched wind), the frosty *buran* (ice wind), and lethal droughts and floods? As Kozhevnikov had pointed out, moreover, in Russia it was a lot harder, given its enormous unused expanses, to convince public opinion that nature had more to fear from humans than the other way around.[17]

Many politically active Soviets viewed nature as an obstacle to socialist construction that had to be conquered. Only a small minority placed equal or greater emphasis on the protection of nature. In the popular literature and the press, antipathy toward harsh nature frequently led authors to anthropomorphize nature.

Nature was portrayed almost as a consciously antisocialist force which needed to be suppressed. More than anything, this failure to despiritualize nature testified to the incomplete fashion in which the scientific revolution had been absorbed into Russian culture, despite a decade of Bolshevik scientific materialism. The prescription offered was enticing: nature had to be transformed and bent to human will—from the roots up.

Almost imperceptibly, from a multitude of disparate sources in the media and politics, a new slogan became colloquial: "the great transformation of nature." This slogan represented a new program wholly to refashion the natural environment. It was yet another example of the peculiar Stalinist attraction to the monumental and of the Soviet fascination with the imagined potentialities of engineering. This leitmotif of heroism was reflected in the literature of the period, which brims with tales of the dreams of the new Soviet technocrats. For these new state-builders, every molecule of nature became transmogrified into raw material for industry and agriculture.

Leonid Leonov's novel *Sot' (Soviet River)* is especially rich in these images. It transports us to magical Karelia, which was opened up to industry only in the 1930s. For the engineer Uvadiev, for example, there was a certain antagonism, even, toward nature: "From the moment when Uvadiev stepped onto the bank, a challenge was cast at the River Sot', . . . and it seemed as though the very earth beneath his feet was his enemy."[18] For the Soviet manager Sergei Potemkin, whose dream was to turn Karelia's pine forests into rivers of newsprint, virgin nature served no purpose. Untapped resources were wasted resources, since to his mind the only way to measure value was in reams of paper, rubles, and kopecks. In the end, Potemkin began to assume the dimensions of an American captain of industry:

> Gradually . . . his dream had swollen. . . . Potemkin sleeps not; he straightens and deepens the ancient beds of rivers, increasing fourfold their carrying capacity, . . . unites three provinces around his industrial infant, . . . opens a paper college. . . . Cellulose rivers flow to foreign lands, the percentage of cellulose in the newspaper world is tripled. The dreams urge on reality, and reality hastens on the dreams.[19]

Elsewhere in the novel, Leonov briefly lifts another veil from the inner life of the new Soviet engineer. A colleague has unexpectedly come upon the protagonist, Burago, gazing at the sky. "Burago is embarrassed," the narrator tells us, "as though there were something shocking for a Soviet engineer in being found looking at the stars."[20]

Maksim Gor'kii took up the war cry of nature-transformation with almost fanatic zeal. *Belomor,* the saga of the construction of the Baltic-White Sea Canal, written under his editorship, handily serves as an ideal complement to Leonov since the action also takes place in idyllic Karelia. Gor'kii's vision:

> Stalin holds a pencil. Before him lies a map of the region. Deserted shores. Remote villages. Virgin soil, covered with boulders. Primeval forests. Too much forest as a matter of fact; it covers the best soil. And swamps. The swamps are always crawling about, making life dull and slovenly. Tillage must be increased. The swamps must be drained. . . . The Karelian Republic wants to enter the stage of classless society as a

republic of factories and mills. And the Karelian Republic will enter classless society by changing its own nature.[21]

Gor'kii called upon the new poets to renounce the admiration of nature. "In the treatment of nature by poets most often rang out—and rings out—feelings of submissiveness, adulation. Praise of nature is praise of a despot," he declared. Gor'kii complained that poets almost as one fell silent at nature's "foul tricks" that "destroy thousands of lives and ruin the fruits of the people's labor." Rather, he intoned, they should have been "summon[ing] humankind to the struggle against Nature, for mastery over her, . . ." something that had never been done before by Russia's cultural confectioners. Poets must now champion "the struggle of collectively organized reason against the elemental forces of nature and against everything 'elemental' . . . in the formation of man. . . ."[22]

"In the Soviet Union," Gor'kii assured the readers of *Pravda* and *Izvestiia*, "scientifically organized reason *has* attained limitless freedom in its battle against the elemental forces of nature" (italics added). In his call to replace elemental nature with a human-contrived "second nature," Gor'kii roused his readers to "cover the sandy steppes with a green carpet, plant forests all over them, irrigate the arid lands with the water from rivers. We must plant trees and shrubs everywhere," he clamored, anticipating the grandiose shelter-belt schemes of the 1940s.[23]

Implicit in these passages from Gor'kii and Leonov is the premise that until nature is actively exploited by humans, it has no value to society. The idea that virgin nature provides valuable ecological services that ultimately enable society to continue to exploit the residual portion of the globe apparently was never considered seriously by these writers, while attempts to find aesthetic value in virgin nature were ridiculed as "submissiveness" and "adulation" or even derided as "quasi-religious behavior." This view of nature devoid of any but the most narrowly utilitarian values harks back to an earlier group of Russian revolutionaries, the Nihilists of the 1860s, who valued things for their immediate, concrete utility to the people, and not for their "abstract" qualities. This utilitarianism, as applied to nature, was typified by Bazarov, the hero of Ivan Turgenev's *Fathers and Sons,* who opines that "Nature is not a temple but a laboratory, and man is there to work."[24]

Another crucial line of thought was expressed in one of Gor'kii's most quoted aphorisms, inserted as the motto for *Belomor:* "Man, in changing nature, changes himself." Indeed, with the short passage of time, it was increasingly agreed that the New Soviet Man could consummate his self-creation only by turning vast nature into his giant plaything. "It seems to me," Gor'kii averred, "that this theme is the fighting theme for our time. . . ."[25] Future Soviet policies amply justified the writer's conviction. Gor'kii's motto became the slogan for a whole era.[26]

Gor'kii exemplified an entire current of "socialist realist" literature which helped to create a new aesthetic and a distinctive place for nature in the regime's symbology. The strong feeling of repulsion it harbored toward the wilderness, as Katerina Clark suggests, was a synecdoche for a disgust with everything "elemental," i.e., outside the rational control of humans. Perhaps nothing better epitomizes the Stalinist worldview than its irresistible craving for total *conscious* mastery over nature, people, and events. It is perhaps worth noting, as Clark has done, that this phobia of spontaneity and obsession with conscious control was no monopoly of Bolshevism but pervaded the political culture of the entire radical Russian intelligentsia of the nineteenth century.[27] Human beings were seen as progressively evolving toward total mastery of the course of life on the planet, supplanting spontaneity everywhere with consciousness, becoming a this-worldly god to replace the toppled gods of religion. (It is hardly surprising that Gor'kii was one of the central figures of the "God-builders" group.)[28]

The first full-scale attempt to realize these heroic visions was made during the years of the First Five-Year Plan. Of the enormous construction projects, the best known is undoubtedly the aforementioned "Belomor," but the most massive was the Volga-Caspian project, which envisioned not merely "petty" changes to promote navigability on the waterways but a wholesale diversion of the flow of Central Russia's rivers to supply water to irrigate its thirsty steppes.[29] Although these projects quickly became matters of concern for the USSR's community of ecologists and other biologists, another kind of project elicited the most worry among those specialists: a proposal to transform the biocenoses of the USSR from their natural states, beginning with the widespread acclimatization of exotic flora and fauna.

ACCLIMATIZATION

For many, acclimatization represented the practical application of nineteenth-century evolutionary doctrines associated with Etienne and Isidore Geoffroy Saint-Hilaire and Lamarck. Brought to Russia and modified by Karl Frantsevich Rul'e, these doctrines taught that organisms could be made to adapt gradually *to* new environments *by* the new environments themselves (including artificial, human-made environments) in a directed and, ultimately, *predictable* way. What was more, the functional adaptations produced by the environment's action could then be hereditarily passed along to the organisms' progeny (the inheritance of acquired characteristics).[30]

The tenacity of the appeal of environmental inductionist doctrines in Russian biology was demonstrated by the persistence of the Rul'e school through his disciples A. P. Bogdanov, S. A. Usov, N. A. Severtsov, and A. N. Beketov and their students, most notably N. F. Kashchenko (named by the Ukrainian Academy of Sciences in 1918 to a new chair for acclimatization as a full member), V. L. Komarov, P. A. Manteifel', and N. M. Kulagin.

One of the first concrete proposals for acclimatization of exotic fauna appeared in a hunting journal in 1915.[31] The author, N. A. Smirnov, a staff member of the Agriculture Department's Hunting and Fishing Section, championed the introduction of the North American muskrat, which, he claimed, would speedily convert the economically unproductive boggy expanses of the Russian North into a lucrative source of exportable, high-quality pelts. However, there was no response to his wartime proposal, and the matter was temporarily dropped. Hunting specialist V.

Ia. Generozov revived the question six years later, when he proposed that a small group of muskrats be introduced to Kafinskoe Lake southeast of Petrograd on an experimental basis. This, too, came to naught, owing to the objections of a number of hunting and fishing specialists who sought to bar the rodent from the Russian mainland.[32] Only the creation of the Central Forest Experimental Station of the RSFSR People's Commissariat of Agriculture in 1922 under the forceful leadership of Boris Mikhailovich Zhitkov put real life into the campaign for acclimatization. Again, the introduction of the muskrat was the pioneering centerpiece of the new campaign; the aquatic rodent had become a symbol for the entire program.

In 1925 Zhitkov took the case for acclimatization once more to the public in *Pushnoe delo* (The Fur Trade).[33] This time, though, conditions were more propitious for a favorable reception of the idea. In particular, prices for pelts in the international market were high and still rising, and both Narkomzem, the People's Commissariat of Agriculture, which employed Zhitkov as director of the Experimental Station's Hunting Biology Section, and Narkomtorg, the People's Commissariat of Trade, which Zhitkov served as a permanent scientific consultant, were enticed by the idea of this promising new source of revenue.

Zhitkov was not content to limit the acclimatization of exotic fauna to the confines of farms and breeding ranches when there were millions of hectares of underutilized virgin territory to transform. He saw no reason why the boundless woodlands of Russia should not be stocked to overflowing with all conceivable valuable life forms from every part of the globe. Cautiously, commencing with a plan to introduce a selection of game animals from similar climatic zones in Canada and South America (his initial efforts focused on the South American nutria as well as the muskrat), Zhitkov mobilized his supporters. Among the *praktiki* and politicos in Narkomzem and Narkomtorg and among the neo-Lamarckians in academic zoology, his plans met with increasing favor.

Nonetheless, by Zhitkov's own account, the idea of acclimatizing the muskrat to Russia was met at first by "violent objections," which became all the more strenuous "when it was proposed to introduce the muskrat not only in the tundra, but in the Ukraine as well."[34] Initially, the most telling arguments derived from ecological thinking. Opponents hoped that by stopping the muskrat, they could derail the entire push for introduction of exotics.

One of the first critiques of Zhitkov's plans appeared in *Pushnoe delo* only three issues after Zhitkov's own article had been published there. "From previous experience of the introduction of various animals and plants in foreign countries and their successful acclimatization to their new habitats," warned veterinary parasitologist Sergei Vasil'evich Kertselli, "we have numerous examples of the extraordinarily pernicious damage [caused by acclimatization], damage which is proportional to the ease with which the new species adapts itself." Kertselli asked the readers to recall the naturalization of the rabbit in Australia and that of the English sparrow in America. "Now, both America and Australia are waging a most bitter war with those alien species," observed Kertselli. Other examples of damaging consequences of acclimatization were the importation of grapevines from America, which brought with them *Phyloxera,* an aphid that nearly wiped out the

French viticultural industry when it spread to nonresistant European vines. Such unexpected and unwanted results could also follow the introduction of the muskrat to continental Russia.[35]

One scenario presented by Kertselli envisioned the destructive possibilities accompanying the penetration of the muskrat to the delta regions of the Volga and Don rivers. Although the diet of the rodent in its native habitat consisted primarily of boggy and aquatic vegetation, it was also known to be quite fond of roe and young fry; the proponents of its acclimatization could not guarantee that the rodent would not alter its feeding habits, shifting principally to fish roe and young, with vegetation becoming only supplementary. This was not inconsequential, since the penetration by the muskrat to spawning grounds of such valuable fish as salmon and sturgeon could cause significant disruption to the Soviet fishing industry.

These likely dangers, partly substantiated by the experiences of the muskrat's introduction in Germany, Hungary, and Czechoslovakia, "compel us to be extremely cautious in approaching [this] problem," wrote Kertselli. "In any case," he warned, "it requires us, in preparation of any massive introduction of the muskrat, to undertake wide-ranging experiments and research, which would graphically indicate any pernicious effects the introduction of the muskrat might have under our conditions." It would be better, he recommended, to get on with the business of putting the game procurement sector aright through the protection of such endangered endemic species as the desman; "experiments with muskrats, deflecting our attention from the urgent, unpostponable measures we need to take to put the hunting sector in order, will create the appearance of intensive work . . . while eliciting a deceptively harmful conviction that we are putting our hunting sector back on its feet."[36]

S. A. Buturlin's objections, in the same vein, referred more explicitly to the ecological notion that the introduction of exotic fauna would destroy the equilibrium of natural communities. "To destroy the equilibrium of living forces forged over the centuries and millennia is an easy thing," he submitted, "but to predict what will emerge from that is not so easy, for the threads that tie all of the living phenomena of the land together are so countlessly numerous, so fine, and, frequently, so unexpected."[37] Buturlin chided those who insisted that, since the muskrat does not seem to cause harm in its North American homeland, it would also prove rather benign in the superficially analogous conditions of the Russian North. Such argumentation he regarded as "naive" demonstrations of ecological ignorance. "They took the bait in Western Europe," he concluded, "and have already shed tears of regret. . . ."[38]

Finally, there were those who objected, in the words of the editors of *Sovetskii sever* (The Soviet North), to "the completely fantastic plans and calculations of profitability that accompanied the agitation in support of the muskrat's acclimatization, . . . claims [which], already shown to be baseless, were of course not promoted by the Central Forest Experimental Station."[39]

Zhitkov's proposal had generated a great deal of discussion among biologists, and not a few sharp exchanges into the bargain. Two specially convened conferences were even held to air the issues, the first on 31 October 1927 at the Society for the Study of the Urals, Siberia, and the Far East, and the second early the next year under the auspices of Gostorg.[40]

Rebutting those critics who pointed to the unsatisfactory experience of the Central European countries, Zhitkov countered that Finland, whose conditions matched those of the Soviet Far North far more closely, was quite happy with its acclimatized muskrats. Besides, he argued, "it is difficult to imagine what sort of perceptible harm the muskrat could bring north of the sixtieth parallel," which he now accepted as the southernmost point for the animal's introduction.[41]

While a majority favored acclimatization, delegates to the first muskrat conference also felt constrained to make an important concession to the voices of caution, recommending that there be preliminary experiments introducing the muskrat under isolated conditions, on an island in the Arctic Ocean, perhaps, or within fenced-in shelters in the Far North.[42]

Even at the second Gostorg conference the proponents of acclimatization still felt constrained to proceed with great circumspection.[43] The need for caution was further underscored by the failure of a first acclimatization attempt involving eleven muskrats purchased from Finland in late 1927 and settled at the Timiriazev Biological Station of the Young Naturalists in Sokol'niki Park: the lone female quickly perished.[44] Thus, when Gostorg proposed that the first party of some five hundred animals scheduled to arrive from Canada in May 1928 be experimentally introduced in the region of Lake Slobodskoe in Arkhangel'sk uezd on the Russian mainland, this plan was rejected by the conference in favor of one using the Solovetskie Islands.[45]

These cautionary tones were also voiced at the Third All-Russian Congress of Zoologists, which met in Leningrad in mid-December 1927. There, the Section on Applied Zoology, in its resolution concerning a talk given by N. I. Dergunov of the Young Naturalists, held that "acclimatization of exotic species must be conducted in a planned fashion, and only pursuant to approval granted by such competent institutions as the Academy of Sciences' Zoological Museum, the Goskomitet, and the RSFSR People's Commissariat of Agriculture, together with ratification by the country's legislative organs."[46] At the same congress, helminthologist A. A. Paramonov additionally warned that under no circumstances should the muskrat be permitted to invade the territory of the native desman, for it would surely outcompete the latter and seal the extinction of that already threatened Russian endemic.[47]

With the rapid and profound developments in politics, economics, and society that came on the heels of the Fifteenth Party Congress, however, the political balance in the field of biology began to alter. In mid-1928, an article by a militant acclimatizer appeared in *Pushnoe delo* that openly criticized the "half-hearted compromises" represented by the resolutions of the two conferences on acclimatization.[48] The next year, Academician N. F. Kashchenko once again revived his propaganda campaign in favor of acclimatization, arguing now that such a program would not only reduce the dependence of the USSR on foreign imports and "proletarianize" the availability of former luxury items (such as subtropical fruits), but would also completely transform nature into the obedient servant of human society:

> The final goal of acclimatization, understood in the broad sense, is a profound rearrangement of the entire living world — not only that portion which is now under the domination of humanity but also that portion that has still remained wild. Generally speaking, all wild species will disappear with time; some will be exterminated, others will be domesticated. All living nature will live, thrive, and die at none other than the will of humans and according to their designs. These are the grandiose perspectives that open up before us.[49]

Within a very short span of time, acclimatization as a program for a miraculous augmentation of nature's productivity gained what amounted to quasi-official status. As in the mid-nineteenth century, acclimatization (and, soon thereafter, Lysenko's vernalization and interspecific hybridization "discoveries") advertised itself as a technological fix for Russian agriculture. Now, as in the 1850s, its appeal was magnified by the crying need to make Russian agriculture more productive, given the impossibility of tampering in any way with the political and economic organization of the countryside. Under post-1928 conditions, the only hope for increased productivity came from technological improvement—agronomic miracles. Acclimatization was in perfect resonance with the new mood of Soviet Russia, its "daring to discount scientifically established norms" in favor of intuitive knowledge. Conditions were ripe for the elevation to official policy of a concrete program that promised to make a reality of the utopian vision—that great transformation of nature—eulogized by Soviet leaders and literati alike. Little did it matter that such visions were based on dubious scientific foundations.

Initially, acclimatization's popularity as a new agronomic approach made great gains, while the inductionist theories of heredity upon which it was based remained in the background. Until the fall of the Deborinites and even later, Mendelian genetic theory was still quite influential in the Communist Academy and elsewhere, not having yet been recognized as a theory that set stringent limits on organisms' abilities to adapt to new environmental conditions and to transmit those adaptations to their progeny. That is, Mendelian genetics was not yet seen as a foe of acclimatization and of the great transformation of nature.

For their part, the geneticists were slow to appreciate the neo-Lamarckian challenge lurking behind the acclimatization campaign. As a matter of fact, one of the acknowledged leaders of the Mendelian school in the Soviet Union, Academician Nikolai Ivanovich Vavilov, had been a warm supporter of introductions, although his conception of the mechanism of that process was necessarily different from that of acclimatization's neo-Lamarckian promoters.[50]

Although Vavilov had devoted his entire life to amassing foreign varieties of cultivars, including many thousands of wild varieties and species, with the aim of utilizing them on Russian soil, his approach to their acclimatization indelibly was colored by his training as a Mendelian geneticist. He put no stock in the ability of plants or other organisms to develop heritable alterations as adaptive responses to new environmental conditions. Instead, for each species of crop plant Vavilov sought to combine the most useful genetic features presented by the numerous varieties and subspecies he had collected in the greenhouses and nurseries of the All-Union Institute for Plant Breeding. This program of *intra*specific hybridization was painstakingly slow, since it was still not clear which genes controlled what traits, whether they were recessive or dominant, or whether particular genes were transmitted singly or were linked in clusters with other genes.

Through late 1931, then, a rather peculiar situation obtained; acclimatization as a program and as an objective was gaining a more and more prominent place in socialist construction, but Soviet officialdom had not yet made it known which version of acclimatization—neo-Lamarckian or Vavilovian—it preferred.

In late 1927, a second group of twenty muskrats arrived from Finland destined for the Solovetskie Islands. In June 1928, thirty-five more muskrats arrived from Ontario at Petropavlovsk-na-Kamchatke and were released on Karaginskii Island in the Sea of Okhotsk. In September and October, 110 more arrived from Finland and ten from America, with 99 released on the Solovetskie Islands and the remainder transferred to the Pushkinskii Breeding Farm near Moscow. In May 1929 from Montreal a steamer brought another thousand or so of the burly rodents, which were again divided between the Solovetskie Islands and the Pushkinskii farm. That autumn, part of the population at the Pushkinskii farm were released into the wild in Krasnoiarsk *krai* and in the Arkhangel'sk and Tiumen' oblasts. In 1932 yet another shipment of muskrats arrived from Finland and England, totaling 1,662 animals, bringing the overall total number imported into the USSR since 1927 to 2,543. Of that number, by 1932 almost 1,650 (plus over 2,000 of their progeny) had been released over the entire Soviet North, from Murmansk Oblast in the west to Kamchatka in the east, and as far south as Buriat Mongolia and Vologda.[51]

Other animals soon became drawn into the acclimatization campaign. The raccoon dog (*Nyctereutes procyonides* Gray), a furry predator native to the Soviet Far East and Manchuria, was introduced at first to the Baikal region, and soon thereafter to the central Urals and parts of the Volga Basin.[52] Also from the Far East, the sika deer found itself the object of a plan to transplant it to the North Caucasus. In connection with this last proposal, the plan's author even had recommended "the complete extermination in the greater portion of the . . . Transcaucasus of the local, Caucasian race of red deer" in order to eliminate a less-valuable potential competitor among the endemic fauna. Also recommended were such "zootechnical" measures as winter feeding of the sika.[53]

With respect to the nutria, which Zhitkov was promoting alongside the musk-rat, efforts directed toward the South American rodent's naturalization picked up steam in 1930 after the Central Forest Experimental Station was transferred from Narkomzem RSFSR ultimately to the Commissariat of Foreign Trade, Narkomvneshtorg USSR. Expeditions to the Caucasus, Dagestan, Kazakhstan, and Turkmenia, staffed by members of Zhitkov's collective, were now funded by the Peltry Association, Soiuzpushnina, to find suitable areas for the animal's introduction. By 1931, several groups of nutria had already been released in the lower reaches of the Kura River in the Caucasus and in the flood plain of the Amu-Dar'ia near Chardzhou.[54]

As for nonmammalian organisms, a call for the all-out acclimatization of fish to basins not native for them was issued at the Fourth All-Union Congress of Zoologists in 1930,[55] while L. A. Zenkevich in 1932 opened a campaign to introduce Black Sea invertebrates (principally Nereids) to the Caspian Sea as a nutritional supplement for the basin's commercial fisheries. In that year also the first grey mullet were introduced into the Caspian.[56]

Finally, the introduction of exotic plants was the subject of A. P. Il'inskii's speech at the 1929 conservation congress and of G. N. Shlykov's report to the VASKhNIL Socialist Agriculture and Stockbreeding Conference in Voronezh in February 1933.[57] It was also the object of ongoing work of the All-Union Institute for Plant Breeding, with which both men were affiliated.

By 1932 acclimatization was a subject for discussion at virtually every major meeting concerned with botany, zoology, or agronomy, and was well on its way to becoming an official state policy. It had prospered because, like the notion of harnessing Russia's rivers, it appealed to the heroic impulse of the times, the drive to subject the elemental to human consciousness and will.

TWELVE

Engineers of Nature

Although the new schemes to alter the face of Russian nature filled Soviet conservationists with considerable apprehension, most upsetting were the increasing suggestions that the *zapovedniki* themselves be co-opted into this campaign. Specifically, spokespersons from the People's Commissariats of Agriculture and Foreign Trade (Narkomzem and Narkomvneshtorg), as well as would-be arbiters of biology, intensified their pressure on the People's Commissariat of Education (Narkompros) and its *zapovedniki* decisively to abandon their traditional emphasis on holistic ecological studies under inviolable conditions. Instead, Narkompros's critics sought to refashion the *zapovedniki* into staging areas not merely for the acclimatization of exotic flora and fauna, but for the "planned reconstruction" of their ecological agglomerations.

ACCLIMATIZATION: THE MUSKRAT'S TEPID WELCOME

As early as the Civil War period, several years before Zhitkov's 1925 article galvanized official support for acclimatization generally, Shillinger had begun to advocate "the necessity of using *zapovednik* territories for the reacclimatization and acclimatization of valuable forms of animals and birds," a position that was not all that surprising in view of Shillinger's training as a hunting specialist. At that time, however, Shillinger said he was "conclusively" rebuked by his fellow conservationists. Accusing him of "scientific ignorance," his colleagues defended the view that any such interference with the natural course of events in *zapovedniki* was "impermissible." The *zapovednik,* in their view, was an inviolable territory, while acclimatization was regarded not as a bold experiment but as "an infestation of . . . alien species."[1] This was also the official viewpoint of Glavnauka, Narkompros's Main Administration for Scientific Institutions.

Undeterred, Shillinger continued to argue "at every available opportunity" for his program, particularly with the aim of developing commercial hunting opportunities. In this he was gradually joined by a growing number of other prominent figures in the Russian game biology field.

In late 1927, at the Third All-Russian Congress of Zoologists, the question of acclimatization in the *zapovedniki* was first publicly posed. By then, proponents of such measures included Professor M. A. Menzbir of Moscow University as well as

Zhitkov and Buturlin. Indeed, specific plans for the introduction of exotic game-birds to the Crimean *zapovednik* already had been proposed.[2]

As reported to the zoological congress by Ivan Ivanovich Puzanov, longtime scientific worker in the Crimean reserve, these plans were greeted with bitter objections from yet other scientists. This group, whose most outspoken representatives included Stanchinskii, Kozhevnikov, Sukachev, V. E. Martino, and botanist V. E. Vul'f, defended the principle of the absolute inviolability of the *zapovedniki* absolutely.[3]

Puzanov sought to mediate between what he considered to be the two extreme positions of precipitous acclimatization and an unyielding defense of absolute inviolability. To those upholding the latter viewpoint Puzanov objected that the vast majority of territories now comprising *zapovedniki,* in his estimation, was no longer virgin and undespoiled, as was presumed; rather, those lands had already been impoverished by the direct and indirect actions of human economic activity. Good examples of this were to be found in the Crimean reserve, where major mammalian species had only recently become extinct, and in the proposed Central Forest *zapovednik,* where beaver had flourished until only a few decades before. An inflexible defense of inviolability, he observed, precluded taking measures to restore the fauna to the variety that existed prior to its impoverishment at the hands of society; such a defense seemed, at the very least, illogical to Puzanov, who considered the worthiness of restoring faunal variety in *zapovedniki* through reacclimatization to be indisputable. Obviously, in his belief that the only "harmonious development" in the *zapovedniki* would come as a result of human management, Puzanov differed cardinally from Kozhevnikov's view that they embodied models of healthy, harmonious nature already.[4]

On the other hand, Puzanov's readiness to intervene in the natural course of events in *zapovedniki* was not unbounded; he rejected a policy of indiscriminate introductions of exotic species into the reserves. Acclimatization of exotics he labeled an exceptional measure which should only be permitted when it involved species from the same general geographical zone. Exotics from other continents and sharply divergent natural communities should remain home, he advised; such acclimatization not only ran counter to aesthetics but also posed the danger of ecological infestation. As a final condition Puzanov insisted that the actual acclimatization experiments be conducted exclusively in the reserves' buffer zones (as opposed to the inner, absolute zones), where human intervention in nature was already permitted on a limited scale but where the experimentally introduced animals could continue to enjoy protection from outsiders.[5]

At the 1929 conservation congress, Puzanov maintained his self-designated middle ground, but the convocation still had its share of defenders of absolute inviolability. First to take the floor in rebuttal to any concessions to the acclimatizers was Smolensk University zoologist Grigorii Leonidovich Grave.[6] He weightily pronounced that *zapovedniki* as such would cease to exist if they were turned into experimental farms. He agreed with Puzanov that reacclimatization was possible, but not the introduction of exotics. Also taking the floor against any human intervention in the reserves was Stanchinskii's future colleague at Askania-Nova,

Boris Konstantinovich Fortunatov, who pithily observed that "an *etalon* must remain undisrupted, or else it ceases to be an *etalon*."[7]

In late autumn 1930, the debate reached a new low, when *Okhrana prirody* published a lengthy letter to the journal's editors. Its author, Vladimir Vladimirovich Karpov, was a relatively minor figure in Soviet biology—a specialist in pest control who had worked on the problem of slug infestation with N. I. Vavilov for the Moscow Provincial Zemstvo before the First World War. Karpov had also been a longtime member of Kozhevnikov's Moscow Province Faunistics Commission,* and had latterly been associated with the Timiriazev Agricultural Academy, the Biological Station of the Young Naturalists organization, Narkomzem's Institute for Correspondence Courses, and the Youth Institute of the Central Committee of the Komsomol.

The prime targets of Karpov's thorned shaft were those conservationists in VOOP who believed that *zapovedniki* should remain inviolate. These he described as

> university professors still having their supporters in our society [i.e., VOOP], [who feel] that we must fence off nature from every human interference, since with the slightest violation of its virgin condition it would allegedly "lose its interest for science." With regard to the *zapovedniki* this means that any sort of economic activity in them would be impermissible, and even the idea of stocking them with wild furbearers or ungulates must be rejected in order not to "infect" the nature of the *zapovednik* with alien elements.[8]

As Karpov characterized it, "a direct consequence of this academic viewpoint [was] the conclusion that game management in *zapovedniki* 'has nothing in common with the cause of conservation.'" This view reportedly was offered at a recent meeting of Moscow State University's Zoological Scientific Research Institute and Zoological Museum specifically convened to discuss the problem of the use of state *zapovedniki* for acclimatization. "Fortunately," Karpov revealed,

> at that meeting there were representatives of a second point of view; as a matter of fact, these were precisely the representatives of economic, fur-breeding, and science-planning organizations. They raised their voices for the right of humans not only to genuflect before nature but also to interfere with its laws, justly noting that man himself is also one of the elements of nature and not an unimportant one at that!

Having presented these overly schematized portraits of the two tendencies vying for control, Karpov rhetorically asked: "To which view ought our young society adhere, so that the cause of conservation is not condemned beforehand to the stagnation in which it has been mired up to now?"

The key to Karpov's answer lay in his deliberate distortion of the intentions of Kozhevnikov's approach and of the latter's conception of the *zapovednik*'s func-

---

*A study group under the auspices first of the Society of Naturalists, Anthropologists, and Ethnographers and then of the Moscow Society of Naturalists (which absorbed the former society circa 1930).

tion. Reducing the "old view" to an absurd caricature, Karpov declared that representatives of the Kozhevnikov viewpoint desired above all

> the preservation of nature in its unchanged state as it was at the moment at which we find it or, in other words, the permanent freezing of existing biocenoses.

However, noted Karpov, "in reality nature is continually changing, and that state in which we now find it today will become something different tomorrow." Why, he demanded to know, "is it so important to preserve existing biocenoses for all time, and why, for example, is growing a young forest in place of the old 'not interesting for science'?"

Karpov's distortion was particularly insidious, for the Kozhevnikov school, not unlike Karpov, nurtured a strong belief in the value of studying a dynamic, evolving nature. Indeed, nothing could have been further from Kozhevnikov's intentions than freezing a biocenosis for eternity at one particular stage of its development; such a position had nothing in common with Kozhevnikov's *etalon* concept, not even with the conviction that *zapovedniki* should be inviolate. Kozhevnikov's central interest, to underscore the point, was precisely to discover the natural laws governing "eternally changing biocenoses."[9]

Perhaps Kozhevnikov's view of change in nature as almost imperceptible, requiring centuries of study in order to uncover its laws, seemed little different from one of a stagnant, unchanging nature, particularly to the impatient breed of socialist constructors. They wanted to see change and to obtain results on the spot. Apparently unable to accept nature as it was, they were led to try to remake it as they felt it should be. Such appears to have been the case with Karpov in his closing call for "rational economic intervention" in the natural life of *zapovedniki:*

> It is evident that the old theory of conservation of nature for nature's sake—a proposition that reeks of ancient cults of Nature's deification—stands in such sharp opposition to both our economic and our scientific interests that there is no place for it in our land of socialism-in-the-making. . . . Not the preservation, come what may, of the existing state of nature, but the rational intervention, study, mastery, and regulation of natural productive forces—that is what should be emblazoned on the banners of our society.[10]

Although the Zoological Museum conference and Karpov's letter, which grew out of it, doubtless put pressure on the defenders of the ecological *zapovednik,* in the short run the latter held firm. In a rejoinder to Karpov's letter, the editors of *Okhrana prirody* showed that they could defend their positions with equal vigor. "Obviously," they taunted, "comrade Karpov was not aware of the new decree [of 20 June 1930][11] or else he would have known that the law provides for the preservation of typical, pristine parcels of nature—*zapovedniki*—for the purposes of *the study of the original conditions of nature prior to their transformation by human activity*" in addition to the organization of other types of reserves, devoted to more utilitarian tasks. "Comrade Karpov is right when he says that man can exterminate the larger animals of a given territory, and with great speed at that, and that he can then settle that territory with new species," wrote the editors, recapitulating Karpov's optimistic plans for transforming nature. However, they concluded trenchantly, man is "powerless to restore those species once they have disappeared," exposing the nature transformers' flawed and one-sided "mastery" of nature.[12]

Despite the renunciation of *zapovednik* inviolability by the new VOOP leader Makarov, the issue of acclimatization in the reserves (and outside of them) remained a live one. Rhetorical concessions failed to satisfy the transformers of nature, who would settle for nothing less than the sacrifice of the virgin *zapovedniki* on the altar of human-willed socialist construction.

THE 1932 FAUNISTICS CONFERENCE

The cancellation of the proposed all-Union conservation congress at Askania-Nova left the Academy of Sciences' Faunistics Conference, organized by I. I. Prezent, as the uncontested arena in which the relationship between biology and socialist construction was to be thrashed out.

With Stanchinskii's fortunes evidently already in decline,[13] the conference, whose slogan declared that science should turn its face toward socialist construction, was conspicuously dominated by Prezent. "The essence of this conference," he announced to the plenum, "is to pose clearly the tasks and the organizational base of science in the period of the construction of socialism." Prezent, who had already formed a distinct notion of those tasks and bases, now authoritatively shared them with his listeners:

> Objects of nature have ceased to be objects of contemplative study. . . . Soviet faunists must become inventors. They must develop concrete projects for the planned transformation of animal communities (cenoses) and for their geographical redistribution. We must master fauna and not only make it work for us, but we must reconstruct it as well so as to enhance its productivity.[14]

Prezent's address was a call to arms for Soviet biologists. Their experiments would "take on grandiose dimensions" and would "acquire a new importance now that they [were] linked with socialist construction."[15] Arguably, Prezent's talk was the most forceful and clearly stated summons to transform nature to be addressed to Russia's biology establishment. However, political developments had not yet progressed to the point where such pronouncements were accepted uncritically.

Makarov also spoke to the conference. Although he conceded the use of the *zapovednik* "to determine the possibility of introducing new life forms to the region for which it serves as an *etalon*," he placed most emphasis on the role of the *zapovednik* as a center for basic ecological research, albeit ultimately directed toward the solution of economic problems. This research did not include the pursuit of "narrowly defined economic activities," which, he charged, were the program of a "utilitarian deviation" that had no place in the *zapovedniki*.

For one reason or another, the hydrobiologists were bolder than the terrestrial ecologists. V. I. Zhadin of the Oka Biological Station laid special emphasis on how he and his fellow hydrobiologists sought to identify the ecological ramifications of large-scale construction projects on rivers, lakes, and other bodies of water. An impressive list of research teams was already conducting an equally impressive variety of studies on the effects of such staples of socialist construction as hydroelectric dams, reservoir dams, locks, navigational canals, drainage canals, irrigation canals, dredging, and water-treatment facilities on the affected ecosystems.[16] It was already clear that dams and other installations could have profound effects on the hydrology of their rivers, affecting flow-rate, temperature, dissolved oxygen, and other gases, and that dams presented obstacles to fish swimming upstream to spawn. The ecological effects of other alterations of water-courses were also thought to be considerable. Nevertheless, lamented Zhadin, the tempo of hydrobiological work "has far from kept pace with that of socialist construction," and it was now essential to direct all available energies in the field of aquatic ecology precisely to the exploration of these problems.

Another participant, Martsynovskii, was more candid. "I must state openly here that we are not yet prepared for the tasks awaiting us," he warned, noting the continuing inability of Soviet ecology to make reliable predictions about the impact of nature-transforming projects on natural communities. To illustrate the destructive potential of a rashly executed transformation of nature he cautioned that the creation of 40,000 ponds along the Volga, as some enthusiasts had recommended, could lead to a malaria epidemic of historic proportions.[17]

Hydrobiologist M. I. Tikhii added his misgivings, noting that Dneprostroi* did not take into account the interests of fishing during the construction. "We have to pose the problem of the impact on fishing *before* the construction is completed," he protested, "and not after the fact, as has been the case in the past."

B. V. Vlastov alerted the delegates to the threat to riverine fauna posed by the recent, frenetic pace of timber floating in Karelia and appealed to them to find some way to neutralize this threat. Others warned that the Black Sea littoral was now menaced by pollution. As D. A. Svirenko, director of the Dnepropetrovsk Biological Station, put it, "The question of the biocenosis is paramount."

Finally, there were those who openly rejected the entire premise of linking science to the needs of socialist construction. Curiously, the most outspoken were the entomologists. A. P. Semenov-tian-shanskii, breaking a long silence regarding conservation matters, asserted that the mighty Soviet hydroelectric projects were exercises in futility, because "all things change, everything flows on." The achievements of socialist construction were mere ephemera, according to him, which had been erected at the price of irreversibly disfiguring nature.[18] His colleague, Professor Mikhail Nikolaevich Rimskii-Korsakov of the Leningrad Forestry Academy, took issue with the new principle that science had to be party-minded. The professor, it was recorded, "threw an open challenge to the conference's entomological section . . . by announcing that 'science has no party, and if it is partisan, then there is nothing for us to do here,' " whereupon he walked out of the meeting.[19]

That the conference "decisively condemned such outbursts" was nothing ex-

---

*The great hydroelectric dam astride the Dnepr River at Zaporozh'e, the largest such project in Europe prior to World War II.

ceptional. Nor was its declaration that "the slogan 'science for science's sake' is noxious to the proletarian state."[20] After all, Semenov-tian-shanskii and Rimskii-Korsakov were well-bred gentlemen-scientists of the old type who never quite accepted the reality of the new order. More disquieting were the invidious comments directed at the methodology and orientation of some of the loyal, yet critical, ecologists. In the hydrobiology section, V. D. Bolkovitianov, director of the Pacific Scientific Institute of the Fishing Industry, launched into a vociferous attack on the application of statistics to biology. His solution for the problems facing Soviet biologists was simple: rely on the guidance of I. I. Prezent's Biological Cabinet of the Communist Academy.[21]

Censured as well was the presentation of D. A. Lastochkin of the Central Scientific Institute for the Fishing Industry. Lastochkin, who spoke on the methods of quantitative measurement of benthos and plankton, themes that closely corresponded to Stanchinskii's interests in productivity and biomass, was severely upbraided for his aloofness from problems of socialist construction. "Where in his talk is there mention of the need for our planned economy's active intervention [in nature]?" asked the critics. "Are we not engineers of nature, summoned to transform its face in the interests of fulfilling the Five-Year Plan . . .?" Lastochkin's whole attempt to provide a picture of the productivity of an aquatic community was painted as a scientific indulgence rather than as the basis for determining rational norms for the fish catch—Lastochkin's own intention.[22]

Even L. A. Zenkevich, professor at Moscow State University and a friend of acclimatization, was called to account for his *omission* of a critique of the theory of equilibrium in nature in his review of the state of marine ecology.[23]

With a definite atmosphere building, the preliminaries at last yielded to the main event: I. I. Prezent himself. Briefly praising Zhadin's speech as "rich in content" (such riches could prove more perilous than impoverishment), Prezent totally passed over Zhadin's caveats concerning the ecological impact of large-scale riverine construction projects. Rather, he drew another conclusion entirely. "Now," he instructed, "the time has arrived to carry out experiments which only the new construction has made possible." Quoting the commissar of agriculture of the USSR, Iakov A. Iakovlev, who had already become Lysenko's principal patron and quite likely Prezent's as well, Prezent concluded:

> The past two years have proved that we, the Bolsheviks, and not our opponents, have truly stood for science, for now even the blind can see that there have never been such grand opportunities for the application of science . . . than as at the present time.[24]

Zhadin, giving his own concluding remarks, sought to counterpose his perspective to Prezent's, yet avoid a potentially catastrophic confrontation. Fortunately, Prezent's expressed praise of his talk, however insincere, presented a tactical opportunity. Appreciatively acknowledging the "very flattering appraisal" of his talk by Prezent, Zhadin pointedly invited the members of his entire brigade to share in the praise. That was a courageous political gesture, for in addition to the hydrobiologists D. E. Beling, G. Iu. Vereshchagin, T. I. Dolgov, and M. I. Tikhii (who had earlier been criticized during the hydrobiology session), his team included

Stanchinskii, who was fast becoming something of Prezent's personal whipping boy. By associating Stanchinskii publicly with Prezent's praise, Zhadin must have hoped to make it much more difficult for Prezent to persecute Stanchinskii. Finally, without directly contradicting Prezent, Zhadin made it evident that the proper place for ecologists was at the side of real engineers, informing their labors with biological good sense, and not, by implication, serving as conjurers of a wholesale transformation of nature.[25] The spirit of resistance, cloaked in protective coloration, was still very much alive.

The faunistics conference had failed to deliver a conclusive victory to Prezent and the camp of the nature-transformers. Even the question of acclimatization in the *zapovedniki* awaited resolution. Nevertheless, the prominence given to attacks on ecology's increasing use of statistical methods and its presumption of the existence of equilibria in natural communities made the position of Soviet Russia's ecologists even more precarious.

Zhadin and his colleagues continued their research into the effects of tampering with the natural course of Soviet rivers and their basins.[26] Although their published pronouncements were far from jeremiads, they still reflected the serious, disquieting misgivings of the hydrobiologists over the pace and direction of socialist construction.

Other conservationists and ecologists were urging greater circumspection as well. At the Congress for the Struggle against Drought, which met in late 1931, A. F. Vangengeim, the former president of VOOP and a meteorologist by profession, tried to impress his fellow delegates with the need to adopt a more realistic assessment of the possibilities of mastery over nature. "The fact that drought is conditioned by the movement of air masses covering . . . millions of square kilometers . . . incontrovertibly means that at our present levels of technology, we cannot prevent the phenomenon of drought itself,"[27] he declared, responding to utopian plans to cover the entire arid southern steppes with a blanket of trees (or perhaps to Prezent's visions of masterminding a wholesale change in the climate through rainmaking[28]). Such measures as the planting of forest strips to diminish the force of the wind during the *sukhovei,* he went on, "must be introduced taking into account the extremely complex constellation of phenomena that would accompany such afforestation."[29]

On the one hand, he explained, the forest itself requires definite climatological conditions and the presence of sufficient moisture in order to thrive. On the other, the afforestation of the arid steppe could deplete the existing soil moisture, even desiccating the deeper layers of the soil. Finally, such afforestation might well be accompanied by a proliferation of arboreal pests of all kinds, previously unknown to the steppe, and with the potential to do great damage to the indigenous flora and fauna. Rather, suggested Vangengeim, Soviet steppe agriculture should concentrate on harnessing local natural energy sources, such as wind and solar power, to undo the harm that other natural forces, such as the *sukhovei* and drought, might do.[30]

Taken together with the ecological-minded objections of other conservationists—to collectivized agriculture based on monocultures, to the Council of Labor and Defense's 31 October 1931 call for increased pelt procurement, and to acclimatization both within and outside the *zapovedniki*—the warnings of Vangengeim and of the hydrobiologists rounded out a picture of a scientific community out of step with the spirit of the age. Indeed, the continuing insistence of the conservationists that the Goskomitet be allowed to exercise real veto power over economic activity in the USSR on the basis of ecological and other conservation-related considerations raised the specter that, like the engineers, the ecologists had mounted a technocratic challenge to the party's monopoly on policymaking. Under these circumstances, it is not surprising that, increasingly, party-minded biologists and philosophers of science directed their energies toward inflicting a mortal wound to the body of ecological thought, in particular to the notions of the web of life and balance of nature.

The botanist Boris Aleksandrovich Keller, who had just been elected to full membership in the Soviet Academy of Sciences, accurately read the tea leaves and completely reversed his warm support for the development of biocenology. "Geobotany," he declared in 1931, referring in fact to the study of plant communities, "developed here under conditions dominated by the bourgeoisie and the gentry landowners and, consciously or unconsciously, carried with it reactionary, class-alien positions which are frequently camouflaged by the hypnotic prestige evoked by the names of such great scientists as Dokuchaev and Morozov." First of all Keller attacked the phytosociological tendency to "bow down before virgin nature." It was not enough simply "to describe and to study vegetation," he lectured, echoing Prezent's refrain; Soviet botanists had to "participate as actively as possible in its reconstruction." In particular, Keller took exception to the view, widespread among ecologists and championed by Sukachev, that the greatest possible harmony and productivity was found in virgin nature, and not in man's cultivated fields.[31]

A respected Soviet plant ecologist, Kh. Kh. Trass, later wrote that Keller's positions "reflected the aspirations of his time. However, if we look at his positions, we see in them as well those tendencies toward dogmatism, absolutism, and one-sidedness which, from the 1930s, began to block the progress of Soviet biology and led to the . . . monopoly of the views of one group of biologists led by T. D. Lysenko."[32] If this judgment of Keller seems harsh, it is because Keller's own abandonment of biocenology for the new, Lysenko-supported biology was almost certainly motivated by careerism.

Holistic ecology had its honest critics as well. They now found that there was a growing market (but, paradoxically, a limited one) for their antiholistic views of nature. Of the opponents of the closed, self-regulating biocenosis, among whom Leontii Grigor'evich Ramenskii, Aleksei Porfir'evich Il'inskii, A. A. Elenkin, and Academician Vladimir Leont'evich Komarov were the most prominent, it was the last who best articulated this current of thought. In the introduction to his opus *The Vegetation of the USSR and Adjacent Countries,* which appeared in 1931, Komarov called for the expurgation of all references to "plant communities" in botanical literature:

> An entire separate discipline, "phytocenology," . . . has been founded. At its core is the
> notion that groups of plants in nature as well as the structure of the vegetation cover

allegedly are much more a consequence of the influence of . . . species of plants on each other than of the influence of environmental conditions.* One reform which must be introduced into the study of vegetation mandates the complete expurgation of . . . phytosociology. The very term *plant community* must be expunged.[33]

Ramenskii, Il'inskii, and Komarov, much like American ecologist Henry A. Gleason, who wrote at about the same time,[34] disputed the existence of discrete communities in nature, much less closed, self-regulating systems characterized by equilibrium. Instead, they believed that the distribution of plant species could be completely explained by means of a species gradient reflecting the greater or lesser presence of necessary environmental conditions required for their propagation. That is, plant distribution was more a function of each individual plant species' adaptation to the sum total of environmental conditions (especially abiotic ones) than of conditioning by the hypothetical laws of presumed ecological communities.

This view, which was revived by American ecologist Robert H. Whittaker and which could have served as a corrective to the holistic excesses of the other side, unfortunately did not play a constructive role. It went too far in the other direction, rejecting as unimportant the influence of organisms in a community on each other and on the substrate itself. Thus, in attributing almost exclusive importance to such abiotic factors as climate, moisture, and temperature (as Lysenko himself did), Komarov, Il'inskii, and their colleagues neglected the sometimes uniquely critical biocenotic roles played by organisms as sources of food, shelter, protection, and even digestive aids with respect to other organisms. (Ramenskii did accord these factors considerable importance, but his sophisticated viewpoint was largely ignored.[35]) In asserting their view of a plastic nature, the antiholists failed to treat seriously the possibility that organisms were dependent for their very survival on the presence of other, specific organisms. The Komarov group's rejection of a "web of life" made their vegetation continuum concept, albeit in the unsophisticated form it assumed during the early thirties, a convenient scientific theory by which a far-ranging rearrangement of nature could be justified.

Thus, by 1931–1932, not only was the holistic approach in biology beginning to be "unmasked" as "bourgeois" science; an alternative view of the structure of nature was likewise struggling to take its place as a "proletarian" approach, much more in concordance with the requirements of socialist construction. These developments were not lost on many Soviet ecologists and conservationists, who now began searching for ways better to integrate their views with the enveloping voluntarist tide.

THE FALL OF ASKANIA

Among the first to disavow any overtly technocratic aspirations on the part of ecologists was Stanchinskii's *Journal of Ecology and Biocenology*. The same editorial that spoke of the "truly boundless possibilities" for biocenology also proclaimed "the need for resolute opposition to that one-sidedness, that arrogance,

*Here Komarov means abiotic factors.

. . . that naive self-conceit of the specialist who claims to have a monopoly on the solution of broad synthetic problems on the basis of his own, limited specialist's perspective." The editors warned,

> Never before has this danger been so openly displayed as now during the current vigorous growth of ecology and biocenology. It is difficult to find either in Europe or in America—and in our Union the situation is still, regrettably, not a whit better—researchers who do not believe that ecology and biocenology are the "central," "decisive," or "fundamental" disciplines of biology. . . . Such claims first of all do harm to ecology and biocenology themselves.

Having washed ecology of the sin of "specialist conceit," the editorial also sought to calm the deep fears of biologists-at-large (and philosophers of biology) that ecology was being taken over by statistics:

> To believe that out of this chaos of opinions [as to what, precisely, constitutes the subject matter of ecology and biocenology] we can find our way with the aid of mathematics alone, with only numerical coefficients or even with the aid of physics and chemistry, is naively to close our eyes to the vast complexity and qualitative uniqueness of those myriad interrelationships between organism and environment and between collectivities of organisms and their environment which give rise to the general principles that govern them.[36]

Evidently, Stanchinskii and his colleagues were sensitive to the fact that reductionist positions in science were now the objects of official condemnation, and that many biologists of both the old school and the new *vydvizhenstvo* generation had backgrounds sadly deficient in mathematics. This deficiency frequently caused those biologists to be intimidated by statistical presentations. Stanchinskii, whose work rested so heavily on the use of statistics and on mathematical symbols to express energy inputs and outputs in natural communities, was doubtless particularly aware of the need to reach out to these groups and to dulcify the threatening image his research presented.

Other ecologists, including Stanchinskii's friend and academic collaborator D. N. Kashkarov, provided even more dramatic demonstrations of political reliability. If, for Henry of Navarre, Paris was worth a mass, then for Kashkarov the prospect of a transfer from remote Tashkent to the chair of vertebrate zoology at Leningrad State University was well worth publicly singing the praises of the great transformation of nature.[37]

The ecologists' self-criticism and professions of humility were not sufficient, however, to stave off the crisis in their young field. By early 1932, a critical juncture had been reached: Prezent already had begun his long association with Lysenko, and their combined forces were capable of moving against the citadel of community ecology, Askania-Nova, and against its leader, Stanchinskii.

The rise of T. D. Lysenko has been treated skillfully elsewhere.[38] However, a number of brief details may be usefully mentioned. Lysenko's first major career advance came in the Ukraine, where desperate officials of that republic's Commissariat of Agriculture (Narkomzem) leapt at the promises made by the young breeder to ensure against further disastrous losses of wheat to winter killing.[39] In the Ukraine as well, at the Ukrainian Institute of Genetics and Selection in Odessa, Lysenko developed the miracle that would gain him even greater fame: vernalization. By 1931 Lysenko had developed a network of patrons both in the Ukrainian Narkomzem and in its subsidiary Ukrainian Academy of Agricultural Sciences (which was loosely linked with VASKhNIL, the Lenin All-Union Academy of Agricultural Sciences).

The summer and fall of 1931 yielded an even more bounteous political harvest for the ambitious young plant breeder. In a decree of 9 July 1931 signed by Iakovlev, the USSR commissar of agriculture, Lysenko was provided with his own press organ, the opportunity to proselytize his agronomic panaceas through structured courses, and 150,000 rubles.[40] Four months later, at the All-Ukrainian Selection Congress which he had addressed, Lysenko was acclaimed by the enthused delegates. Protesting that Lysenko's "outstanding scientific work" had not received "adequate attention from other scientific research institutions," the delegates now insisted that his "agroecological" studies be included in the work plans of these institutions.[41]

By the end of the year, Lysenko was granted direct access to Commissar Iakovlev,[42] whose support of the agronomist only seemed to increase. Consequently, by the time that Prezent and Lysenko began their potent collaboration, Lysenko was already politically very well placed, both in Khar'kov and in Moscow, and his work was championed as a model for emulation by other scientific centers. Prezent, meanwhile, had attained a not insignificant degree of influence in academic politics, although the political sources of his support to 1932 are more of a mystery than those of Lysenko.

Although Prezent alone was not able to transform Soviet zoologists into an obedient squadron of biological "engineers" and "inventors," supported by Lysenko he now could draw upon another set of political resources. The first use to which those new resources were put was an all-out attack on Stanchinskii's ecological research at Askania-Nova in the Ukraine.

Prior to Stanchinskii's appointment as scientific director at Askania, the complex had been racked by dissension and intense rivalry among its disparate units. In particular, the sheep-breeding and livestock hybridization programs and those for the acclimatization and domestication of exotic fauna had repeatedly tried to oust from the reserve the research units that were pursuing more theoretical themes in biology and to seize the remaining virgin steppe for their more practical purposes. These units were all under the general supervision of Mikhail Fedorovich Ivanov and were in collusion with the reserve's grain-growing sector. They also had the active support of key staffers in the Ukrainian Narkomzem.

The reorganization of Askania-Nova in 1929 proceeded along lines other than those envisioned by the utilitarian sectors and their Narkomzem allies. Askania was launched on a new, ecological course under Stanchinskii.[43] At first, the future of theoretical ecological studies at Askania seemed inspirited. Stanchinskii's Scientific Steppe Institute received substantial subsidies in the form of hard-currency loans[44] and, for the first time, zoologists and botanists at the reserve no longer worked as

isolated units but as parts of a collaborative team studying the ecological dynamics
of the feathergrass-fescue community. Data were collected to test further Stanchinskii's novel notions about energy flow in natural systems, articles were published,
and materials were assembled for a full-length monograph.[45] From the *zapovednik*
itself Stanchinskii's teams fanned out to other sites from the Dnepr in the west to the
Molochnaia in the east, including other *zapovedniki*.[46] Soon, it was hoped, ecologists also would include in their observations cultivated lands, pasturelands, and
other types of agricultural land in order to compare their efficiencies in transforming
solar energy into organic matter with that of the virgin steppe already under study.[47]
Even Ivanov's 200,000-head flock of sheep had been thinned to a mere 10,000, and
the controversial grainfield in the Dorenburg tract of the reserve was detached and
handed over to a sovkhoz.[48]

Stanchinskii was at the height of his career. From 1929 he was chief of the
Vertebrate Zoology *kafedra* at Khar'kov State University. Founder of the university's Zoological-Biological Scientific Institute and head of the institute's Ecological Division, he became the magnet for an entire company of student followers. He
served as editor-in-chief of the USSR's first ecology journal, and, among Soviet
scientists at large, he was the acknowledged leader in community ecology. He was
entrusted with organizing not only a panel on biocenology for the Fifth Congress of
Zoologists but also the congress itself, which was set for 1933 in Khar'kov. Finally,
it was to Stanchinskii that his fellow conservationists turned to organize the first
all-Union conservation congress at Askania-Nova for September 1931.

Ironically, just as Stanchinskii was basking in the accolades of his colleagues
at the Fourth Congress of Zoologists in Kiev, an event in Khar'kov whose importance was not recognized at the time set the stage for an undoing of the
ecologist's lifework. On 23 March 1930 the Council of People's Commissars of the
Ukraine placed Askania-Nova under the direct authority of the Ukrainian Commissariat of Agriculture "for employing [the reserve] in the development of measures for agricultural improvement." Day-to-day authority for the management of
Askania was delegated to the All-Ukrainian Academy of Agricultural Sciences,
which was subordinate to the commissariat. In the process, the collegial interagency
administration that had governed the *zapovednik*'s affairs since 1922 was abolished
(followed soon thereafter by the abolition of the Ukrainian Narkomzem's Scientific
Advisory Committee and *its* conservation commission). Although this decision was
protested to the Council of People's Commissars of the Ukraine by N. A. Skrypnik,
the people's commissar for education in the Ukraine, the protest was rejected and
the measure stuck.[49]

Until the summer of 1931 there was little evidence at Askania of the elimination by decree of all Narkompros and other non-Narkomzem input in the reserve's
administration or work program. Nonetheless, Stanchinskii's position there was
increasingly imperiled. For one thing, since March 1930 he had been serving at
the sufferance of officials of Narkomzem of the Ukraine, and they, it should be
noted, were becoming increasingly disappointed by the failure of Stanchinskii's
ecological energetics to produce any agricultural miracles. Secondly, although
forced temporarily into the background, Ivanov's sheep- and hog-breeding pro-

grams, his hybridization experiments, and the work on acclimatization were still very much a presence at Askania. With heightened interest on the part of agricultural officials in the possibilities of new miracle hybrids of livestock and in acclimatization and domestication of exotic fauna as a technological fix for the problems of Soviet agriculture, Ivanov's work now garnered increasingly favorable attention. This was especially true when Ivanov's putative practical achievements in stock breeding were juxtaposed with the tarnished promise of Stanchinskii's ecological studies. In addition, Ivanov undoubtedly chafed at the decimation of his sheep-breeding operation and sought to get even with Stanchinskii for being relegated to a humiliatingly minor role at Askania since 1929.

The end of the summer of 1931 was the beginning of the end for Stanchinskii's Scientific Steppe Institute. The first serious blow came with the arrival of a high-powered commission dispatched by Narkomzem of the Ukraine. It was composed of Oleksei Nikanorovich Sokolovskii, president of the Ukrainian Academy of Agricultural Sciences; A. M. Slipanskii, vice-president; and N. I. Vavilov, who still nurtured hopes of molding Lysenko into a rigorous agricultural scientist.[50] The panel after several days' inspection released its startling conclusion: "Askania must be an Institute for Acclimatization and Hybridization as its basic profile."[51] With this decision to create a wholly new institution to dominate Askania, the effects of the reserve's 1929 reorganization were reversed. Since the reserve was placed in March 1930 under the direct rule of the Ukrainian Academy of Agricultural Sciences and Narkomzem of the Ukraine (with the abolition of the Askania Commission), there was no means to appeal this grim move; Stanchinskii dutifully yielded, adding his signature to those who assented to the panel's recommendations. The only hope now was to salvage as much of his own work as possible in the shadow of this new hybrid institute, even if it were to be on a much more modest scale than previously. Moreover, there was little that could be done now that the utilitarians had unbridled legal sway over Askania.

The new All-Union Institute for Agricultural Hybridization and Acclimatization of Fauna was established by a decree of the All-Union and Ukrainian Narkomzems on 30 September 1931.[52] Lysenko may well have played a role in this transformation of Askania, particularly through his connections with Iakovlev, with the Ukrainian Academy of Agricultural Sciences,[53] and, ironically, with Vavilov.[54] However, the key force in mobilizing support for the institute's establishment was likely to have been Ivanov, who now saw his opportunity to bring to life his vision of the agronomists' paradise. Not surprisingly, Ivanov was appointed the institute's first scientific director.

As its director and supporters liked to boast, the institute was the first of its kind in the world. Its roots in the Russian Lamarckian acclimatization tradition were broadly hinted at by F. F. Bega, the reserve's overall director, who noted as early as 1933 that the institute was brought into being "to solve those questions upon whose threshold the naturalist-experimenters of the nineteenth century were poised, . . . namely, the mastery of the processes and techniques of the directed creation of new life forms."[55] Ivanov wrote in a similar vein at about the same time:

There is a pressing urgency to transform the entirety of our primitive and unproductive livestock-breeding sector into a highly productive one. . . . The resolution of this problem may be attained not only by means of selection, better methods of feeding, upkeep and breeding, and by means of acclimatizing the best foreign varieties and interbreeding them with our own best, BUT ALSO BY MEANS OF CREATING ENTIRELY NEW VARIETIES AND SPECIES of domesticated animals on the basis of INTERVARIETAL, INTERSPECIFIC, and INTERGENERIC HYBRIDIZATION as well as through the acclimatization and domestication of as yet untamed wild species of animals.[56]

Indeed, Bega, in one of the most forceful anti-Mendelian statements prior to Lysenko's open break with Mendelian genetics, noted that the institute was specifically charged with conducting broad-scale experiments in interspecific hybridization *despite* "all of the pseudoscientific assertions of the old capitalist school"[57] of geneticists who continued to insist on the existence of genetic boundaries between species. Ironically, the Mendelian Vavilov was one of the midwives of the institute.

To accomplish these agricultural miracles the institute was richly endowed. For its first year of operation the institute was allotted one million rubles for hybridization alone.[58] Additionally, it inherited 20,000 hectares of virgin steppe, formerly used for pasturing and hay-mowing; 6,000 hectares of cultivated lands; the zoo, which was transformed into a purely demonstration satellite of the institute; 8,000 sheep; 200 horses; 400 head of cattle; and a large number of Ivanov's "pure-line" hogs.[59] Stanchinskii's Scientific Steppe Institute, now an almost accessorial yet still autonomous part of the Askania combine, retained its two modest parcels of virgin steppe totalling 6,300 hectares, which were temporarily supplemented (for a portion of 1932) by the affiliation of the Chernomorskie and Primorskie *zapovedniki*.[60]

As in the 1920s there was again a situation of intense rivalry between the scientific and the applied (and outright economic) tendencies within Askania. The reserve's divided legacy of extensive agriculture, sheep breeding, acclimatization, and now ecology was simply too unwieldy to survive, observed one of its staff scientists.[61] In fact, it survived as such for only a few months.

The Acclimatization and Hybridization Institute was riding the crest of interest in the production of agricultural miracles. Mikhail Ivanovich Kalinin, titular chief of state of the USSR, was one of its first visitors. Unfortunately for Stanchinskii, I. I. Prezent was another. Less than six months after the February 1932 faunistics conference, ironically at a time when the "leftist" deviation had finally been quashed in the *kraeved* society and VOOP, Stanchinskii's enterprise at Askania was on the ropes. Speaking with the authority of the Communist Academy, we are told, but now possessing the political clout to make good on his words (thanks to his association with Lysenko), Prezent pronounced the sentence of death on the Scientific Steppe Institute after a two-week stay at the reserve complex:

We must give Askania a single profile. Up until now, in reality, *only* the Institute for Hybridization and Acclimatization had a *clear* idea of its tasks. The same could not be said about the Steppe Institute. These two institutes were alien to one another by the content of their work, and only territorial proximity conferred any sort of "collaborative status" on them. . . . Askania must become a mighty center for hybridization and acclimatization, not only for animals alone but also for plants. We must expand this institution so that animals may remain the *leading* and decisive element of Askania, while the inviolable steppe must be transformed from a parcel "protected from man" into a base for the introduction of new crop varieties.[62]

As Askania's director, Bega, told the First All-Union Conservation Congress several months later, "Any commentary on this, it is evident, is superfluous."[63] His listeners evidently well understood why.

The liquidation of the Scientific Steppe Institute was Prezent's first big triumph over the ecologists. However, the events at Askania still seemed reversible to the Soviet Union's harried band of conservationists and ecologists. They looked to the All-Union Conservation Congress, set at last for late January 1933 (after repeated postponements), to rescue Askania and, with it, the future of the ecological profile of the *zapovedniki.*

THIRTEEN

The First All-Union Conservation Congress

The First All-Union Conservation Congress, which was really the second great congress for the movement, convened in the depths of the Moscow winter. On 25 January 1933 its 190 voting and nonvoting delegates were called to order by V. T. Ter-Oganesov, who was now secretary of the USSR Central Executive Committee's Committee on Academic Institutions and a leader of its Science Section.

A brief comparison with the 1929 congress discloses the vast journey traversed by Soviet society in just four years. The presidium of the congress, numbering more than twenty, still had some familiar faces, including P. G. Smidovich, V. N. Makarov, Ter-Oganesov, N. M. Kulagin, A. V. Fediushin, V. V. Stanchinskii, F. F. Shillinger, and A. P. Protopopov. However, there were several new members, including P. I. Valeskaln of the All-Union Association of Workers of Science and Technology (Varnitso), an early supporter of Lysenko, and A. N. Sudarikov of the USSR People's Commissariat of the Forest Industry. These leaders, together with the host of officials from among the rank-and-file delegates representing the People's Commissariats of Agriculture (Narkomzem), Foreign Trade (Narkomvneshtorg), and Supplies (Narkomsnab), were the éminences grises of the assembly.

The sharpest changes were among the delegates themselves. As a group, the 92 voting delegates to the 1933 congress (the only group for which we have data) differed noticeably from the 124 delegates to the 1929 congress in a number of important respects. They were considerably less well-educated; only 35 percent of them had received higher education as compared with 75 percent of the delegates to the 1929 congress. A mere 12 percent of the 1929 congress's members had claimed party membership as against 37 percent in 1933. And one-third of the voting and nonvoting delegates to the 1933 congress were described as civil servants.

After the proclamation of the ritual greeting to Stalin in the name of the congress and the announcement of the composition of the congress's working and honorary presidiums, the chairperson, Smidovich (representing the central government, as he had in 1929) took the floor. Although Smidovich began by enjoining the conservation organizations to tie their work closely to economic development, the latter portion of his address contained a somewhat opaque, yet identifiable defense of basic research as a legitimate aspect of conservation.[1]

With Makarov's keynote address which followed, however, the congress was plunged directly into an unvarnished examination of the fate of the *zapovedniki* as ecological research bases. Initially, Makarov, the VOOP leader, continued his long-standing strategy of protective coloration. Indeed, he took special pains to demonstrate that the People's Commissariat of Education (Narkompros) had conclusively rejected the "fetish of the inviolability of the *zapovedniki*."[2] He admitted that "there was still a group of individuals who feel that 'human influence on the natural course of natural processes [in the *zapovedniki*] is out of the question,' " even conceding that, "at one time, even the Goskomitet [the interagency conservation committee] shared the same point of view." But Makarov stressed that now, "for us, this line is completely unacceptable, and we gave and will give a decisive rebuff to such tendencies."[3]

Partisans of absolute inviolability were further accused by Makarov of distorting the intent of Engels's article "The Role of Labor in the Transformation from Ape to Man" to justify their discredited position. After reading aloud the disputed passage he explained:

> In this way Engels allegedly indicates that nature "avenges" man for its improper use. People, in referring to Engels's words, lose sight of two things. First, Engels had in mind not socialist society . . . but the plunderous, unplanned, irrational economy of the capitalist system. Second, Engels by this passage warns . . . that prior to exploiting [any resource] it is necessary—dozens of times—to weigh and deliberate what economic consequences, what consequences for the culture . . . this exploitation will bring, and it is necessary to study not simply the short-term but also the long-range consequences of such use. Engels teaches us dialectically to *foresee* the consequences of human intervention in nature. He did not prohibit intervention. . . . [nor] did he say that man must not regulate the course of natural processes, must not submit natural forces to his will.[4]

As concerned one of the hotly contested forms of human intervention in the *zapovedniki,* the acclimatization of exotic biota,[5] Makarov likewise agreed—in principle—that such acclimatization was permissible in either the absolute or the buffer zones.[6]

Much of Makarov's firmness against the partisans of inviolable *zapovedniki* was motivated, paradoxically enough, by his desire to protect the very existence of the ecological reserves from those who would destroy them completely. By disavowing the opponents of modified human intervention in the reserves, Makarov hoped to demonstrate to all that

> the reproach that Narkompros and the Goskomitet occupied the position of taking a "contemplative approach" to nature, only an observer's stance, . . . is completely false and today does not have a leg to stand on.[7]

Those who leveled such charges, as had participants of a recently concluded conference of Narkomvneshtorg's Peltry Association (Soiuzpushnina), were described by Makarov as "people who are unwilling to take the facts of the matter into account." For the benefit of the representatives of the economic organs at the congress Makarov reiterated Narkompros's rejection of "science for science's sake" and "research for the sake of research," so that there could be no further distortion of the commissariat's public position.[8]

Makarov's disclaimers, appeals, and verbal concessions, however, did little to dampen the ardor of conservation's enemies, who were better represented at this congress than at the previous one. After Makarov's talk, S. V. Turshu, the plenipotentiary of Narkomvneshtorg in the Crimean ASSR, demanded that Narkompros be stripped of its conservation functions, particularly the system of *zapovedniki*.[9]

Turshu's initial assault was countered by V. I. Smirnov, delegate of the Mid-Volga *zapovednik*, who protested that the reserves' transfer to economic organs would "lead them to complete and utter ruin."[10] Unperturbed, the economic organs returned to the attack. S. A. Petrushin, who represented hunting affairs for Narkomvneshtorg, launched into a vehement castigation of the Narkompros reserves:

> The scientific workers of the *zapovedniki* have thus far failed to learn both the new tasks which confront the *zapovedniki* and the new direction that the reserves should take. They have not put those things into practice and seem incapable of linking their scientific research with economic requirements. . . .[11]

With a touch of ridicule reminiscent of his quip at the 1929 gathering ("Let Narkompros carry on its scientific research itself. We shall carry on other work"), Petrushin accused the *zapovedniki* of being havens for irrelevant academics:

> The situation which up to now has prevailed [in the *zapovedniki*] is unthinkable. It is impermissible that scientific workers of the reserves could occupy themselves with whatever on earth they pleased—only not with work!

"We must expose this state of affairs," he concluded, ominously, "so that this congress may inaugurate a new period in the life and operations of the *zapovedniki*."[12]

Ivan Vasil'evich Sosnin, a former lecturer at Irkutsk State University's Faculty of Law and Economics and now also representing Narkomvneshtorg at the congress, demanded that the applied approach represented by his commissariat's *zapovedniki* be imposed on those of Narkompros.[13] Also chiming in for the transfer of the Narkompros *zapovedniki* to the economic organs were V. P. Maleev, acclimatization theorist, and F. F. Bega, the director of Askania-Nova, which was now completely taken over by the All-Union Institute for the Hybridization and Acclimatization of Fauna.[14]

Makarov's protective-coloration strategy, it was painfully obvious, had failed to curb the desire of the representatives of the economic organs to destroy the ecological orientation of the Narkompros reserves; now Makarov took the floor in rebuttal. While again seeking to protect his left flank by continuing to reject the doctrine of inviolability, Makarov tried to portray Narkompros's position as that of the embattled middle, trying to prevent the triumph of an equally unreasonable utilitarianism. "We must not view this question one-sidedly, as several comrades have done here, viewing the *zapovedniki* from the narrow perspectives of game procurement, game breeding, or forestry," he instructed. "We must struggle against such an approach, because our *zapovedniki* are far from being merely game procurement stations or centers for pasture research. The *zapovednik* is valued [first of all] for its holistic attributes."[15]

Makarov explained that the *zapovednik* was a place in which the individual elements gained their importance from being parts of the whole and that the reserves, alongside their other functions, "justifiably occupy themselves with far-reaching theoretical problems." Acknowledging the objections of the impatient, Makarov conceded that "the scientific levels of our *zapovedniki* do not yet permit us to resolve those problems, the resolution of which would allow humanity to control the processes of living nature. . . ." This failure he attributed to "an as yet poor mastery of dialectical materialism." Nonetheless, he emphasized, this shortcoming, which was by no means a monopoly of the "nonparty comrades," did not affect the validity of the Narkompros system's unique approach to the use of protected territories; that approach had as much right to exist as the equally distinctive applied one practiced by the economic organs.[16]

Sosnin's proposal to transfer all USSR *zapovedniki* to Narkomvneshtorg was specifically denounced by Makarov. If the approach argued by the economic organs was taken to its logical conclusion, he said,

> then we must reject *zapovedniki* completely as scientific research institutions. If we take such a position, then we must . . . state honestly, without any wavering, that we must turn over the entire system of *zapovedniki* to the appropriate economic agencies: Soiuzryba, Narkomvneshtorg, etc., according to the reserves' individual profiles.[17]

However, Makarov cannily noted, such a divestiture inescapably would be accompanied by tremendous confusion. Owing to the presence of a variety of important resources within the territories of each of the reserves, the very same *zapovednik,* from the economic point of view, could well be claimed by any number of economic agencies and commissariats, he argued. Who would be competent to decide, for example, whether the Crimean *zapovednik* should be classified primarily as a source of timber, in which case it would be assigned to the Forest Industry Commissariat, or as a game preserve, where affiliation with Narkomvneshtorg would be more appropriate? Each *zapovednik* would dangle like an apple of discord before the acquisitive clutches of the economic organs.[18]

Capping his rebuttal to the utilitarians Makarov in rather uncomplimentary terms evaluated the sorry record of the economic agencies' administration of *zapovedniki* now or previously under their jurisdiction. It was ironic, he noted, that the directors of the Lapland, Lopatkinskii, and even the Voronezh reserves were forced to turn to the Goskomitet for material assistance because of the failure of Narkomzem and Narkomvneshtorg to provide it. For agencies seeking to take on increased responsibilities, theirs were hardly reassuring credentials.[19]

Another voice raised in clear opposition to the economic organs was that of Stanchinskii, who discerned in Sosnin's talk "a profoundly bureaucratic stridency."

"I do not consider Narkomvneshtorg to be an agency of little importance," offered Stanchinskii, signaling that even basic researchers had a certain regard for the economic organs. However, he flatly rejected "view[ing] the entire world from the standpoint of the interests of the People's Commissariat of Foreign Trade." To Sosnin's declaration that it was essential to transfer all of the Narkompros *zapovedniki,* Stanchinskii responded with a rebuke: "Comrades of Narkomvneshtorg! Start by putting your own *zapovedniki* in good running order . . . first!"

Like Makarov, Stanchinskii offered the utilitarians an olive branch if they chose to accept it. But with his offer went a warning of resistance to the economic organs' claims to hegemony over the Soviet *zapovedniki:*

> You are in error, however, when you seek to force [our] *zapovedniki* to work according to your plan. You have flatly directed: "Here is our plan. Be so kind as to start work on it." . . . But even if you offered us enough funding, it would still make no sense to us that we should occupy ourselves with *your* problems to the exclusion of everything else. . . .

For Stanchinskii the justification of his stand was simple; each agency was charged by the government with its own specific tasks in a fruitful division of labor. So long as the 20 June 1930 decree on *zapovedniki* remained in effect and until the charters of the Narkompros *zapovedniki* were abrogated by governmental decree, those *zapovedniki* were not only entitled but bound to continue with their ecological work as *etalony.*[20]

Stanchinskii and Makarov were immediately supported by their colleagues. A. A. Shummer, director of the Chernomorskie *zapovedniki,* Ivan Nikolaevich Bulankin[21] of the Ukrainian Narkompros, and Fediushin of Narkompros of the Belorussian SSR added their voices to the rising chorus of resistance to the menace of takeover. So, significantly, did A. A. Umnov, leader of the hunting cooperative union,* which was also in the process of being liquidated at the instigation of Narkomvneshtorg. More ecological even than the ecologists, Umnov now brazenly advocated the abolition of all *zakazniki* and *zapovedniki* that functioned merely as game preserves, declaring that the only protected territories his organization considered to be worthwhile were "*zapovedniki* in which scientific research was conducted." Thus, Russia's organized hunters once again came to the aid of ecologically oriented conservation in its hour of need, this time as partners in adversity.[22]

One perspicacious participant, ecologist S. Ia. Sokolov of the Academy of Sciences' Botanical Institute, laid part of the blame for the current debacle on Narkompros's policy of making concessions to its utilitarian opponents. Under pressure, he charged, Narkompros had disavowed the very organizational aspects of its reserves that made them unique—pure research under conditions of inviolability—while now conceding, if only rhetorically, the salient importance of applied projects and even active human intervention. By that very combination of

---

*Vsekokhotsoiuz, which had been renamed Soiuzokhottsentr not long before the congress.

concessions, argued Sokolov, Narkompros had handed their enemies a weapon of damaging power, for now the economic organs could challenge Narkompros's *zapovedniki* to live up to their renunciation of inviolability and basic research. As more suitable managers of such utilitarian reserves, the economic commissariats had the perfect justification to "demand the transfer of the *zapovedniki* to themselves." Now, when Narkomvneshtorg's Sosnin rose to demand such a transfer as the legitimate representative of game management and procurement, Narkompros found that it had compromised the very principles that best argued against those claims.[23]

"TRIM IT DOWN TO SIZE!"

If the discussion over the fate and function of Soviet *zapovedniki* was being conducted largely in generalities, events at Askania had shown that outside the conference hall the battle for the *zapovedniki* was already raging in earnest. Askania-Nova had become the symbol of the great contest in Soviet conservation. Activists knew that if Askania were lost for good to the acclimatizers and stock breeders, ecological work in the other *zapovedniki* might be similarly imperiled. A defeat in the struggle for Askania could even conceivably open the way to a successful takeover of the *zapovedniki* of the republican Commissariats of Education by the economic organs—the wolf outside the door. Understandably, interest in the reserve's fate was exceptionally high.

Leading off the discussion on this *zapovednik* was Askania's director, Bega, who outlined the sequence of events leading to the creation of the Hybridization and Acclimatization Institute and the subsequent liquidation of Stanchinskii's Scientific Steppe Institute. These developments he viewed with a considerable degree of approbation. The only outstanding question, it seemed, was what to do with the approximately six thousand hectares of virgin steppe now that the ecological institute had been closed down. In connection with this Bega passed along the recommendation of I. I. Prezent, who, it appears, had been taking a continuing interest in developments at Askania: the virgin steppe should be used as a bridgehead for the acclimatization of exotic plants.[24]

While trying to reassure the sceptical conservationists that any acclimatization would be pursued in harmony with the goal of preserving this last portion of virgin steppe (how this was to be done Bega did not reveal), Bega intimated that even were the pristine conditions of the steppe to be degraded, it would not be a tragic loss for science; after all, even the authoritative plant geographer E. M. Lavrenko had written that the Askania steppes were typical only of a small strip of feathergrass steppe in the southern Ukraine and were hardly to be viewed as an *etalon* for the agriculturally much more important steppe lands to the north and east.

Stanchinskii replied to the assertions of his director. Although he still worked at Askania, Stanchinskii came to the congress not as a delegate of his home reserve nor even of its superordinate agency, Narkomzem of the Ukrainian SSR, but rather of the Ukrainian Commissariat of Education, in whose name he now spoke. The Education Commissariat contended that because the abolition of the Steppe Institute and, together with it, of Askania's remaining virgin steppe was a conservation issue, and since the decrees of 1926 and 1928—theoretically still in force—provided that no conservation matters in the Ukraine could be decided without the commissariat's participation, the ongoing reorganization at Askania was illegal, pure and simple. Amid scattered heckling, Stanchinskii "in the name of Narkompros of the Ukrainian SSR" warned the congress of the impending mortal danger to the Askania steppe:

> Narkompros does not doubt that the questions of hybridization and livestock breeding are of pressing importance for our socialist economy. However, from this it does not follow that those problems, which can be investigated at any institution within the jurisdiction of Narkomzem, must be solved only at Askania-Nova. . . . If the director of the *zapovednik* is to direct his attention to the development of economic matters, these will surely become blown all out of proportion. This is not in the interests of our cause, and our task is to *not* allow this to happen![25]

A. P. Protopopov, an ex-Civil War commissar and VOOP activist, noted the particular outrage of the conversion of Askania into a stockbreeding station, since Askania was not just any *zapovednik* but one which was "at the forefront of institutions of its kind."[26] This argument was given more force by Stanchinskii's close collaborator, S. I. Medvedev, who outlined the basic thrust of the Steppe Institute's recent research. Exhorting the delegates speedily to put right the situation, Medvedev warned that "any interruption, no matter how comparatively short, could have an unexpectedly negative effect on the research," which required continuity. If the congress failed, then Askania would end up fulfilling "the petty errands of the economic organs." What better proof of this could there be, he asked, than the proposal to establish a Machine-Tractor Station (MTS) at the reserve?[27]

Another official delegate of the Ukrainian Narkompros, I. N. Bulankin, also had something to say on Askania. Though Bulankin was only thirty-two years old and had been a member of the Communist Party from the time of the Lenin call-up in 1924, he did not share some of the cruder intellectual and attitudinal attributes of so many others of his background. Without a trace of equivocation, Bulankin proceeded to explain the mentality that reduced Askania to its present circumstances:

> It is clear to us why [the Steppe Institute] was liquidated; it was because [Narkomzem] did not appreciate why the Steppe Institute was valuable to itself as well. There are people who are often guided exclusively by the interests of the present day. They have to this day viewed *zapovedniki* as being somehow suspect. "It is repugnant when land lies idle," they say; "on the one hand, it is not exploited, while on the other. . . . What *is* this scientific research that cannot promise to give us so many centners of grain tomorrow?"[28]

Bulankin attributed these attitudes to a failure to understand the necessity of basic research for technological progress, in this case progress in agriculture. His exploration of the impatient utilitarian mind and its unrealistic expectations of science went far toward explaining one of the basic reasons behind Askania's debacle. It was not, however, the whole story; there was the further complication of the hard currency loan.

The matter of the loan was first broached by Mikhail Solomonovich Shalyt. An ecologist with a keen and rigorous mind, Shalyt had been among the most prominent of the biologists at Askania before Stanchinskii and his great trophic dynamics project pushed him into the background. Whatever the impulse, Shalyt now saw his opportunity to expose the past four years as a waste of the people's money. In 1929, he recalled, Stanchinskii was granted an enormous sum of money in hard currency credits by the government to pursue his research at Askania (this money was in the form of a loan which had to be repaid).[29]

Presumably, the loan originally was to have been repaid from the profits earned by the reserve's 10,000-hectare grain-growing parcel at Dorenburg. Those lands, however, were transferred to a sovkhoz in 1931 and there seemed to be no way to finance repayment.[30] Logically, it was up to the chief executive of the reserve to find an alternate means of repayment, although Stanchinskii, in his capacity of scientific director, had cosigned for it along with the director, Bega. For Stanchinskii's personal and scientific enemies, though, it was far simpler to lay the entire responsibility for the debacle at his door alone.

One of those most eager to do so was the director himself, who was described by Shalyt as having "washed his hands of the whole affair."[31] "It must be understood," Bega said in his own defense (now it was he who was heckled), "that the Steppe Institute had inflated itself into such a white elephant in the region between Kherson and Melitopol' that a decision was finally made: trim it down to size!" Concluding his apologia Bega claimed that he had done everything possible to aid Stanchinskii's research, but that it was not his fault "if it did not all hang together."[32]

Another who saw the Steppe Institute as partly the author of its own troubles was B. K. Fortunatov, the longtime Askania scientist who had recently made some dramatic gestures of accommodation with the reserve's new bosses. Fortunatov observed that Stanchinskii had chosen the site for his ecological studies poorly, since there were so few immediately practical implications that could be derived from a study of the "unrepresentative" and "biologically impoverished" Askania steppe, especially at such a cost. Fortunatov, obviously, had completely missed the point behind Stanchinskii's selection of Askania, for Stanchinskii's criteria were not the Askania steppe's potential value for the acclimatization of exotic fauna and flora nor their representativeness vis-à-vis the Soviet Union's chief crop-growing regions. Nor was Stanchinskii seeking at this time to study areas whose fauna played, actually or potentially, a great role in agriculture or in the economy (be they pests or "useful" fauna). Rather, Stanchinskii chose Askania because its simple, "impoverished" biocenoses offered, he believed, the most convenient conditions for developing and refining his new paradigm in biology. As Stanchinskii so often (and unsuccessfully) tried to explain, only with the development of a more powerful theoretical knowledge of the workings of nature could there be significant improvement in practical affairs.

Yet, his work was persistently misinterpreted. Some, including the careerists Bega, M. F. Ivanov, and Prezent, cynically depicted it as scientific self-indulgence. For their part, the bureaucrats of Narkomzem of the Ukraine misinterpreted Stanchinskii's research in a more benign way. Deceiving themselves, they had failed to understand that investing in Stanchinskii's research was not likely to yield "so many centners of grain tomorrow" but that it was an investment in the future of Soviet agriculture that would begin to pay dividends only after perhaps the passage of a generation. So, even in the matter of the hard currency loan, Bulankin's explanation of the causes of Askania's downfall was confirmed: the inability of the powers that be to see beyond the next day.

In his remarks Makarov came right to the point. Bluntly, he accused the economic organs of trying to transform the *zapovedniki* into "narrow agricultural extension stations." In so doing, Makarov challenged his adversaries once and for all to abandon the facade that those farms *(khoziaistva)* going under the name *zapovedniki* still had anything to do with conservation. Certainly, the economic organs could turn Askania into a hybridization and acclimatization farm, he granted,

> but then it is necessary to come right out and say that [they] have no use any longer for *zapovedniki*, that they have lost all of their importance. . . . It is not necessary to deceive anyone. [They] should discuss the problem and then come right out and say: "At this stage of socialist economic development *zapovedniki* have outgrown their usefulness and are no longer needed."

"Apparently, however," Makarov remarked with a combination of derision and frustration, "no one is either willing or able to say these things, and nothing really can be proved."

Makarov's summation conveyed the feeling that nothing short of the future of conservation was in the balance. "Askania-Nova stands on the threshold of the negation of the very idea of *zapovednost'*," he warned, astonishingly invoking the word which commonly denoted the anathematized concept "inviolability," and continued:

> If this comes to pass, there will be no sense in speaking of the "*zapovednik*" Askania-Nova, for in reality it will have ceased to exist. Instead, we should speak of the Institute for Hybridization and Acclimatization occupying the territory of Askania-Nova.[33]

Although the economic organs had greatly increased their presence at this congress, delegates sympathetic to the positions of Narkompros still constituted a large majority. This fact was reflected in the resolutions which dealt with Askania and with the plight of the *zapovedniki* generally.

On the question of Askania, the congress urged the creation of a competent commission composed of representatives of the USSR and Ukrainian Commissariats of Agriculture, VASKhNIL, and the Ukrainian Academy of Agricultural Sciences, the USSR Academy of Sciences, the Communist Academy, the Ukrainian Narkompros, the Committee for Scientific and Educational Institutions of the USSR

Central Executive Committee, the Ukrainian conservation organs, the proposed all-Union conservation organs, and Makarov, who was to represent the congress. This commission would be empowered to decide the future organizational fate of Askania. The proposal for such a commission, with its delicate balance of organizations friendly and unfriendly to recent developments there, was a response to a similar suggestion of Bega's. However, Bega's proposed review panel would have been composed only of representatives of the Communist Academy, VASKhNIL, and the Central Executive Committee science committee. Such a commission, with its built-in two-to-one majority in favor of the most recent reorganization, was regarded as unacceptable by the congress, and the roster of organizations named in the resolution was seen as a compromise.[34]

Because Makarov's Goskomitet exercised no legal authority in the Ukraine, and an all-Union conservation organ was still only a hope, the convocation of such a commission was the only means by which the conservationists could reestablish *zapovednost'* at Askania. Thus, with no power to do otherwise, the congress pledged itself "not to prejudice the organizational decisions" to be made by the commission. It did go on record notwithstanding that it regarded as "fundamentally essential to preserve the work being done on the holistic study of the arid steppe" and that "in any event, the congress underscores the absolute necessity of preserving the existing areas of virgin steppe in an inviolate condition."[35] Stanchinskii had won an arresting moral victory; in the face of attacks at the congress by the economic organs and, offstage, by Prezent, the unity of the conservationists had held.

THE GENERAL PLAN FOR THE RECONSTRUCTION OF FAUNA

Askania-Nova was in crisis, and therefore the debate over its future and that of the entire network of *zapovedniki* assumed an importance even greater than would have been the case under normal circumstances. Nevertheless, there were other matters on the congress's agenda, too, that cast their own pall on the future of conservation and ecology in the USSR. Of these, the most overshadowing was a general plan for the reconstruction of fauna.

If Prezent had sounded the call for Soviet biologists to enroll in a top-to-bottom transformation of nature, it remained for lesser minions concretely to work out the details. Accordingly, after the usurpation of Askania by the Hybridization-Acclimatization Institute, the old scientific staff, including Fortunatov and Stanchinskii, was assigned the task of developing the theoretical basis and practical recommendations for a Soviet acclimatization policy. One of the first products was Fortunatov's General Plan for the Reconstruction of Economically Important Fauna of European Russia and the Ukraine, which he now presented at the conservation congress.

Although the idea of a general plan was not original to Fortunatov—the acclimatization enthusiast Kh. S. Veitsman developed a similar plan for the fauna of the Caucasus and the Crimea in the summer of 1932 during discussions he led at the new Sukhumi Institute for the Acclimatization of Fauna[36]—Fortunatov not only extended its territorial scope but was the first to present such a plan to a broad audience of biologists. More importantly, from our perspective, he was first to sketch out the ecological principles that would justify such a reorganization of existing natural communities.

At the core of Fortunatov's argument was the belief that the "gigantic fodder base" of the USSR was going to waste owing to undersettlement by game. "We have an evidently gigantic disproportion between the nutritional opportunities provided by the wild areas of our country, on the one hand, and a fauna, which, as a result of a complex historical process, has become impoverished both numerically and from the standpoint of variety," he asserted.[37]

In addition to the predatory activities of human society that had contributed to this impoverishment Fortunatov also suggested that nature itself had imperfectly populated its wilderness. Zoogeographical accidents and the existence of topographical barriers sometimes thwarted the settlement of a suitable area by a particular species of animal, thereby preventing that region from attaining a greater biological productivity, he argued. In support of this belief Fortunatov cited the absence of squirrels from the Caucasus, although there was an apparently plentiful food base there for the rodent. According to Fortunatov, in fact, nature was riddled with such empty habitats (pustye stasii):

> We see in nature a whole series of what I would describe as biologically empty places, nutritional opportunities of occasionally vast territorial scope going unused simply owing to an absence there of fauna capable of taking advantage of them.[38]

Proceeding from this, Fortunatov now outlined a general plan for introducing an entire roster of exotics to regions that putatively presented suitable nutritional opportunities to assure their successful acclimatization. For the European Russian North, he recommended the wide acclimatization of the muskrat, already under way; the acclimatization of the musk-ox to the Kola Peninsula (it was once thought to have inhabited the area); the introduction of the Kamchatka otter, the Kolyma marmot, and the North American raccoon; and the reacclimatization of the beaver and the restoration of the moose and reindeer to their former ranges. For the Central Forest Region, Fortunatov suggested the reacclimatization of the moose, the roe deer, and the capercaillie and the introduction of the maral deer and the baibak marmot. For the forest-steppe and the Ukraine, measures included the acclimatization of the sika deer from the Far East and Manchuria and an ambitious attempt to genetically reconstruct and then reacclimatize the aurochs—the progenitor of domestic cattle. For the steppe region, the saiga, the korsak, and the baibak were to be reacclimatized. For the northern Urals, sable were to be brought in from the Baikal region and red fox from Kamchatka, while voles and hamsters were to be introduced as their food base. Mountain goats and mountain sheep were to be introduced to the southern Urals from Siberia.[39]

Actually, much of Fortunatov's plan consisted only of the reacclimatization of such vanishing endemics as moose, saiga, and European bison to areas from which they had only recently been eliminated by hunting and other human activities. It is not too far-fetched to view this relative emphasis on the need to reacclimatize endemics over the acclimatization of complete exotics as another instance of protective coloration. Although Fortunatov explained this emphasis by pointing both to the Soviet state's inability to finance the importation of a great number of costly exotics from abroad and to the possibility of the displacement of existing species by introduced competitors (such a risk would be lessened in reacclimatization), the second argument seems more convincing. This seems particularly likely in light of the later denunciation of Fortunatov by the Lysenkoite director of Askania, Aleksandr Ageevich Nurinov, for allegedly having followed the discredited Stanchinskii line.[40]

Under the protective coloration of the ambitious banner of the general plan, it seems, Fortunatov had cooked up a recipe for relative ecological caution. This was borne out by his lack of enthusiasm for acclimatizing the American mink and the raccoon dog on ecological grounds, his opposition to the introduction of the sika deer to the Caucasus as a competitor to the local red deer, his criticism of "chaotic, local" patterns of faunal reconstruction, and his failure to mention the extermination of "harmful" species in his plan.[41]

Fortunatov's presentation was accompanied by a report on the same theme by his colleague at the Moscow Zoo (Fortunatov was also affiliated with that institution), P. A. Manteifel'. Manteifel' devoted the major segment of his talk to a discussion of the physiological aspects of acclimatization, although he, too, had a list of high-priority animals for introduction. Significantly, his list included the mink and the raccoon dog, whose trial acclimatization he urged on a "massive scale" in the Caucasus zapovednik. "We must regard zapovedniki . . . as production units," he concluded, "and not as institutions cut off from life."[42]

Not everyone was immediately enamored with the theory of ecological empty places. Stanchinskii, responding first, noted the absence of a solid theory of biocenoses which could assist in predicting what trophic and other ecological relationships would be affected by the acclimatization of an exotic. "It is here that we have our greatest weak spot," he warned, "indeed, a total lapsis."

Stanchinskii took Fortunatov to task for simply selecting a score or so of mammalian species—out of a hat, it almost appeared—and then deciding where they might be successfully and profitably introduced. Such an approach was simplistic, he objected. The problem was extraordinarily complex in its ecological dimension alone. Moreover, if socialism were to remain synonymous with planning and rationality, any plan for the reconstruction of nature would first have to be coordinated with the actual economic needs of the country; it was first essential to find out from the planning and economic organs what sorts of raw materials were in sharpest demand, and only then proceed to draft plans to augment biological productivity to meet those needs. Finally, an institutional base for such systems-oriented planning barely existed; the Sukhumi Acclimatization Institute in the Abkhazian ASSR, which pretended to such a planning role, had only been established not long before. (Stanchinskii conspicuously omitted mention of Askania-Nova as such a planning base because he obviously hoped that the Hybridization and Acclimatization Institute would soon be dissolved and his Scientific Steppe Institute reinstated.)

For all of these reasons, then, Stanchinskii rejected Fortunatov's general plan as no plan at all. "We are not only unprepared to draft a general plan," he insisted, "but we should totally own up to the fact that . . . we are entering the Second Five-Year Plan with insufficient material to speak of . . . even *any* plan for the reconstruction of our fauna.[43]

While Stanchinskii was exceptive to Fortunatov's proposal, he was positively dismissive toward the remarks of Manteifel', which he described as "having failed to satisfy me in any regard." For a scientific paper, Stanchinskii found the presentation "quite subjective"; what scientific conclusions there were had been "hastily arrived at" and were scarcely credible.[44] Then again, Manteifel' was an authentic charlatan, whereas Fortunatov was merely playing at it.

Another strong voice for caution was that of G. A. Kozhevnikov. Appealing to Mendelian genetics, Kozhevnikov observed that the acclimatizer might select individuals for acclimatization from an unsuitable population or simply from an unsuitable genotype; these would fail to thrive under the new conditions. He cited the authority of N. I. Vavilov and the community of classical geneticists as to the inability of animals to adapt limitlessly to new conditions or to pass along these individual, conditioned adaptations to their progeny. Acclimatization was therefore a matter of genetic luck, even if it could be made safe for the ecological community that was to play host to the exotic.[45]

Kozhevnikov also provided direct evidence to buttress his claims that acclimatization was a failure in practice; at the Sukhumi Acclimatization Institute—where, ironically, he finally found work after abandoning active duties at Moscow State University—all of the anthropoid apes introduced from Africa had perished. Aligning himself with Stanchinskii's reservations specifically, Kozhevnikov concluded that Soviet biologists should prudently confine themselves to the limited reacclimatization of recently vanished fauna until a solid theory of acclimatization was developed.[46]

To the side of Kozhevnikov and Stanchinskii came S. A. Severtsov. Although he would later critique Lamarckian biology from the antiteleological standpoint of classical genetics,[47] much in the spirit of Kozhevnikov's remarks, he limited his comments at the congress to an ecological critique of Fortunatov's "overly simplistic" approach. Acclimatization, he stated, "ultimately boils down to the problem of surrogate species." The implication here was that the successful introduction of one species into an established ecological community could proceed only at the expense of existing members of that community, whose niches would be usurped by the more vigorous newcomers.[48]

The appeals for caution by conservationists in turn provoked rebuttals from the proacclimatization camp. Kulagin, whose advocacy of conservation had always been colored by a certain utilitarianism, contested the arguments advanced by Kozhevnikov. Bogdanov's favorite during his declining years, Kulagin now faithfully defended the Lamarckian heritage of his mentor, declaring:

The geneticists believe that some animals have genes enabling them to adapt while others lack them, and that attempts to acclimatize the latter will end in failure. Where do these animals get these genes? It is as if they appear out of the blue! We cannot share such a view.[49]

Actually, Kulagin's position did not constitute a total rejection of the concept of the gene as the bearer of the organism's heredity; he was only arguing that genes were also responsive to the influence of the environment. "Viewed in this way," he announced, "genetics does not stand in the way of acclimatization."[50]

Even though it was then known that chromosomes, at least, were altered when exposed to x-rays—thanks to the experiments of American Herman J. Muller and Russians D. D. Romashov, G. A. Nadson, and G. S. Filippov—geneticists still could not accept the contention of the Lamarckian acclimatizers that the genetic material of the organism could change in an adaptive way in response to new environmental conditions. This belief the geneticists rejected as teleological, and Kulagin's attempt to reconcile Mendelian and environmentalist beliefs on heredity in support of acclimatization was doomed to founder on this crucial point.[51]

While Kulagin tried to defend Fortunatov's proposals, other enthusiasts felt they did not go far enough. P. P. Smolin, of the Young Naturalists, complained that Fortunatov touched only on the positive side of faunal reconstruction, ignoring the equally pressing need to exterminate such harmful life forms as the wolf, the wolverine, and the lynx:

In the final analysis the composition of our fauna must reflect social goals; a specific complex of [natural] objects must be created which will provide the maximum usable productivity (*effekt*), and all of those species that will impair that productivity must be reduced in number to a greater or a lesser degree.[52]

Both Kulagin's and Smolin's remarks were noteworthy in the development of biological thought under Stalin. If Kulagin's talk and the eventual responses to it served to clarify the opposition of classical genetics to acclimatization, then Smolin's comments portended biology's wholesale rejection of the concept of the holistic natural community in favor of a view of nature as a place where "harmful" and "useful" species were randomly associated. Moreover, the "usefulness" or "harmfulness" of individual species was assessed solely from the standpoint of the present day. The utilitarian champions of this dualistic framework completely ignored the possibility that unknown future discoveries might transform a "harmful" species into a "useful" one, or that a particular species might have an entire range of impacts on human society. They totally disregarded criteria of usefulness other than those that were defined by the immediate economic requirements of socialist construction.

Now Makarov entered the fray on the side of the advocates of caution. Although he restated his earlier endorsement—in principle—of the need for acclimatization, Makarov suggested that the time for such a program on a mass scale had not yet come. Such an all-out effort, he warned, "is an extremely dangerous thing in terms of the consequences it might have for our economy," and therefore urged that acclimatization should be limited for the time being to small-scale trials. He, too, concluded with the observation that "we have not yet developed a theory of acclimatization or reacclimatization."[53]

Fortunatov was a man in the middle. Fearful that his continued employment at Askania would be jeopardized by any overt indication of sympathy for the conservationist position, Fortunatov in his closing arguments refuted Stanchinskii's call for caution, his remarks hinting at the duress affecting Soviet scientists:

> Caution is a fine thing, and if we could afford to wait, say, an entire Five-Year Plan until . . . this problem is worked out in detail, we would certainly obtain the best resolution of this problem. But are we the masters of our own schedules? No! The reconstruction of fauna has already begun, and it is forging ahead full-speed on an enormous scale. Already millions have been invested, and huge shipments of animals and birds have been transferred from one place to another.[54]

Manteifel', too, was in a hurry, although by contrast to Fortunatov his haste was a product of an early and genuine enthusiasm for transforming nature. Having dismissed Stanchinskii's objections, Manteifel' tackled Severtsov's warning against introducing possible competitor species to ecosystems where they might threaten the survival of endemics. Perhaps he thought that he made short work of Severtsov when he optimistically proclaimed:

> Competitor species! Yes, let them compete, but let us calculate the food base to ensure that it will be adequate for them both.[55]

As it turned out, Manteifel' 's simplistic ideas about plenitude in nature were just then being undermined, for at Moscow State University the brilliant G. F. Gauze had designed an elegant series of experiments proving that when two species having largely overlapping habitat and nutritional requirements were brought together in the same system, one species would inevitably drive the other to extinction (the competitive-exclusion principle, as it was later christened by Garrett Hardin).[56] Anywhere else, such controverting experimental results would have made responsible government officials and the scientific community think twice about the wisdom of acclimatization. However, Gauze's findings, while acclaimed by the worldwide community of biologists, posed no obstacle to acclimatization in the Soviet Union. Not only was "practice" superior to theory; some practices took precedence over other practices. Gauze soon found it expeditious to abandon his ecological experiments for the less exposed work of developing antibiotics, while the juggernaut of acclimatization rolled on.

Still, the delegates searched desperately for some politically safe yet effective deterrent to the great transformation of nature. As the scope for protective coloration seemed to contract inexorably, the cautious majority showed itself capable of great ingenuity and subtlety. First, the framers of the resolution on acclimatization recommended that all of the zoological parks of the USSR come under the direct control of the Goskomitet, thereby undercutting Manteifel' 's power base at the

Moscow Zoo. Secondly, while the resolution gave its qualified approval to a circumspect policy of acclimatization, zoos were designated as the key institutions to carry out that policy. Saddling the zoos with this task would accomplish two major objectives simultaneously: it would exempt the *zapovedniki* from serving as such acclimatization bases and would prevent the early dispersal of introduced exotics into the wild.

Underscoring their determination to preserve the Narkompros *zapovedniki* as ecological *etalony* and to shield them from any direct or indirect economic use, including acclimatization, the delegates decided that it was high time to distinguish clearly between the two types of *zapovedniki*. There were, first, those *zapovedniki* that were

> territories, set aside for the protection of various genetic resources, comprising the most characteristic natural features of the region from an economic-geographical point of view, conducting on their territory holistic scientific research and setting for themselves the goal of the discovery, in a dialectical-Marxist way, of those regularities that determine the individual development of every element in the *zapovednik,* their mutual interrelationships, their . . . dynamics, . . . thereby solving a number of problems in general biology chiefly of an ecological nature. . . .

Second, there were *zapovedniki* that were "protected territories of the type of '*rezervaty'*." They were

> subject to the jurisdiction of agencies representing a particular branch of the economy and which have been established to restore depleted, commercially important species of animals and plants or to conduct mass-scale experiments in acclimatization, reacclimatization, hybridization, or captive breeding, etc., so that these . . . species can be made available for exploitation in the shortest time possible. . . .[57]

In this way, the congress tried once again to resolve the unsettled matter of the taxonomy of protected territories, which had contributed to the present predicament of the Narkompros *zapovedniki*.

Finally, in a drastic move to secure the Narkompros reserves against their enemies, the delegates recommended the reserves' jurisdictional reorganization. Although the majority of delegates supported the republican Commissariats of Education in their struggle with the economic organs, this did not imply backing for continued Narkompros jurisdiction over conservation matters. The conflict over Askania-Nova exposed the impotence of the Education Commissariats. Only a powerful, all-Union agency could defend conservation interests—if anything could.

In speech after speech, the simmering desire to abandon the tutelage of the Education Commissariats for that of either the USSR Central Executive Committee or the USSR Council of People's Commissars now boiled over into an insistent clamor. Even Makarov and Bulankin, who, respectively, represented the Commissariats of Education of the RSFSR and the Ukraine, had been won over to the necessity of such a course. While there must have been many twinges of regret over leaving the nest that had served conservation so well, when it was resolved to seek the transfer of the republican Goskomitets and *zapovedniki* to the USSR Central Executive Committee there was hardly a peep of resistance.

Logically, it was correspondingly decided to expand the scope of VOOP's activities to an all-Union competence as well. A new organizational committee for the proposed All-Union Society for the Promotion of the Development and Conservation of Natural Resources was named, containing twenty-four founder-members drawn from both ends of the conservation spectrum, including Smidovich, Ter-Oganesov, Makarov, Shillinger, Stanchinskii, Bega, the delegate of the People's Commissariat of the Forest Industry of the USSR, Kulagin, Bulankin, and even a number of communist factory workers.

More interesting was the selection of the new society's honorary members (reminiscent of the old Tsarist-era practice of finding patrons for new academic societies from among the members of the Imperial family). Klim Egorovich Voroshilov and Semen Budennyi, two old friends of Askania-Nova from the Civil War, were chosen, as was N. V. Krylenko, apparently remembered with gratitude for his services against the "left deviation" during the Cultural Revolution. Two honorary members from the world of science were Academicians N. I. Vavilov and B. A. Keller, the first at the apogee of his career as president of the Lenin All-Union Academy of Agricultural Sciences and the latter a fast-rising star in the Academy of Sciences proper. Others came from the political sphere. The choices, however, betrayed a degree of political naiveté on the part of the conservationists. By 1937, only Keller, Budennyi, and Voroshilov remained in good political odor; the others, if they had not already, were soon to succumb to the grim fate of repression in the second half of the 1930s.

With the conclusion of the congress, the conservation cause in the Soviet Union truly stood at another crossroads. The alternatives were clearly symbolized by two images: Askania as the ecological research center it had been, briefly, under Stanchinskii, and Askania as the hybridization and acclimatization farm it had now become.

FOURTEEN

Conservation without Ecology: Nature Protection in the Age of Lysenko

To the increasing apprehension of established naturalists, I. I. Prezent had carved himself a handsome niche indeed, beating the drum for what he saw as a creative, activist biology. According to his understanding of science and society, the development of science under capitalism was necessarily impeded by restricted research opportunities and by the cloistered autonomy of theory, untested by practice. During the Tsarist period, for example, such eminent researchers as plant physiologist K. A. Timiriazev were forced to conduct their experiments on crimped, inadequate plots. Particularly backward were the sciences that studied what Prezent referred to as "so-called wild nature": faunistics, geobotany, and biocenology. Mirroring the low level of economic development generally in prerevolutionary Russia, which Prezent said had "failed to demand of science a deep study of the laws of animal and plant life in 'wild nature,' " these disciplines had failed to develop experimental field techniques. Moreover, naturalists compounded this regrettable state of affairs by their commitment to the credo "Study first, experiment later," the hallmark of the "bourgeois" scientific method.[1]

The triumph of revolutionary socialism in Russia, however, now provided all needed conditions not simply to rectify these deficiencies but also to far outstrip capitalist natural science, enthused Prezent. As USSR Commissar of Agriculture Iakovlev had declared at a recent plenum of his commissariat, it was now possible to solve problems in a short time. Experiments, such as determining where cotton can grow, would not drag out over periods of many years on tiny trial plots, depriving society of any immediate benefits; rather, the commissar announced, now "we perform our experiments on tens of thousands of hectares."[2] To this Prezent added that the transformation of nature through economic development itself constituted one gigantic experiment; broad changes in whole populations—indeed, in entire landscapes—could now be studied at one go.[3]

Aside from the creation of novel research opportunities, socialism enhanced scientific development by reconciling theory and practice, Prezent held, with practice as the criterion of scientific truth. While "bourgeois" practitioners of the scientific method might have found this reconciliation indistinguishable from their own belief in the validating role of the experiment, Prezent had something extra in mind. Only "socioeconomic practical mastery"—results on a mass scale—could

211

authentically validate the truth of a scientific theory. Thus, results of the laboratory, of the small experimental plot, or even of observations in the field could carry only meager significance as compared with the results of trial plantings or acclimatization carried out over hundreds of thousands of hectares. (There was no small irony here, since Lysenko's original demonstrations of the conversion of seasonal wheats were conducted in a couple of flower pots, and, in any case, could never successfully be repeated under laboratory conditions. As David Joravsky has pointed out, scientific "truth" was now held hostage by those responsible for reporting the results of the massive new economic "experiments"; as the "Lysenko affair" has revealed, gross inaccuracies in reporting led to the official validation of preposterous biological notions.)

Despite the propitious conditions for science so obligingly provided by Soviet power, Prezent complained that there were still potent forces blocking progress. Chief among them were a number of natural scientists, relics of prerevolutionary patterns of thought. Instead of inspiring society with passion "to revolutionize the life of plants and animals," as Iakovlev had enjoined, they sought to inculcate "a passive 'love of nature.' "[4]

At the basis of this passive, contemplative, even obsequious approach to nature was the holists' erring belief, in Prezent's opinion, that unexploited ecological systems embodied a natural harmony which could be as easily shattered by socialist economic activity as by capitalist. Indeed, charged Prezent, there existed "a modest group of scientists who, adhering to the theory of harmonious equilibrium," claimed that nature would take its revenge on those who defied its limits, and who even claimed that socialism was aggravating this danger.[5] It was as if they had outfitted nature "in a police officer's tunic," he observed, seeking in nature some strict deus ex machina to obstruct social and economic changes that they found unpalatable.[6]

One such adherent singled out for criticism by Prezent was agronomist B. Demchinskii, whom he accused of purveying an agronomic philosophy which sought "the protection of free nature from the hand of man, with man *passively availing himself* of nature's bounty but in no way *transforming* her. . . ." Demchinskii, who, like other conservation-oriented scientists, had trotted out Engels's famous paragraph from "The Role of Labor" in support of his positions, had argued in a book published in 1932 that organisms were always in equilibrium with their environment. Consequently, agriculturally motivated transformations either in the environment or in the organism would always reduce the organism's fitness and disrupt the harmony that prevailed before. In a withering review, Prezent charged that Demchinskii's ideas were "leading to the practical rejection of . . . all types of acclimatization of crops," indeed, to the abandonment of all cultivated agriculture. Demchinskii's view of selection stations was caricatured as "unique types of *zapovedniki* where the 'enfeebling' influence of agriculture would be eliminated." Prezent identified the danger of Demchinskii's book as dual: it simultaneously distorted Marxism and sabotaged socialist construction. It was no less than "a refined form of wrecking." "We must strike a hard, Bolshevik blow against Demchinskii's book," Prezent urged, ". . . because Demchinskii is not alone."

Indeed, Prezent spared neither ink nor paper in alerting Soviet society to the threat of those who would place "a theoretical land mine under our [socialist] construction." Another prominent target of his fulminations was Stanchinskii's ally at Askania and chairperson of the Ukrainian Committee for the Protection of Monuments of Nature (UKOPP), A. A. Ianata, who had committed the unpardonable sin of opposing any expansion of the arable land at the expense of virgin steppe or its use in the acclimatization of introduced varieties—obviously a reference to Ianata's defense of Askania-Nova as an ecological *zapovednik*. Prezent concluded his polemic with a clever play on the title of Engels's controversial article, certain that "the . . . overwhelming mass of Soviet scientists, . . . our entire Soviet public opinion, will strike a telling blow at this slander of Marxism, this antiagricultural tendency, this philosophy of the *transformation of man into ape*" (italics added).[7]

ECOLOGY'S DIALECTICAL RESPONSE

A reasonably astute lot, Soviet ecologists began to modify both the substance and the presentation of their positions in the face of this barrage. Much of this modification was aimed at salvaging ecology's basically holistic framework by taking Marxian philosophical critiques into account and by expurgating teleological and philosophically idealist points of doctrine. V. Bukovskii, for instance, shielded his defense of the notion of the *relative* self-containment of the biocenosis by ostentatiously contesting those who considered it to be *absolutely* so.[8]

In a similar vein, Bukovskii assailed Pachoskii's well-known efforts to analogize plant communities with human society. Those like Beklemishev, who had compared the biocenosis to an individual organism, or Thienemann, who had gone even further, terming the biocenosis an actual organism of the second order, were likewise challenged. However, these sallies were not the wanton work of an academic vandal. As with his argument against the total closure of the ecological community, Bukovskii used the extreme, reductionist positions of Thienemann, Pachoskii, and Beklemishev as foils to offset his dialectical middle-ground position that ecological communities do indeed "possess a certain ability for self-regulation," though not in the same sense as that of an organism.[9]

Having demonstrated his dialectical credentials, Bukovskii, saving his most potent artillery for last, now turned to his chief targets: the antiholistic partisans of the vegetation continuum theory. This group, led by Elenkin, Ramenskii, Komarov, and Il'inskii, saw "no competition" and "no mutualism," according to Bukovskii, but instead held that all changes in the vegetation were brought about by such external factors as climate, geological disturbances, and the like. By stressing the overwhelming dependence of vegetation cover on abiotic factors and downplaying the biotic ties among the plants themselves and between them and other biota, the antiholists thereby minimized or even denied any side effects of tampering with living nature. Such a plastic view lent itself far better to the aims of the great transformation of nature than did the holistic view, even Bukovskii's modified one. Fearing the implications of the triumph of the antiholistic view, therefore, Bukovskii pressed his attack. With ironic cunning, he branded the vegetation continuum group the intellectual heirs of the great German ecologist Karl Möbius (actually the spiritual father of the holistic camp), in particular to the view of the biocenosis as "a morphologically static entity, frozen and immobile." What had emerged from their theorizing was nothing other than "a mechanist theory of the equilibrium of biocenoses," a description which could not have failed to bring to mind Bukharin's similar theory of socioeconomic development, so derisively damned by Stalin in 1929.[10] Bukovskii was able to tag Elenkin and his colleagues in this fashion because the antiholists themselves had originally, anomalously called their concept the "theory of dynamic equilibrium." In fact, though, the only "dynamism" in their model was supplied by exogenous forces—there was no provision for any internal, dialectical development of the ecological community—while *equilibrium* was a particularly inappropriate choice, since it implied the existence of a system, which the antiholists denied. (They would have been far more precise had they described vegetation as being in a condition of stasis, according to their theory.) Nevertheless, the antiholists themselves had handed Bukovskii his terminological ammunition, and he did not stint in associating them with the undesirable notion of "equilibrium," the very charge that had previously dogged the holists.

We may view Bukovskii's essay as an elegant exercise in scientific politics. By repudiating extreme positions, he was able to defend modified holism as a reasonable position, by contrast. Moreover, by attacking Pachoskii, Beklemishev, and Thienemann (two of whom did not live in the USSR at the time), he had inflicted no more damage to ecology than had already been done, if, indeed, the well-taken Deborinite critiques are to be regarded as damaging. Finally, he was gambling that the powers that be would opt for dialectical science, as embodied in holistic ecology, over its mechanist rival, despite the latter's more congenial implications for the great transformation of nature. With the stakes so high, Bukovskii saw nothing wrong in shifting the odds a little more in his favor, blurring the continuum group's actual opposition to holism by linking the group with the holistic attribute *equilibrium*, the term most associated with ecological opposition to nature-transforming schemes.

Acutely aware of the need to make his views more palatable to the prevailing mood, Stanchinskii, too, modified and developed his ecological views, emphasizing different elements from those stressed in his talk and articles of 1930 and 1931. Like Bukovskii, though, Stanchinskii found a dialectical approach not merely politically expedient, but intellectually fertile.

By no means abandoning trophic dynamics as the key to understanding ecological communities, Stanchinskii now took pains to underscore the historical and dynamic nature of his concept of the biocenosis, as opposed to the teleological, structuralist, or static ones that had fallen into extreme disrepute. To clarify his notion of an ecological system, a crucial point, Stanchinskii spelled out how his views diverged from those of the other schools. His rejection of teleological positions was unambiguous; the biocenosis, unlike a living organism, did not develop along a specific path as a result of preexisting genetic instructions. Rather, he proposed a view of the biocenosis as a system of species whose mutual, historical adaptation to each other and to the abiotic environment they shared (and created) was dialectical, unplanned, unpredictable, and unduplicatable. The development of the biocenosis, like a kaleidoscope, was the product of the emergence of new evolutionary facts through this unending flux of interactions.

Yet, within this sea of myriad interactions of the biocenosis there were major, architechtonic units—biocenotic systems of species tied to each other by particularly dependent relationships in a food web.[11] Sometimes these cenotic systems constituted semiautonomous instances of vertical integration, trophic ladders in miniature. But sometimes they were unbelievably complex and overlapping, and Stanchinskii commenced work on a study and illustrated taxonomy of these cenotic systems.[12]

Having defended trophic dynamics as a progressive, historical, dialectical approach to biocenology, Stanchinskii next sought to dissociate clearly his notion of the existence of a "proportionality" in the biocenosis from the discredited concept of "equilibrium," which he now rejected as "formalistic." Partisans of such views, noting (as he so recently had) the persistence of numerical proportionalities among the populations of various species in natural communities as well as the apparent fluctuation of those populations around a norm, rushed to conclude that the biocenosis was therefore in a state of equilibrium. Furthermore, they pointed to this equilibrium as confirmation of the alleged ability of the biocenosis to regulate itself or even organize energy use in the most effective way. Stanchinskii made it clear that he now regarded those ideas as "idealistic concepts" and "metaphysical approaches" to the problem.[13]

By contrast, Stanchinskii advanced his more dialectical notion of proportionality. Not denying the existence of states of equilibrium in biocenoses over the short term, he nevertheless pointed out their relative and transmutating nature, buttressing his argument with a short passage from Engels's *Anti-Duhring*. Since, according to Stanchinskii, the equilibrium observed in nature was "no equilibrium in the ordinary sense," not even a "relative equilibrium," he suggested that the use of the term to describe the properties of biocenoses be eschewed altogether. Rather, he proposed, the biocenosis was marked by a "property of proportionality," which reflected the system's organic, harmonious continuity with past and future states:

> In distinction to a system in equilibrium, the biocenosis remains in constant development owing to its internal . . . dynamics . . . leading to transformations, . . . to evolution expressing itself first of all in so-called successional stages of biocenoses. It is not equilibrium, . . . but in fact *an absence of equilibrium that is characteristic for biocenoses.*[14]

Finally, Stanchinskii insured himself against the charge that he construed the biocenosis as a closed, self-contained system. Much like Bukovskii, he pointed to the "dual" or even "multiple citizenship" of fauna of neighboring biocenoses as evidence in support of his contention. Not infrequently, he observed, animals and birds engaged in migrations that took them even to distant systems on other continents; sometimes, organisms evolved so as to spend only a portion of their complex life cycle in any one particular habitat. While these organisms constituted "a theoretical and practical difficulty for the biocenologist," lamented Stanchinskii, all the same "they seem to make it impossible to set boundaries for individual biocenoses." In this way, Stanchinskii and his colleagues sought to shield what was valuable in the new ecology from attack by jettisoning speculative elements and by highlighting the concordance of the remainder with dialectical thought. They had also demonstrated the intellectual courage to abandon the neat, a priori schema of the structuralists, and to embrace the fact that reality was disappointingly messy. This was a particularly brave choice, since it meant abandoning the quest to transform ecology into a fully predictable, powerful exact science like physics, which was one of the few things that now offered ecology any hope of gaining real legitimacy.[15]

Not surprisingly, Stanchinskii also concluded that a demonstration of self-criticism would, under the circumstances, not be a bad thing. Speaking for the field as a whole in an introduction to materials he prepared for the Fifth Congress of Zoologists, he criticized the Fourth Congress for proceeding "along the old, well-trodden path of bourgeois science."[16]

Having abandoned hope that the great transformation would quietly vanish from the Soviet scene, Stanchinskii persevered in his efforts to at least underlay it with some genuine scientific foundation. In order to master the management of biocenoses, he warned, it was above all necessary to gain an understanding of healthy, pristine biocenoses in nature. The alternative, he noted, was there for all to see: ugly, disrupted seminatural environments.

Similarly, if "until recently acclimatization was conducted in a nakedly empirical way, without any theoretical foundations," a theoretical development of the problem now emerged as "a necessity of the first order."[17] Before long the opportunity to develop such a foundation was thrust upon him.

After the Scientific Steppe Institute was liquidated in the summer of 1932, Stanchinskii, along with the other scientific staff members at Askania, was assigned to develop a theoretical basis for acclimatization. The challenge for him now was to fulfill his assignment while preserving the integrity of his ecological views. As he wrote in the preface to his "Theoretical Foundations of the Acclimatization of Fauna: Tasks, Means, and Methods," no doubt with a twinge, "socialist science places completely new demands on scientists unheard of in bourgeois science." These new demands weighed heavily on Stanchinskii's project, particularly in light of the evolution of his scientific views.[18]

Acclimatization—which Stanchinskii defined broadly as the resettlement by humans of wild or domesticated animals from their natural habitats to new ones, their survival in the new habitats, and their continued ability to produce fertile offspring—was, for him, particularly fraught with problems. For one thing, not every species could live everywhere, while not every animal capable of living in new conditions would retain its economically desirable qualities in those new conditions. Secondly, there were also biocenotic limitations to acclimatization: the domesticated cow could not be introduced to wide regions in Africa because of lethal diseases transmitted by the tsetse fly. Thirdly, there was the old ecological objection that an introduced exotic could imperil the host community, becoming a serious pest or weed.[19]

Permeating the entire problem was the complex nature of acclimatization: a synergistic interplay of the principles of classical genetics and community ecology. It was no accident, therefore, that Stanchinskii held up the "grandiose research work conducted by Academician N. I. Vavilov" as a model of scientifically guided acclimatization.[20]

To introduce order into an area previously characterized by "the most general and superficial observations," Stanchinskii set out his own thoughts on acclimatization in the form of a systematized taxonomy. All of the logically possible categories of acclimatization were listed and evaluated.

The first category, which he termed *phenotypical acclimatization,* was marked by an absence of any changes in the introduced form's genotype, or genetic structure. That sometimes included even an absence of changes in the organism's phenotype (observable traits), in which case he labeled the process endophenotypical acclimatization. According to Stanchinskii, the Norway rat, in its peregrinations from Asia to North America via Europe, and the Asiatic mongoose, introduced to Jamaica, were examples of such acclimatization, not having undergone any observable changes in their genetic makeup. This broad category also embraced ecologically plastic species, whose heredity did not change from generation to generation, but whose populations permanently enjoyed the capacity to undergo nonheritable adaptations in their observable traits, which process Stanchinskii had earlier designated morphosis. This variety of phenotypical adaptation he labeled *exotypical acclimatization,* an example of which was the ability of many varieties of sheep to grow longer wool in moister climates; their genetic makeup allowed for a whole range of potential phenotypical expressions, depending upon environmental conditions.[21]

Even when working with ecologically plastic species, however, the ecologist needed to remain aware that some of its geographical races or subspecies might be more adaptive than others. Since each of these subgroups had different nutritional and other requirements arising out of their individual evolutionary histories in geographical isolation from each other, each constituted what Stanchinskii called a separate ecotype. It was the job of the acclimatization zoologist to identify the ecological requirements for each ecotype of a species and then use that information to match the most suitable ecotype to its correspondingly suitable new habitat.

Phenotypical acclimatization, Stanchinskii averred, was the only type of acclimatization that could be attempted with any assurance of success (at least from the point of view of the introduced plant or animal), since it was the only type that fell within the adaptive limits presented by the organism's genetic coding.

The only other form of successful acclimatization he broadly termed *genotypical acclimatization* because it was based on changes in the introduced form's genetic structure that enabled it to thrive in its new environment. Such changes in the genetic material could come about either through naturally occurring mutations (ecotypical genoacclimatization) or through the creation of a hybrid variety by mating introduced forms with local varieties (mixotypical genoacclimatization).[22]

As concerned the first course, hoping for an adaptive natural mutation in the genetic structure of an introduced form could prove a costly and exhausting endeavor, Stanchinskii cautioned, given both the infrequency of natural mutations and the unlikelihood that they would prove adaptive. Combining the genes of already adapted local races with introduced varieties, as Vavilov was doing, carried far greater assurances of success. Glaringly excluded from the entire discussion was any mention of Lamarckian-style acclimatization.[23]

Turning then to ecological considerations, Stanchinskii emphasized that what was desired was a search for "optimal"—meaning adequate—conditions for the introduction of biota, and not "supraoptimal" ones, which would fail to provide natural checks on the exotics and would allow them to become pests. With a great deal of insight he observed that the physiological optima of the exotic might not always coincide with the economic and social desiderata of society; indeed, there was no guarantee that, finding itself in physiologically optimal conditions, the exotic form would even retain its economically valuable features that motivated its introduction in the first place.[24]

Finally, Stanchinskii confronted the "theory of ecologically empty places." Conceding their existence in principle, he noted however that, in the "overwhelming majority of cases," ecologically analogous areas to which exotics might successfully be introduced were already populated by analogous fauna, i.e., by ecological types (ecotypes) that had similar nutritional and other requirements. An exotic could be integrated into the natural community only if it were more highly differentiated than the native forms, so that it could realize a truly vacant niche (intercenotic inhabitation). Otherwise, successful acclimatization of the exotic would proceed only at the expense of local forms which could not compete as successfully for the disputed resources—Gauze's competitive-exclusion law, called by Stanchinskii "exhabitation." In the worst case, successful introduction might cost the stability of the biocenosis as a whole (suprainhabitation). Such drastic outcomes might prove more harmful than beneficial.[25]

Although Stanchinskii's essay was characterized by rigorous, unrelenting logic, neither that nor its protective coloration could redeem it, or him, in the eyes of his persecutors. His theory of acclimatization became a personal disaster. Virtually omnipotent only three years earlier, Stanchinskii had now been relegated at Askania to virtual serfdom at the Hybridization-Acclimatization Institute.

The acclimatization essay was the evidence Stanchinskii's enemies needed to clinch his downfall. Now the blows came crashing down on his head with increasing savagery. The publication of his magnum opus on the trophic dynamics of the Askania steppe, which had already been typeset, was suddenly halted. "It was denounced as a bagatelle, and all further research was foreclosed as 'not having any practical importance,' " Stanchinskii's former colleagues N. T. Nechaeva and S. I. Medvedev related. Not surprisingly, the critics of his research were T. D. Lysenko and I. I. Prezent, who had reached their verdict after a sweep through Askania in the summer of 1933.[26]

In a *cri de coeur,* Medvedev, citing the "extremely important conclusions" reached by Stanchinskii and his team that were contained in his book, appealed to the All-Ukrainian Academy of Agricultural Sciences to cease its persecution of his mentor. But that proved unavailing.[27]

By 1934, Stanchinskii had been "exposed" by a party purge committee and arrested. Among the other victims of this campaign were Medvedev himself, A. A. Ianata, ecologist A. P. Gunali, I. V. Goncharov (who lost his party membership), and even B. K. Fortunatov, who had offered the plan for faunal transformation. With crude vehemence they were denounced as "mongrels of human society" and "wreckers" by Askania's new director, A. A. Nurinov, a fervent Lysenko supporter. Of special interest was the diagnosis by the party purge committee that Stanchinskii had deviously wormed his "counterrevolutionary, pernicious theories" into the published transactions of the institute and had posed, with his students, as progressive Soviet scientists.[28]

Protective coloration was no longer protective. Stanchinskii, who was accused of placing the acclimatization work of the institute "on crutches" and of trying to sabotage the hog-breeding work of M. F. Ivanov,[29] watched his career collapse. Like Kozhevnikov (who had died just one day before the conclusion of the 1933 conservation congress), Stanchinskii was routed from his academic posts. Arrested and unable to publish, Stanchinskii relinquished the editorship of the *Journal of Ecology and Biocenology* to his old friend D. N. Kashkarov, who had proved politically more adept. After an absence from public and academic life for four years, Stanchinskii resurfaced in the late 1930s as a senior scientific worker at the Central Forest *zapovednik,* where his old friend, reserve director G. L. Grave, gave him refuge. He finished out his working life at the *zapovednik,* perishing in total obscurity in the small town of Vologda in 1942 in flight from the advancing Nazis. Along with the stillbirth of trophic dynamics in Russia, almost certainly one additional consequence of Stanchinskii's downfall was the cancellation of the Fifth All-Union Congress of Zoologists, Anatomists, and Histologists, which he had been scheduled to host in Khar'kov in 1933.

After the departure of the "wreckers," the All-Union Institute for the Agricultural Hybridization and Acclimatization of Animals at Askania-Nova became a formidable base of support for Lysenko and Prezent in their drive for control over all of biology. With 150 scientific workers, a staff of 2,000, and 5,438,000 rubles,[30] it was a prize that was worth the trouble. The reserve now began to generate loyal minions of Lysenko and Prezent for "acclimatization" to other academic institutions. A prominent example was Academician-to-be L. K. Greben'.

At the Ecological Conference of the Academy of Sciences' Botanical Institute, which met in January 1934 to discuss the "problem" of the biocenosis, Prezent revealed why Stanchinskii's ecological research at Askania had to be discontinued. Not astonishingly, foremost among these reasons was that Stanchinskii's "reactionary" ecological views argued the existence of natural limits to the ability of human culture to transform nature. Stanchinskii had mistakenly taken the existing geographical distribution of organisms to be the only biologically viable pattern, according to Prezent. Based on this view, Stanchinskii had concluded that in order to acclimatize plants or animals to a new habitat, it was necessary to find new conditions analogous to the original ones.

However, Prezent objected, "the existing habitat conditions and the optimal ones for the organism far from always coincide." In his search for the organism's physiologically "optimal" conditions Prezent totally disregarded Stanchinskii's sophisticated warning about confounding biological and economic optima, and declared: "we must in no way limit ourselves to a search for analogous habitats in our selection sites for introduction."[31] Drawing on Darwin's observation that animals and plants were far from absolutely adapted to their local conditions, Prezent asserted that "nature is considerably richer in its possibilities—when . . . controlled by human culture—than it has itself managed to actualize on the face of the earth."[32]

A second highly objectionable aspect to Stanchinskii's work was his great reliance on mathematics: the use of symbolic expressions to describe natural systems and processes and the statistical analysis of data collected by sampling techniques. Unfortunately for Stanchinskii (who, ironically, had already moved away from the dream of reforming ecology into a fully mathematized, exact science), Prezent and Lysenko had concluded that such methods had no place in the biological sciences. As Prezent asserted at the ecological conference:

> Ecology is a biological science, and its methods, consequently, must be biological. It is impermissible to allow mathematics to usurp the content of biology. This must be particularly stressed. . . . We are interested in concrete knowledge, not in algebraic symbols that efface the specifically biological content [of Soviet ecology].

In particular, Prezent berated the tendency in contemporary ecology—in great measure a legacy of Stanchinskii's—to substitute the study of productivity or "biomass" for what Prezent called "the regularities governing concrete biological subjects."[33] Here, according to Prezent, the error of a mathematical approach was compounded by the apparent bootlessness of productivity studies. Deftly he developed his observation:

> Can anyone say that all "biomass" has equal economic weight? If, thanks to the absence of essential conditions . . . a plant becomes lushly woody, thereby producing a considerable "biomass," but fails to develop to sexual maturity, is this "biomass" biologically as valuable as the "biomass" of grain? Are we interested, really, in each and every "biomass"?

These commonsensical doubts on the utility of productivity studies served as the natural introduction to an attack on Stanchinskii's research at Askania, which Prezent characterized as "the most glaring example of the sterility of mathematical methods" in biology. Pointing to poster-diagrams from Stanchinskii's studies showing the fluctuations of the biomass of the autotrophs and heterotrophs of the Askania steppe over time, Prezent asked:

What can we understand from this that will aid us in gaining true mastery over the vegetation and faunal "cover"? Can these overcomplicated mathematical calculations, this integral, give us even the most minute concrete indication? Of course not! This is—a mathematical game, not scientific research. It is just a game of scientific formulae.

Effective as this critique was in trivializing Stanchinskii, there was a larger point to Prezent's barbs. That point was simple: mathematical methods should henceforth be kept out of biology. In support of this view, Prezent capped his lengthy talk with a pungent excerpt from a letter by Goethe:

I consider mathematics the highest, most useful science when it is appropriately applied. However, I do not agree with its use in those matters where it has no business. In such cases, that noble science becomes nonsense. It is as if something exists only if it can be proved mathematically. It would truly be preposterous if someone refused to believe in the love of his sweetheart because it could not be mathematically demonstrated.[34]

It is interesting to speculate just why Prezent trained such heavy fire on the mathematization of biology. In all likelihood, he and Lysenko only commanded a rudimentary understanding of mathematics.[35] Ignorance of mathematics alone would certainly be adequate to explain why such men, with their aspirations to arbitership in biology, sought to bar quantitative studies. (How could they effectively police what they could not decipher?) Yet, it seems, additional factors may have come into play. For one thing, there may well have been a genuine philosophical objection to statistical methods from the standpoint of Marxian dogma. That has been suggested by Barrington Moore, Jr., who argued that the statistical concept of probability was seen to be at odds with many Marxists' conviction that all phenomena were inexorably determined.[36] A historian of French science, Charles Gillispie, has argued a different kind of link between scientific styles and ideology. In his view, mathematics was rejected by "Jacobin" biology in the 1790s because of its reductionist, mechanist implications, to which the dynamic, change-oriented revolutionary ideology was averse.[37] Prezent had been, after all, a Deborinite. His invocation of Goethe seems to indicate that within the Bolshevik tradition, so heavily influenced by the example of the French Revolution, the traditions of "Jacobin" science were still very much alive. It should also be noted that the reaction against the application of mathematics to biology was not limited to the Soviet Union. In the West, as a consequence of Alfred J. Lotka's formal mathematical models of predator-prey relations, soon to be overturned by Gauze, ecologists quickly became disenchanted with such attempts to express biological behavior. What particularly rankled was the seeming arrogance of the mathematician-ecologists, their penchant for a priori theorizing, and the main inference drawn from their work that population dynamics operated in great measure independently of specific environments. By the mid- to late-1930s, particularly among the old guard, field-oriented ecologists, this antimathematical reaction had attained significant

proportions. While Prezent and Lysenko may or may not have shared these princi-
pled objections to the algebraicization of ecology, their position was attractive to the
many Soviet scientists who doubtless did.[38]

Prezent's warnings about the use of mathematics in biology, it would seem,
were not empty threats. V. V. Alpatov's work on the role of densities in the
regulation of animal populations was attacked as "a formalist, mechanist school."
The statistically based attempts of S. A. Severtsov to correlate fertility with
longevity in animals were denounced as well. G. F. Gauze's highly original
experiments in population dynamics (which, incidentally, represented a vast improvement over Lotka because they *did* take into account the properties of the
specific environment) likewise were declaimed. That, it seems certain, motivated
him to abandon ecology for microbiology. Even D. N. Kashkarov, who had
expiated his old errors and even had joined the party late in life, was not exempted
from criticism for his support for the notion that animal populations were self-
regulating within a biocenotic equilibrium.[39] Although Nechaeva and Medvedev
may have overstated the case when they asserted that "theoretical research in
biology, including ecology and biocenology, was excluded from work plans not
only of Askania-Nova but of all scientific institutions for two decades at the very
least,"[40] it is irrefutable that the conceptual development of those sciences was
significantly retarded.

Ecological energetics (trophic dynamics) as such wholly disappeared from
the research agendas of Soviet scientific institutions after the purge of Stanchinskii,
and the great ecologist was almost never cited in scientific literature. Nevertheless, it proved impossible for the new arbiters of biology to achieve an airtight
surveillance of the field. Productivity studies, some of which were influenced by
Stanchinskii's work, continued to be quietly pursued in *zapovedniki* and at academic biological stations on a limited basis.[41] One such study, by Viktor S. Ivlev
at the Astrakhan' *zapovednik*, examined the energy consumption and efficiency
of oligochete worms in the Caspian Sea littoral; it was subsequently used by
Raymond L. Lindeman (under the supervision of G. Evelyn Hutchinson) in his independent development of ecological energetics in the United States in the early
1940s.[42]

After the conclusion of the ecological conference, Prezent became known as a
thoroughgoing blackguard among Soviet scientists. Whatever genuinely valid criticisms of biology he offered, and there indeed were some, became completely
overshadowed by his reputation as an unscrupulous and ambitious climber. This
impression was soon further reinforced by his campaign, together with Lysenko,
against the Mendelian geneticists.

For Prezent, and for acclimatization theory, the problem of the objections to
acclimatization from the standpoint of genetics, as expressed by Kozhevnikov and
Stanchinskii, was unfinished business. The classical geneticists had even raised
objections to the Lysenkoist belief that new species could be created through
hybridization, which allegedly "softened up" the conservative forces of inheritance,
allowing the transforming power of the environment to refashion the heritable
characteristics of the offspring of such a union. Before he was expelled from

Askania-Nova in 1934 along with Stanchinskii, geneticist A. S. Serebrovskii had voiced strong reservations about such unsystematic beliefs:

> It is clear that the scientist has no right to work haphazardly—on the off-chance that something interesting will come of it—just as the architect does not have the right to assemble the beams and the bricks hodge-podge in the hope that by pure chance a building that is good for something will emerge from the effort.[43]

Clearly, such doubters of Soviet practice as Serebrovskii could no longer be tolerated. Yet, in the matter of acclimatization and hybridization, "practice" still outran theory. As late as 1934, for example, even as acclimatization attained significant economic importance and was poised to co-opt even the *zapovedniki,* Prezent still continued to denounce "Mechano-Lamarckism" as a petty-bourgeois pseudoscience based on teleological principles.[44] Only toward the close of 1934 did Prezent make an abrupt about-face and begin to attack the concept of the gene as itself metaphysical.[45] (Although in 1931 he had attacked geneticists Kol'tsov and Filipchenko for their role in promoting eugenics, that objection concerned the social applications of theory, and not the theory itself). It did not take long for Prezent's realization—that Mendelian-Morganist genetics, like ecology before it, had placed itself in opposition to socialist construction by its insistence on the existence of limits in nature—to blossom into an all-out assault on genetics; correspondingly, acclimatization was elevated to a "new science."[46] By 1936, B. M. Zavadovskii was describing how "the recently touted suppositions [of geneticists] about the alleged existence of sharp barriers between different animal species" had been demolished by experiments conducted at the Askania Hybridization and Acclimatization Institute.[47] Lysenko's brand of Lamarckism, officially referred to as Michurinism, gradually attained official status as the only acceptable explanation for evolutionary change.[48]

CONSERVATION AFTER THE 1933 CONGRESS

It remains now briefly to conclude this early history of the conservation movement in Russia with a discussion of the fate of the movement itself and of the *zapovedniki* after the 1933 conservation congress. The congress, if it revealed nothing else, demonstrated the existence of a de facto state of war between the conservationists and the economic organs of the country. Even the party stalwart P. G. Smidovich had criticized the "hell-or-high-water production orientation" of the latter.[49] Indeed, from the outset of the Five-Year Plans, conservationism had been a movement under siege. Nothing illustrated this better than V. N. Makarov's lament to the congress that "it was exceedingly difficult for us to try to prove that bureaucratic interests must give way to the broad interests of the state. We were forced to appeal on a whole series of matters to the RSFSR Central Executive Committee, the prosecutor-general, and others in order to stop the actions of one economic organ or another."[50]

The lesson to be drawn from this, he continued, was that "direct protection of nature and direct opposition to . . . distortions of . . . Soviet [policy] . . . still must be exercised" and that it was "still too early to state that the direct protection of . . . objects [of nature] is an unnecessary thing."[51] Therefore, he concluded,

> those comrades who hold that "conservation of nature" as such is obsolete, that in our conditions there is no need to concern ourselves with the question of the protection of nature, can be relegated, at the very least, to those who are unfamiliar with the practical side of this work.[52]

Nevertheless, the adversaries of protected territories persisted. The focus of their efforts remained the divestiture of the Narkompros *zapovedniki* and their reassignment to the economic commissariats. After the congress, in the spring of 1933, it increasingly appeared that those efforts would be crowned with success. Conditions were ripe for such an outcome: Stanchinskii and his following of conservationist-ecologists had lost their power base, and Narkompros RSFSR itself was in the throes of yet another reorganization designed to constrict its sphere of competence to strictly educational matters.[53]

Beginning in March 1933, the Goskomitet was almost totally preoccupied with the question of the future of the *zapovedniki* in the RSFSR. The problem had already attracted the attention of the leaders of the RSFSR Council of People's Commissars, which appointed a special commission headed by its deputy chairperson, Turar Ryskulovich Ryskulov, to study the matter. The commission recommended that a main *zapovednik* administration of the RSFSR be created to replace the Goskomitet, and that this new organ be directly attached to the RSFSR Council of People's Commissars. A draft of a decree to that effect was then drawn up.

When, on 20 May 1933, the RSFSR Council of People's Commissars decided the question, however, Ryskulov's conclusions were not adopted. Instead, the council decided to award the *zapovedniki* to Narkomzem RSFSR (now, suddenly, back into the picture), which was also to oversee the proposed main administration for *zapovedniki*. A crushing blow to the conservationist camp, the draft proposal was officially approved by the Council of People's Commissars on 27 July 1933 and was routinely forwarded to the All-Russian Central Executive Committee.

Here, however, the story had a surprise ending. Far from rubber-stamping the decision of its executive body, the Secretariat of the Central Executive Committee, which had independently examined the draft as early as 15 July, now balked. Doubtless Smidovich had been hard at work pulling strings.

With this impasse, another interagency committee, chaired by Daniil Egorovich Sulimov, chairperson of the RSFSR Council of People's Commissars, and including Smidovich, A. S. Bubnov, and Nikolai Vasil'evich Lisitsyn (deputy people's commissar for the RSFSR Workers' and Peasants' Inspectorate) was called into being to reconcile viewpoints and to produce a final draft. Once again, Smidovich brought his political influence to bear in the service of the cause he loved. Evidently, this was not for naught. When the new decree was finally published as law in *Izvestiia* on 29 August 1933, Narkomzem RSFSR had been deleted as the organ of supreme oversight for *zapovednik* matters; in its place was named the Presidium of the All-Russian Central Executive Committee.[54]

Smidovich, a member, took personal charge as the first chairperson of the Committee for Zapovedniki of the Presidium of the All-Russian Central Executive Committee, in effect replacing N. M. Kulagin, who had served to the end as the de jure chief of the now-defunct Goskomitet. Makarov retained his role as nominal deputy chairperson and effective day-to-day administrator of Russia's conservation affairs.

Happy as that outcome was, it still fell short of the conservationists' program maximum. Most activists had pinned their hopes on transferring the conservation apparatus to an all-Union organ and not a republican-level one. Despite the avid support of V. T. Ter-Oganesov, the secretary of the USSR Central Executive Committee's Committee on Academic Institutions, efforts to interest his parent body in assuming responsibility for conservation foundered. By the autumn of 1933 it was clear that the conservationists would have to settle for half a loaf.[55]

Despite their evident good intentions, there was little that Smidovich and Makarov could do to insulate the *zapovedniki* further from the encroachments of socialist construction. By late 1934 the reserves of the new Committee for Zapovedniki had already gone far toward becoming the *zapovedniki* of the future envisioned by the acclimatization enthusiast Kh. S. Veitsman. Such "*zapovedniki* of a completely new type" were to serve as "models of what the creative will of man can do with nature under socialism." Rather than being laboratories *of* nature, the reserves would now serve as laboratories *in* nature, where scientists would strive to create "prototypes of the nature of the future," varying the scope of the changes induced in the various experimental settings so that they would reflect an entire spectrum of future environments—some located further into the utopian communist future than others.[56] On the immediate agenda of such *zapovedniki* were the tasks of acclimatization and reacclimatization of animals and plants, while just ahead beckoned

> the questions of the restoration and development of climate and of the hydrological regime, especially in resort areas; questions of drought control, flood control, and of combatting the *sukhovei* and other phenomena that imperil the harvest. . . .[57]

Topping off this ambitious program was a call for the development of a massive shelter-belt of vegetation and forests on the parched steppes—later to be christened the Stalin Plan for the Great Transformation of Nature.[58]

With the publication of the new decree on *zapovedniki* of 1 April 1934,[59] Veitsman's vision became an emerging reality. While the direct economic exploitation of the reserves was still prohibited by the new statute, their primary objective was now redefined as "the protection and numerical increase of genetic resources in nature, especially valuable from the economic or scientific points of view." The supplementary tasks—"the identification of new natural resources and the solution of the problems of the acclimatization and reacclimatization of wild animals and plants"—only underscored the startling reversal.

New *zapovedniki* were created and old ones redirected to the narrow objective of abetting the increase of one or a few target species of fauna, mainly ungulates or furbearers. The Okskii, Khoperskii, and Kliazminskii *zapovedniki* were created for the specific protection of the desman, for example, while the Seven Islands reserve was established for the downbearing eider duck.

In addition to serving as *rezervaty* for the propagation of valuable game, the former Narkompros *zapovedniki* were now burdened with acclimatization functions in earnest. In almost every *zapovednik,* from 1934 on, exotics of all description were introduced, notably sika deer, raccoon dog, and European bison.[60] With the 1940 decree on *zapovedniki,* which superseded that of 1934, the extermination of wolves and other predators was added to the list of primary functions of the reserves. Extensive tourism (which reached 40,000 annually, for example, in the Caucasus *zapovednik*) contributed to the despoliation of the system, as did wholesale utilitarian abuses such as the pasturing of livestock, mining, timbering, and illegal hunting, all catalogued in an unpublished report by Makarov in 1940.[61] These counted as abuses only because they were committed by outsiders; under the rubric of Kiselev's old notion of *"zapovednoe khoziaistvo"* the *zapovedniki* already were permitting their own staffs to conduct the very utilitarian activities for which Makarov condemned the illegal interlopers.[62] By the late 1930s, there was almost nothing to distinguish the former Narkompros reserves from those of the Narkomvneshtorg system.[63] Indeed, nothing could have been more natural when, in 1939, the latter were absorbed by the Committee on Zapovedniki, now reorganized as the Main Administration for Zapovedniki under the RSFSR Council of People's Commissars.[64]

As for VOOP, the All-Russian Society for Conservation, efforts to elevate its status to that of an all-Union organization got nowhere (though it was also transferred from Narkompros RSFSR to the RSFSR Central Executive Committee). Its membership, which had peaked in 1932–1934 at about 15,000, now began a slow decline;[65] even the infusion of eight "proletarians" into the twenty-seven-member executive council failed to imbue the society with any greater dynamism.[66]

Late in 1933 an article evaluating VOOP was featured in the Varnitso journal *Front nauki i tekhniki* (The Front of Science and Technology).[67] Judging from the author's comments, the society failed to meet the challenge of the times; there had been little improvement since N. V. Kirillova and the Workers' and Peasants' Inspectorate identified VOOP's deficiencies three years earlier. "The society continues to be isolated from the masses," reproved the author, M. Nadezhdin, and it was now time for VOOP to put an end once and for all to its ivory tower and preservationist stance. "It was proper for the old 'nature lovers' to rail against the 'barbaric, impermissible, and offhand' treatment of nature in the era of the capitalists and the *pomeshchiki,*" continued Nadezhdin, "but now that the masters of the country are the workers and the peasants, things are different, and such criticism is not justified."[68]

It is unclear whether VOOP voluntarily took Nadezhdin's advice. However, one thing is beyond dispute: beginning only one year after the minatory article and continuing for six years thereafter, not a critical word was heard from VOOP. Nor could it have been. From 1935 to 1948, the society's house organ, the anthology *Nature and the Socialist Economy* (*Priroda i sotsialisticheskoe khoziaistvo,* formerly the twice-monthly *Okhrana prirody*) fell into an unexplained silence, which was punctuated only once, in 1941.

Perhaps the last VOOP publication to appear in the 1930s was the proceedings of the 1933 All-Union Congress on Conservation. Makarov, who edited the volume, noted in its preface that all of the work of the congress was permeated by one general idea,

> to place the cause of conservation at the service of the socialist construction of the USSR, . . . having subjected to deep criticism all precongress positions in the matter of conservation and having decisively condemned the principle of human nonintervention in the course of the natural processes of the *zapovedniki* as a reactionary principle opposed to the dialectical view of nature, her laws, and the role of people in nature. . . .[69]

While G. A. Kozhevnikov did not survive to witness this forced rejection of his principles—and, indeed, of his lifework—Makarov did survive to witness the collapse of *his*. The policies of the 1930s and 1940s, far from enhancing the Soviet economy and providing a model of nature for the future, wreaked havoc not only in the *zapovedniki* but also in surrounding regions, where many newly acclimatized forms swarmed. The attempt to nullify the environmental resistance and other regulatory factors that prevented the uninhibited increase of favored species also led to ecological debacles. The suppression of natural selection pressures on game animals, particularly ungulates, led to their inordinate increase at first. At the same time, because the feeble and poorly adapted individuals were no longer culled from the population by effective predation (wolves were exterminated in great campaigns), the genetic load of the deer, moose, and other ungulate populations also rose, leading to the birth of a great number of defective individuals. That set the stage for the collapse of population structures and for subsequent huge die-offs. The abnormally high densities of the animals led to massive epidemics, which spread to the surrounding livestock that were illegally pastured on *zapovednik* territory. Feral dogs moved in to occupy the niche vacated by the wolves; over vast stretches of European Russia they posed grave health and security problems for livestock and even humans. The ecological coddling of select, economically valuable species even led at times to situations where the simplified, degraded ecosystems could no longer support even as many of the animals as they had originally.[70]

After the war, in the climate of intense international tension, Lavrentii Beria, the secret police chief, began to accuse the *zapovedniki* along the Soviet Union's heavily wooded borders of sheltering spies and anti-Soviet partisans. Pressure on the *zapovedniki* increased still further after the regime, during the near-famine conditions of the late 1940s, sought ways of increasing land for agriculture and logging.[71]

Taking his cue from the times, the new director of the RSFSR Main Administration for Zapovedniki and Makarov's immediate superior, A. V. Malinovskii, a forester with reputed connections to Beria, proposed a plan in 1950 calling for the liquidation of two-thirds of the *zapovedniki* (with 85 percent of their total area). The lands taken out of the *zapovednik* system, according to this plan, were to be distributed to state farms and to the Ministry of the Lumber Industry. What Malinovskii stood to gain from this was the elevation of the truncated remainder of the system from a republican-level organ to an all-Union state committee—a significant personal promotion.[72]

Makarov now tried to mobilize public opinion against the liquidation. Personal appeals to Stalin were made by prominent public figures, including Arctic explorer Dmitrii Papanin and conservation's old friend Klim Voroshilov. It was too late. The liquidation went through in 1951, and a 1952 statute on *zapovedniki* codified the status of the surviving reserves as essentially that of experimental agricultural stations. Of 128 *zapovedniki* with an aggregate of 12.5 million hectares (0.56 percent of the territory of the USSR), only 40 remained, with a mere 1,465,000 hectares (0.06 percent of the USSR's total area).[73] Makarov was dismissed as deputy chairperson of the Main Administration (now the USSR State Committee on Zapovedniki), having survived to see the policy of human intervention in the life of the reserves taken to its inevitably absurd extreme. By the year of his death, 1953, Makarov's strategy of protective coloration was in ruins.

Conclusion

Ecological conservation's moment in the Soviet sun was tragically brief. Changes in the cultural and political atmosphere, which favored that approach during the New Economic Policy, worked strongly against it by the late 1920s and early 1930s. By analyzing first the success and then the subsequent collapse of ecological conservation in the Soviet Union we are led to examine Soviet culture through an important new prism; crucial linkages of professional groups, institutions, agencies, and values come into view.

When the Bolsheviks took power in late 1917 a modest conservation movement was already established in Russia. United by journals, societies, a quasi-governmental commission, and an informal network of professional ties, its adherents held a variety of beliefs arguing the necessity of nature protection. Three basic positions—pastoralist, ecological, and utilitarian—may be identified.

The pastoralist view is represented best in Russia by the writings of A. P. Semenov-tian-shanskii, I. P. Borodin, and V. E. Timonov. The pastoralists valued nature for aesthetic and moral reasons. We can best describe this view as anti-modernist. Repelled by modern industrial society—capitalist or socialist—its adherents sought to return to an idealized, organic, agrarian golden age when humanity had not yet despoiled the earth.

The implication of the pastoralist view was that humankind is a pathological element that by its very presence disrupts the preexisting harmony of nature. In its purest form, the pastoralist ideal was a world without civilization, though pastoralist theorists did not take their views to this logical extreme. Rather, they emphasized that nature is valuable in itself, irrespective of its utility to humans, and that other living things have an equal right to existence.

The pastoralist view also took a distinctive stance with respect to human nature. Humans were regarded as having originally been children of nature (despite, paradoxically, their current status as pathological outcasts). As a result, they had aesthetic needs that only nature could satisfy. By removing themselves from nature and by destroying virgin nature itself, humans were denying themselves the ability to satisfy those needs and were distorting their own nature into the bargain. The Industrial Human had become, in fact, denatured.

In Russia, the pastoralist view was deeply influenced by German neo-romanticism. In particular, the Germans and the Swiss inspired the fledgling Russian conservation movement with programmatic and organizational models.

The great influence that Hugo Conwentz, Germany's most illustrious conservation activist, had on Borodin accounted in large measure for the Russian movement's early emphasis on landscape protection. German influence also revealed itself in the patriotic flavor of the Russian aesthetic conservationists and in their accent on the value of the "unique."

The second basic position of conservationists, the ecological view, is epitomized by G. A. Kozhevnikov and V. V. Stanchinskii. This view presented itself as sanely materialistic, in contrast to the pastoralist view, which at times approached a religious sensibility. Held almost exclusively by natural scientists, particularly those involved in the new science of ecology (with supporters among such enlightened Bolsheviks as A. V. Lunacharskii), this position viewed nature as having a distinctive structure characterized by interdependence among its biotic components and by a state of relative equilibrium or, at least, proportionality. With no real place for humans in their harmonious "natural" systems (as if humans were somehow unnatural), adherents of the ecological view were deeply convinced that civilization, if it continued to disrupt the balance of natural communities at current rates, would destroy itself.

Emphasizing nature's fragility, defenders of the ecological view warned of the possibilities of an ecological collapse. This warning sounded a concern not so much about the survival of other life forms for their own sake as about the consequences for civilization that a breakdown in natural ecosystems might bring. Accordingly, scientists who held this evidently anthropocentric view, pointing to the dangers of an ecological breakdown, claimed a policymaking role in economic matters and resource use, arguing that only their scientific expertise could ensure that growth would remain within the possibilities afforded by healthy nature. This led them into the heresy of technocratism during the Soviet period.

Although Kozhevnikov and Stanchinskii were modern, politically progressive scientific materialists, it is tempting to speculate about the degree to which their opposition to Stalinist economic policies on ecological grounds was, like that of the pastoralists, a protest rooted in social and aesthetic antipathy toward the emerging new order. Ecological conservation may well have been a protective coloration for educated society's struggle against collectivization, loss of intellectual autonomy, and the shabby "proletarianization" of everyday life, and for natural and cultural diversity and aesthetic values.

The third position, the utilitarian, is also known as "wise use." Growth-oriented and state-oriented, proponents of wise use sought to introduce the principle of sustained yield wherever applicable and to make resource use generally more efficient. Utilitarians tended to define resources narrowly, however, based on the limiting criteria of current-day economic utility. Excluded from their concern were recreational and aesthetic amenities and living and nonliving things whose economic value was as yet unproved. The more extreme utilitarians even divided life forms schematically into "useful" and "harmful" categories, with the latter slated for extermination.

Because they were not preoccupied with the integrity of ecological systems, wise-use partisans were much more apt to accept the goals and methods set by established political authority. Lenin embodied this mentality to a great extent, although he supported ecological conservation. So did geologist A. E. Fersman and zoologist N. M. Kulagin. Even adherents of this view, however, were pushed into a technocratic posture by the irrationalities of Stalin-era policies; Leonid Leonov's *The Russian Forest* provides an unexcelled depiction of this development.

While all these conservation tendencies were present before the Revolution, the utilitarian and pastoralist ones especially flourished; the tsarist government was concerned with revenue matters, while there was ample scope for privately organized, aesthetically oriented efforts as well. By contrast, the Soviet period saw the gradual dominance of the ecological approach to conservation. A sympathetic regime established *zapovedniki* that were unique in their functions as centers of ecological research and as *etalony*. This may be explained as a consequence of a sharp change in the values of the new rulers, leading to changes in the political culture. Such figures as Lenin, Lunacharskii, F. N. Petrov, and V. T. Ter-Oganesov exemplified that segment of the Old Bolshevik intelligentsia that regarded socialism's double mission to be enlightenment and the rational organization of social and economic life on the basis of science. Not surprisingly, these leaders greeted ecological *zapovedniki* warmly, for Kozhevnikov's program appealed to both missions. By providing a materialist, scientific explanation for complex natural phenomena, ecological science would enlighten. And by establishing the permissible and recommended parameters of economic activity for specific natural regions on the basis of *etalon* studies, ecologists would help promote a rational and self-sustaining economy. Above all others, the People's Commissariat of Education (Narkompros) became the institutional guardian of this sense of mission.

Despite early successes, ecological conservation's position was never really secure. Undermining it was a battery of adverse forces. Some had dogged conservation generally from its beginnings in the tsarist period, while others were of newer vintage. Whatever their origin, all of them operated with an exaggerated intensity during the stressful years of the Cultural Revolution and its immediate aftermath, often acting in concert or in complex, interconnected ways.

Among the most important factors barring success for ecological conservation were new priorities and missions linked with the First Five-Year Plan, supplanting the older, Lenin-era priorities. While utilitarian currents were well represented in Lenin's government, particularly in the Commissariats of Agriculture and Foreign Trade and in the Supreme Council of the National Economy, their influence was counterbalanced by Lenin's personal solicitude for Narkompros. By the late 1920s, though, with the Stalinists' capture of the levers of power, narrow utilitarianism decisively triumphed as a central element in a new constellation of missions. Among the other new missions that supplanted the old were vocationalism, working-class upward mobility *(vydvizhenstvo),* hyperindustrialization, and a radical transformation of nature, both human and nonhuman.

Among the more immediate ramifications of these mission changes was a redistribution of power among Soviet institutions. From the Civil War days, there had been a simmering rivalry between Narkompros, which had attracted Soviet *kulturträger* to its banner, and the economic commissariats, which championed production values. While this rivalry had been kept in check, for the most part, through the mid-twenties, by early 1928, following the fateful Fifteenth Congress of the All-Russian Communist Party (Bolsheviks), relations took a sharp turn for the worse. The moderation of Bukharin's allies at the helm of the Commissariat of Agriculture (Narkomzem) never had translated into a sympathy for ecological conservation. Now those leaders were either unwilling or unable to restrain their logging trusts, which were intent on preventing the creation of the Central Forest and other *zapovedniki* that they accused of pursuing "science for science's sake." With the removal of the Bukharin sympathizers from Narkomzem and the rise to paramountcy of the All-Russian Council of the National Economy (VSNKh) in 1929, the rivalry became an all-out war. To those promising the most un-compromising growth rates belonged the victory and the spoils. Correspondingly dramatic was the collapse of Narkompros as a powerful and authoritative actor in the realm of public policy, symbolized by Lunacharskii's resignation as commissar in September 1929. His departure was precipitated by the rejection of his commit-ment to humanistic education and to cultural pluralism and autonomy, and it promoted a further decline of programs nourished by those values. Specifically, his resignation deprived the conservation movement of a committed protector. As a result of these developments, the State Interagency Committee for Conservation (Goskomitet) became, in effect, only a relatively small department within a relative-ly unimportant commissariat. The search for truly authoritative, union-wide status for a Soviet conservation agency still goes on.

The larger changes of the late 1920s also threatened to obliterate con-servationists' hopes of moderating development on the basis of their scientific expertise. With their holistic tenets about the existence of relatively self-contained natural communities that embodied unbroken "webs of life" and were characterized by a natural balance, community ecologists argued that there were strong limits to humankind's ability to tamper safely with nature. Advancing ecological arguments, they were among the last to continue to oppose collectivization publicly. Further-more, the All-Russian Society for Conservation (VOOP), as well as the Gosko-mitet, found itself in almost continual opposition to the policies and procurement targets of the various economic commissariats and agencies. The two groups drifted perilously close to setting themselves up as a technocratic opposition to the party. Similar suspected technocratic aspirations among Soviet engineers had been dealt with ruthlessly, and the conservationists hardly endeared themselves to the regime by their behavior. Unfortunately, they had little choice. The alternative was to abandon their critical posture and to become apologists for what they believed to be irrational policies.

Another feature of the new Stalin era was the Soviet leadership's search for agronomic miracles. This feature explains the support provided by such figures as USSR People's Commissar of Agriculture Ia. A. Iakovlev for acclimatization. As in the 1850s, acclimatization represented a technological fix for unproductive Russian agriculture. If peasants had to be organized into collective farms for political reasons, then the only means of raising agricultural productivity were technological improvements. Acclimatization and the General Plan for the Transformation of the

Economically Valuable Fauna of European Russia and the Ukraine were advertised as just such potential agronomic miracles, and they were seized upon by a regime desperate for quick successes.

The regime's adoption of almost unlimited faith in the power of applied science coincided with a commitment to breakneck industrialization: the attainment of the fastest growth rate possible. In many ways, this commitment was motivated by the growing fear that if the Soviet Union failed soon to catch up and overtake the West, it would succumb to the encircling capitalist powers. Ironically, the Soviets looked to the West in formulating their objectives. The very premise underlying Stalin's admonition to the engineers to overtake the West was that the Soviets would be competing in the production of the same social output: industrial production and, especially, defense capacity. Precisely in this period of the First Five-Year Plan the Soviets made their long-term commitment to prove the superiority of their system by showing that it was more efficient than the capitalist system in attaining the objectives of the latter! This marked a fateful departure from those ways in which Marx, Bukharin, Lunacharskii, and even Lenin believed that socialism would constitute an advance over capitalism. The combination of an exclusive reliance on applied science and the single-minded pursuit of economic growth in gross terms alone would have spelled out grave danger for the goal of rational resource management based on an ecological understanding of nature.

In line with this, the late 1920s and early 1930s marked an evolution in the criteria for scientific legitimacy. Although Lenin certainly had strong ideas about the nature of physical reality growing out of equally strong epistemological convictions, he never sought to impose them on others as official, party-endorsed dogma. All scientific findings could be legitimate, so long as they did not invoke nonmaterial (or nonenergetic) explanations, stood the test of empirical verification or professional consensus, and did not represent a challenge to the Marxian world view. By the late 1920s, however, the scope of legitimate science narrowed. With the victory of the Deborin faction in the Communist Academy, a new criterion of good science was pronounced: active employment of the dialectical method in investigations and explicit elucidation of scientific findings in dialectical terms.

This new criterion itself yielded, however, to another by the early 1930s, a consequence of several crucial pronouncements by Stalin in late 1929. The new standard for approved science was the doctrine of the primacy of practice, which really meant that all scientific doctrines had to accord with, if not justify, the specific social and economic policies of the regime. While the criterion of dialecticity did not substantively obstruct the development of ecological theory, that of the primacy of practice proved crippling. Again, there was no way to reconcile the holistic conceptions of the ecologists with the massive, earth-moving projects of the Stalin period.

Stalin's advent to power also fostered a radical reinterpretation of the concept of "the mastery of nature." The Bolsheviks, as heirs to both the Russian revolutionary intelligentsia and Marxian traditions, had succeeded to important philosophical impulses of the Enlightenment. One was the impulse to desacralize and demystify nature. Desacralization of nature made it ideologically possible for humans to strive to dominate and to transform it. Like Bacon, Marx, and Engels, NEP Russia had viewed nature coldly, unsentimentally; yet, like those three thinkers, it understood that "nature, in order to be commanded, had to be obeyed." Natural laws could not be altered, only learned and utilized for the benefit of human society, as Lenin and so many others had said. Flowing from this view of nature was strong backing during the Lenin and NEP years for basic research into the structure of nature; only a fuller understanding of the structure of nature and its laws could permit society to extend its abilities to wrest greater bounties from nature.

Marx had made one other important point about the relationship of nature and humanity: that humans and nature, or, rather, culture and nature, are not two distinct forces at loggerheads with one another, but are one. As one Soviet philosopher of science explained, "Nature does not oppose humanity as something equal to itself and eternally unchanging. . . . It is not an abstract reality with eternal 'natural vocations.' "

Yet, much as Stalin-era attitudes owed to these classical Marxian positions, they diverged markedly on crucial points. Though Bacon's exhortation to master nature rang out throughout Stalin's Russia, it was no longer thought necessary to study and obey nature's laws in pursuit of that mastery. Moreover, while Soviet Marxist philosophers rejected the notion that humans and nature were things apart, real-life Stalin-era attitudes often did set nature apart from people as a hostile force. One need only turn to the works of Gor'kii, Maiakovskii, and other literati of the time for evidence.

One reason for this antipathy toward and contempt for nature flowed from another impulse within the Russian Marxist (and radical intelligentsia) tradition: its phenomenology of the human being. Viewed as the climax of evolution, human beings were seen as progressively, relentlessly evolving toward total mastery of the course of life on the planet, becoming a this-worldly god to replace the toppled gods of religion. Pavel Akselrod epitomized this view when he spoke of paving the way "for a race of gods on earth, of beings endowed with an all-powerful reason and will, consciousness and self-consciousness, capable of grasping the world with their thoughts and ruling it."

This blind optimism, which reached its height in the Stalinist thirties, viewed the transformation of nature by society as the sine qua non of human self-perfection. Owing itself perhaps as much to a Russian Orthodox millenarianism as to Marx, this transformist mentality represented the polar extreme of anthropocentrism; nature had only instrumental value as a prop for human self-creation. Indeed, nature was regarded as an enemy to be conquered in the course of the creation of the totally man-made socialist environment: truly, a world without nature as we know it.

One related aspect of the Stalinist view of humans stands out from our study. Humans were seen as beings in whom culture so outweighed biology as to almost efface it. Aesthetic and moral sensibilities, moreover, were merely the reflections of a transient cultural conditioning and hence were invalid guides to practical action. The only important human needs, so it seemed, were those that could be reduced to quantifiable, material, economic needs; acquiring "higher-order" knowledge at the feet of party mentors was important as well. In progressing toward their "species-essence," according to the Stalinists, human beings were also progressively effacing nature, both in the wild and within themselves.

Parochially, the view that nature was not useful until it was exploited or transformed disregarded all of the benefits conferred on human society by the healthy functioning of wild (or second-growth) natural systems. Additionally, it presupposed that total human management of nature—at current levels of scientific knowledge—could substitute adequately for the intricate and recondite processes of nature itself. Moreover, there was an implicit view that nature was amenable to such profound reorganization and mastery. By contrast with the ecological view, impatient Marxists, particularly during the impetuous drive to modernize and industrialize, preferred a simpler view of nature as merely an aggregate of forms that could be rearranged at will. Further, partisans of the transformist approach rejected ecological teachings by dividing life forms into "useful" and "harmful" categories based on narrowly construed, transitory criteria of economic utility. With these views, of course, the ecologists could hardly agree. The triumph of transformism as an officially sanctioned credo effectively blighted the prospects of a conservation movement that was fearful of the pace at which nature was being altered.

Another factor in conservation's debacle was its inability to extend its appeal beyond educated society. Ecologists and conservationists were unable to demonstrate significant practical benefits arising from their research in *zapovedniki* to a regime and a political public that now derided "science for science's sake." Only a few *zapovedniki* had actually commenced research into community ecology. Most were still mired in the tedious work of inventorying their fauna and flora. What recommendations there were from conservation-oriented ecologists smacked of technocratic presumptiveness, especially when they involved opposition to collectivization or to the heroic construction projects of the First Five-Year Plan.

It would be unfair, however, to lay all or even most of the responsibility for the social isolation of the conservation movement at the doorstep of the conservationists themselves. The vast majority of Soviet citizens—workers and peasants—were too preoccupied with the calamitous and brutal changes of the early 1930s to worry about the survival of esoteric life forms or the protection of threatened ecological communities. Moreover, there was a pervasive impression among Soviets of all social strata that, because of the vast size of the Soviet Union, nature could not possibly be in any danger. Indeed, it seemed to many that people were in danger from nature in the USSR and not the other way around.

The situation may be sharply contrasted with that of the United States or Germany during the same period, each of which boasted a mass conservation movement. In the United States, a large, prosperous, and mobile middle class formed the bedrock of a public constituency for recreational amenities in nature—which found expression in the national parks. In Germany, protection of the landscape (*Landschaftspflege*) was an outgrowth of intense attachment to the local village and its environs. Functionally, this patriotism supported a pretty, well-husbanded landscape, important in such a densely settled land. With the exception of the Baltic region and other scattered areas, the Russian Empire and the Soviet

Union lacked these conditions; other, specifically Russian conditions did not support a mass movement for conservation on the scale observed elsewhere.

Other difficulties arose out of a failure to delineate clearly a taxonomy of protected territories. Because a clear classification scheme of protected territories had never been agreed upon, during the 1920s and 1930s both the Commissariat of Education and the Commissariats of Agriculture and Foreign Trade continued to designate their respective protected territories as *zapovedniki* despite profound differences in their functions and regimes. This gave rise to confusion in the public mind as to the specific nature of *zapovedniki*, obscuring the unique character of the *zapovedniki* belonging to the Narkompros system. The failure to distinguish terminologically between the reserves of Narkompros and those of the economic commissariats also permitted the latter to wage a debilitating campaign for hegemony over all Soviet *zapovedniki*. (Narkompros responded with a similar claim.) While this campaign did not result in an institutional victory for the economic commissariats (their high-water mark came with the raiding of three important Narkompros *zapovedniki* in 1929, which were restored to Narkompros the following year), it was a crucial factor in the ultimate conversion (from 1934) of the ecologically oriented Narkompros *zapovedniki* to reserves modeled after the game-management *zapovedniki* of the economic commissariats.

Finally, the viability of *zapovedniki* organized as *etalony* was damaged by overloading these reserves with conflicting functions. It was not clearly realized at the time that the *etalon* function of the reserve was in potential conflict with the use of the reserve to protect endangered life forms. While the former function required a regime of total inviolability, the latter often required human intervention in the natural events of the *zapovednik* in order to safeguard or restore the essential conditions necessary for the preservation of the endangered life form. A number of other problems, such as how to determine the appropriate boundaries for an *etalon*, also stemmed from ecology's ongoing doctrinal confusion. All of these factors conspired to undermine confidence among both staff and public in the *etalon* role of the *zapovedniki*.

It is important to emphasize that these difficulties proved so damaging to ecological conservation precisely because of a radical shift in the political culture: the demise of NEP. While no decree of the Council of People's Commissars records this occurrence, which was more a historical process than an event, by 1929 NEP was in its death throes; by 1933, the Soviet Union was a different universe. While recent scholarship, supported by this study, has shown that the seeds of Stalinist values had already sprouted by the mid-1920s—in the Red Army, in the economic commissariats, and even in Narkompros's State Academic Council—the NEP period was characterized by the absence of full-powered state mobilization and by a correspondingly high degree of bureaucratic autonomy. These features enabled Narkompros, with its increasingly minority-status mission, to support such pioneering programs as ecological conservation. Such support proved untenable after the state, through such arbiters and agents as I. I. Prezent and the All-Union Association of Workers of Science and Technology (Varnitso), embarked on a sweeping social mobilization to promote a new mission and new values.

Conservationists tried to overcome this constellation of adverse factors in a number of ways. From 1930, VOOP earnestly tried to recruit peasants and workers. Through the schools, particularly through the observance of Bird Day and Arbor Day, the conservation movement likewise tried to reach the minds of the young. Finally, and most central to our study, the most politically astute conservationists and their patrons in the party adopted a strategy of protective coloration, giving rhetorical support to the goals of socialist construction and making tactical concessions where it was thought necessary while attempting to salvage as much of the ecologically informed conservation program as possible. Unfortunately, one concession—renouncing the *zapovedniki*'s "fetish" of inviolability—proved too drastic, and the entire strategy ultimately ended in failure. Nonetheless, for twenty years (until the *zapovedniki* were largely liquidated in 1951) protective coloration remained serviceable, and it is unlikely that the alternative—all-out resistance to the economic commissariats and the arbiters of biology—would have worked any better. As Soviet historians might have put it, the objective conditions for an influential conservation movement had not yet arrived.

Appendices

Soviet *Zapovedniki:* Affiliation, Area, and Administrative Status,
1925–1933

Republic	State zapovedniki		Local zapovedniki		Total	
	Num-ber	Area in hectares	Num-ber	Area in hectares	Num-ber	Area in hectares
RSFSR						
1925						
Narkompros	6	337,000	7	37,417	13	374,417
Narkomzem	1	540,000*	2	14,077	3	554,077
Total	7	887,000	9	51,494	16	918,494
1929						
Narkompros	6	428,439	22†	170,388	28	598,827
Narkomzem	3	1,346,477*	10	1,710,000*	13	3,056,477
Narkomzdrav			1	10,000	1	10,000
Total	9	1,774,916	33	1,890,388	42	3,665,304
1933						
Narkompros	12	2,495,039	21†	203,788	33	2,698,527
Narkomvneshtorg USSR	3	1,346,477*	10‡	1,710,000	13	3,056,477
Narkomzdrav			1§	10,000	1	10,000
Far East Affiliate, USSR Academy of Sciences			1	17,000	1	17,000
Local Karelian Agencies			2	19,300	2	19,300
Total	15	3,841,516	35	1,960,088	50	5,801,604
Belorussian SSR 1925 through 1933						
Narkomzem	1	65,000			1	65,000
Ukrainian SSR						
1925						
Narkompros			2	1,800	2	1,800
Narkomzem	1	42,000‖	2	2,430	3	44,430
Total	1	42,000	4	4,230	5	46,230
1929						
Narkompros			5#	2,310	5	2,310
Narkomzem	3	75,700‖	2	2,430	5	78,130
Total	3	75,700	7	4,740	10	80,440

Republic	State _zapovedniki_		Local _zapovedniki_		Total	
	Num-ber	Area in hectares	Num-ber	Area in hectares	Num-ber	Area in hectares
1933						
Narkompros			5	2,310	5	2,310
Narkomzem	3	59,700	2	2,430	5	62,130
Total	3	59,700	7	4,740	10	64,440
Azerbaidzhan SSR						
1925						
Narkompros			1	500	1	500
1929 and 1933						
Narkompros			1	500	1	500
Narkomzem	1	50,000	1	28,380	2	78,380
(in 1933, the Narkomzem _zapovedniki_ were under the jurisdiction of Narkomvneshtorg of the USSR)						
Total	1	50,000	2	28,880	3	78,880
Georgian SSR						
1925						
Narkompros			1	821	1	821
1929 and 1933						
Narkompros			3	14,344**	3	
Turkmenian SSR						
1929						
Turkmenian Affiliate of the USSR Academy of Sciences			1	25,200	1	25,200
1933						
Narkompros	1	69,700			1	69,700
Turkmenian Affiliate of USSR Academy			1	25,200	1	25,200
Total	1	69,700	1	25,200	2	94,900
Uzbek SSR						
1929						
Narkomzem	1	5,400			1	5,400
1933						
Narkomzem			1††	5,400	1	5,400

Republic	State zapovedniki		Local zapovedniki		Total	
	Number	Area in hectares	Number	Area in hectares	Number	Area in hectares
USSR overall						
1925						
All Narkompros	6	337,000	11	40,538	17	337,538
All Narkomzem	3	647,000	4	16,507	7	663,507
Total	9	984,000	15	57,045	24	1,041,045
1929						
All Narkompros	6	428,439	31	187,402	37	615,841
All Narkomzem	9	1,542,577	13	1,740,810	2	3,283,387
Narkomzdrav			1	10,000	1	10,000
Academy of Sciences			1	25,200	1	25,200
Total	15	1,971,016	46	1,963,412	61	3,934,428
1933						
All Narkompros	13	2,564,739	30	220,942	43	2,785,681
All Narkomzem	4	124,700	3	7,830	7	132,530
Narkomvneshtorg of USSR	4	1,396,477	11	1,738,380	15	3,134,857
USSR Academy of Sciences			2	42,200	2	42,200
Karelian local agencies			2	19,300	2	19,300
Total	21	4,085,916	48	2,028,652	69	6,114,568

SOURCES: V. V. Alekhin, [Listing and brief description of *zapovedniki*], typewritten MS., 1 p. [n.d., ca. 1932], Moscow University Archives, fond 207, op. 1; V. G. Averin, in *Vserossiiskii s"ezd po okhrane prirody,* pp. 48–53; K. P. Blagosklonov, A. A. Inozemtsev, and N. V. Tikhomirov, pp. 421–425 (table 19); V. N. Makarov, "Zapovedniki," *BSE,* 1st ed., vol. 26, cols. 238–246; A. F. Mil'chenko, in *Vsesoiuznyi s"ezd po okhrane,* p. 133; *Vneshniaia torgovlia v SSSR,* 2 pts. (Moscow-Leningrad, 1936); Komitet po zapovednikam pri prezidiume VTsIK, *Nauchno-metodicheskie zapiski,* 1938, vol. 1, no. 1; M. P. Potemkin, in *Vserossiiskii s"ezd po okhrane prirody,* p. 18; M. P. Rozanov, "Zapovedniki za granitsei i v SSSR," in *Izvestiia Tsentral'nogo biuro Kraevedeniia,* 1929, no. 10, esp. pp. 17–23; N. F. Reimers and F. R. Shtil'mark, *Osobo okhraniaemye,* pp. 41–49 (tables 2 and 3); S. A. Severtsov, "Zapovedniki SSSR"; A. P. Vasil'kovskii, comp., "Perechen' uchastkov"; Vsesoiuznyi institut nauchno-tekhnicheskoi informatsii po sel'skomu khoziaistvu, *Obzor literatury,* 1967, no. 14 (85); K. D. Zykov, D. Nukhimovskaia, and F. R. Shtil'mark, "Razrabotka i sovershenstvovanie perspektivnogo plana sozdaniia zapovednikov v RSFSR," in *Geograficheskoe razmeshchenie,* pp. 89–90 (table 4).

*This area includes the extensive buffer zones *(okhrannye zony)* of the reserves as well as their zones of absolute inviolability.

†Includes Kungurskie peshchera reserve (300 ha.), whose status is unclear.

‡Includes seven *zapovedniki* (in excess of 2,500 ha.) noted by Severtsov in 1929 but unconfirmed for 1933.

§Existence unconfirmed for 1933.

‖The entire Askania complex. In 1930, 16,000 ha. of grainfields were transferred to local sovkhozes, leaving 26,000 ha., mostly uncultivated steppe (including an absolute zone of 6,600 hectares).

#Includes Akademicheskaia step' (area unknown) and Dikan'skaia step' (affiliation with Ukraine Narkompros probable).

**Area of Lagodekhi in 1929 unavailable; 13,283 ha. (present area) assumed.

††Zaaminskii jurisdiction unclear; consigned in table to Narkomzem UzSSR as local *zapovednik*.

NOTE: V. P. Semenov-tian-shanskii, "Geograficheskoe izuchenie Sovetskogo Soiuza," in F. N. Petrov, ed., *Desiat' let Sovetskoi nauki*, pp. 276–277, lists the following as well: Lakhtinskii Forest *zapovednik*, near Leningrad; a local beaver *zapovednik* in Smolensk Province, liquidated in 1927; a *zapovednik* on Khortitsa Island in the Dnepr; stalactite caves near Novaia Ladoga; and a small *zapovednik* for relict vegetation in Luzhskii *uezd*, Leningrad Province. However, these reserves are not listed by any other contemporary sources and were juridically almost certainly *pamiatniki prirody* (monuments of nature) having no budgets or staff.

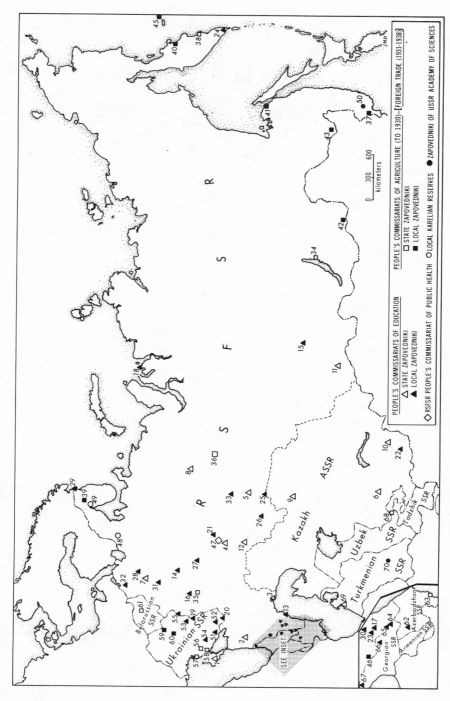

Zapovedniki of the USSR in 1933. Numbers are keyed to Appendix 2.

Zapovednik	Actual date established	Date organized as local *zapovednik**	Date organized as state	Area in hectares
		RSFSR		

I. Narkompros
  A. State

Zapovednik	Actual date established	Date organized as local	Date organized as state	Area in hectares
1. Crimean	1917	1923	1923	21,138[j]
2. Caucasus	1917	1924	1924	335,000[i]
(280,000[g]; 337,000[f]; 350,000[a,d])				
3. Astrakhan'	1919	1919	1927†	22,794[j]
4. Penza (Mid-Volga)‡	1919		1919	3,967[j,n]
			(1927)‡	6,000[a]
5. Il'menskii	1920		1920	15,000[a,d,n]
6. Aksu-Dzhebagly	1925	1925	1927	30,540[d]
(30,000[j]; 35,000[a])				
7. Central Forest	1927	1928	1931	60,000[j]
(35,000[a,d,f,n])				
8. Pechoro-Ilychskii			1930	1,000,000[a,d,f]
(1,300,000[n])				
9. Naurzumskii			1930§	15,000[t]
(200,000[d]; 250,000[a])				
10. Alma-atinskii			1931§	13,000[t]
11. Altai			1932	1,000,000[d,f,n]
(1,500,000[a])				
12. Buzulukskii bor			1932	3,600[n]
(5,000[f])				

  B. Local

Zapovednik	Actual date established	Date organized as local	Date organized as state	Area in hectares
13. Uch-kosa	1916	n.a.		58,000[g]
(60,000[a]; 80,000[p])				
14. "Zhivaia kniga"	1923	1923		27[j]
15. Krasnoiarskii ("Stolby")	1924[j]	1924[j]; 1925[h]		3,960[j]
(3,000[n])				
16. "Galich'ia gora"	1925	1925		16[j]
17. Samurskii	1925[j]	1925[j]		2,700[j]
18. Olenii Island	1925[j]	1925[j]		n.a.
19. "Les na Vorskle"	1925	1925; 1923[j]		174[j]
(1,000[a])				
20. Donetskii	1926[j]	1926[j]		1,000[j]
21. Tatarskii natsional'nyi ("Raif")	1926[j]	1926[j]		730[j]

Zapovednik	Actual date established	Date organized as local	Date organized as state	Area in hectares
		zapovednik*		
22. Dzhety-suiskii	1926[j]	1926[j]		20,000[j]
23. Gunibskii	1926[j]	1926[j]		1,368[j]
24. Lopatkinskii	1927[j]	1927[j]		3,000[d]
25. Troitskii	1927	1927		1,510[j,n]
26. Bashkirskii	1927[ll]	1930		15,000[g]; 85,000[all]
27. Iambirskii	1928[j]	1928[j]		165[j]
28. Zhelezninskii	1928[j]	1928[j]		143[j]
29. Lake Mogil'noe	1929[i]	1929[i]		n.a.
30. Parabochevskii	n.a.	n.a.		2,000[j]
31. Zvenigorodskii ("Gorodok")	n.a.	n.a.		n.a.[j]
32. Pushkinskii	n.a.	n.a.		295[j]
33. Kungurskie peshchera[#]	n.a.	n.a.		300[n]

II. Narkomzem
  A. State

34. Barguzinskii (573,000**[e])	1916		1926†	540,000**[j]
35. Voronezhskii		1923	1927	6,477**[j]
36. Kondo-Sos'vinskii (843,000[e]; 1,500,000[a])	1929		1929	800,000[j,d,n]

  B. Local

37. Kedrovaia pad'	1916	1924		7,600[j]
38. Kronotskii (1,000,000[a,n]; 1,120,000[e])	1927	1930[a]		1,500,000**[i]
39. Laplandskii ("Chunatundra") (250,000[a])	1929[j]	1930[h]		200,000[n,f]
40. Utkinskii	n.a.	n.a.		n.a.[j]
41. Peschanyi po-luostrov	n.a.	n.a.		n.a.[j]
42. Lakes Zun-Torei and Barun-Torei	n.a.	n.a.	n.a.	n.a.[j]
43. Lake Teploe	n.a.	n.a.		n.a.[j]
44. Karamzin Island	n.a.	n.a.		n.a.[j]
45. Mednyi Island	n.a.	n.a.		n.a.[j]
46. Ten local zapovedniki in the Kabardino-Balkarian Autonomous Republic (counted as one)	1929[j]	1929[j]		2,500[j]

III. Narkomzdrav

47. Urianbashskii	n.a.	n.a.		10,000[j]

IV. Karelian††
  A. State
    none

Zapovednik	Actual date established	Date organized as local zapovednik*	Date organized as state	Area in hectares
B. Local				
48. "Kivach" (1,888[f])		1931		2,500[n]
49. Kandalakshskii (22,046[m])		1932		16,800[n]
V. USSR Academy of Sciences (Far Eastern Division)				
A. State				
none				
B. Local				
50. Ussuriiskii (Suputinskii) (16,500[m])	1912	1932		17,000[n]

Ukrainian SSR

I. Narkompros				
A. State				
none				
B. Local				
51. Kamennye mogily	1925[j]	1925[j]		600[j]
52. Khomutovskaia step'	1925[j]	1925[j]		1,200[a]
53. Mikhailovskaia tselina (202[m]; 240[b])	1928	1928		220[k]
54. Akademicheskaia step'	n.a.	n.a.		n.a.[j]
55. Dikan'skaia leso- step'	n.a.	n.a.		150[k]
II. Narkomzem				
A. State				
56. Askania-Nova ("Chapli") (43,000[d])	1898		1919	42,000[r]
57. Chernomorskii ("Pes- chanye")‡‡	1924		1927	8,700[j]
58. Primorskie (Azovo- Sivashskii)‡‡	1924		1927	25,000[j]
B. Local				
59. Koncha-Zaspa (713[a])	1921[j]	1921[j]		250[j]

Zapovednik	Actual date established	Date organized as local zapovednik*	Date organized as state zapovednik*	Area in hectares
60. Kanevskii ("imeni Shevchenko")	1923[j]	1923[j]		2,180[a]

Belorussian SSR

I. Narkompros: none
II. Narkomzem
  A. State

61. Belorussian (Berezinskii)	1925		1925	65,000[j]

Azerbaidzhan SSR

I. Narkompros
  A. State: none
  B. Local

62. Gëk-gël'skii	1925	1925		500[s]

II. Narkomzem
  A. State

63. Kyzyl-Agach (120,000[a])	1929		1929	50,000[d]

  B. Local

64. Zakatal'skii	1929	1929		28,380[s]

Georgian SSR

I. Narkompros
  A. State: none
  B. Local

65. Lagodekhi	1912	1928[h]		13,283[m]
66. Akhmetovskii (600[k])	1925[j]	1925[j]		821[j]
67. Pitsundskii	1926[j]	1926[j]		240[j]

Uzbek SSR

I. Narkompros: none
II. Narkomzem
  A. State

68. Zaaminskii	1926	1933[§§]	1926	5,400[k]

Turkmenian SSR

I. Narkompros
  A. State

69. Gasan-kuli (Krasno- vodskii) (70,000[f])			1932	69,700[c,m]

II. Narkomzem: none
III. Turkmenian Affiliate of the USSR Academy of Sciences (local)

70. Repetekskii	1912	1928		25,200[j]

SOURCES: See Appendix 1.

*Founding dates from Reimers and Shtil'mark unless otherwise noted. De facto existence often antedated official establishment.

†Astrakhan and Barguzinskii were regarded as state *zapovedniki* long before measures were taken to codify this status.

‡Founded 1919 as Penza; greatly expanded in 1927 and reorganized as Mid-Volga.

§Did not begin operations until 1934–1935 owing to opposition from local authorities.

‖Bashkirskii, at first a 15,000-ha. reserve associated with Il'menskii *zapovednik*, became an autonomous local *zapovednik* in 1930 with 83,400 ha.

#Although Kungurskie peshchera in the Urals (a network of limestone caves) became a state *zapovednik* in 1943, it is unclear whether prior to that it was a local *zapovednik* or a *pamiatnik prirody*.

**Totals include buffer zones.

††Planned in late 1920s but not launched until 1931, when Narkomzem had lost its responsibilities in game protection and management; under jurisdiction of local authorities.

‡‡Temporary merger, during 1932, of the Chernomorskie and Primorskie *zapovedniki* with Askania-Nova.

§§During the period 1930 to 1933 the Zaaminskii *zapovednik* ceased operations. It was reopened in 1933, most likely as a local *zapovednik*.

ªAlekhin. Unreliable except for steppe parcels.

ᵇAverin. He also mentions a Parasotskii *zapovednik* in the Ukraine (155 ha.), but it apparently was a *zakaznik*.

ᶜBlagosklonov et al. Contains some errors regarding dates of establishment.

ᵈMakarov. Omits many smaller reserves.

ᵉ*Vneshniaia torgovlia v SSSR.*

ᶠKomitet po zapovednikam pri prezidiume VTsIK.

ᵍPotemkin.

ʰReimers and Shtil'mark. Based on Shtil'mark's work in archives; one of the best chronologies available. Areas of reserves not provided.

ⁱRozanov. Based mainly on Severtsov, but Caucasus calculation is based on personal involvement with the reserve.

ʲSevertsov. Based on examination of Glavnauka's files by a knowledgeable insider; best general directory for 1929.

ᵏVasil'kovskii. List of existing and prospective protected territories; consulted when no other sources were available.

ᵐVsesoiuznyi institut. Gives areas for 1967; used in absence of contemporary data.

ⁿZykov et al. Based on Shtil'mark's archival research. As reliable as Reimers and Shtil'mark; provides original areas for RSFSR *zapovedniki* still in existence. Figures rounded off.

ᵖComments of N. N. Shul'zhenko, delegate of Dagestan Cultural Institute, at 1929 conservation congress (*Vserossiiskii s"ezd po okhrane*, p. 39).

ʳZavadovskii and Fortunatov, p. 24, give 45,000 desiatins (41,190 ha.); Kolod'ko and Fortunatov, p. 6, have 40,000 ha.; and Askania director F.F. Bega put it at 43,000 ha. in report to 1933 conservation congress, referring to pre-1931 area (*Vsesoiuznyi s"ezd po okhrane*, p. 94). Cropland and pastureland accounted for about 26,000 ha., of which 6,600 were inviolable (the Scientific Steppe Institute). In 1931, 16,000 ha. of cropland was transferred to state farms.

ˢP. Koval'skaia-Il'ina, report to 1933 congress (*Vsesoiuznyi s"ezd po okhrane*, p. 66).

ᵗMil'chenko.

ACRONYMS

AKADTsENTR: A major administrative subdivision of Narkompros, responsible for science and the arts; formally established on 11 February 1921. Its responsibilities were divided between Glavnauka and Glavlit in 1922.

Glavmuzei: Glavnyi komitet po delam muzeev (Main Committee for Museum Affairs). Not a true *glavk* (main administrative subdivision in a commissariat) but subsidiary first to AKADTsENTR and then to Glavnauka. Until 1923, conservation affairs were handled by a subdepartment in Glavmuzei.

Glavnauka: Glavnoe upravlenie nauchnymi, nauchno-khudozhestvennymi, muzeinymi i po okhrane prirody uchrezhdeniami Narkomprosa RSFSR (Main Administration for Scientific Institutions, the Arts, Museums, and Conservation of Narkompros). Originally subordinated to AKADTsENTR, it became an autonomous *glavk* in 1922. In 1930 it was reorganized as the commissariat's Scientific Sector. Glavnauka exercised immediate jurisdiction over the Conservation Department from 1924 through 1927 and over the department's successor, the conservation section of its Department for Scientific Institutions, from 1927 to 1934. It also bore a general responsibility for the operations of the Goskomitet.

Goskomitet: Gosudarstvennyi mezhduvedomstvennyi komitet po okhrane prirody (State Interagency Committee for Conservation).

Gostorg: State wholesale network for internal wholesale trade under the auspices of Narkomtorg.

Narkompros: Narodnyi komissariat po prosveshcheniiu (People's Commissariat of Education) [of RSFSR, Ukrainian SSR, and other republics].

Narkomsnab: Narodnyi komissariat snabzheniia (People's Commissariat of Supplies) [of the USSR, RSFSR, and other republics].

Narkomtorg: Narodnyi komissariat vnutrennei i vneshnei torgovli (People's Commissariat of Trade). In 1930 it was divided into an all-Union Narkomvneshtorg and the Narkomsnab system.

Narkomvneshtorg: Narodnyi komissariat vneshnei torgovli (People's Commissariat of Foreign Trade of the USSR).

Narkomzdrav: Narodnyi komissariat zdravookhraneniia RSFSR (People's Commissariat of Public Health of the RSFSR).

Narkomzem: Narodnyi komissariat zemledeliia (People's Commissariat of Agriculture) [of the RSFSR, Ukrainian SSR, etc., and of the USSR].

NEP: New Economic Policy introduced by Lenin in 1921. Also designates the period from 1921 (the end of the Civil War) to 1928–1929.

OKRAM: Obshchestvo kraevedov-marksistov pri Kommunisticheskoi Akademii (Society of Marxist-Kraevedy).

Rabkrin: People's Commissariat of the Workers' and Peasants' Inspectorate [of the RSFSR, etc. and of the USSR].

SNK RSFSR [Sovnarkom RSFSR]: Sovet narodnykh komissarov RSFSR (RSFSR Council of People's Commissars).

Soiuzpushnina: All-Union Peltry Association of Narkomvneshtorg of the USSR.

TsBK: Tsentral'noe biuro kraevedeniia (Central Bureau for the Study of Local Lore).

Tsentrokhota: Hunting Subdepartment of Narkomzem RSFSR.

UKOPP: Ukrainskii komitet po okhrane pamiatnikov prirody (Ukrainian Committee for the Protection of Monuments of Nature).

Varnitso: Vsesoiuznaia assotsiatsiia rabotnikov nauki i tekhniki dlia sodeistviia sotsialis-ticheskomu stroitel'stvu (All-Union Association of Workers of Science and Technology for the Promotion of Socialist Construction).

VASKhNIL: Vsesoiuznaia akademiia sel'sko-khoziaistvennykh nauk imeni V. I. Lenina (Lenin All-Union Academy of Agricultural Sciences).

VOOP: Vserossiiskoe obshchestvo okhrany prirody (All-Russian Society for Conservation).

VSNKh: Vysshii sovet narodnogo khoziaistva (Supreme Council of the National Economy) [of the RSFSR, USSR].

VTsIK: Vserossiiskii tsentral'nyi ispolnitel'nyi komitet (All-Russian Central Executive Committee). The official parliamentary body of the RSFSR. TsIK was the corresponding institution on the all-Union level.

GLOSSARY

acclimatization: The introduction or naturalization of a nonnative plant or animal to a region.

biocenology: The study of natural communities.

biocenosis: A natural ecological community. *Ecosystem,* while not absolutely synonymous, is a closely related term.

etalon: A baseline, standard, model, or prototype.

exotic: A nonnative life form, opposite of endemic.

glavk: A department (major subunit) within a people's commissariat.

kraeved: A person who engages in *kraevedenie.*

kraevedenie: The study of local lore, geography, ethnology, fauna, or other local characteristics (from *krai*).

krai: Region; a large Soviet territorial unit or territory (as in Yukon Territory).

oblast: A Soviet territorial unit roughly equivalent to a province.

okhotnichii zapovednik: A game-management *zapovednik;* a preserve dedicated to promoting the increase of the population of select species of game; used by Narkomzem and Narkomvneshtorg to describe their preserves.

okhrana prirody: Conservation; nature protection.

pamiatnik prirody: Monument of nature; a protected territory in the Soviet Union, generally occupying a small area and having no permanent staff or funding.

phytosociology: The study of plant communities, which were thought to share many structural and functional attributes with human societies.

zakaznik: A protected territory established generally for five to ten years during which all or only part of its natural components may be protected.

zapovednik: A permanently established protected territory with its own staff and funding.

zapovednost': Inviolability (from *zapoved',* a commandment).

ABBREVIATIONS USED IN NOTES AND BIBLIOGRAPHY

AMGU: Arkhiv Moskovskogo Gosudarstvennogo Universiteta (Archives of Moscow State University)

BKhOLP: *Biulleten' Khar'kovskogo obshchestva liubitelei prirody*

BNKP: *Biulleten' Narkomprosa RSFSR*

BSE: *Bol'shaia Sovetskaia Entsiklopediia*

EG: *Estestvoznanie i geografiia*

EM: *Estestvoznanie i marksizm*

ENKP: *Ezhenedel'nik Narkomprosa RSFSR*

ESS: *Estestvoznanie v sovetskoi shkole*

FNT: *Front nauki i tekhniki*

IKORGO: *Izvestiia Kavkazskogo otdeleniia Imperatorskogo russkogo geograficheskogo obshchestva*

ITsBK: *Izvestiia Tsentral'nogo biuro kraevedeniia*

IVSORGO: *Izvestiia Vostochno-Sibirskogo otdeleniia russkogo geograficheskogo obshchestva*

MOIP: *Biulleten' Moskovskogo obshchestva ispytatelei prirody.* Otdel biologicheskii.

NMZ: *Nauchno-metodicheskie zapiski Komiteta* [later, *Glavnogo upravleniia*] *po zapovednikam pri prezidiume VTsIKa* [later, *pri Sovete narodnykh komissarov RSFSR;* later still, *pri Sovete ministrov RSFSR*]

NVT: *Nasha vneshniaia torgovlia*

OP: *Okhrana prirody*

OPZD: *Okhrana prirody i zapovednoe delo v SSSR*

PB: *Problemy biotsenologii* [Trudy sektora ekologii Vseukrainskogo zoologo-biologicheskogo instituta pri Khar'kovskom gosudarstvennom universitete]

PD: *Pushnoe delo*

PSKh: *Priroda i sotsialisticheskoe khoziaistvo*

PZM: *Pod znamenem marksizma*

SB: *Sovetskaia botanika*

SK: *Sovetskoe kraevedenie*

TBSIIU: *Trudy botanicheskogo sada pri Imperatorskom Iur'evskom universitete*

TIGA: *Trudy Gosudarstvennogo nauchnogo instituta sel'skokhoziaistvennoi gibridizatsii i akklimatizatsii zhivotnykh* (Askania-Nova)

TsGA RSFSR: Tsentral'nyi gosudarstvennyi arkhiv RSFSR (Central State Archives of the RSFSR)

TsGAOR: Tsentral'nyi gosudarstvennyi arkhiv Oktiabrskoi revoliutsii (Central State Archives of the October Revolution)

TVAS: *Trudy Vserossiiskogo iubileinogo akklimatizatsionnogo s"ezda*

TVSOM: *Trudy Vtorogo vserossiiskogo s"ezda okhotnikov v Moskve*

VEB: *Voprosy ekologii i biotsenologii*

VEK: *Vtoraia ekologicheskaia konferentsiia po probleme "Massovoe razmnozhenie zhivotnykh i ikh prognoz"*

VFK: *Trudy Vsesoiuznoi faunisticheskoi konferentsii Zoologicheskogo instituta* [AN SSSR]

VRSOP: *Trudy Pervogo vserossiiskogo s"ezda po okhrane prirody*

VRZAG: *Trudy Tret'ego vserossiiskogo s"ezda zoologov, anatomov i gistologov*

VSSOP: *Trudy Pervogo vsesoiuznogo s"ezda po okhrane prirody*
VSZAG: *Trudy Chetvertogo vsesoiuznogo s"ezda zoologov, anatomov i gistologov*
VT: *Vneshniaia torgovlia*
ZhEB: *Zhurnal ekologii i biotsenologii*
ZZh: *Zoologicheskii zhurnal*

NOTES

ONE. MONUMENTS OF NATURE

1. See N. F. Reimers and F. R. Shtil'mark, *Osobo okhraniaemye prirodnye territorii,* p. 24, and G. P. Dement'ev, "Zhivotnyi mir i ego okhrana," *OPZD,* 1956, no. 1, p. 79.

2. Philip R. Pryde, *Conservation in the Soviet Union,* pp. 9–10.

3. Ibid.

4. Lyell's book appeared as *Osnovnye nachala geologii* and Marsh's as *Chelovek i priroda.* One Russian who was likely to have been influenced by the conservationist message of Marsh was Anton Chekhov.

5. N. F. Kashchenko, "Razvitie chelovecheskogo gospodstva nad organizovannoi prirodoi," p. 21.

6. From I. D. Lukashevich, *Neorganicheskaia zhizn' zemli* (1911), quoted in I. P. Gerasimov, ed., *Priroda i obshchestvo* (Moscow: Nauka, 1968), p. 135.

7. From the General Survey of 1775–1804 to 1880, the forests of the central and southern regions of European Russia were diminished by almost one-quarter. See A. A. Maksimov, "Istoriia razvitiia sel'skokhoziaistvennogo landshafta v lesnoi zone Evropeiskoi chasti SSSR," *OPZD,* 1962, no. 7, p. 122, based on M. I. Ivanovskii, *Ocherki po ekonomicheskoi geografii lesa* (Moscow-Leningrad, 1926).

8. Anton Chekhov, *The Wood Demon: A Comedy in Four Acts,* trans. by S. S. Koteliansky (New York: Macmillan, 1926), pp. 36–38.

9. For references, see L. P. Sabaneev, compiler, *Ukazatel' knig i statei okhotnich'iago i zoologicheskogo soderzhaniia.*

10. Kashchenko, "Razvitie," p. 9.

11. See Reimers and Shtil'mark, *Osobo okhraniaemye,* p. 26.

12. Pryde, p. 12.

13. The law's critics included forestry experts N. I. Faleev, *Lesnoe pravo* (St. Petersburg: I. D. Sytin, n.d.), and M. Orlov, *Ob osnovakh russkogo gosudarstvennogo lesnogo khoziaistva,* (Petrograd, 1918).

14. See Maksimov (n. 7 above), p. 121.

15. V. N. Makarov, *Okhrana prirody v SSSR,* 1947, pp. 31–32.

16. These categories were recognized by conservationists at the time; see V. I. Taliev, *Okhraniaite prirodu!* (Khar'kov, 1913), and A. A. Silant'ev, compiler, *Okhrana zverei i ptits, poleznykh v sel'skom khoziaistve.*

17. A. A. Silant'ev, "Zhivotnye, preimushchestvenno zveri i ptitsy, poleznye v sel'skom khoziaistve."

18. For a discussion of this law, see Silant'ev, *Okhrana,* p. 6.

19. Duma Law no. 2396 of 25 October 1916, "Ob ustanovlenii pravil ob okhotnich'ikh zapovednikakh."

20. See G. Bryzgalin, "O sobolinykh zapovednikakh v Sibiri," *BKhOLP,* 1917, no. 1, pp. 61–63.

21. These approaches also had indigenous roots in the sentimentalist Russian Humane Society.

22. The usage of *Naturdenkmal,* coined by Alexander von Humboldt, was revived by German conservation leader Hugo Conwentz and then borrowed by Russian conservation pioneer Ivan Parfen'evich Borodin, who was close to Conwentz.

23. See I. P. Borodin, "Okhrana pamiatnikov prirody," pp. 300–306.

24. See, for example, *Shchadite nashi pamiatniki prirody! Vozzvanie Rizhskogo obshchestva estestvoispytatelei,* p. 8. This pamphlet was also published in German by the *Rigascher Zeitung.*

25. When the speech was published the following year, its title was simply "Okhrana pamiatnikov prirody," which was far more congenial to its aesthetically motivated message.

26. Borodin, "Okhrana pamiatnikov prirody."

27. On the Sharashskie cliffs, see M. V. Knorina, "Pamiatniki nezhivoi prirody," p. 102. The Khortitsa society is described by Borodin, "Khortitskoe obshchestvo okhranitelei prirody."

28. For a discussion of this tradition, see Genrietta Isaakovna Dokhman, *Istoriia geobotaniki v Rossii*.

29. N. I. Kuznetsov, "Obzor rabot po fitogeografii Rossii za 1889 g.," *Ezhegodnik Russkogo geograficheskogo obshchestva*, 1890, vol. 1, p. 168. Quoted in Dokhman, p. 127. Kuznetsov later was active through the Russian Geographical Society in the establishment of protected territories in the Caucasus. The earliest non-Russian proposal for the preservation of natural areas in the interests of scientific study I have been able to locate is A. C. Haddon, "The Saving of Vanishing Data," *Popular Science Monthly*, 1903, vol. 62, pp. 222–229.

30. G. N. Vysotskii, "Rastitel'nost' Veliko-Anadol'skogo uchastka," *Trudy Ekspeditsii, snariazhennoi Lesnym Departamentom pod rukovodstvom V. V. Dokuchaeva*, 1898, vol. 2, no. 2, p. 48. Cited in Dokhman, p. 112.

31. There are no full-length biographies of Kozhevnikov and few articles about him; see B. N. Mazurmovich, "Grigorii Aleksandrovich Kozhevnikov," in his *Vydaiushchiesia otechestvennye zoologi*, pp. 171–176, and Kozhevnikov's obituary, in *ZZh*, 1933, vol. 12, no. 4, written by S. I. Ognev.

32. G. A. Kozhevnikov, "O neobkhodimosti ustroistva zapovednykh uchastkov dlia okhrany russkoi prirody," p. 24.

33. Ibid., pp. 24–25, and id., "O zapovednykh uchastkakh," p. 374.

34. Because such game preserves were characterized by extensive management measures "designed to maintain the forest in a particular condition" or "even to improve it from the standpoint of the forester" and therefore contradicted "*the idea of the preservation of nature in its primordial inviolate state*," Kozhevnikov vehemently objected to referring to such preserves as *zapovedniki* or *zapovednye uchastki*. See his "O zapovednykh," p. 373.

35. Kozhevnikov, "O neobkhodimosti," p. 25.

36. *TVAS*, no. 1, *Obshchie sobraniia s"ezda*, p. 28.

37. *TVSOM*, esp. pp. 46–55 and 243–1248. Although Kozhevnikov was gratified to find support for his ecologically based belief that no animal should be declared "outside the protection of the law," his utilitarian opponents, led by Silant'ev and V. V. Dits, carried the day, adopting, by a vote of 32–16, a resolution supporting the continued killing of leopards, snow leopards, tigers, and wolves year-round.

38. Kozhevnikov, "O zapovednykh," pp. 373–374.

39. *TVAS*, p. 28.

40. "Predstavliaiut li parka dlia zashchity pamiatnikov prirody opasnost' dlia lesovodstva?"

41. Kozhevnikov, "O zapovednykh," p. 376.

42. *Dnevnik dvenadtsatogo s"ezda russkikh estestvoispytatelei i vrachei v Moskve (s 28-ogo dekabria 1909 g. po 6-oe ianvaria 1910 g.)*, F. N. Krasheninnikov, ed. (Moscow, 1911), pp. 146–149. Notable among those supporting this proposal were Georgii Fedorovich Morozov, father of Russian forest biocenology, Ivan Vasil'evich Novopokrovskii, and Mikhail Ivanovich Golenkin. So did the brilliant plant ecologist V. N. Sukachev, "Ob okhrane prirody Zhegulei," *Zapiski Simbirskogo oblastnogo estestvenno-istoricheskogo muzeia*, 1914, no. 2. A similar program for the creation of scientific reserves was advanced by botanist Vladimir Mikhailovich Savich, "Lesnye zakazniki i ikh gosudarstvennoe znachenie," *Vestnik Tiflisskogo botanicheskogo sada*, 1910, no. 18, pp. 40–44. Savich's piece was noteworthy because it implied the superior adaptability of primordial varieties *and* ecological communities over the agricultural ones with which humans replaced them.

43. See, for example, A. P. Semenov-tian-shanskii, "O zapovednikakh prirody," *Novoe vremia*, 11 (24) December 1913, p. 4, in which he states: "Zapovedniki must provide a broad and instructive picture of that natural harmony and that natural equilibrium characteristic of communities . . . [which exists] until the disruption of the conditions for their existence with

the arrival of humans on the scene." Of course, it must be kept in mind that, for Semenov-tian-shanskii, "nature's harmony" was instructive not merely (or even chiefly) in the scientific sense, but in the aesthetic and moral senses as well.

44. The relatively more destructive effect of *khutor* agriculture with respect to virgin nature was argued by Silant'ev, *Okhrana zverei*, p. 23.

45. This point was emphasized by a student of Dokuchaev's, Novopokrovskii, in comments at the Twelfth Congress and a talk to the experimental agriculture conference in Novocherkassk in early May 1911; AMGU, fond 200, undated MS., 3 pp., typed carbon.

46. L. S. Belousova, "Iz istorii okhrany botanicheskikh pamiatnikov prirody v Rossii," p. 34, and Borodin, "Okhrana pamiatnikov prirody," p. 313.

47. See "Okhrana prirody na Kavkaze" and "Khronika." On the other private lands, see Reimers and Shtil'mark, *Osobo okhraniaemye*, p. 29.

48. (V. N. Taliev), "Otchet o deiatel'nosti Obshchestva za vremia s 24-ogo sentiabria 1911 g. po 1-oe marta 1912 g.," *BKhOLP*, 1912, no. 1, p. 4.

49. *BKhOLP*, 1914, no. 1, pp. 34ff.

50. Ibid., p. 34.

51. G. A. Kozhevnikov, *Mezhdunarodnaia okhrana prirody*.

52. V. A. Dubianskii, ed., *Mirovaia okhrana prirody* (Petrograd: Postoiannaia Prirookhranitel'naia Komissiia pri Imperatorskom Russkom Geograficheskom Obshchestve, 1915). Trans. from French by E. Eremina.

53. Ibid., pp. 18–29, and Kozhevnikov, *Mezhdunarodnaia*, p. 53.

54. Kozhevnikov, *Mezhdunarodnaia*, p. 53.

55. Ibid. For the full passage, see Dubianskii, p. 42.

56. In 1912 A. N. Mazurmovich called for the protection of interesting geological formations, urging that such sites be "torn out of the barbaric hands of the capitalists" and be declared "national property." (Quoted in Knorina, p. 103.)

57. Kozhevnikov, "O neobkhodimosti," p. 26.

58. A. P. Semenov-tian-shanskii, "O priiutakh prirody i ikh znachenii v srednei Rossii."

59. Kozhevnikov, "O zapovednykh," p. 377.

TWO. CONSERVATION AND REVOLUTION

1. V. I. Taliev, "Da zdravstvuet novaia, svobodnaia Rossiia!" p. 65. Taliev's views bear a striking resemblance to those of V. I. Vernadskii, who also underscored free thought (and conservation) as central elements in the making of the new, rational order. See Kendall E. Bailes, "Science, Philosophy and Politics in Soviet History: The Case of Vladimir Vernadskii," *The Russian Review* 40 (July 1981), no. 3, pp. 278–299.

2. V. I. Taliev, "Khronika," *BKhOLP*, 1917, no. 2, p. 66.

3. Ibid.

4. V. I. Taliev, "Okhrana prirody," cols. 1163–1164.

5. Ibid.

6. Ibid., col. 1164.

7. N. V. Sharleman', "Poslednye dni evropeiskogo zubra."

8. B. Zakharov, "Sud'ba zubrov Belovezhskoi Pushchi," *BKhOLP*, 1917, no. 1, p. 64.

9. S. A. Sidorov, *Vymiraiushchie zhivotnye*, p. 9.

10. Ibid., p. 8.

11. G. A. Kozhevnikov, "Doklad," August 1917, AMGU, fond 200.

12. Ibid.

13. Taliev, "Khronika," p. 68, and id., "Okhrana prirody," col. 1162. Among the founder-members of the Moscow Society were geneticist N. K. Kol'tsov and zoologist N. M. Kulagin.

14. On the conference, see Taliev, "Okhrana prirody," cols. 1161–1162.

15. Ibid.

16. F. R. Shtil'mark and G. S. Avakov, "Pervyi proekt geograficheskoi seti zapovednikov dlia territorii SSSR," *MOIP,* 1977, no. 2, pp. 153–156.

17. Shtil'mark and Avakov, p. 156.

18. Taliev, "Okhrana prirody," col. 1163.

19. Ibid., col. 1164.

20. N. Troitskii, "Krymskii gosudarstvennyi zapovednik, ego znachenie i istoriia," *Krymskii gosudarstvennyi zapovednik* (sbornik), no. 1 (Moscow: Otdel okhrany prirody pri Glavnauke, 1927), pp. 14–15.

21. Taliev, "Okhrana prirody," col. 1163.

22. See, for instance, Zigurds L. Zile, "Lenin's Contribution to Law: The Case of Protection and Preservation of the Natural Environment."

23. V. I. Lenin, *Sobrannye sochineniia,* 3d ed., vol. XXII, p. 453.

24. Lenin further elaborated in an address to the Communist delegates to the All-Russia Central Council of Trade Unions on 11 April 1921:

> in order to protect the sources of our resources, we must act in accordance with scientific-technical laws. For example, if the subject is the renting out of forests we must see to it that the forestry industry conducts itself properly. If we are talking about oil, then we must organize against spillage. Thus, it is necessary to enforce adherence to scientific-technical laws and to the principle of rational exploitation.

See V. I. Lenin, *Sobrannye sochineniia,* 4th ed., vol. XXXI, p. 478.

25. Iu. N. Kurazhkovskii, *Ocherki prirodopol'zovaniia* (Moscow, 1969), p. 44.

26. Iu. N. Kurazhkovskii, *Vladimir Il'ich Lenin i priroda,* p. 15. Sukachev's book's full title was *Bolota, ikh obrazovanie, razvitie i svoistva: Sbornik lektsii tret'ikh dopol'nitel'nykh kursov dlia lesnichikh* (St. Petersburg, 1914).

27. Kurazhkovskii, *Vladimir,* pp. 20–21 and 25.

28. Decree of 9 November 1917. SU RSFSR 1917–18, no. 1, text 3.

29. Quoted in Iu. P. Kravchuk, "V. I. Lenin o lesakh," *Okhrana prirody Moldavii,* 1970, no. 8, p. 13.

30. Kravchuk, p. 14. Kravchuk claims that Lenin was acutely aware of the need for forest protection and was said to have frequently cited agrarian economist F. A. Shcherbina, who had chronicled post-Emancipation deforestation (p. 15).

31. SU RSFSR 1918, no. 42, text 522, esp. Articles 77 and 78.

32. *Lesogotovitel'naia politika: posobie dlia lesogotovitel'nykh-politicheskikh kursov* (Moscow: Glavleskom-Glavpolitprosvet, 1921), p. 76.

33. P. Ia. Gurov, ed., *Lesnoi kodeks RSFSR (v voprosakh i otvetakh).*

34. A fascinating transcription of this commission's proceedings is in *Lesa respubliki,* 1918, no. 17–19, pp. 996–997. On the collapse of the first hunting law draft, see G. A. Kozhevnikov, "Ob"iasnitel'naia zapiska k proektu dekreta ob okhote," p. 2, undated, handwritten MS., AMGU, fond 200.

35. SU RSFSR 1919, no. 21, text 256.

36. Ibid.

37. F. F. Shillinger, "Dokladnaia zapiska," typed, signed, undated MS., AMGU, fond 200.

38. N. N. Pod"iapol'skii, "Vladimir Il'ich i okhrana prirody." On Lunacharskii's curatorship of education and cultural affairs through the early 1920s, see Sheila Fitzpatrick, *The Commissariat of Enlightenment: Soviet Organization of Education and the Arts under Lunacharsky* (Cambridge: Cambridge University Press, 1970).

39. Such a proposal, incidentally, had been advanced before the World War by Astrakhan's scientific societies but was rebuffed by the Tsarist authorities.

40. Pod"iapol'skii, "Vladimir," pp. 36–38.

41. Petrov's comments are cited in K. N. Blagosklonov and V. G. Geptner, "Leninskie printsipy okhrany prirody," *ZZh,* 1970, vol. 49, no. 4, p. 488.

42. Pod"iapol'skii, "Vladimir," p. 38.

43. SU RSFSR 1921, no. 65, text 492.

44. Article Four specifically conferred such responsibility on Narkompros's Museum Department (Glavmuzei).

45. "Otchet o deiatel'nosti gosudarstvennogo komiteta po okhrany pamiatnikov prirody v 1920 g.," typed carbon, unsigned, undated, AMGU, fond 200.

46. Ibid.

47. On the genesis of the Il'menskii *zapovednik*, see I. V. Paramonov and N. P. Korobochkin, *Nikolai Mikhailovich Fedorovskii* (Moscow, 1979).

48. L. K. Shaposhnikov and Vladimir Borisov, "Pervye meropriiatiia sovetskogo gosudarstva po okhrane prirody." The decree defined the *zapovednik* as "national property designated exclusively for the fulfillment of scientific and scientific-technical tasks of the nation." The reserve was, so far as I am aware, the first governmentally established protected territory for such a use. See Robert P. McIntosh, "Pioneer Support for Ecology," *BioScience*, February 1983, vol. 33, no. 2, pp. 107–112.

49. F. F. Shillinger, "Dokladnaia zapiska," typed, signed, undated carbon, AMGU, fond 200.

50. SU RSFSR 1920, no. 66, text 297.

51. Not far from the already existing Barguzinskii *zapovednik* on the east coast of Lake Baikal. An expedition to the Barguzin *zapovednik* in summer 1922 found the reserve in a deplorable state (S. S. Turov, "K voprosu o Barguzinskom sobolinnom zapovednike [otchet o poezdke letom 1922 goda]," pp. 3–4), while Shillinger, in a letter to the Goskomitet to be read at its meeting of 4 February 1922 (typed, undated, AMGU, fond 200), characterized the Baikal'skii *zapovedniki* as "dead in its tracks." The consequences of this mismanagement were great, since Lenin was personally following the fate of these reserves and his disillusionment with their management led to a complete cutoff of appropriations for conservation generally for 1922.

52. See, for example, Turov and Shillinger (n. 51 above) or Shillinger, "Losi i proekt Muromskogo zapovednika."

53. S. A. Buturlin, "Okhotnich'e delo v SSSR," p. 18, mentioned that by 1925 there was a "lone specialist" in the subdepartment.

THREE. CONSERVATION UNDER THE NEP

1. See n. 49, chap. 1.

2. F. R. Shtil'mark, "Razvitie zapovednogo dela posle Oktiabrskoi revoliutsii," p. 24.

3. See n. 49, chap. 1.

4. F. F. Shillinger, "V goskomitet po okhrane pamiatnikov prirody," (Pamiatnaia zapiska), c. early 1922, AMGU, fond 200.

5. "Vypiska, Protokol 56-ogo zasedaniia Gosudarstvennogo komiteta po okhrane pamiatnikov prirody," 12 November 1921, AMGU, fond 200.

6. Ibid.

7. Ibid.

8. "Protokol no. 5. Zasedanie Prezidiuma Glavmuzeia ot 17-ogo noiabria 1921 g.," in folder "Dokladnaia zapiska Glavmuzeia," AMGU, fond 200.

9. F. F. Shillinger, "Eshche o vsesoiuznom organe po okhrane prirody," *OP*, 1930, no. 8–10, pp. 179–180.

10. G. M. Krzhizhanovskii, chairman of Gosplan, declared that "a proper role for conservation is essential for the healthy development of our country" and recommended the creation of a strong central organ for conservation. This information was provided by F. R. Shtil'mark. The original document may be found in TsGA RSFSR, fond 2306, op. 1, delo 1988, list 17.

11. M. P. Rozanov, "Zoologicheskaia ekspeditsiia Glavnauki v Kavkazskom zapovednike," *OP*, 1928, no. 3, p. 13.

12. P. E. Vasil'kovskii, "Nazrevshii vopros," p. 33.

13. *ENKP*, 28 July 1923, no. 7 (36), pp. 2–3.

14. This expression was used by A. P. Semenov-tian-shanskii, "Muzei tsentral'nye i oblastnye i ikh vzaimootnosheniia."

15. A. P. Semenov-tian-shanskii, *Taksonomicheskie granitsy vida i ego podrazdelenii: Opyt tochnoi kategorizatsii nizshikh taksonomicheskikh edinits,* (St. Petersburg, 1910).

16. S. I. Ognev, "A. P. Semenov-tian-shanskii," p. 126.

17. A. P. Semenov-tian-shanskii, "Svobodnaia priroda, kak velikii zhivoi muzei, trebuet neotlozhnykh mer ograzhdeniia," col. 201.

18. A. P. Semenov-tian-shanskii, Speech to the Section on Natural Science, 7 September 1921, in *Vserossiiskii s"ezd liubitelei mirovedeniia, Pervyi* (Petrograd, 1921), p. 195.

19. Semenov-tian-shanskii, "Svobodnaia," col. 213.

20. Semenov-tian-shanskii, Speech to the Section on Natural Science, pp. 195–196.

21. Semenov-tian-shanskii, "Svobodnaia," cols. 200, 213–214.

22. Ibid., cols. 212 and 214.

23. V. E. Timonov, "Okhrana prirody pri inzhinernykh rabotakh."

24. Semenov-tian-shanskii, "Svobodnaia," cols. 200, 209.

25. Loren R. Graham, *The Soviet Academy of Sciences and the Communist Party, 1927–1932* (Princeton, 1967), pp. 32–33.

26. See David Joravsky, *Soviet Marxism and Natural Science, 1917–1932*.

27. V. T. Ter-Oganesov, Foreword, *Krymskii gosudarstvennyi zapovednik: ego priroda, istoriia i znachenie. Sbornik* (Moscow: Glavnauka, 1927), p. 4.

28. Some scholars, notably Zigurds L. Zile, "Lenin's Contribution to Law," have argued that the conservation achievements in the Lenin period have been vastly overrated in recent Soviet accounts and represented nothing innovative or durable. In light of the new data presented here, a much more positive appraisal of the Lenin period may be defended.

FOUR. THE LIMITS TO GROWTH

1. Gosplan SSSR, *Kontrol'nye tsifry narodnogo khoziaistva SSSR na 1927/1928 g. (Postanovlenie prezidiuma Gosplana ot 25-ogo avgusta 1927 g.)* (Moscow, 1928), p. 145. Also, Postanovlenie SNK SSSR no. 189, 2 February 1928, "O merakh k uporiadocheniiu lesnogo khoziaistva," in *Izvestiia TsIK SSSR*, 7 April 1928, no. 83.

2. Narkomzem RSFSR, *Otchet deiatel'nosti za 1924–1925 gg.,* (Moscow, 1926), p. 393.

3. Nauchno-issledovatel'skii institut monopolii vneshnei torgovli, *Ezhegodnik vneshnei torgovli za 1931 god,* pp. 598–599.

4. A. S. Emel'ianov, "Sostoianie pushnogo khoziaistva SSSR k desiatoi godovshchine oktiabr'skoi revoliutsii."

5. Such *zapuski* were in fact declared with respect to sable hunting in Kamchatka in 1925 and the Far East *krai* in 1927 and to polecat hunting in 1927 in the Astrakhan' *krai*, to cite notable examples.

6. SU·RSFSR 1926, no. 24, text 154, "Ob ogranichenii promysla morskikh kotikov i morskikh bobrov," and SU RSFSR 1927, no. 102, text 684.

7. There are now more than 130,000 beaver in the USSR, descendants of those few dozen—ample testimony to the success of Narkomzem's operation. See A. G. Bannikov, *Po zapovednikam Sovetskogo soiuza* (Moscow, 1974), p. 140.

8. *Priroda*, 1928, no. 2, p. 173.

9. *PD*, 1928, no. 5, p. 1.

10. A. V. Fediushin, "K osnovaniiu Berezinskogo zapovednika," pp. 3–4.

11. N. M. Kulagin, *Uchet pushnykh zverei v SSSR* (Leningrad, 1928), pp. 5 and 12. As a result of overharvesting, sable take declined from 18,945 in 1924–1925 to an estimated 11,000 in 1926–1927. See also id., "K voprosu o vremennom zaprete dobychi sobolia v predelakh SSSR."

12. By January 1924 the price of an average pelt was 259.9 percent that of 1913. See P. A. Berlin and V. G. Groman, eds., *Entsiklopediia russkogo eksporta*, vol. 3, *Izvestiia Torgovogo predstavitelia SSSR v Germanii pri uchastii NKVT na Ukraine i Tsentrosoiuza* (Berlin, 1925), p. 4.

13. *PD*, 1927, no. 1 (21), p. 138, and *Ezhegodnik vneshnei torgovli za 1931 god*, pp. 405–418.

14. Cited in S. A. Buturlin, "Okhotnich'e delo v SSSR," p. 16.

15. Iu. A. Kudriavtsev, *Puti stroitel'stva okhotkhoziaistva* (Moscow, 1929), pp. 46–53.

16. Editorial, *PD*, 1928, no. 10, pp. 1–2.

17. Editorial, *PD*, 1928, no. 5.

18. B. M. Zhitkov, "Raboty Biologicheskoi stantsii TsLOS Narkomzema."

19. *Biotechnics (biotekhnika)* was a term invented by the Germans *(technische Biologie)* referring to the array of techniques employed by scientists to increase the fecundity of animals or to otherwise transform them: artificial insemination, acclimatization, and, later, vernalization. From the early 1930s through the 1950s biotechnics was vaunted as a science in its own right by P. A. Manteifel', N. P. Lavrov, I. I. Prezent, and T. D. Lysenko; these claims, however, were ridiculed as empty by other Soviet scientists.

20. P. A. Manteifel' (1882–1960) was a longtime official at the Moscow Zoo who devoted his research to practical problems of game biology. From 1929 he headed a department at the Moscow Furs and Skins Institute and became one of the most zealous advocates of biotechnics, acclimatization, and other aspects of the great transformation of nature. As such, he was a close ally of Lysenko and Prezent, both of whom signed his obituary in the March 1960 issue of *Agrobiologiia*.

21. N. P. Lavrov (b. 1903) was a student of Zhitkov's and a central figure in the acclimatization campaign as its historian and documentarian.

22. "Khronika," *Okhotnik*, 1925, no. 2, p. 27.

23. After the shake-up of March 1928, there were new and tougher faces in Narkomzem. A. P. Smirnov was replaced as people's commissar by Stalin ally N. A. Kubiak, while Smirnov's deputy, Bukharin supporter A. I. Sviderskii, was pushed out, only to land up at Narkompros.

24. V. I. Vernadskii, "Ocherednaia zadacha v izuchenii estestvennykh priozvoditel'nykh sil."

25. S. A. Sidorov, *Vymiraiushchie zhivotnye*.

26. See, for instance, *Dnevnik Vsesoiuznogo s"ezda botanikov, Tretii, Rezoliutsii* (Leningrad, 1928), p. 327. At the Third All-Russian Congress of Zoologists, Anatomists, and Histologists (December 1927) no fewer than eight speeches were devoted in full or in part to nature protection. See "Khronika po okhrane prirody," *Kraevedenie*, 1928, no. 1.

27. The first board of officers elected to the TsBK included D. N. Anuchin as honorary president, S. F. Ol'denburg as president, and V. V. Bogdanov as vice-president. Later officers included V. P. Semenov-tian-shanskii and N. Ia. Marr (vice-presidents), D. O. Sviatskii (scholarly secretary), and A. F. Vangengeim (editor of the bureau's *Izvestiia*). Only with the advent of P. G. Smidovich to the presidency of TsBK in 1926 did its directorate include a nonacademic, in this case a Bolshevik politician (and even he was trained as an engineer).

28. P. G. Smidovich, "Kraevedenie na putiakh sotsialisticheskogo stroitel'stva," in Smidovich and G. M. Krzhizhanovskii, eds., *Sotsialisticheskoe stroitel'stvo i kraevedenie* (Moscow, 1930), pp. 7 and 25.

29. *ITsBK*, 1928, no. 3, p. 10.

30. Total income for VOOP, 1 October 1927 to 14 April 1929, was 8,887 rubles; *OP*, 1929, no. 5, pp. 127–128.

31. The responsibility for the day-to-day management of Glavnauka's *zapovedniki*, which had been lodged with its Department of Conservation, was transferred to the Department of Scientific Institutions in 1927 when budget cutbacks forced the elimination of the Conservation Department.

32. *Piatnadtsatyi s"ezd VKP(b), dekabr' 1927 goda, Stenograficheskii otchet, chast' vtoraia* (Moscow, 1962), p. 929.

33. M. P. Potemkin, "Kraevedenie i okhrana prirody," p. 4.

34. Ibid., p. 5.

35. *Ustav Vserossiiskogo obshchestva okhrany prirody* (Moscow, 1925). The society was empowered to hold discussions; conduct public meetings and debates; organize excursions, laboratories, experimental stations, museums, exhibits, libraries, and university courses; monitor changes in natural conditions and compliance with conservation decrees; publish its proceedings; organize congresses; obtain leases; rent all types of property; and conclude contracts.

36. "Zasedanie VOOP 15-ogo fevralia 1925 g. (Pamiatki k dokladam)," AMGU, fond 200. Semashko's position is readily understandable. The sanitoriums of his commissariat were most immediately threatened by the increasing frequency of mudslides down the southern slopes of the denuded Crimean uplands, and there was the real fear that the Crimea's role as the Riviera of the Soviet Union could be buried in an avalanche of mud.

37. "Pervyi otchet deiatel'nosti VOOP," *OP*, 1928, no. 1, p. 29.

38. Other speakers included N. N. Pod"iapol'skii and F. N. Petrov. See "Pervyi otchet" and USSR Society for Cultural Relations with Foreign Countries (VOKS), *Weekly News Bulletin*, 29 October 1925, no. 18–19, p. 14.

39. Soviets remained fascinated with the U.S. national parks during the 1920s, as evidenced by D. N. Kashkarov's "Natsional'nye parki SShA," I. I. Puzanov's translations of Theodore Roosevelt's reminiscences of Yellowstone, and other literature.

40. After the death of Conwentz, the new head of the Prussian Statstelle für Naturschutz und Naturschutzdenkmalpflege, Walther von Schoenichen, was made an honorary member of VOOP. VOOP was also represented at the Kassel conservation fair (Naturschutztag) in August 1927 with an exhibit that included forty-five photographs and a map of the USSR marked with the locations of *zapovedniki*. See "Otchet deiatel'nosti VOOP, Vtoroi," *OP*, 1928, no. 1, p. 29.

41. "Otchet o deiatel'nosti VOOP, Tretii," *OP*, 1929, no. 4, p. 127.

42. "Koordinirovannyi plan rabot VOOP i TsBK," *OP*, 1930, no. 1, pp. 5–6.

43. B. P. Ditmar, "Okhrana prirody v Rossii: istoricheskii ocherk."

44. Kh. G. Shaposhnikov, "Kavkazskii gosudarstvennyi zapovednik."

45. V. P. Nalimov, "Sviashchennye roshchi udmurtov i mari."

46. G. A. Kozhevnikov, "Zadachi okhrany prirody v SSSR," p. 6.

47. "Ot redaktsii *Okhrany prirody*," *OP*, 1928, no. 1, p. 3.

48. See *Sektsiia okhrany prirody Krasnoiarskogo geograficheskogo obshchestva, Listochki*, 1927 (May), no. 1, and *OP*, 1929, no. 4, pp. 109–110.

49. From *Pochemu nuzhno zashchishchat' zhivotnykh?* (n.p., n.d.). See also "Kratkii obzor deiatel'nosti Vseukrainskogo obshchestva zashchity zhivotnykh i rastenii (ZhIVRAS) za 1925–1927 gg."

50. "Ob uchastii detuchrezhdenii Sotsvosa v provedenii kampanii 'Den' lesa' v 1924 godu," Tsirkuliar no. 23, published in *ENKP*, 1924, no. 9 (27 April), pp. 22–24.

51. G. A. Kozhevnikov, *Shkol'nyi uchitel' i okhrana prirody*, p. 15.

52. Ibid.

53. On Bird Day, see A. Peresvetov, "Edinaia shkola i delo okhrany prirody," *OP*, 1928, no. 4, pp. 19–20, and "Den' ptits," *OP*, 1928, no. 1, pp. 16–19.

54. A photograph of the Ivanovo-Voznesensk demonstration is on the cover of *OP*, 1929, no. 3.

FIVE. THE GOSKOMITET AND THE *ZAPOVEDNIKI*

1. SU RSFSR 1925, no. 70, text 559, "Ob okhrane uchastkov prirody i ee otdel'nykh proizvedenii, imeiushchykh preimushchestvenno nauchnoe ili kul'turno-istoricheskoe znachenie," published in *ENKP*, 1925, no. 51 (101), pp. 2–4.

2. These co-signatories included Deputy Commissar of Education Varvara Nikolaevna Iakovleva, Deputy Chairman of Gosplan RSFSR A. M. Essen, Deputy Commissar of Agriculture A. I. Sviderskii, Deputy Commissar of Public Health K. G. Mukhtarov, Deputy Commissar of Finance R. Ia. Levin, Deputy Chairman of VSHNKh RSFSR A. P. Brykov, and People's Commissar of Internal Affairs A. G. Beloborodov. The instructions were published in *ENKP*, 1926, no. 36, pp. 4–7.

3. Apparently, situations where Narkompros would have to appeal against the decisions of the Goskomitet majority were obviated by the commissariat's ability to cast a pocket veto over all such decisions.

4. M. P. Potemkin, Speech, *VRSOP*, p. 11. A more optimistic appraisal was provided by S. A. Severtsov, scholarly secretary of the Goskomitet, who put the total number of local commissions at thirty-three by late 1927; see Severtsov, "O mezhduvedomstvennykh komissiiakh po okhrane prirody."

5. "Ob organizatsii mezhduvedomstvennykh komissii po okhrane prirody (Tsirkuliar no 5000/82)," *ENKP*, 1928, no. 16.

6. "Ob organizatsii mezhduvedomstvennykh komissii po okhrane prirody i napravlenii ikh raboty (Tsirkuliar no. 50/001/19)," *ENKP*, 1929, no. 1.

7. V. T. Ter-Oganesov, "Industrializatsiia SSSR i voprosy organizatsii nauki," *Nauchnyi rabotnik*, 1926, no. 9, pp. 11, 15–19.

8. S. A. Severtsov (1891–1947) was first docent, then professor at Moscow State University. In addition to his conservation-related activities in Glavnauka and the Goskomitet, he taught courses in zoology, evolutionary theory, general ecology, the biological bases of game management, and conservation.

9. V. V. Perovskii (1875–?) turned up in 1931 as a censor for the State Publishing House OGIZ, with responsibility for *kraeved* literature.

10. G. R. Eitingen (1899–?) was professor of forestry at the Timiriazev Agricultural Academy and director of its Experimental Forestry Station. He represented the RSFSR Workers' and Peasants' Inspectorate on the Goskomitet. In the early 1950s, he rejected charges by other scientists that his work incorporated concepts developed by Lysenko.

11. S. S. Perov (1889–?) was professor of chemistry at the Vologda Dairy Industry Institute, an affiliate of VSNKh, director of the Agricultural Section of the State Polytechnical Museum in Moscow, and deputy director of the State Timiriazev Scientific Research Institute for the Study and Propagation of the Natural-Science Bases of Dialectical Materialism (not to be confused with the Timiriazev Agricultural Academy).

12. See S. A. Severtsov, "O deiatel'nosti Goskomiteta po okhrane prirody."

13. Severtsov, "O mezhduvedomstvennykh," p. 25. State *zapovedniki* were established by acts of the central government and were usually included in the republican budget. Local *zapovedniki* were established and funded by local governments.

14. V. Dolgoshov, "O sud'be Tsentral'nogo lesnogo zapovednika."

15. Ibid.

16. Severtsov, "O deiatel'nosti."

17. "Khronika," *OP*, 1929, no. 2.

18. Ibid., no. 4, pp. 125–126.

19. For 1925–1926 Glavnauka's budget was 1,038,000 rubles; V. T. Ter-Oganesov, "Industrializatsiia SSSR," p. 12. The figure quoted by Martyn Liadov (director of Glavnauka in 1929) for 1927–1928 was 12,744,300 rubles (see his "Zadachi organizatsii i puti razvitiia nauchno-issledovatel'skoi raboty v SSSR," in *Tretii Vsesoiuznyi s"ezd nauchnykh rabotnikov, Sputnik delegata* [Moscow, 1929], p. 150). Although it appears curious that Glavnauka received a tenfold increase in its budget over two years, I have been unable to locate any more definitive data.

20. V. Sergiev, "Vystavka Glavnauki," *Narodnoe prosveshchenie*, 1926, no. 1, p. 116.

21. See, for example, I. I. Puzanov, *Po nekhozhennomu Krymu*, p. 193.

22. A listing of scientific studies conducted in the *zapovednik* is provided by V. I.

Dobrokhotov and A. M. Ermolaev, *Astrakhanskii gosudarstvennyi zapovednik: Kratkaia istoriia, sovremennoe sostoianie i rabota v 1935 g.*, pp. 141–143.

23. M. P. Rozanov, "Zoologicheskaia ekspeditsiia Glavnauki v Kavkazskii zapovednik," *OP*, 1928, no. 3, p. 13.

24. A. G. Diunin, briefly director of the Caucasus *zapovednik*, stated that its budget was increased to 89,000 rubles for 1928–1929, when its staff numbered fifty, including five scientists; *VRSOP*, pp. 169–171. The budget for the Il'menskii *zapovednik* rose to 33,283 rubles in 1928–1929 and the budget for the Middle Volga *zapovednik* increased from 19,040 rubles in 1927–1928 to 29,432 rubles in 1928–1929; *VRSOP*, pp. 77–78.

25. G. A. Kozhevnikov, "Ob"iasnitel'naia zapiska po zaprosu Gosplana o nauchno-issledovatel'skoi rabote Otdela okhrany prirody pri Glavnauke Narkomprosa ot 15-ogo sentiabria 1923 g. za no. 792," TsGA RSFSR, fond 2307, op. 8, ed. khr. 281, listy 143–146, cited in Shtil'mark and Avakov, p. 148 (see n. 16, chap. 2).

26. The six state reserves and their areas (in hectares) were Caucasus, 280,000; Crimean, 21,138; Astrakhan', 22,900; Il'menskii, 15,500; Penza, 170; and Kosino, 60. Source: Kulagin, "Sovremennoe," p. 112. Also, the Decree of SNK RSFSR and VTsIK, 17 February 1925, in *Kraevedenie*, 1925, no. 1, pp. 194–200, lists institutions then under Glavnauka's jurisdiction.

27. The seven local reserves and their areas (in hectares) were Galich'ia gora, 16; Olenii ostrov, 1,000; Aksu-Dzhebagly, 30,540; Stolby, 3,960; Samurskii, 2,700; Zhivaia kniga, 27; and Les na Vorskle, 174. Principal source: S. A. Severtsov, "Zapovedniki SSSR."

28. A listing of these reserves is in the appendices.

29. Thirty-one (with 187,402 hectares) belonged to local branches of the republican Commissariats of Education, thirteen (with 1,740,810 hectares) to local branches of the republican Commissariats of Agriculture, and two to other local jurisdictions.

30. Narkomzem's territorial advantage was largely on paper. It was a direct result of the creation of poorly staffed and financed reserves of immense size in the formerly game-rich taiga zones of Siberia and the northern Urals.

31. D. K. Solov'ev, *Tipy organizatsii, sposobstvuiushchikhsia okhrane prirody* (Petrograd, 1918), p. 4.

SIX. THE *ZAPOVEDNIKI* AND COMMUNITY ECOLOGY

1. Two excellent surveys of early Russian community ecology are Kh. Kh. Trass, *Geobotanika: istoriia i sovremennye tendentsii razvitiia*, and G. I. Dokhman, *Istoriia geobotaniki v Rossii*.

2. V. V. Alekhin, *Chto takoe rastitel'noe soobshchestvo?* p. 75. In the early 1890s Iosif Konradovich Pachoskii coined the term *fitosotsiologiia* (phytosociology) for the new science of plant communities, although systems or organisms had already been referred to as sociological phenomena in, for example, the limnological writing of D. M. Rossinskii.

3. Donald Worster, *Nature's Economy: The Roots of Ecology*.

4. Dokhman.

5. Ibid., esp. pp. 55–58.

6. G. F. Morozov, "Soderzhanie i zadachi obshchego lesovodstva," *Isvestiia Lesnogo instituta*, 1904, no. 11, p. 152; quoted by Dokhman, p. 56.

7. G. S. Karzinkin, "Popytka prakticheskogo obosnovaniia poniatiia biotsenoza," *ZZh*, 1927, vol. 7.

8. Pachoskii's precepts were synopsized by Trass, *Geobotanika*, pp. 35–36, based on Pachoskii, *Opisanie rastitel'nosti Khersonskoi gubernii*, I. *Lesa* (Kherson, 1915). Dokhman, p. 18, concurs in this reading. Although Pachoskii subsequently published works with such sociologizing titles as *Osnovy fitosotsiologii* (Kherson, 1921) and "Sotsial'nyi printsip v rastitel'nom tsarstve," my reading of the latter finds no attempt by Pachoskii explicitly to compare plant and human societies or to impute a class structure to human society. Evidently,

the strident ideological flavor of his earlier work left an ineradicable impression that impugned all of phytosociology.

9. Trass, *Geobotanika*, p. 53.

10. Ibid., p. 50. Sukachev had written in his *Rastitel'nye soobshchestva*, p. 56: ". . . we see in the structure of the community a striving to utilize as fully as possible the productive forces of the environment. To this last principle, first advanced by Pachoskii, we may add the notion advanced by him recently that at the basis of plant communities is the principle of the good of the whole, and not that of its individual constituent elements."

11. Trass, *Geobotanika*, pp. 62–63.

12. Ecological themes occupied an increasingly prominent place in the papers and discussions at the All-Russian and All-Union Congresses of Zoologists, Anatomists, and Histologists through the early 1930s. And, when botanists were asked by the Russian Botanical Society to define themselves by their primary subspecialty, 129 indicated geobotany, 43 phytosociology, and 28 ecology, for a total of 200, or over 10 percent of subspecialties named; A. E. Zhadovskii, comp., *Adresnaia kniga botanikov SSSR* (Leningrad, 1929), p. 6.

13. G. A. Kozhevnikov, "Znachenie Kosinskogo zapovednika," p. iii.

14. G. A. Kozhevnikov, "Kak vesti nauchnuiu rabotu v zapovednikakh," p. 15.

15. Ibid., p. 13.

16. Ibid., pp. 14–19.

17. Kozhevnikov, "Znachenie," p. i.

18. G. A. Kozhevnikov, "Zadachi okhrany prirody v SSSR," p. 6.

19. Ibid.

20. Ibid.

21. Kozhevnikov, "Kak vesti," p. 13.

22. Kozhevnikov, *Shkol'nyi uchitel'*, p. 32.

23. "Ot redaktsii," *OP*, 1928, no. 1, p. 2.

24. See, for instance, the remarks of N. N. Pod"iapol'skii in "Okhrana prirody i sel'skoe khoziaistvo," *OP*, 1928, no. 1, pp. 14–16.

25. A. L. Brodskii, *Okhrana prirody v Turkestane*, pp. 5ff. Brodskii here remarkably anticipated the ideas of F. R. Shtil'mark and N. F. Reimers by more than fifty years.

26. See M. N. Kolod'ko, "Pervyi stepnoi gosudarstvennyi zapovednik 'Chapli'," in Kolod'ko and B. K. Fortunatov, eds., *Stepnoi zapovednik Chapli—Askania-Nova, Sbornik statei* (Moscow, 1928), p. 7.

27. For information on Askania-Nova in the nineteenth century, see V. V. Stanchinskii, "Chapli (Askania-Nova)," and M. M. Zavadovskii, "Obshchii ocherk i istoriia razvitiia Askanii-Nova," in Zavadovskii and B. K. Fortunatov, eds., *Askania-Nova: Stepnoi zapovednik Ukrainy, Sbornik statei*.

28. On Askania during the Civil War, see B. K. Fortunatov, "Dva goda Askanii-Nova (1921–1922)," in Zavadovskii and Fortunatov; Kolod'ko, "Pervyi stepnoi" (n. 26 above); and P. K. Kozlov, "Sovremennoe polozhenie zooparka 'Askania-Nova,' " pp. 467–468.

29. Kolod'ko, "Pervyi stepnoi," pp. 31–32. The text of the decree is reproduced there. See also Fortunatov, "Dva goda Askanii-Nova," p. 64.

30. Fortunatov, pp. 74–76.

31. "V obshchestve akklimatizatsii," *Priroda i okhota na Ukraine*, 1924, no. 1–2, pp. 205–206 and 210–215.

32. I. K. Pachoskii, "Nabliudeniia nad tselinnym pokrovom v Askanii-Nova v 1923 g.," *Visti derzhavnogo stepovogo zapovidnika Chapli*, 1924, vol. 3, p. 17.

33. Ibid., p. 34.

34. "V obshchestve," p. 203.

35. B. K. Viktorov, "Pervyi zapovednik imeni Kh. G. Rakovskogo (byvshii Askania-Nova)," *Priroda i okhota na Ukraine*, 1924, no. 1–2, pp. 207–209.

36. "V obshchestve," p. 211.

37. Kolod'ko, "Pervyi," p. 34.

38. Ibid., p. 35.

39. *Spravochnik: Na puti v Askaniiu,* p. 24.

40. Ibid., p. 31.

41. Kolod'ko, "Pervyi stepnoi," pp. 18 and 28.

42. Ibid., p. 20. Seven thousand tourists came in 1925 and thirty thousand in 1927.

43. "M. F. Ivanov," *Liudi russkoi nauki,* vol. 3 (Moscow, 1961), pp. 844–851.

44. M. F. Ivanov, "Po povodu stoletiia sushchestvovaniia Askaniia-Nova (1828–1928)," *Biulleten' Zootekhnicheskoi opytnoi stantsii v goszapovednike 'Chapli' (byvshaia Askania-Nova),* 1928, no. 4, cited in "Pis'mo v redaktsiiu," *OP,* 1929, no. 2, pp. 55–56.

45. See V. F. Levitskii, "Sel'skoe khoziaistvo Askanii-Nova (Chapli) v sviazi s perspektivami orosheniia doliny Dnepra," pp. 89–91.

46. Ibid.

47. "Pis'mo v redaktsiiu," p. 56 (n. 44 above).

48. Ibid.

49. *VRSOP,* p. 56.

50. Ibid.

51. Ibid., pp. 49 and 56.

52. Ibid., p. 49.

53. These others included the Primorskie *zapovedniki* (which had been incorporated into Askania by V. O. Zitte in 1923 but were detached in 1927 and incorporated into a single *zapovednik)* and the Koncha-Zaspa, Kanev-Shevchenko, and Lower Dnepr *zapovedniki.*

54. "O pamiatnikakh kul'tury i prirody," *UKOPP, Zbirnik,* no. 1, *Okhorona pam'iatok prirodi na Ukraini* (Khar'kov, 1927), pp. 89–90; it was signed by Petrovskii and Chubar'.

55. Biographical information about Stanchinskii may be found in B. N. Mazurmovich, "V. V. Stanchinskii," *Vydaiushchie,* pp. 268–273, and N. T. Nechaeva and S. I. Medvedev, "Pamiati V. V. Stanchinskogo."

56. V. V. Stanchinskii, *Izmenchivost' organizmov i ee znachenie v evoliutsii,* p. 3.

57. Stanchinskii's idea of a dualistic system of inheritance, involving two types of chromosomal material (one behaving according to Mendelian regularities, the other responding to environmental stimuli), has intriguing parallels in the thinking of German biologist Richard Goldschmidt (the Grundstock hypothesis).

58. Stanchinskii, *Izmenchivost',* p. 5.

59. V. V. Stanchinskii, "O nekotorykh osnovnykh poniatiiakh zoologii v svete sovremennoi ekologii." Vernadskii called this "stuff" *vidovoe veshchestvo,* or species-stuff. It is related to the term *biomass* but is not identical.

60. V. V. Stanchinskii, "K metodike kolichestvennogo izucheniia biotsenozov travianistykh assotsiatsii," *ZhEB,* 1931, vol. 1, no. 1, p. 133.

61. See Sharon E. Kingsland, *Modeling Nature: Episodes in the History of Population Ecology* (Chicago: University of Chicago Press, 1985).

62. V. V. Stanchinskii, "O nekotorykh," p. 42.

63. Ibid.

64. The existence of biocenoses was assumed by most ecologists of the time. Exceptions were L. G. Ramenskii, a forerunner of the gradient analysis approach, and American Henry Allen Gleason.

65. V. V. Stanchinskii, "O znachenii massy vidovogo veshchestva v dinamicheskom ravnovesii biotsenozov," p. 89. This seminal article was rediscovered by Professor Richard Brewer of Western Michigan University.

66. Stanchinskii, "O nekotorykh," p. 42.

67. Stanchinskii, "O znachenii," p. 90.

68. Stanchinskii, "O nekotorykh," p. 43.

69. "Ot redaktsii," *ZhEB,* 1931, vol. 1, vyp. 1, p. 6. Stanchinskii was the journal's editor-in-chief.

70. Stanchinskii, "O znachenii," p. 94.

71. Stanchinskii, "K metodike," pp. 133–137, with illustrations.

72. N. T. Nechaeva and S. I. Medvedev, "Pamiati V. V. Stanchinskogo," p. 112.

73. "Otchet o nauchnoi rabote S. V. Kirikova v Berezinskom zapovednike (s 11.X. po 28.XII–1929 goda) predstavlennyi v Belorusskoe lesnoe upravlenie," in A. V. Fediushin, "K osnovaniiu," p. 9.

74. S. A. Severtsov, "Zapovedniki SSSR," OP, 1929, no. 2, p. 51.

75. Ibid.

76. See "Vypiska iz protokola no. 4 zasedaniia Prezidiuma Gosudarstvennogo komiteta okhrany prirody," 21 January 1927, signed by S. A. Severtsov, TsGA RSFSR, fond 2306, op. 69, ed. khr. 1412. See also note from Narkompros RSFSR to SNK RSFSR no. 691-55 of 30 April 1927, signed by Deputy-Commissar Iakovleva, ibid. The original Narkomzem position is set out in "Ob utverzhdenii polozheniia o Voronezhskom Gosudarstvennom okhotnich'em i bobrovom zapovednike" (Memorandum of Narkomzem RSFSR to SNK RSFSR, signed by M. I. Latsis), ibid., list 1-a.

77. "Ob Astrakhanskom gosudarstvennom zapovednike," Decree of 24 November 1927, in Izvestiia TsIK SSSR, 1928, no. 4 (5 January).

SEVEN. THE CONSERVATION CONGRESS OF 1929

1. VRSOP, p. 7. Specifically, the idea was generated by the presidium of the Goskomitet. About 60 percent of the congress' total cost of 3,780 rubles was borne by Narkomzem RSFSR, Narkomtorg RSFSR and SSSR, and the Hunters' Cooperative Union.

2. Ibid.

3. A party member since 1908, P. G. Smidovich (1874–1935) served as chairman of the Moscow Soviet during 1917 and 1918. During the Civil War, he directed the Energy Department of VSNKh RSFSR and was a member of the delegation that negotiated a peace with Poland. As a member of VTsIK's presidium he was in charge of all matters relating to conservation. He headed VTsIK's Committee for Zapovedniki, created in 1933, and served as president of the nongovernmental Society of Friends of Green Cities.

4. VRSOP, p. 125.

5. Ibid., p. 10.

6. P. P. Smolin (1897–1975), a founder of KIuBZ (Club of Young Biologists of the Moscow Zoo) in 1923, soon became an activist in the Komsomol's Young Naturalist movement, helping to organize its first congress in 1925. During the thirties he worked as a game specialist in the Northern Game and Hunting Station in Arkhangel'sk, where he studied the recently introduced muskrat. After a tour as scientific director of the Crimean zapovednik (1935–1939) and an enlistee in the Red Army, Smolin worked for the Darwin Museum in Moscow and led the youth section of the All-Russian Conservation Society (to 1966).

7. VRSOP, p. 151.

8. Ibid., p. 125.

9. OP, 1928, no. 1, p. 3.

10. Ter-Oganesov relinquished his conservation responsibilities at that time with the elimination of the Conservation Department in Narkompros. Potemkin assumed many of those responsibilities as the specialist in charge of conservation affairs in the Department of Scientific Institutions, which absorbed the defunct Conservation Department. He occupied the Goskomitet vice-chairmanship ex officio as the highest ranking conservation official of Narkompros RSFSR.

11. VRSOP, p. 16. The total prewar catch was fewer than 67,000 seals annually.

12. Ibid.

13. Ibid. Almost all of the lake's more valuable commercial fish—omul, pike-perch, and carp-bream—had been replaced by such less desirable varieties as pope and roach.

14. Ibid., p. 17.

15. Ibid.

16. Ibid., pp. 132 and 82–83.

17. Ibid., p. 130.

18. Ibid., pp. 192–193.

19. Ibid., p. 13.

20. In late 1927, F. N. Petrov was replaced as head of Glavnauka by Martyn Nikolaevich Liadov. Liadov's position, however, was shaky; he was replaced in early 1930 by Ivan Kapitonovich Luppol.

21. No decree on this can be located in the 1929 *Sobranie uzakonenii i rasporiazhenii raboche-krest'ianskogo pravitel'stva RSFSR,* probably because it was rescinded so quickly. The ruling is mentioned in the SNK RSFSR Decree of 4 May 1930 which rescinded it.

22. *VRSOP,* pp. 172–175.

23. Ibid., p. 13.

24. Ibid., p. 133.

25. Ibid., pp. 101–102.

26. Ibid., p. 191.

27. Ibid., p. 25.

28. Ibid., p. 19.

29. Ibid., p. 22.

30. Ibid., p. 172.

31. Ibid., p. 23.

32. Ibid., p. 86.

33. Ibid., p. 89.

34. Ibid.

35. Ibid., p. 91.

36. Ibid., p. 90.

37. Ibid., pp. 119, 123.

38. Ibid., p. 121.

39. Ibid., p. 123.

40. Ibid., p. 92.

41. Conversation with Andrei Aleksandrovich Nasimovich, 18 April 1980, in Moscow.

42. *VRSOP,* p. 31.

43. Ibid., pp. 122–123.

44. Ibid., p. 123.

45. Ibid.

46. Ibid., p. 122.

47. Ecologists still cannot predict the minimal territories required to preserve viable tracts of many of the world's biological communities. In the Amazon Basin, the Brazilian government, in conjunction with the World Wildlife Fund, is engaged in a project to determine empirically the relationship between the area of intact tropical moist forest and the *number* of species whose survival that area can guarantee. These efforts, informed by island biogeography and patch-dynamics theory, have yielded only imprecise results owing to the limitations of models. Attempts to substantiate, much less identify and protect, discrete biocenoses have been even less promising. A good example of this is the experience of the International Biological Program of the late 1960s and early 1970s, a "descendant" of Soviet *zapovednik* studies.

48. *VRSOP,* p. 121.

49. Ibid. In this, Fortunatov foreshadowed the more empirical approach exemplified by the Amazon reserves project, as described in n. 47 above. Again, the crucial difference is that the Soviet discussion focused on the preservation of systems, whereas island biogeography focuses on the survival of numbers of species (as a function of area).

50. Ibid.

51. Ibid., pp. 194–195.

52. Ibid.

EIGHT. THE CULTURAL REVOLUTION COMES TO BIOLOGY

1. Law adopted by the Fourth Session of TsIK SSSR in 1929, quoted in A. F. Vangengeim, "Kraevedenie v bor'be za urozhai," *ITsBK,* 1929, no. 4, p. 1.

2. S. V. Pokrovskii, Preface, in V. D. Sokolov, *Okhrana prirody i povyshenie urozhainosti,* p. 3.

3. A. A. Teodorovich, "Problema urozhainosti i okhrana prirody."

4. Written in June 1876 and published in 1896 in *Die Neue Zeit,* the essay warned against impetuous human transformation of nature.

5. See *OP,* 1930, no. 1, p. 4.

6. N. N. Pod"iapol'skii, "Industrializatsiia sel'skogo khoziaistva i ocherednye zadachi okhrany prirody."

7. Ibid., p. 49. As early as 1927, S. A. Buturlin had argued against the hasty sowing of the virgin lands on ecological grounds. See Iu. N. Kurazhkovskii, *Ocherki prirodopol'zovaniia* (Moscow: Mysl', 1969), p. 83.

8. Pod"iapol'skii, "Industrializatsiia."

9. Early in 1930, the society's *sovet* (governing council) decided to create a special commission to negotiate anew with Narkomzem RSFSR and the other obstructing parties regarding the future of the Central Forest *zapovednik.* See E. G. Bloshenko, "Khronika," *OP,* 1930, no. 4, pp. 89–90.

10. A. I. Grishin, Letter to the Editor, *OP,* 1930, no. 8–10, p. 215.

11. See Loren R. Graham, "Science and Values: The Eugenics Movement in Germany and Russia in the 1920s," *American Historical Review,* 1977, vol. 82, no. 5, pp. 1133–1164.

12. B. E. Raikov (1880–1966) was a natural-science methodologist and historian of science. He was professor at the A. I. Gertsen Leningrad State Pedagogical Institute from 1918 until his arrest c. 1931 and again, after his rehabilitation, from 1945 to 1948. President of the Society for the Propagation of Natural-Science Education, he edited its journals during the two decades prior to his arrest. He also wrote a biographical study of Russia's first evolutionary biologists. See T. A. Lukina, *B. E. Raikov: 1880–1966.*

The Young Naturalists group was founded in Moscow in 1918. The group later came under the curatorship of Narkompros and the Komsomol. Its purpose was "to assist the party . . . in the mastery of nature in the interests of socialist construction," according to *BSE,* 1st ed. (Moscow, 1931), vol. 65, p. 241. In 1929, the group had 65,000 members.

13. There was as yet no Biological Faculty at Moscow State University, and the various biological sciences, to 1930, were subsumed under the Physical-Mathematical Faculty's Biology Department *(Kafedra).*

14. M. R—na, "Revoliutsiia v institutakh fizmata 1 MGU," *Varnitso,* 1930, no. 2, pp. 79–81.

15. Ibid., p. 81.

16. Kozhevnikov was president of the Moscow branch of the Society for the Propagation of Natural-Science Education, which Raikov headed.

17. A. V. Nemilov, "Zametki uchenogo."

18. Ibid.

19. Alexander Vucinich, *Science in Russian Culture: 1861–1917,* vol. 2 (Stanford, 1970), esp. pp. 12–15 (discussion of the Nihilists' attitudes toward science).

20. Ibid. See also Vucinich, *The Empire of Knowledge* (Berkeley: University of California Press, 1984), esp. p. 48.

21. See Loren R. Graham, *Science and Philosophy in the Soviet Union* (New York: Knopf, 1972), chap. 2.

22. See David Joravsky, *Soviet Marxism and Natural Science, 1917–1932.*

23. Ibid., p. 163 and passim.

24. Ibid., pp. 153–155.

25. See Graham, *Science and Philosophy*, pp. 13–14, and Diane Paul, "Marxism, Darwinism, and the Theory of the Two Sciences."

26. For the early activities of these societies, see *EM*, 1929, no. 3, p. 204, for the Russian group and *EM*, 1930, no. 2–3, p. 165, for the Ukrainian.

27. They included geneticists I. I. Agol, A. S. Serebrovskii, and N. P. Dubinin and experimental biologist M. M. Zavadovskii.

28. Quoted in I. I. Bugaev, "Fitosotsiologiia ili fitotsenologiia?"

29. Criticism of the conclusion that nonidentical beings in nature and in society necessarily had to be regarded as endowed with unequal rights may be found in Theodosius Dobzhansky, "Is Genetic Diversity Compatible with Human Equality?" *Social Biology*, 1973, vol. 20, pp. 280–288.

30. Trass, *Geobotanika*, p. 68.

31. Ibid., p. 53. In a letter of 9 March 1965 to Trass, V. N. Sukachev, a disciple of Pachoskii's in the 1920s, wrote:

> As is known, some of our "philosophers" exercised a similarly negative influence on [ecological] work. . . . I regret the fact that we were forced in the 1930s to renounce the term *phytosociology* to describe our field. . . . The fact that a few tried to draw far-reaching, unfounded parallels between phytosociology and sociology should not have served as the basis for rejecting the term. . . ."

32. Bugaev, "Fitosotsiologiia," p. 79.

33. Ibid., p. 90. Pachoskii's notions about the biocenosis borrowed heavily from the ideas of Herbert Spencer.

34. Ibid., p. 81.

35. Ibid.

36. Ibid., p. 92.

37. Graham, *Science and Philosophy*, p. 209.

38. E. V. Ryzhkova, "Akademik Isai Izrailovich Prezent," p. 98.

39. Conversation with Mark Popovsky, 17 February 1981, New York City.

40. Ryzhkova, "Akademik," pp. 98–99.

41. Popovsky conversation.

42. Ryzhkova, "Akademik," p. 99.

43. I am indebted to Samuel Rakhlin for the applicability of the term *avos'* to describe this mentality.

44. J. V. Stalin, "A Year of Great Change," *Works* (Moscow: Foreign Languages Press, 1951), vol. 12, p. 135.

45. J. V. Stalin, "Concerning Questions of Agrarian Policy in the USSR," *Works* (Moscow: Foreign Languages Press, 1951), vol. 12, p. 161.

46. Ernst (Arnost) Kol'man, a Czech emigré, served as general overseer of science within the Central Committee from about 1930.

47. In 1928, however, he *did* publish a monograph on the origin of speech in humans.

48. Nechaeva and Medvedev, p. 111. The quotation marks are the authors'.

49. Ibid.

50. Iu. D. Tsinzerling, "Pervaia proizvodstvennaia konferentsiia geobotanikov i floristov, 25 fevralia-2 marta 1931 g." At the time, the term *geobotany* was still largely synonymous with *phytocenology*.

51. I. I. Prezent, *Klassovaia bor'ba na estestvenno-nauchnom fronte* (Moscow-Leningrad: Obshchestvo biologov-marksistov pri Leningradskom otdelenii Kommunisticheskoi Akademii, 1932), pp. 33, 39–40.

52. Zhores Medvedev, *The Rise and Fall of T. D. Lysenko* (New York, 1968), trans. by I. Michael Lerner, p. 10, and Lukina, pp. 78–79. Raikov was permitted to return to Leningrad only in 1945. See Lukina, pp. 81–85.

NINE. PROTECTIVE COLORATION

1. The February speech featured the slogan "Technology decides everything." Stalin's letter to the editors of *Proletarskaia revoliutsiia,* which appeared in the sixth issue for 1931, inaugurated the purge of the Communist intelligentsia and abolished the proletarian literary and artistic organizations. His call to stop the baiting of the old intelligentsia was most clearly announced in a speech published 23 June 1931 in *Vechernaia Moskva.*

2. These Bolshevizers included Academician Boris Aleksandrovich Keller; future Academicians V. R. Vil'iams and A. I. Oparin; Professors E. L. Sepp, B. M. Zavadovskii, and L. M. Sabsovich; and A. V. Nemilov, V. P. Bushinskii, and A. I. Vishinskii. But the Varnitso inner circle also included two future victims of Stalin-era politics—N. I. Vavilov and N. M. Tulaikov—and zoologist A. L. Brodskii.

3. K. Kviatkovskii, "Nauchnye obshchestva pered sudom sovetskoi obshchestvennosti," p. 56.

4. B. M. Zavadovskii (1895–?) was an experimental biologist and head of the Biology Department at Sverdlov Communist University.

5. Kviatkovskii, "Nauchnye obshchestva," pp. 56–57.

6. K. Kviatkovskii, " 'Nauchnye' bolota," p. 53.

7. E. K. Sepp, "Neobkhodimo reorganizovat' nauchnye obshchestva," p. 20.

8. Loren R. Graham, *The Soviet Academy of Sciences and the Communist Party, 1927–1932* (Princeton, N.J.: Princeton University Press, 1967), chap. 3.

9. Sepp, "Neobkhodimo," pp. 20–21.

10. For MOIP's history, see S. Iu. Lipshits, *Moskovskoe obshchestvo ispytatelei prirody za 135 let ego sushchestvovaniia, 1805–1940.*

11. Kviatkovskii, " 'Nauchnye' bolota," p. 53.

12. Quoted in V. F. Karpych, "Bor'ba za marksizm v sovetskom kraevedenii."

13. Ibid.

14. These are retrospective thoughts of I. G. Klabunovskii on the struggle for a "Soviet" *kraevedenie; FNT,* 1932, no. 6, pp. 108–109. In addition to his activist work in the local lore movement, Ivan Grigor'evich Klabunovskii was director of the Information Department of Narkompros's Main Administration for Organization and Planning.

15. Pinkevich was an educational theorist and rector of the Second Moscow University, as well as a professor at the Moscow Institute of Scientific Pedagogy. Sheila Fitzpatrick, *Education and Social Mobility in the Soviet Union, 1921–1934* (Cambridge, 1979), pp. 140, 219, and passim, characterizes him as a "sober and learned Marxist professor" and an early target of the "radical" attacks of V. N. Shul'gin. In light of Fitzpatrick's assessment, it seems plausible that his attacks on the inclusion of preservationism and conservation in the scope of *kraevedenie* were a preemptive attempt to excise those aspects of *kraevedenie* most glaringly out of step with the Cultural Revolution in order to forestall even more destructive assaults by radical elements.

16. A. P. Pinkevich, "Predmet sovetskogo kraevedeniia."

17. I. M. Grevs (1860–1941) was the author of numerous historical works, including studies of ancient Roman agriculture and the private life of Turgenev.

18. S. S. Ganeshin (1879–1930) was a specialist in botanical geography, curator of the Academy of Sciences' Botanical Museum, and professor at the Leningrad Agricultural Institute. He represented the Academy of Sciences at the 1929 All-Russian Congress on Conservation, and died only months after the publication of Pinkevich's article, having lost his way on a mountain expedition.

19. Pinkevich, "Predmet," p. 10.

20. Pinkevich, "Predmet," p. 20.

21. G. M. Krzhizhanovskii, "Sotsialisticheskoe stroitel'stvo i kraevedenie," in G. M. Krzhizhanovskii and P. G. Smidovich, eds., *Sotsialisticheskoe stroitel'stvo i kraevedenie, Sbornik* (Moscow, 1930), p. 28.

22. Confirmation of the supposition that the changes effected by the TsBK were largely

cosmetic may be seen in a 1931 analysis by M. P. Potemkin, "Desiatyi Plenum TsBK," *SK*, 1931, no. 2, p. 4:

Both in the keynote speeches and in the debates it was revealed with full force that the resolutions of the Fourth Kraeved Conference adopted while the influence of the "old-timer" *kraevedy* was still great, contain . . . a whole collection of unclear, incomplete or, in some cases, just plain incorrect formulations.

23. See, for example, "Informatsiia o deiatel'nosti TsBK za aprel'-mai 1930 g.," *OP*, 1930, no. 6, p. 29.

24. V. N. Balandin, "Sotsialisticheskaia rekonstruktsiia i zadachi kraevedcheskikh organizatsii v oblasti okhrany prirody," *SK*, 1930, no. 11–12, p. 23.

25. Ibid.

26. V. Luchnik, "Bibliograficheskie zametki."

27. See the Rabkrin report in *OP*, no. 11–12, p. 56. Also see "Postanovlenie kolegii NK RKI RSFSR ob obsledovanii i chistke TsBK ot 26-ogo oktiabria 1930 g" (Protokol no. 46, p. 5), *SK*, 1930, no. 10–11, pp. 55–56.

28. Kviatkovskii, " 'Nauchnye' bolota," p. 53.

29. Potemkin, "Desiatyi," p. 2.

30. P. G. Smidovich had declared his intention to resign because of poor health and overwork. The true reasons were revealed later by N. V. Krylenko, "O rabote OKRAM i polozhenie na kraevedcheskom fronte," *SK*, 1932, no. 5, p. 20.

31. Potemkin, "Desiatyi," p. 2.

32. Despite the fact that *Sovetskoe kraevedenie* was supposedly the joint publication of the TsBK and the Society of Marxist-Kraevedy (OKRAM), this arrangement was reflected neither in the composition of the editorial board of the journal nor in its work plan or content. As a consequence, charged its radical critics from OKRAM, major ideological errors continued to find their way into the journal.

33. Kviatkovskii, "Nauchnye obshchestva," p. 57.

34. Kviatkovskii, " 'Nauchnye' bolota," p. 54.

35. Kviatkovskii, "Iskopaemye ot nauki," *Za kommunisticheskoe prosveshchenie*, 1931, no. 65.

36. "Postanovlenie prezidiuma TsBK ot 25-ogo marta 1931 g. po povodu stat'i Kviatkovskogo 'Iskopaemye ot nauki,' pomeshchesnnoi v no. 65 gazety *Za kommunisticheskoe prosveshchenie*," *SK*, 1931, p. 64.

37. V. Karpych, "Pod znamia bol'shevistskoi partiinosti! (Po-novomu rabotat', po-novomu rukovodit')," *SK*, 1931, no. 7–8, p. 10.

38. *FNT*, 1932, no. 6, pp. 108–109.

39. Karpych never cited the two articles by name; his charges may have been woven of whole cloth.

40. Vasil'ev and Karpych, "Kraevedenie," p. 3.

41. Krylenko, a hunter and first head of Tsentrokhota, was also an honorary member of VOOP and later served on the VTsIK Komitet po zapovednikam, whose first chairman was Smidovich. He and Smidovich seem to constitute the core of a circle whose other members may have included Turar Ryskulov (onetime chairman of SNK RSFSR) and others.

42. Vasil'ev and Karpych, p. 3.

43. M. P. Potemkin, "Odinnadtsatyi Plenum TsBK," *SK*, 1931, no. 11–12, p. 6.

44. On Savel'ev and Smidovich, see V. I. Zlobina, ed., *Vospitanniki Moskovskogo universiteta—soratniki V. I. Lenina*.

45. *SK*, 1932, no. 5, p. 20, and M. P. Potemkin, "Nado ispravit' politicheskie oshibki."

46. "Osobye postanovleniia XI Plenuma TsBK 25–28-ogo marta 1932 g.," *SK*, 1932, no. 5, p. 37.

47. The commission was liquidated on 26 September 1930. See *OP*, 1930, no. 8–10, p. 219.

48. See *SK,* 1931, no. 7–8, pp. 93 and 96. The old Conservation Section was renamed Productive Forces, however, as a concession to Stalinesque rhetoric.

49. "Rezoliutsiia po dokladu predstavitelia TsBK tovarishcha Potemkina 'O kraevedches-koi rabote,' priniataia sessiei Goskomiteta sodeistviia razvitiiu prirodnykh bogatstv, 28-ogo dekabria 1931 g.," *SK,* 1932, no. 5, p. 40.

50. Membership reached its peak early in 1931, at 115,000, organized in 2,700 cells and affiliates ("Postanovlenie Prezidiuma TsBK 25-ogo marta 1931 g.," p. 64) but had declined to 50,000–60,000 members in 1,500–2,000 affiliates by early the next year (I. G. Klabunovskii, "Cherez sovetskoe kraevedenie—k osvoeniiu estestvennykh bogatstv strany," *SK,* 1932, no. 5, p. 6).

51. *OP,* 1930, no. 1, p. 17.

52. *OP,* 1930, no. 1, p. 17. In actual fact, the purge of the central commissariats conducted in the winter of 1929–1930 by Rabkrin RSFSR was rather mild. As Sheila Fitzpatrick noted in "Cultural Revolution as Class War," in Fitzpatrick, ed., *Cultural Revolution in Russia, 1928–1931* (Bloomington: Indiana University Press, 1978), p. 11, that purge was aimed at the removal of corrupt officials and deadbeats; the social theme was relatively muted. Therefore, we may view Kirillova's comments about VOOP's fate hanging in the balance as tinged with a certain degree of hyperbole.

53. Kviatkovskii, " 'Nauchnye' bolota," p. 54.

54. Ibid.

55. *OP,* 1930, no. 1, p. 17.

56. Ibid.

57. The first occupational breakdowns, calculated as of March 1926, revealed that professors alone constituted 25 percent of VOOP's membership of 1,013, with the white-collar and civil servant group another 50 percent. See "Pervyi otchet VOOP," *OP,* 1928, no. 1, p. 29.

58. "Tretii otchet VOOP," *OP,* 1929, no. 4, p. 127. In 1929, educators accounted for only 12.4 percent of the membership, with the white-collar and civil servant group an additional 31.8 percent. Workers constituted only 1.4 percent.

59. *Okhrana prirody* cheerfully reported the establishment of each new rural branch of VOOP, but these were clearly the exception. See *OP,* 1930, no. 7, p. 176, and no. 8–10, p. 217, for lists of new branches.

60. A. A. Teodorovich, Letter to the Editorial Board, *OP,* 1930, no. 2, p. 19.

61. Ibid.

62. *OP,* 1931, no. 1–3, p. 49.

63. Workers constituted only 1.4 percent of the membership in April 1929 and 4.3 percent in October 1930, according to the third and fourth annual reports. By 1931, however, as reported by M. Nadezhdin, "Obshchestvo bez aktiva," p. 78, workers represented 9.4 percent. This figure rose only to 10.2 percent in 1934, as per *PSKh,* 1934, vol. 7, p. 213.

64. According to the remarks of Manteifel', *VSSOP,* p. 75, membership, which stood at 7,000 in early 1930 (and which reached 9,639 in October of that year), grew to 14,000 by 1932. By 1934, though, membership stood only slightly higher, at 15,093 (*PSKh,* 1934, vol. 7, p. 213).

65. See the first through fourth annual reports of VOOP.

66. "Chetvertyi otchet VOOP," *OP,* no. 8–10, p. 219.

67. *OP,* 1930, no. 4, p. 89. The first course was given at Moscow University in 1930–1931 by ecologist S. A. Severtsov, and was attended by such prominent future scientists as Academician Gordei Bromlei, G. F. Gauze, A. A. Nasimovich, N. A. Gladkov, S. S. Folitarek, and G. V. Nikol'skii. Conversation with A. A. Nasimovich, Moscow, April 10, 1980.

68. Students constituted 58.3 percent of the total membership at that time. Workers accounted for 4.3 percent, peasants 8.5, and the white-collar and civil servant group 16.3 (a dramatic decline from the 1920s). Professors and teachers were not listed as such, but

presumably accounted for a good share of the "other" and "no information" categories, which together totaled 12.6 percent.

69. "Chetvertyi otchet VOOP," p. 220.

70. Ibid.

71. *OP,* 1930, no. 1, p. 17 and "Chetvertyi otchet VOOP," p. 217. These figures, however, may be noncomparable, depending on whether the January 1930 amount includes Komsomols or not.

72. *OP,* 1929, no. 4, p. 129.

73. A. V. Segal' (1894–1935), a party member from 1917, was an ecologist and organic chemist at the Polytechnical Museum's Agricultural Laboratory. From 1926, he was scholarly secretary of Glavnauka and from 1931 of the USSR Academy of Sciences' Institute of Organic Chemistry.

74. *OP,* 1930, no. 8–10, p. 219.

75. A special VOOP commission was created to try to reach an accord with Narkomzem RSFSR and other agencies that were obstructing the establishment of the *zapovednik. OP,* 1930, no. 4, p. 89, and no. 8–10, p. 219.

76. *OP,* 1930, no. 8–10, p. 219, and editorial, "K voprosu ob okhrane mest zimovok vodoplavaiushchei i bolotnoi dichi," *OP,* 1930, no. 7, p. 154.

77. See F. F. Shillinger, "Informatsionnyi doklad o rabote Pechosko-Ilychskoi ekspeditsii VOOP 1929 g.," *OP,* 1929, no. 6, p. 167; also *OP,* 1930, no. 8–10, pp. 219–220.

78. *OP,* 1930, no. 3, pp. 63–68.

79. B. Lovetskii, "Neobkhodimo ozhivit' rabotu Sozh," *PSKh,* 1930, no. 1–3, p. 52.

80. V. V. Karpov was president of the Circle of Young Biologists of the Moscow Zoo (whose mentor was P. A. Manteifel') during the late 1920s and early 1930s. He was also a longtime member of the Society for the Study of the Fauna of Moscow Province, whose president was Kozhevnikov.

81. "Chetvertyi otchet VOOP," p. 223.

82. Short biographical articles about Makarov include S. S. Turov, "V. N. Makarov"; an obituary by G. P. Dement'ev; and a critical study, F. R. Shtil'mark, "Vasilii Nikitich Makarov (k dvadtsatiletiiu so dnia smerti)."

83. V. N. Makarov (1887–1953), born into a peasant family in Vladimir Province, enrolled in the Moscow Teachers' Institute at age eighteen. In his first year there, Makarov, a sympathizer with the Socialist Revolutionaries, was elected to the institute's strike committee. Soon, his revolutionary activity eclipsed his studies. Apprehended by the Tsarist police, he was exiled from Moscow, but returned after one year and reenrolled, graduating in 1908 with a specialty in natural-science teaching. After three years of teaching in Kostroma, he returned to Moscow to upgrade his skills at the Moscow Commercial Institute, graduating in 1916. During the Revolution and afterward he served as school inspector for the Bauman District in Moscow. As one of the founders of the Educational Workers' Union (Rabpros), he served on its Presidium from 1919 to December 1924, and was a deputy to the Moscow Soviet from 1922 to 1924. From 1925, when he was first accepted as a candidate member of the party, until 1930, when he emerged as a senior research associate in Narkompros's Scientific Sector, there is no information about his activities. Actually, his involvement in conservation dates to 1917, when he worked (until 1919) in the Russian Geographical Society's Permanent Conservation Commission editing V. P. Semenov-tian-shanskii's plans for a network of reserves.

84. V. N. Makarov, "Nashi zadachi," p. 2.

85. Ibid., p. 3.

86. Ibid.

87. Quoted in Kviatkovskii, " 'Nauchnye' bolota," p. 55.

88. The speaker, V. M. Sverdlov, secretary of Varnitso, referred to such societies as the Marxist-Kraevedy (OKRAM), the Materialist-Biologists, etc.

89. Kviatkovskii, " 'Nauchnye' bolota," p. 58.

90. No information is available concerning the circumstances of Kozhevnikov's relocation c. 1930 to the Sukhumi Primate Acclimatization Institute.

91. "O deiatel'nosti VOOP v 1932 g.," *PSKh*, 1932, vol. 5, p. 222.

92. See, for example, articles by Berkutov, Vorob'ev, and Sil'vestr in *PSKh*, 1931, vol. 4, and by Puzanov and Sobolevskii, 1932, vol. 5.

93. See *PSKh*, 1931, vol. 4, pp. 49 and 163, and 1932, vol. 5, p. 229, for details on this involvement.

94. N. N. Pod"iapol'skii, "Eshche o znachenii okhrany tseliny."

TEN. CONSERVATION AND THE FIVE-YEAR PLAN

1. SU RSFSR 1930, no. 9, text 108.

2. SZ SSSR 1930, no. 45, text 465.

3. SZ SSSR 1929, no. 59, text 550.

4. Gosplan SSSR. *Kontrol'nye tsifry narodnogo khoziaistva na 1929/30 god* (Moscow, 1930), p. 527.

5. A brief but suggestively glum commentary on the situation in the Crimea during this period is provided by L. A. Alferov, "Krymskie lesa i osnovnoi vopros ikh sokhraneniia."

6. N. Savin, "Iz Smolenskoi oblasti," *OP*, 1930, no. 4, pp. 87–88.

7. "O sostoianii lesnogo khoziaistva Zapadnoi oblasti," *OP*, 1930, no. 8–10, p. 210.

8. Reprinted in *PSKh*, 1931, no. 4–5, pp. 103–104.

9. For a particularly anguished commentary on the situation in the Crimea, see I. I. Puzanov, "Okhrana prirody v Krymu."

10. SU RSFSR 1930, no. 9, text 109.

11. A. Lavrov, "K voprosu o regulirovanii srokov okhoty," *OP*, 1930, no. 7, pp. 163–164, seems to indicate that the functions of creating *zakazniki* had passed to VSNKh RSFSR's All-Union Forest Industry Syndicate (Lespromkhoz), while in the Kazakh ASSR, the syndicate's local branch was cited as issuing a hunting decree in May 1930 (see "Godovoi otchet Kazakhskogo komiteta po okhrane prirody, pamiatnikov stariny i isskustva," *PSKh*, 1931, no. 1–3, p. 51).

12. SZ SSSR 1930, no. 41, text 223.

13. SZ SSSR 1930, no. 45, text 460.

14. Postanovlenie Narkomtorg SSSR, "O zagotovke pushniny i mekhsyr'ia v 1930–1931 godu," dated 18 September 1930. See *Zakonodatel'stvo i administrativnye rasporiazheniia po torgovli*, 1930, no. 56, p. 11.

15. Postanovlenie kollegii Narkomsnab SSSR ot 31-ogo dekabria 1930 goda no. 366, "O zagotovke pushniny i mekhsyr'ia v 1931 godu." See *Zakonodatel'stvo i administrativnye rasporiazheniia po torgovli*, 1931, no. 3, p. 1.

16. Postanovlenie EKOSO RSFSR ot 3-ogo sentiabria 1931 goda no. 286, "Ob utverzhdenii 'Polozhenie o komitete po delam okhotnich'ego khoziaistva pri Narkomsnabe RSFSR.' " See *NVT*, 1931, no. 1–2, p. 7.

17. Ibid.

18. E. G. Bloshenko, "Iz materialov Goskomiteta," *PSKh*, 1931, no. 4–5, p. 99.

19. See *NVT*, 1931, no. 12, p. 10.

20. Prikaz Narkomvneshtorg SSSR no. 657 ot 24-oktiabria 1931 goda, in *VT*, 1931, no. 23, p. 25.

21. Ibid. As of 1932, sixty production-hunting stations had been organized, including at least four devoted to acclimatizing the muskrat. See V. A. Perevalov, "Proizvodstvenno-okhotnich'i stantsii (POS-y) i ikh stroitel'stvo v 1932 godu," *Sovetskii sever*, 1933, no. 5, p. 31. The average size of these stations was nearly one million hectares.

22. *Ezhegodnik vneshnei torgovli za 1931 god*, p. 626.

23. *NVT*, 1931, no. 12, p. 10; no. 24, pp. 21–22; and 1932, no. 5, pp. 21–24, for example.

24. *NVT*, 1931, no. 12, p. 10.

25. *VT*, 1932, no. 5, p. 23.

26. *VT*, 1933, no. 4, p. 11.

27. *NVT*, 1931, no. 6, p. 8.

28. *NVT*, 1931, no. 9.

29. *NVT*, 1932, no. 5, p. 23.

30. "Obzor deiatel'nosti Gosudarstvennogo mezhduvedomstvennogo komiteta sodeistviia razvitiiu prirodnykh bogatstv za 1932 god (II, III, i IV kvartaly)," *PSKh*, 1932, vol. 5, p. 226.

31. Ibid., p. 228. The Goskomitet called the incident "a particularly disgusting violation of the law on hunting" and proposed a temporary ban on the harvesting of sea lions and the creation of a marine *zapovednik*.

32. Postanovlenie SNK RSFSR ot 1-ogo ianvaria 1931 goda, "O merakh okhrany pereletnoi dichi," *PSKh*, 1931, no. 1–3, pp. 53–54.

33. *OP*, 1930, no. 4, pp. 91–92, and "Obzor deiatel'nosti Gosudarstvennogo . . . v 1932 godu. . . ." pp. 225–226.

34. N. M. Kulagin, chairman of the Goskomitet, wrote of "the extremely impermissible attitude on the part of several agencies . . . to the requests by the Goskomitet that they submit reports on their activities. . . ." The agencies included Narkomvneshtorg, Narkomzem, and VSNKh. See "O rabote Goskomiteta za 1931 god," *PSKh*, 1931, no. 9–10, p. 251.

35. Postanovlenie VTsIK i SNK RSFSR ot 20-ogo iunia 1930 goda, "Ob okhrane i razvitii prirodnykh bogatstv RSFSR." Published in *OP*, 1930, no. 6, pp. 150–152.

36. This state of affairs was worriedly noted by the Fourth All-Union Congress of Zoologists, meeting in Kiev in May 1930, in its resolution speaking to conservation matters. See *OP*, 1930, no. 6, p. 123.

37. "Khronika," *OP*, 1930, no. 3, p. 68.

38. *PSKh*, 1931, no. 4–5, p. 98.

39. See the remarks of Mil'chenko in *VSSOP*, p. 46.

40. *PSKh*, 1931, no. 4–5, p. 100. At the 1933 conservation congress, the nearby Buzulukskii bor *zapovednik* was described by V. I. Smirnov, director of the Mid-Volga *zapovednik*, as "in the process of being destroyed" by forestry organs. See *VSSOP*, p. 147.

41. *PSKh*, 1931, no. 4–5, p. 101.

42. Ibid., p. 94. At the Bashkirskii *zapovednik*, the Okskii Combine, then under construction, claimed rights to one million cubic meters of wood, and tried to liquidate the reserve to gain access to its forests. See *VSSOP*, p. 147.

43. See the remarks of Shummer in *VSSOP*, p. 137.

44. *PSKh*, 1931, no. 4–5, p. 98.

45. Ibid. A similar protracted negotiation over the boundaries of the Kyzyl-Agach *zapovednik* in Azerbaidzhan, involving the Goskomitet and its adversaries in the Narkomsnab system and lasting over three years, ultimately ended with an agreement to *expand* the boundaries from those originally proposed in 1929. See "Obzor deiatel'nosti Gosudarstvennogo . . . v 1932 godu . . .," p. 219.

46. Bloshenko, "Iz materialov Goskomiteta," *PSKh*, 1931, no. 4–5, p. 100.

47. Ibid., p. 98.

48. *PSKh*, 1931, no. 4–5, p. 103.

49. SU RSFSR 1930, no. 9, text 109, "Polozhenie ob okhotnich'em khoziaistve RSFSR."

50. On 11 April 1930, the Malyi SNK RSFSR (Inner Council of People's Commissars) reviewed the question of the three *zapovedniki* (Caucasus, Astrakhan', and Crimean) and decided by decree to restore them to the jurisdiction of Narkompros. See *OP*, 1930, no. 4, p. 90.

51. See German Kreps, Foreword, O. I. Semenov-tian-shanskii, *Laplandskii zapovednik*, p. 9.

52. "Rezoliutsii Vsesoiuznogo soveshchaniia UPOL-NKVT o vzaimootnosheniiakh mezhdu UPOL-NKVT i eksportnymi ob"edineniiami," *VT*, 1932, no. 16, p. 8.

53. "Ob okhrane i razvitii prirodnykh bogatstv," pp. 150–152.

54. (V. N. Makarov), "K soveshchaniiu sektorov nauki soiuznykh respublik o postanovke

dela okhrany prirody v RSFSR (materialy v tseliakh informatsii)," *PSKh*, 1931, no. 4–5, p. 97.

55. Ibid.

56. F. R. Shtil'mark, "Vasilii Nikitich Makarov."

57. Postanovlenie kolegii Narkompros no. 689 ot 28-ogo noiabria 1931 goda, "O Gosudarstvennom Kavkazskom zapovednike," *BNKP*, 1931, no. 55, pp. 2–4.

58. Postanovlenie Narkompros no. 7444 ot 19-ogo avgusta 1931 goda, "Polozhenie o Pechorsko-Ilychskom Zapovednike," *BNKP*, 1931, no. 35, pp. 12–13.

59. "Tezisy doklada V. N. Makarova na sessii Goskomiteta v dekabre 1931 goda," *PSKh*, 1931, no. 9–10, p. 246.

60. Ibid., p. 247.

61. Ibid.

62. Ibid., p. 246.

63. The Caucasus *zapovednik*'s planned budget for 1931, for example, rose to 655,000 rubles (although part of the rise reflected rather considerable inflation). See *PSKh*, 1931, no. 1–3, p. 48. By contrast, total funding for all Narkomvneshtorg *zapovedniki* across the USSR for 1932 amounted to a meager 200,000 rubles (*VSSOP*, p. 67).

64. "Obzor deiatel'nosti Gosudarstvennogo . . . v 1932 godu . . .," p. 246.

65. Postanovlenie SNK RSFSR ot 4-ogo maia 1930 goda, reprinted in *OP*, 1930, no. 4, p. 96. The others were a steppe *zapovednik* in the Central Black Earth Oblast, composed of noncontinguous parcels with an aggregate area of approximately 10,000 hectares, including buffer zones; the Naurzum-Karagach Forest-Steppe *zapovednik* in the Kustanai Okrug of the Kazakh ASSR, with an area of approximately 185,000 hectares; the Sikhote-Alin *zapovednik* in the Far East Territory with an area of about one million hectares; the Altai *zapovednik* with an area to 600,000 hectares; and the Pechoro-Ilych *zapovednik* with an area of greater than one million hectares.

66. These six *zapovedniki* were the Alma-atinskii (400,000 hectares), to be upgraded from local status; the Borovoe (100,000 ha.); the Borzhomskii (18,000 ha.) in the Transcaucasus SFSR; the Karakalinskii [Turkmenian SSR] (50,000 ha.); the Katunskii (100,000 ha.); and the Chuiskii (250,000 ha.). See "Obzor deiatel'nosti Gosudarstvennogo . . . v 1932 godu . . .," p. 217.

67. See V. N. Makarov, "Tezisy doklada Narkomprosa RSFSR na pervom Vsesoiuznom s"ezde: 'O sostoianii raboty v oblasti okhrany prirody RSFSR i perspektivy ee razvitiia vo vtoroi piatiletke,' " AMGU, fond 200. Apparently as a result of the protracted struggle between conservation organs and the economic agencies, Makarov scaled down his projections of the area of some of the *zapovedniki* on the planning boards. He gives the planned area for the Alma-atinskii *zapovednik*, for example, as 50,000 hectares (p. 6). In this plan for the Second Five-Year Plan attention was redirected toward the creation of gigantic Siberian *zapovedniki*, including the proposed Ussuriiskii (250,000 ha.), Kamchatskii (250,000 ha.), Saianskii (500,000 ha.), Eniseiskii (200,000 ha.), Poliarnyi (1,000,000 ha.), Chukotskii (500,000 ha.), Anadyrskii (400,000 ha.), Verkhoianskii (500,000 ha.), and Odokminskii (500,000 ha.), as well as similarly large Central Asian ones, the Fergana Valley (250,000 ha.), Kalmytskii (300,000 ha.), and Saksaulovo-Pustinnyi (500,000 ha.) *zapovedniki* (p. 10).

68. "Rezoliutsiia po dokladu V. N. Makarova 'Proizvodstvennyi plan Gosudarstvennogo Mezhduvedomstvennogo komiteta sodeistviia razvitiiu prirodnykh bogatstv RSFSR i Sektora nauki Narkompros po etomu razdelu raboty na 1931 god," *PSKh*, 1931, no. 4–5, p. 45.

69. Ibid.

70. The Scientific Sector, created on 1 June 1930 from the old Glavnauka, was led during the early 1930s by Ivan Kapitonovich Luppol, who, while sympathetic to conservation, lacked the ardent zeal for that cause of Glavnauka's former chief, F. N. Petrov. On the organizational changes within Narkompros, see *Nauchnoe slovo*, 1930, no. 7–8, p. 116.

71. "Rezoliutsiia po dokladu V. N. Makarova," p. 46.

72. But not exclusively. *Zapovednik* director G. Kreps credited the involvement of the Goskomitet with keeping the Laplandskii reserve vital during the period 1930–1935.

73. "Obzor deiatel'nosti Gosudarstvennogo . . . v 1932 godu . . .," pp. 223–224.
74. "O rabote Gosudarstvennogo mezhduvedomstvennogo komiteta sodeistviia razvitiiu prirodnykh bogatstv RSFSR," Report, signed by Deputy People's Commissar of Education M. Epshtein, 21 December 1931, in *BNKP*, 1932, no. 1, pp. 4–5.
75. (Makarov), "K soveshchaniiu sektorov nauki," p. 95.
76. "Obzor deiatel'nosti Gosudarstvennogo . . . v 1932 godu . . .," pp. 223–224.
77. Ibid.
78. "Iz materialov Goskomiteta," p. 100.

ELEVEN. THE GREAT TRANSFORMATION OF NATURE

1. The Soviets' important contributions to community ecology were noted by J. Richard Carpenter in his exhaustive annotated bibliography, "Recent Russian Work on Community Ecology," *Journal of Animal Ecology*, 1939, vol. 8, pp. 354–386.
2. V. V. Stanchinskii and T. V. Radionova, "K ustanovleniiu biotsenologicheskikh poniatii i biotsenologicheskoi terminologii," p. 79.
3. "O programmnykh dokladakh piatogo s"ezda po voprosam biotsenologii," *VSZAG*, p. 27. Zernov, incidentally, was first to introduce Möbius's term *biocenosis* into Russian usage, in 1912.
4. "Po voprosam, sviazannym s prepodavaniem v VUZ-akh zoologicheskikh i blizkikh k nim distsiplinii," Ibid., p. 20.
5. Originally published as *Sreda i soobshchestvo*.
6. D. N. Kashkarov, *Environment and Community*, pp. 14–15.
7. V. Bukovskii, "Naselenie bespozvonochnykh Krymskogo bukovogo lesa (Biotsenologicheskii ocherk)," *Komitet po zapovednikam, Nauchnye trudy Krymskogo gosudarstvennogo zapovednika*, Seriia 2, 1936, no. 1, p. 6.
8. V. Bukovskii, "Puti zoologicheskikh issledovanii v zapovednikakh," p. 9.
9. In *Narkompros RSFSR, Sektor nauki, Biulleten' nauchno-issledovatel'skogo instituta zoologii moskovskogo gosudarstvennogo universiteta imeni M. N. Pokrovskogo*, 1933, no. 1, p. 7, Kozhevnikov is listed as a member for 1931 of the institute's Laboratory of Ecology and of the Study of Useful Vertebrates. It is not clear from this whether he was in Moscow at this time or at the Sukhumi Primate Acclimatization Institute, with which he was affiliated at some point between late 1929 and early 1933.
10. G. F. Gauze, "The Ecology of Populations," *Quarterly Review of Biology*, 1932, vol. 7, no. 1, pp. 27–46.
11. S. A. Severtsov, "Ob issledovanii biologii razmnozheniia v zapovednikakh," pp. 142–143. This seems to be the first use in the Soviet Union of the carrying capacity concept as applied to individual species.
12. Ibid., pp. 145–148.
13. N. A. Troitskii, "Rol' Kavkazskogo gosudarstvennogo zapovednika v izuchenii pastbishch i v voprose ratsionalizatsii gorno-pastbishchnogo khoziaistva," in A. I. Molodchikov, ed., *Gosudarstvennyi Kavkazskii zapovednik: Sputnik ekskursanta*, (Rostov-on-Don, 1931), p. 45.
14. These pioneers included V. V. Alpatov, G. F. Gauze, G. V. Nikol'skii, S. I. Medvedev, N. T. Nechaeva, A. A. Nasimovich, A. N. Formozov, V. S. Ivlev, G. G. Vinberg, E. M. Vorontsov, K. K. Fasulati, M. P. Bozhko, O. I. Semenov-tian-shanskii, G. A. Novikov, and a host of others.
15. "Ot redaktsii," *ZhEB*, 1931, vol. 1, no. 1, p. 7.
16. *Istoriia Vsesoiuznoi kommunisticheskoi partii (Bol'shevikov), Kratkii kurs* (Moscow: Pravda, 1938), p. 300. This is the famous "*tekhnika reshaet vse*" (technology will solve everything) speech in which Stalin complained that throughout history Russia had been "beaten for her backwardness."
17. See G. A. Kozhevnikov, "Zadachi okhrany prirody v SSSR," p. 6.
18. Leonid Leonov, *Sot'* (London, 1931), p. 50. Trans. by Ivor Montagu.

19. Ibid., p. 67.

20. Ibid., p. 354.

21. Maxim Gorky et al., *Belomor,* p. 306.

22. M. Gor'kii, "Iz stat'i 'O biblioteke Poeta,' " in *Gor'kii i nauka: stat'i, pis'ma i vospominaniia* (Moscow, 1964), pp. 56–57. This piece appeared in both *Pravda* and *Izvestiia* on 6 December 1931.

23. Maksim Gor'kii, "O bor'be s prirodoi," in *Gor'kii i nauka,* pp. 59–60.

24. As Ralph E. Matlaw notes in the Norton Critical Edition of *Fathers and Sons* (New York, 1966), p. 33, Bazarov is quoting from the dissertation of Chernyshevskii, *The Aesthetic Relations of Art to Reality* (1855), "the bible of the radicals."

25. Gor'kii, "O bor'be s prirodoi," p. 60.

26. See Raymond A. Bauer, *The New Man in Soviet Psychology* (Cambridge: Harvard University Press, 1952) and Katerina Clark, *The Soviet Novel,* for discussions of the place of voluntarism in the Soviet Union and the Stalinist *Weltanschauung.*

27. Katerina Clark, *The Soviet Novel: History as Ritual* (Chicago: University of Chicago Press, 1981).

28. See Nina Tumarkin, *Lenin Lives! The Lenin Cult in Soviet Russia* (Cambridge: Harvard University Press, 1983), p. 20.

29. The official bravado surrounding these projects is well reflected in *Nashi dostizheniia,* a journal of the early 1930s edited by Gor'kii.

30. On K. F. Rul'e (1814–1858), see B. E. Raikov, *Russkie biologi-evoliutsionisty do Darvina,* vol. 3, esp. pp. 307–355. For an exploration of nineteenth-century Russian interest in acclimatization, see Douglas R. Weiner, "The Roots of 'Michurinism': Transformist Biology and Acclimatization as Currents in Russian Life Science," *Annals of Science,* 1985, vol. 42, pp. 243–260.

31. N. A. Smirnov, "Ob odnom iz akklimatizatsionnykh opytov," *Nasha okhota,* 1915, no. 1.

32. V. Ia. Generozov, *Razvedenie kuropatok, dikikh utok i fazanov,* (n.p., 1921), cited in N. P. Lavrov, *Akklimatizatsiia ondatry v SSSR,* p. 20.

33. B. M. Zhitkov, "Ondatra i vozmozhnost' ee rasprostraneniia na Sibirskom severe."

34. B. M. Zhitkov, "Ob itogakh rabot Tsentral'noi biologicheskoi okhotnich'e-promyslovoi stantsii v Pogono-Losinom ostrove za desiatiletie 1922–1931 gody.," p. 50.

35. S. Kertselli, "K voprosu ob akklimatizatsii v SSSR ondatry."

36. Ibid.

37. S. A. Buturlin, "Osvoenie chuzhezemnykh zverei," quoted in I. Grossman, "Neobkhodimo uskorit' vypusk ondatry," p. 23.

38. Ibid.

39. Zhitkov, "Ob itogakh," p. 50.

40. V. A. Sytin, "Na dispute ob ondatre."

41. Zhitkov, "Ob itogakh," p. 50.

42. Sytin, "Na dispute."

43. "V Gostorge RSFSR," *PD,* 1928, no. 5, p. 70.

44. Lavrov, *Akklimatizatsiia ondatry,* p. 21.

45. "V Gostorge RSFSR," p. 70.

46. *VRZAG, Tretii,* p. 24.

47. Ibid., p. 401. To a certain extent, Paramonov's fears were realized when the muskrat extended its range southward to the basins of the Volga and Voronezh rivers.

48. Grossman, "Neobkhodimo."

49. N. F. Kashchenko, "Rol' akklimatizatsii v protsesse pod"ema proizvoditel'nykh sil SSSR," p. 5.

50. Vavilov's own Institute for Applied Botany and New Crops, later renamed the All-Union Institute for Plant Breeding, had a Department of Naturalization (Acclimatization) consisting of three sectors: dendrological, ornamental, and subtropical.

51. Lavrov, *Akklimatizatsiia ondatry,* pp. 21–22.

52. N. P. Lavrov, *Akklimatizatsiia i reakklimatizatsiia pushnykh zverei v SSSR*, p. 111, and K. N. Blagosklonov et al., *Okhrana prirody*, p. 323.

53. E. L. Markov, "Ob akklimatizatsii v Zakavkaz'e ussuriiskogo piatnistskogo olenia."

54. Zhitkov, "Ob itogakh," p. 51.

55. *VSZAG*, p. 15.

56. See L. A. Zenkevich and Ia. Birshtein, "O vozmozhnykh meropriiatiiakh povysheniia produktivnykh svoistv Kaspii i Arala," *Rybnoe khoziaistvo SSSR*, 1934, no. 3, cited in L. A. Zenkevich, "Ob akklimatizatsii v Kaspiiskom more novykh kormovykh (dlia ryb) bespozvonochnykh i teoreticheskie k nei predposylki," *MOIP*, 1940, vol. 49, p. 19.

57. G. N. Shlykov, "Problema novykh kul'tur," *Trudy sessii VASKhNIL, posviashchennoi podniatii urozhainosti i razvitiia sotsialisticheskogo zhivotnovodstva (Voronezh, 15-ogo do 20-ogo fevralia 1933 g.* (Voronezh, 1933–1934), pp. 32–58.

TWELVE. ENGINEERS OF NATURE

1. F. F. Shillinger, "Krymskii poluostrov, ego rol' i znachenie v SSSR," p. 76.

2. See I. I. Puzanov, "O granitsakh akklimatizatsii, dopustimykh v zapovednikakh," *VRZAG*, pp. 402–403.

3. Sukachev had unmistakably declared to the Third All-Union Congress of Botanists that under no circumstances should the introduction of exotic plants or animals into *zapovedniki* be allowed; see the abstract of his speech "Ob organizatsii botanicheskikh rabot v zapovednikakh po okhrane prirody," in *Dnevnik Vsesoiuznogo s"ezda*, p. 129. He was joined in this sentiment by N. N. Pod"iapol'skii, who had written that "many *zapovedniki* established by Western European peoples were ruined because they [introduced] exotic plants . . . and animals in them." See his *Chto daet priroda trudovomu narodu*, p. 11.

4. Puzanov, "O granitsakh," pp. 402–403.

5. Ibid., p. 404.

6. G. L. Grave (1872–?), in the late 1920s, was a senior assistant in the Zoology Department at Smolensk University and assistant curator of the Smolensk State Museum. In the 1930s, he became director of the Central Forest *zapovednik* and provided a safe haven for his erstwhile colleague Stanchinskii after the latter's removal from Askania and arrest.

7. *VRSOP*, p. 121.

8. V. V. Karpov, Letter to the Editors.

9. Preservationism required the active management of protected territories in order to maintain desired natural conditions in the face of inevitable natural change and downstream effects; Kozhevnikov's approach, while maintaining inviolability, was premised on observing the dynamic change of ecological systems over time, hardly a static view.

10. Karpov, Letter, p. 216.

11. SU RSFSR 1930 no. 30 text 397. Postanovlenie VTsIK i SNK RSFSR, "Ob okhrane i razvitii prirodnykh bogatstv RSFSR." The decree, which set out the functions of the *zapovedniki*, chiefly as *etalony*, did not include acclimatization as a legitimate function (other, secondary functions listed were protection of wildlife, water quality, and climate; recreation; and promoting the economic utilization of hitherto unused natural resources). "Acclimatization parks" were mentioned separately in the decree as another category of protected territory.

12. Editors' reply, *OP*, 1930, no. 8–10, p. 216

13. Stanchinskii was to have hosted the aborted conservation congress.

14. E. Kir'ianova, "Vsesoiuznaia faunisticheskaia konferentsiia," p. 454, quoting Prezent's remarks at the conference.

15. Ibid., p. 457.

16. V. I. Zhadin, "Biotsenoticheskoe i faunisticheskoe issledovanie raionov i ikh biotopov v sviazi s khoziaistvennymi rabotami, izmeniaiushchimi uslovii sushchestvovaniia vodnykh zhivotnykh," *VFK, Sektsiia gidrobiologicheskaia*, p. 34.

17. These and others' remarks following are quoted from *VFK, Sekstiia gidrobiologiche-skaia*, pp. 41–46.

18. Kir'ianova, "Vsesoiuznaia," p. 458. Later, in November 1933, at the specially convened interdisciplinary session of the Academy of Sciences devoted to the problem of the reconstruction of the Volga-Caspian system, Semenov-tian-shanskii proved similarly outspoken in his opposition to megalithic engineering schemes. See *Akademiia nauk, Noiabrskaia sessiia 1933 g. Problemy Volgi i Kaspii*, vol. 2 (Leningrad, 1934), pp. 223–224. Given the times, his brashness is something to marvel at.

19. Kir'ianova, "Vsesoiuznaia," p. 458.

20. Ibid.

21. V. D. Bolkhovitianov, "O zadachakh, stoiashchikh v oblasti biologicheskikh issledovanii ryb, morskogo zveria, i bespozvonochnykh, v sviazi s ratsional'noi postanovkoi rybnogo khoziaistva Sovetskogo Soiuza na vtoruiu piatiletku," *VFK, Sektsiia gidrobiologicheskaia*, pp. 14–15.

22. *VFK, Sektsiia gidrobiologicheskaia*, p. 77.

23. Ibid., p. 80.

24. Ibid., p. 42.

25. Ibid., p. 47. Zhadin remarked: "It is not at all by accident that [comrade Prezent] called us engineers in these matters because we are linked with practical engineering. All of us work in institutes which are directly involved with studies for industry. I and my other comrades are directly involved with all drafting activities for hydroelectric construction, and . . . for that reason, consider it necessary that faunists work in close touch with industry." Notably, there is not a word in this passage about biologists needing to become "engineers of biocenoses" and the like. As students of Soviet history know all too well, what is omitted may be just as significant as what is explicitly stated.

26. See V. I. Zhadin, "Vliianie gidrotekhnicheskikh sooruzhenii na biologicheskii rezhim i faunu rek," *Priroda*, 1937, no. 12, pp. 50–58.

27. "Iz vystupleniia A. Vangengeima na s"ezde po bor'be s zasukhoi: 'Zasukha, sukhovei, i bor'ba s nimi,' " *FNT*, 1931, no. 12, pp. 73–74.

28. See Prezent's vivid remarks as quoted in David Joravsky, *The Lysenko Affair*, p. 80.

29. "Iz vystupleniia," p. 74.

30. Ibid.

31. B. A. Keller, "Metodologiia geobotaniki v stroitel'stve sotsializma," in *Programma dlia geobotanicheskikh issledovanii*, (Leningrad, 1932), pp. 7–8, quoted in Trass, *Geobotanika*, p. 68.

32. Trass, *Geobotanika*, p. 68.

33. V. L. Komarov, *Rastitel'nyi mir SSSR i sopredel'nykh stran* (Moscow-Leningrad, 1931), pp. 14–15, quoted in Trass, *Geobotanika*, p. 53.

34. Gleason's seminal article, "The Individualistic Concept of the Plant Association," *Bulletin of the Torrey Botanical Club*, 1926, vol. 53, pp. 1–20, is a joy to read. On Gleason, see Robert McIntosh, "Henry A. Gleason: 'Individualistic Ecologist,' 1882–1975: His Contributions to Ecological Theory," *Bulletin of the Torrey Botanical Club*, Sept.–Oct. 1975, vol. 102, no. 5, pp. 253–273.

35. See T. A. Rabotnov, "L. G. Ramenskii kak geobotanik," *MOIP*, 1978, vol. 83, no. 6, pp. 126–133, and Robert P. McIntosh, "Excerpts from the Work of L. G. Ramenskii," *Bulletin of the Ecological Society of America*, 1983, vol. 64, pp. 7–12.

36. "Ot redaktsii," *ZhEB*, 1931, vol. 1, no. 1, pp. 12–13.

37. See D. N. Kashkarov, "Izuchenie zhivotnogo mira pustyn' Srednei Azii i Kazakhstana v proshlom i zadachi ego v nastoiashchem i budushchem," in *Khoziaistvennoe osvoenie pustyn' Srednei Azii i Kazakhstana, Sbornik* (Tashkent, 1934).

38. David Joravsky, *The Lysenko Affair*. See also Zhores A. Medvedev, *The Rise and Fall of T. D. Lysenko*; Nils Roll-Hansen, "A New Perspective on Lysenko?" *Annals of Science*, 1985, vol. 42, no. 3, pp. 261–278; Semen Reznick, *Doroga na eshafot* (Paris-New York: "Tret'ia volna, 1983); Dominique Lecourt, *Proletarian Science: The Case of Lysenko*

(London: New Left Books, 1977); and Loren R. Graham, "Genetics," in his *Science and Philosophy in the Soviet Union*.

39. Joravsky, *The Lysenko Affair*, p. 61.

40. "Postanovlenie kollegii Narkomzem SSSR ot 9-ogo iuliia 1931 goda, Protokol no. 33," in *Biulleten' iarovizatsii*, 1932, vol. 1. no. 1, pp. 71–72.

41. Ibid., pp. 74–75.

42. Conversation with Mark Popovsky, 12 February 1981, New York City.

43. V. Pleskov, *Oazis v stepi (Chapli—Askania-Nova)* (Moscow, 1931), p. 12.

44. According to M. S. Shalyt. See *VSSOP*, p. 104.

45. Nechaeva and Medvedev, "Pamiati," pp. 111–112.

46. Ibid., p. 112.

47. Ibid.

48. *VSSOP*, p. 106.

49. Remarks of F. F. Bega, director of Askania-Nova, in *VSSOP*, p. 108.

50. Vavilov's presence on the panel may be explained by his interest in the problems of introduction, adaptation, and ecotypes, and by the fact that, after 1930, Narkomzem of the Ukraine, along with all of the other republican Commissariats of Agriculture, fell under the overall purview of the All-Union Commissariat of Agriculture. Correspondingly, the Ukrainian Academy of Agricultural Sciences came under the jurisdiction of VASKhNIL, of which Vavilov was president.

51. Nechaeva and Medvedev, "Pamiati," p. 110.

52. *VSSOP*, p. 110.

53. See Reznik, *Doroga* (n. 38 above), esp. pp. 35–36.

54. Reznik, *Doroga,* and Roll-Hansen, "A New Perspective on Lysenko?" (n. 38 above).

55. *VSSOP*, p. 109.

56. M. F. Ivanov, Foreword, *TIGA,* 1933, vol. 1, p. 7.

57. F. F. Bega, "Institut sel'sko-khoziaistvennoi gibridizatsii i stepnoi akklimatizatsii zhivotnykh v Askanii-Nova," p. 12.

58. *VSSOP*, p. 109.

59. Bega, "Institut," p. 13, and also his remarks in *VSSOP*, pp. 96–97.

60. *VSSOP*, pp. 96–97.

61. Ibid., p. 106.

62. Ibid., p. 110.

63. Ibid.

THIRTEEN. THE FIRST ALL-UNION CONSERVATION CONGRESS

1. *VSSOP*, p. 9.

2. Ibid., p. 48.

3. Ibid., pp. 25–26.

4. Ibid., p. 26. Engels's passage had indeed become a bone of contention in the early 1930s.

5. Makarov conceded that the question even led to "fights within the Goskomitet." See ibid., p. 27.

6. Ibid., p. 48.

7. Ibid., p. 27.

8. Ibid., pp. 219 and 314.

9. Ibid., p. 38.

10. Ibid.

11. Ibid., p. 39.

12. Ibid.

13. Ibid., p. 212.

14. Ibid., p. 41.

15. Ibid., p. 48.

16. Ibid., p. 49.

17. Ibid., p. 219.

18. Ibid. The same point was made by Krasnobryzhev, director of the Caucasus *zapovednik* (p. 45).

19. Ibid., p. 50.

20. Ibid., pp. 219–220.

21. I. N. Bulankin (1901–1960), a biologist specializing in the biochemistry of proteins, was a member of the Ukrainian Academy of Sciences from 1951. A graduate of Khar'kov Pedagogical Institute (in 1926), Bulankin taught there from 1934 to 1945, when he became rector of Khar'kov State University. Bulankin had long been concerned with the disruptive consequences of the struggle between Narkompros and the economic commissariats. See a report on his remarks to Ukrainian botanists in A. V. Fomin, "Ukrainskaia botanicheskaia konferentsiia ot 6-ogo po 10-oe maia 1931 g. v Kieve," *SB*, 1933, no. 2, p. 85.

22. *VSSOP*, p. 43.

23. Ibid., p. 318.

24. Ibid., p. 98.

25. Ibid., p. 99.

26. Ibid., p. 101.

27. Ibid., p. 102.

28. Ibid., pp. 55–56.

29. Ibid., p. 102.

30. Ibid., p. 106.

31. Ibid., p. 104.

32. Ibid., p. 111.

33. Ibid., p. 107.

34. Ibid., p. 112.

35. Ibid.

36. B. K. Fortunatov, "O general'nom plane rekonstruktsii promyslovoi fauny evropeiskoi chasti RSFSR i Ukrainy," p. 90.

37. *VSSOP*, pp. 318–319.

38. Ibid., p. 321.

39. Ibid., pp. 323–337.

40. A. A. Nurinov, "Vyshe klassovuiu bditel'nost' v nauke," p. 9.

41. *VSSOP*, pp. 323–337.

42. Ibid., p. 345.

43. Ibid., p. 346.

44. Ibid.

45. Ibid., p. 348.

46. Ibid.

47. S. A. Severtsov, "Darvinizm i ekologiia," wrote: "Taking into account all the conditions of the struggle for existence, it is scarcely possible to believe that the physiological effect of abiotic factors on an organism will result in directed, adaptive alterations. . . ."

48. Severtsov's remarks were summarized in *VSSOP*, p. 353.

49. Ibid.

50. Ibid.

51. Early Soviet work on chemical- and x-ray-induced mutagenesis has been explored by Valerii Nikolaevich Soifer, *Molekuliarnye mekhanizmy mutagenezisa* (Moscow: Nauka, 1969).

52. *VSSOP*, p. 350.

53. Ibid., p. 353.

54. Ibid., p. 355.

55. Ibid., p. 357.

56. See Kingsland, chap. 7, "Gause and the Russian Connection," in her *Modeling Nature* (n. 61, chap. 6).

57. *PSKh*, 1933, vol. 6, pp. 185–186.

FOURTEEN. CONSERVATION WITHOUT ECOLOGY

1. I. I. Prezent, Kommunisticheskaia akademiia, Institut filosofii. *Materialy nauchnoi sessii: k piatidesiatiletiiu so dnia smerti Marksa* (Moscow-Leningrad: OGIZ, 1934), pp. 358–359.

2. Quoted in I. I. Prezent, *Klassovaia bor'ba na estestvenno-nauchnom fronte* (Moscow-Leningrad, 1932), p. 59. I am grateful to David Joravsky for sharing this material with me.

3. *Materialy*, pp. 357–358, and Prezent, *Klassovaia*, p. 45.

4. Prezent, *Klassovaia*, pp. 39–40.

5. *Materialy*, p. 361.

6. Prezent, *Klassovaia*, p. 2.

7. I. I. Prezent, "Protiv vredneishei 'filosofii agronomii,' " p. 202.

8. V. Bukovskii, "K kritike osnovnykh problem i poniatii biotsenologii," p. 81.

9. Ibid., pp. 81 and 83–85.

10. Ibid., pp. 84 and 88.

11. V. V. Stanchinskii, "K ponimaniiu biotsenoza," pp. 25–27, provides a taxonomy of the categories of trophic interrelationships observed during his field research at Askania, together with schematic illustrations of these patterns. Of particular interest are Stanchinskii's speculations on the influence played by evolving cenotic systems on the process of species formation. With all things being equal, hypothesized Stanchinskii, the degree to which a biocenosis was already ramified would determine what opportunities it could offer to potentially new species. The more settled an ecosystem, the more specialized a newcomer would need to be to realize a niche. These ideas find a modern resonance in the thinking of G. E. Hutchinson, R. A. MacArthur, and others.

12. Ibid., p. 26.

13. Ibid., p. 24.

14. Ibid., p. 26.

15. Stanchinskii prefigured the concept of the ecosystem first advanced by Arthur G. Tansley, "The Use and Abuse of Vegetational Concepts and Terms," *Ecology*, 1935, vol. 16, pp. 284–307.

16. Stanchinskii, "Teoreticheskie osnovy," p. 33.

17. Ibid., p. 35.

18. Ibid.

19. Ibid., p. 34.

20. Ibid., p. 38.

21. Ibid., p. 42.

22. Ibid., p. 46.

23. At this time, the noted Mendelian geneticist, A. S. Serebrovskii, was a colleague of Stanchinskii's at Askania.

24. Stanchinskii, "Teoreticheskie osnovy," p. 53.

25. Ibid., pp. 55–56.

26. Nechaeva and Medvedev, "Pamiati," p. 112. Nechaeva's first scientific work perished along with Stanchinskii's. Conversation with Nina Trofimovna Nechaeva, June 6, 1986, Moscow.

27. S. I. Medvedev, "Kompleksnost' pri ekologo-biotsenologicheskikh issledovaniiakh," p. 58.

28. A. A. Nurinov, "Vyshe klassovuiu bditel'nost' v nauke," p. 8.

29. Ibid., p. 10.

30. L. K. Greben', "Itogi nauchno-issledovatel'skoi raboty instituta gibridizatsii i akklimatizatsii zhivotnykh za 15 let," *Trudy Vsesoiuznoi akademii sel'sko-khoziaistvennikh nauk*

imeni V. I. Lenina, 1937, no. 11, pt. 1, *Itogi nauchno-issledovatel'skoi raboty instituta gibridizatsii i akklimatizatsii zhivotnykh za 15 let.* (VI Plenum sektsii zhivotnovodstva, 19–24 maia 1936 g.), E. F. Liskun and Ia. M. Berzin, eds., p. 11.

31. *SB*, 1934, no. 3, p. 59.
32. Ibid., pp. 59–60.
33. Ibid.
34. Ibid., pp. 61–62.
35. This has been noted by Loren Graham and Conway Zirkle. To effectively monitor the philosophical implications of the scientific work of biologists, Prezent and Lysenko would have had either to become knowledgeable in mathematics or to proscribe its use in biology. They chose the latter course.
36. Barrington Moore, Jr., *Terror and Progress, USSR* (New York: Harper Torchbooks, 1966), pp. 146–147.
37. Charles Gillispie, "The *Encyclopédie* and the Jacobin Philosophy of Science: A Study in Ideas and Consequences," in Institute for the History of Science [1957, University of Wisconsin], *Critical Problems in the History of Science: Proceedings,* ed. Marshall Clagett (Madison: University of Wisconsin Press, 1959), pp. 255–308.
38. Aspects that particularly rankled—at least in the West—were the seeming arrogance of the mathematician-ecologists; the fact that many of them "invaded" the field from physics, statistics, and chemistry; their penchant for a priori theorizing; and the main inference from their work that population dynamics operated in good measure independently of the environment. Moreover, many field ecologists held that because real ecological phenomena were unique, there could be no prediction or modeling of natural phenomena. See Kingsland, *Modeling Nature* (n. 61, chap. 6).
39. See esp. I. I. Prezent, "Zakon edinstva organizma i uslovii sushchestvovaniia"; A. P. Markevich, "Sostoianie i zadachi sovetskoi ekologii zhivotnykh"; and N. V. Minin, "O nekotorykh idealisticheskikh ucheniiakh v ekologii." Markevich's attack was the most comprehensive and the most extreme, concluding, p. 22, that "The task of ecologists in the USSR is to rid Soviet science once and for all of the influence of the erroneous and pernicious theories of formalistic ecology."
40. Nechaeva and Medvedev, "Pamiati," p. 113.
41. Likely to have been influenced by Stanchinskii's ideas were hydrobiologists G. G. Vinberg, S. A. Zernov, V. S. Ivlev, and M. V. Ermolaev.
42. Raymond L. Lindeman, "The Trophic-Dynamic Aspect of Ecology," esp. p. 403.
43. A. S. Serebrovskii, "Gibridizatsiia zhivotnykh kak nauka," *TIGA*, 1933, vol. 1, no. 1, p. 27.
44. See I. I. Prezent, ed., *Leningradskii Gosudarstvennyi Universitet, Kafedra dialektiki prirody i evoliutsionnogo ucheniia, Khrestomatiia po evoliutsionnomu ucheniiu* (Leningrad, 1935). After a discussion of Paul Kammerer's experiments and other alleged proof of the inheritance of acquired characteristics, Prezent wrote (p. 485):

> All of the above data together with the theoretical considerations outlined above lead to the inescapable conclusion: *somatic induction with the production of adequate* [i.e., permanent and heritable] *alteration is impossible.*"

See also pp. 495, 498, and 499.

45. I. I. Prezent, "Uchenie Lenina o krizise estestvoznaniia i krizise burzhuaznoi biologicheskoi nauki." While continuing to pan Lamarckism and the theory of the environmental induction of hereditary change, Prezent in this work began to make his break with Mendelian genetics. Citing Michurin's experiments as evidence against Lotsi and Bateson (and A. S. Serebrovskii, we might add), Prezent affirmed the possibility of the creation of viable new life forms through transspecific hybridization. For Prezent, this constituted the overthrow of the Mendelian principle by a higher authority: I. V. Michurin. The lesson to be learned from this, concluded Prezent, was that an overreliance on mathematics leads to erroneous,

formalistic conclusions, and that the necessary and, indeed, ultimate, corrective is practice (pp. 250–252). He also noted (p. 255) that while "the geniuses of science" Weissman, De Vries, Mendel, and Morgan had made giant contributions to biology, the "metaphysical and idealistic sides of their teachings . . . have thrown genetics into crisis."

46. B. M. Zavadovskii, *Zhivaia priroda v rukakh cheloveka (zapiski okhotnika za gormonami)* (Moscow, 1935), p. 16.

47. Ibid. These experiments involved crossing geese with ducks, antelope with deer, etc. As Serebrovskii had predicted, though, the general problem of hybrid sterility was never solved by the Lysenko group.

48. Although Lysenko and his followers amply criticized Mendelian genetics by name, they never elaborated their own theory of heredity or of evolutionary change in a clear, systematic way. Nevertheless, as Graham points out in *Science and Philosophy*, pp. 228–230, Lysenko—though denying that he was a "Lamarckist"—did state that he considered a materialist theory of evolution "unthinkable without recognition of the inheritance of acquired characteristics" (from T. D. Lysenko, *Izbrannye sochineniia* [Moscow, 1958], vol. 2, p. 48.). Other followers of Lysenko and Prezent, however, were more explicit in linking themselves with the teachings of Lamarck. Thus, Markevich, at the Kiev Ecological Conference of 1950, attacked ecologist D. N. Kashkarov for writing in his textbook *Osnovy ekologii zhivotnykh* (Moscow, 1945), p. 279: "We must now decisively overturn the Lamarckian interpretation. The organism is plastic. It has the ability to change under the influence of the environment. But we have no proof of the heritability of these transformations. . . ."

49. *VSSOP*, p. 9.

50. Ibid., p. 29.

51. Ibid., p. 24. Makarov buttressed his argument by citing a number of the most glaring recent violations of conservation laws by the economic organs, and assured the delegates that "dozens more examples could be cited."

52. Ibid.

53. See the decree SU RSFSR 1933, no. 52, text 277 of 25 October 1933, "O reorganizatsii Narkomprosa RSFSR."

54. This account is taken from E. G. Bloshenko, "Obzor deiatel'nosti Gosudarstvennogo Mezhduvedomstvennogo Komiteta sodeistviia razvitiiu prirodnykh bogatstv RSFSR za pervoe polugodie 1933 g.," *PSKh*, 1933, vol. 6, p. 180.

55. Ibid.

56. Kh. S. Veitsman, "Zapovednik budushchego," p. 106.

57. Ibid., p. 107.

58. See V. A. Kovda, *Great Construction Works of Communism and the Remaking of Nature* (Moscow: Foreign Languages Press, 1953; original Russian edition, 1951), as an example of the numerous works of the early 1950s that extolled this plan.

59. This decree superseded that of 20 June 1930.

60. See, for example, V. A. Arsen'ev, "Akklimatizatsionnaia rabota v zapovednikakh"; K. P. Filonov, *Dinamika chislennosti kopytnykh zhivotnykh i zapovednost'* (Moscow: Lesnaia promyshlennost', 1977); and Lavrov, *Akklimatizatsiia i reakklimatizatsiia.*

61. V. N. Makarov, "O neobkhodimosti soiuznogo zakonodatel'stva," Undated MS., c. 1940, 6 pp. typed carbon, AMGU, fond 200.

62. Salient are S. S. Arkhipov, "Ob organizatsii zapovednogo khoziaistva," *NMZ*, 1938, no. 1, "Formy zapovednogo khoziaistva," *NMZ*, 1939, no. 2, and "Instruktsii dlia organizatsii zapovednogo khoziaistva."

63. For the classic description of how Narkomvneshtorg believed a reserve should be managed, see *Nauchno-issledovatel'skii institut vneshnei torgovli, Vneshniaia torgovlia v SSSR* (Moscow, 1936), pt. 2, p. 36, and then compare with Arkhipov (n. 62 above).

64. Despite the qualitative changes in the *zapovedniki* observed after 1933, V. N. Makarov continued to expand the network of reserves at an energetic pace. In the RSFSR, the number of state *zapovedniki* by 1939 had reached twenty-five with an aggregate area of 8,428,000 hectares. For a list of *zapovedniki* for that year, consult Makarov, "Spravka o

rabote komiteta po zapovednikam pri SNK RSFSR/1939, no. 2," undated MS. c. 1939, 5 pp. typed carbon. AMGU, fond 200.

65. On 1 January 1930 VOOP membership (2,533) was at an eight-year nadir. See A. G. Giller, "Otchet o rabote Vserossiiskogo obshchestva okhrany prirody za 1938–1947 gg.," *Okhrana prirody, Sbornik,* 1948, no. 1, p. 19.

66. Although important projects were started—preparation of a list of endangered species and sea-bird nesting sites—these efforts languished. See S. Fridman, "Otchet Vserossiiskogo obshchestva okhrany prirody. O deiatel'nosti v 1934 g.," *PSKh,* 1934, vol. 7, p. 215.

67. M. Nadezhdin, "Obshchestvo bez aktiva."

68. Ibid., p. 78.

69. V. N. Makarov, Predislovie, *VSSOP,* p. 5.

70. See K. P. Filonov, "Dinamika chislennosti."

71. Conversation with A. A. Nasimovich, 18 April 1980, Moscow.

72. Ibid., and A. V. Malinovskii, "Zapovedniki Sovetskogo soiuza," *Dostizheniia nauki i peredovogo opyta v sel'skom khoziaistve,* 1953, no. 7, pp. 72–77.

73. Reimers and Shtil'mark, *Osobo,* p. 39.

SELECTED BIBLIOGRAPHY

I. PERIODICALS CONSULTED

Agrotekhnika (Vseukrainskaia akademiia sel'sko-khoziaistvennykh nauk and Narkomzem of the Ukrainian SSR), 1932–1933.

Akademiia nauk SSSR. Institut istorii estestvoznaniia i tekhniki. Trudy, 1947–1961.

Biulleten' iarovizatsii (Ukrainskii institut selektsii), 1932.

Botanicheskii sad Imperatorskogo Iur'evskogo universiteta. Trudy, 1910–1914.

Botanicheskii zhurnal, 1916–.

Estestvoznanie i geografiia, 1896–1916.

Estestvoznanie i marksizm (Kommunisticheskaia akademiia. Assotsiatsiia institutov estestvoznaniia), 1929–1932.

Estestvoznanie v shkole (Obshchestvo rasprostraneniia estestvenno-nauchnogo obrazovaniia), 1918–1929.

Estestvoznanie v sovetskoi shkole (Organ uchebno-metodicheskoi sektsii Narkomprosa), 1927–1932.

Front nauki i tekhniki (Varnitso), 1929–1938.

Geograficheskoe obshchestvo SSSR. (Imperatorskoe russkoe geograficheskoe obshchestvo). *Kavkazskoe otdelenie. Izvestiia*, 1911–1915.

Geograficheskoe obshchestvo SSSR. Krasnoiarskoe otdelenie. Sektsiia okhrany prirody. Listovki, 1917–1929.

Geograficheskoe obshchestvo SSSR. Postoiannaia Prirodookhranitel'naia komissiia. Trudy, 1915–1918.

Gosudarstvennyi zoologicheskii muzei pri Moskovskom gosudarstvennom universitete. Sbornik trudov, 1934–1937.

Iugoklimat. Sbornik po voprosam akklimatizatsii, 1929–1930.

Izvestiia Tsentral'nogo ispolnitel'nogo komiteta SSR, 1918–1935.

Kavkazskii gosudarstvennyi zapovednik. Materialy, 1935–1936.

Khar'kovskoe obshchestvo liubitelei prirody. Biulleten', 1912–1917.

Kommunisticheskaia akademiia. Vestnik, 1922–1935.

Kraevedenie (Tsentral'noe biuro kraevedeniia), 1923–1929.

Lesa respubliki, 1918.

Lesnoi dukh, 1910–1916.

Lesnoi zhurnal, 1910–1918.

Moskovskii gosudarstvennyi universitet. Uchenye zapiski, 1940–.

Moskovskii kraeved (Obshchestvo izucheniia Moskovskoi oblasti), 1927–1930.

Moskovskoe obshchestvo ispytatelei prirody. Otdel biologicheskii. Biulleten', 1940–.

Nasha okhota, 1907–1916.

Nauchnoe slovo, 1928–1931.

Nauchnye osnovy okhrany prirody, 1970–1975.

Nauka i ee rabotniki, 1920–1922.

Okhota i okhotnich'e khoziaistvo, 1955–.

Okhotnik, 1925–1929.

Okhrana prirody (Vserossiiskoe obshchestvo okhrany prirody), 1928–1941. In January 1931 renamed *Priroda i sotsialisticheskoe khoziaistvo*.

Okhrana prirody. Sbornik (Vserossiiskoe obshchestvo okhrany prirody i sodeistviia razvitiiu prirodnykh bogatstv), 1948–1951.

Okhrana prirody i zapovednoe delo v SSSR, 1956–1962.

Okhrana prirody na Urale, 1960–1967.

Pod znamenem marksizma, 1922–1944.

Priroda (Akademiia nauk SSSR), 1916–.

Priroda i okhota, 1882–1888.

Priroda i okhota na Ukraine (Vseukrainskii soiuz okhotnikov i rybolovov), 1924.

Problemy marksizma (Kommunisticheskaia akademiia. Leningradskoe otdelenie), 1928–1934.

Pushnoe delo (Vsesoiuznyi pushnoi sindikat), 1925–1930.

RSFSR. Glavnoe upravlenie po zapovednikam pri prezidiume VTsIK'a (later, *-pri Sovete narodnykh komissarov RSFSR* [1939], *-pri Sovete ministrov RSFSR* [1940]). *Nauchno-metodicheskie zapiski*, 1938–1949.

RSFSR. Komitet po zapovednikam pri prezidiume VTsIK'a (renamed later as above), 1934–1940.

RSFSR. Narodnyi komissariat po prosveshcheniiu. Ezhenedel'nik (also entitled *Biulleten'*), 1922–1935.

RSFSR. Narodnyi komissariat po prosveshcheniiu. Sektor nauki. Nauchno-issledovatel'skii institut zoologii Moskovskogo gosudarstvennogo universiteta imeni M. N. Pokrovskogo. Biulleten', 1933–1936.

RSFSR. Narodnyi komissariat zemledeliia. Planovaia komissiia. Trudy zemplana, 1924–1927.

Russkoe obshchestvo akklimatizatsii zhivotnykh i rastenii. Trudy, 1888–1913.

Sovetskaia botanika, 1933–1947.

Sovetskii sever (Komitet Severa pri prezidiume VTsIK'a), 1930–1935.

Sotsialisticheskaia rekonstruktsiia i nauka, 1934–1936.

Tsentral'noe biuro kraevedeniia. Izvestiia, 1925–1929.

V masterskoi prirody (Otdel edinoi shkoly Narkomprosa RSFSR), 1919–1929.

Ukrainian SSR. Narodnyi komissariat po prosveshcheniiu. Nauka na Ukraine, 1926–1927.

Ukrainian SSR. Narodnyi komissariat po prosveshcheniiu. Ukrains'kii komitet okhorani pamiatok prirodi na Ukraini. Zborniki, 1927.

Ukrainian SSR. Narodnyi komissariat zemledeliia. Dosvidnii viddil. Komissiia okhorani prirodi. Materiali, 1928.

USSR. Narodnyi komissariat snabzheniia. Biulleten', 1931–1935.

Vneshniaia torgovlia (also found as *Nasha vneshniaia torgovlia*), 1931–1935.

Voprosy ekologii i biotsenologii, 1934–1940.

Vsesoiuznaia akademiia sel'sko-khoziaistvennykh nauk imeni V. I. Lenina. Gosudarstvennyi nauchnyi institut sel'sko-khoziaistvennoi gibridizatsii i akklimatizatsii zhivotnykh (Aska-nia-Nova). Trudy, 1933–1935.

Vseukrainskii zoologo-biologicheskii institut pri Khar'kovskom gosudarstvennom universitete. Sektor ekologii. Trudy, 1933.

Zemlevedenie, 1914–1929.

Zhurnal ekologii i biotsenologii, 1931–1934.

Zoologicheskii zhurnal, 1916–1940.

II. CONFERENCE PROCEEDINGS

Akademiia nauk SSSR. *Noiabr'skaia sessiia, 1933 g. Problemy Volgi i Kaspii.* 2 vols. Leningrad, 1934.

Akademiia nauk SSSR. Zoologicheskii institut. *Trudy Vsesoiuznoi faunicheskoi konferentsii Zoologicheskogo Instituta, 3-8-ogo fevralia 1932 g.* 3 vols. Leningrad, 1933–1934.

Aviatsiia v bor'be s vrediteliami sel'skogo i lesnogo khoziaistva. Materialy Pervoi vsesoiuz-noi aviakhimicheskoi konferentsii v Moskve, noiabr' 1930 g. Moscow, 1932.

Biologicheskaia konferentsiia Azovo-Chernomorskogo kraia i Severnogo Kavkaza, 1-ogo ianvaria 1934 g. Rezoliutsii i materialy. Rostov-on-Don, 1934.

Ekologicheskaia konferentsiia po probleme "Massovoe razmnozhenie zhivotnykh i ikh prog-noz." Pervaia. Kiev, 1940.

———. *Vtoraia.* 3 parts. Kiev, 1951.

Imperatorskoe Russkoe geograficheskoe obshchestvo. Postoiannaia prirodookhranitel'naia komissiia. *Mirovaia okhrana prirody.* [Published as Vypusk 2 of the Commission's Occasional Papers.] Edited by V. A. Dubianskii. Translated from the French by E. Eremina. Petrograd, 1915.

S"ezd russkikh estestvoispytatelei i vrachei v Moskve, s 28-ogo dekabria 1909 g. po 6-oe ianvaria 1910 g. Dvenadtsatyi. Dnevnik. Edited by F. N. Krasheninnikov. Moscow, 1911.

S"ezd russkikh estestvoispytatelei i vrachei v Tiflise, s 16-ogo po 24-oe iunia 1913 g. Tiflis, 1914.

Tomskii universitet. *Nauchnaia konferentsiia. Piataia. Sektsiia zoologii i gidrobiologii. Materialy. Sbornik posviashchen N. F. Kashchenko.* Tomsk, 1954.

Voprosy kraevedeniia. Sbornik dokladov prochitannykh na Vserossiiskoi konferentsii nauchnykh obshchestv po izucheniiu mestnogo kraia v Moskve v dekabre 1921 g. Moscow, 1923.

Vserossiiskaia konferentsiia zoologov, anatomov i gistologov. Pervyi. Trudy. Petrograd, 1923.

Vserossiiskaia sel'sko-khoziaistvennaia i kustarno-promyshlennaia vystavka 1923 g. Almanakh. Moscow, 1923.

Vserossiiskii iubileinyi akklimatizatsionnyi s"ezd. Trudy. Vyp. 1. *Obshchie sobraniia s"ezda.* Edited by N. Iu. Zograf. Moscow, 1909.

Vserossiiskii s"ezd liubitelei mirovedeniia. Pervyi. Petrograd, 1921.

Vserossiiskii s"ezd okhotnikov v Moskve s 17-ogo do 25-ogo noiabria 1909 g. Vtoroi. Trudy. Moscow, 1910.

Vserossiiskii s"ezd po okhrane prirody. Pervyi. Trudy. Edited by B. P. Ditmar and S. A. Severtsov. Moscow, 1930.

Vserossiiskii s"ezd zoologov, anatomov i gistologov. Vtoroi. Trudy. Moscow, 1925.

Vserossiiskii s"ezd zoologov, anatomov i gistologov. Tretii. Trudy. Moscow, 1928.

Vsesoiuznaia akademiia sel'sko-khoziaistvennykh nauk imeni V. I. Lenina. *Sessiia VASKhNIL'a, posviashchennaia podniatiiu urozhainosti i razvitiiu sotsialisticheskogo zhivotnovodstva, Voronezh, s 15-ogo do 20-ogo fevralia 1933 g.* Voronezh, 1933–1934.

Vsesoiuznaia konferentsiia po ekologii zhivotnykh. Tretii. Tezisy dokladov. Kiev, 1954.

Vsesoiuznyi geograficheskii s"ezd v Leningrade s 11-ogo po 18-oe aprelia 1933 g. Pervyi. Trudy. Leningrad, 1934.

Vsesoiuznyi s"ezd botanikov. Vtoroi. Dnevnik. Moscow, 1926.

———. *Tretii. Dnevnik.* Leningrad, 1928.

Vsesoiuznyi s"ezd nauchnykh rabotnikov v Moskve. Fevral' 1929 g. Tretii. Sputnik delegata. Moscow, 1929.

Vsesoiuznyi s"ezd po okhrane prirody. Pervyi. Trudy. Edited by A. G. Giller and V. N. Makarov. Foreword by V. N. Makarov. Moscow, 1935.

Vsesoiuznyi s"ezd zoologov, anatomov i gistologov v Kieve, s 6-ogo po 12-oe maia, 1930 g. Chetvertyi. Trudy. Edited by I. I. Shmal'gauzen. Kiev-Khar'kov, 1931.

III. ARCHIVAL SOURCES

Charles Christopher Adams Archive for the History of Ecology, Western Michigan University, Kalamazoo.

Bakhmetev Archives, Columbia University, New York. V. I. Vernadskii and Valerii Petrovich Semenov-tian-shanskii Manuscript Collections.

Central State Archive of the Russian Socialist Federated Soviet Republic, Moscow, USSR (TsGA RSFSR). Fond 2307, opis' 6. Materials relating to the creation of the Voronezh state *zapovednik.*

Archive of Moscow State University, Moscow, USSR. Fond 200. Materials on the history of conservation in Russia and the USSR; personal papers of Professor Grigorii Aleksandrovich Kozhevnikov. Fond 207. Personal papers of Professor Vasilii Vasil'evich Alekhin.

IV. BOOKS AND DISSERTATIONS

Akademiia nauk SSSR. Komissiia ekspeditsionnykh issledovanii. *Spisok zapovednikov po svedeniiam imeiushchimsia v AN SSSR. Osvedomliaiushchii biulleten',* no. 8 (69). Leningrad, 1929.

Alekhin, Vasilii Vasil'evich. *Askania-Nova: zamechatel'nyi oazis v stepiakh Tavridskoi gubernii.* Moscow, 1912.
———. *Chto takoe rastitel'noe soobshchestvo?* Moscow, 1924.
Anuchin, D. N. *Okhrana pamiatnikov prirody.* St. Petersburg, 1914.
Astrakhanskii gosudarstvennyi zapovednik: K dvadtsatiletiiu Astrakhanskogo gosudarstvennogo zapovednika. Sbornik statei. Moscow, 1940.
Blagosklonov, K. N.; Inozemtsev, A. A.; and Tikhomirov, V. N. *Okhrana prirody.* Moscow: Vysshaia shkola, 1967.
Brauner, Adol'f Adol'fovich. *Ocherk akklimatizatsii sel'sko-khoziaistvennykh zhivotnykh v prichernomorskikh-Azovskikh stepiakh.* Odessa, 1928.
Brodskii, Abram L'vovich. *Okhrana prirody v Turkestane.* Tashkent, 1923.
Bryzgalin, G. A., and Zakharov, B. A. *Chto takoe natsional'nye parki i dlia chego oni uchrezhdaiutsia?* Khar'kov, 1919.
Buturlin, S. A. *Okhotnichii zakonoproekt: Razbor "Proekta pravil ob okhote" v redaktsii mezhduvedomstvennogo soveshchaniia s predlozheniem nekotorykh izmenenii.* St. Petersburg, 1909.
Den' lesa. Sbornik. Moscow: Novaia derevnia, 1923.
Dergunov, Nikolai. *Kak organizovat' den' ptits.* Moscow, 1928.
Dobrokhotov, Vladimir Ivanovich. *Astrakhanskii gosudarstvennyi zapovednik.* 2d ed. Moscow, 1940.
———, and Ermolaev, A. M. *Astrakhanskii gosudarstvennyi zapovednik: Kratkaia istoriia, sovremennoe sostoianie i rabota v 1935 g.* Moscow, 1936.
Dogel', Valentin Aleksandrovich. *Zubry i vopros ob ikh sokhranenii v nastoiashchee vremia.* Moscow, 1927.
Dokhman, Genrietta Isaakovna. *Istoriia geobotaniki v Rossii.* Moscow: Nauka, 1973.
Dvadtsat' let Kavkazskogo gosudarstvennogo zapovednika. Sbornik. Moscow: Glavnoe upravlenie po zapovednikam pri Sovete ministrov RSFSR, 1947.
Dzens-Litovskii, A. I., ed. *Na novykh putiakh kraevedcheskoi raboty. Sbornik statei.* Moscow, 1926.
Feoktistov, K. Kh. *Polozhenie ob okhrane lesov respubliki i instruktsii lesnoi strazhi po okhrane prirody.* Leningrad, 1924.
Genko, N. K. *K statistike lesov Evropeiskoi Rossii.* St. Petersburg, 1888.
Gladkov, N. A. *Okhrana prirody v pervye gody sovetskoi vlasti.* Moscow, 1972.
Glinskii, Frants Antonovich. *Belovezhskaia pushcha i zubry.* Belostok, 1899.
Gor'kii i nauka. Sbornik. Moscow: Nauka, 1964.
Gorky (Gor'kii), M. et al. *Belomor: The Construction of the Great White Sea-Baltic Canal.* New York and London: Smith and Haas, 1935.
Gosplan SSSR. *Kontrol'nye tsifry narodnogo khoziaistva SSSR na 1927/1928 god: Postanovlenie prezidiuma Gosplana ot 25-ogo avgusta 1927 g.* Moscow, 1928.
———. Tsentral'noe upravlenie narodno-khoziaistvennogo ucheta. Sektor ucheta kadrov, kul'tury i nauki. *Nauchno-issledovatel'skie uchrezhdeniia i nauchnye rabotniki SSSR.* Moscow, 1934.
Gosudarstvennyi Kavkazskii zapovednik: Sputnik ekskursanta. Rostov-on-Don, 1931.
Graham, Loren R. *Science and Philosophy in the Soviet Union.* New York: Random House, 1972.
Gratsianov, V. I. *Kratkii ocherk istorii Imperatorskogo russkogo obshchestva akklimatizatsii zhivotnykh i rastenii za piat'desiat' let sushchestvovaniia, 1857–1907.* Moscow, 1907.
Greben', L. K. *Akademik M. F. Ivanov i ego raboty po vvedeniiu novykh porod zhivotnykh.* 2d. ed. Moscow, 1956.
Grossgeim, A. A. *Rol' zapovednikov v khoziaistve strany.* Baku, 1929.
Gurov, P. Ia., ed. *Lesnoi kodeks RSFSR (v voprosakh i otvetakh).* Moscow, 1924.
Hayden, Sherman Strong. *The International Protection of Wildlife.* New York: Columbia University Press, 1942.

Heiss, L. *Askania-Nova, Animal Paradise in Russia; Adventure of the Falz-Fein Family*. London: Bodley Head, 1970.

Iampol'skii, M. L. *Okhrana prirody i shkola*. Rostov-on-Don, 1929.

Il'menskii gosudarstvennyi zapovednik. Sbornik. Moscow: Glavnoe upravlenie po zapovednikam pri Sovete narodnykh komissarov RSFSR, 1940.

Ivanov, Mikhail Fedorovich. *Izbrannye sochineniia*. 2 vols. Moscow: Sel'khozgiz, 1957.

Ivanova, N. K. *Akademik M. F. Ivanov: Zhizn' i deiatel'nost'*. Moscow, 1953.

Joravsky, David. *The Lysenko Affair*. Cambridge: Harvard University Press, 1970.

———. *Soviet Marxism and Natural Science, 1917–1932*. New York: Columbia University Press, 1961.

K ankete po okhrane prirody Studencheskogo nauchnogo kruzhka "Liubiteli prirody" v gorode Kazani. Kazan', 1926.

Karpych, V. F., and Klabunovskii, I. G., eds. *Za marksizm v sovetskom kraevedenii. Sbornik*. Moscow-Leningrad, 1931.

Kashkarov, D. N. *Environment and Community: A Course of Lectures Read at the Middle Asian State University*. Translated from the Russian by Michael Poggenpohl. Albany, N.Y.: New York State Education Department and the Works Project Administration, 1935.

———. *Sreda i soobshchestvo*. Moscow: Medgiz, 1933.

Keller, B. A. *Preobrazovateli prirody rastenii Timiriazev, Michurin, Lysenko*. Moscow, 1944.

Kern, E. E. *Les i ego znachenie v prirode: Vvedenie k izucheniiu osnovnogo zakona o lesakh 27-ogo maia 1918 g*. Petrograd, 1919.

Khar'kovskoe obshchestvo liubitelei prirody. *Otchet o deiatel'nosti*. Khar'kov, 1915.

———. *Otchet o deiatel'nosti*. Khar'kov, 1916–1917.

Khrustalev, Vladimir Mikhailovich. "Sozdanie i deiatel'nost' sistemy gosudarstvennykh zapovednikov v RSFSR, 1917–1937 gg." Dissertation for *kandidat* degree, Moscow Historical-Archival Institute, 1984.

Kolod'ko, M. N., and Fortunatov, B. K., eds. *Stepnoi zapovednik Chapli—Askania-Nova. Sbornik statei*. Moscow, 1928.

Koval'skaia-Il'ina, P. V. *Okhrana prirody v naselennykh mestakh*. Moscow, 1930.

Kozhevnikov, Grigorii Aleksandrovich. *Mezhdunarodnaia okhrana prirody*. Moscow, 1914.

———. *Otchet ob iubileinom zasedanii Imperatorskogo russkogo obshchestva akklimatizatsii zhivotnykh i rastenii*. Moscow, 1909.

———. *Shkol'nyi uchitel' i okhrana prirody*. Moscow: Glavnauka, 1926.

Kozlov, P. K. *Askania-Nova*. Petrograd, 1915.

Kozlova, E. *Askania-Nova*. Petrograd, 1923.

Krestianin, okhraniai prirodu! In the series "Nauchno-populiarnaia literatura po okhrane prirody." Moscow: Narkompros, 1925.

Krymskii gosudarstvennyi zapovednik: ego priroda, istoriia i znachenie. Sbornik. Foreword by V. T. Ter-Oganesov. Moscow: Glavnauka, 1927.

Kulagin, Nikolai Mikhailovich. *Zhivotnye organizmy kak proizvoditel'naia sila prirody*. Petrograd-Moscow, 1925.

———. *Zubry Belovezhskoi pushchi*. Moscow, 1919.

Kurazhkovskii, Iurii Nikolaevich. *Vladimir Il'ich Lenin i priroda*. Astrakhan', 1969.

———. *Zapovednoe delo v SSSR*. Rostov-on-Don, 1977.

———, compiler. *Iz istorii okhrany prirody v Astrakhanskom krae. Materialy i deiatel'nosti V. I. Lenina i ego soratnikov v oblasti okhrany prirody*. Astrakhan', 1958.

Kuznetsov, N. I. *Okhrana pamiatnikov prirody na Kavkaze*. Tiflis: Kavkazskoe otdelenie RGO, 1911.

Larina, Vera Gennad'evna. "Vserossiiskoe obshchestvo okhrany prirody, 1924–1941." Dissertation for *kandidat* degree, Moscow Historical-Archival Institute, 1982.

Lavrov, Nikolai Petrovich. *Akklimatizatsiia i reakklimatizatsiia pushnykh zverei v SSSR*. Tomsk, 1964.

————. *Akklimatizatsiia ondatry v SSSR*. Moscow, 1957.
Leonov, Leonid. *The Russian Forest*. Translated from the Russian by Bernard Isaacs. Moscow: Progress, 1966.
Lipshits, S. Iu. *Moskovskoe obshchestvo ispytatelei prirody za 135 let ego sushchestvovaniia, 1805–1940*. Moscow: MOIP, 1940.
————, ed. *Russkie botaniki. Biograficheskii-bibliograficheskii slovar'*. 4 vols. Leningrad-Moscow, 1947–1952.
Lukina, T. A. *Boris Evgen'evich Raikov, 1880–1966*. Leningrad, 1970.
Makarov, Vasilii Nikitovich. *Okhrana prirody v SSSR*. 1st ed. Moscow: Goskul'tposvetizd, 1947.
————. *Okhrana prirody v SSSR*. 2d ed. Moscow, 1949.
————. *Zapovedniki SSSR*. Moscow: Sel'khozgiz, 1940.
Maleev, Vladimir Petrovich. *Teoreticheskie osnovy akklimatizatsii*. Leningrad: VASKhNIL, 1933.
Markgraf, Otto Vasil'evich. *Russkii zoopromyshlennyi park*. St. Petersburg, 1903.
Mazurmovich, B. N. *Vydaiushchiesia otechestvennye zoologi*. Moscow, 1960.
Miliutin, V. P., ed. *Sel'sko-khoziaistvennaia entsiklopediia*. 4 vols. Moscow, 1932–1935.
Morozov, Georgii Fedorovich. *Uchenie o lese*. St. Petersburg, 1912.
Nasimovich, Andrei Aleksandrovich, ed. *Preobrazovanie fauny pozvonochnykh nashei strany*. Moscow: MOIP, 1953.
Nasimovich, A. A., and Isakov, Iu. A., eds. *Opyt raboty i zadachi zapovednikov SSSR*. Moscow: Nauka, 1979.
Nauchno-issledovatel'skii institut monopolii vneshnei torgovli. *Ezhegodnik vneshnei torgovli za 1931 god*. Moscow-Leningrad, 1932.
Nauka i nauchnaia rabota SSSR. Moscow: Akademiia nauk SSSR, 1928.
Novikov, G. A., ed. *Ocherki po istorii ekologii*. Moscow, 1970.
Novopokrovskii, I. V. *K organizatsii stepnogo zapovednika v Donetskom okruge*. Novocherkassk, 1927.
————. *Kratkii otchet o deiatel'nosti Novocherkasskogo otdeleniia Russkogo botanicheskogo obshchestva po organizatsii na Donu stepnykh zapovednikov*. Novocherkassk, 1919.
Ob okhrane prirody. Moscow: Glavnauka, 1928.
Obshchestvo biologov-marksistov [pri Kommunisticheskoi akademii]. *Protiv mekhanisticheskogo materializma i men'shevistskogo idealizma v biologii*. Moscow, 1931.
Okhrana prirody. Moscow: Glavnauka, 1926.
Okhrana prirody. Moscow: Glavnauka, 1929.
Okhrana prirody Tsentral'no-Chernozemnoi polosy. Voronezh: VOOP, 1974.
Okhraniaite les. Agitsbornik. Moscow: Doloi negramotnost', 1925.
Ostrovitianov, K. V., ed. *Organizatsiia nauki v pervye gody sovetskoi vlasti, 1917–1925 gg.* Moscow, 1968.
Paramonov, A. A. *K biologii vykhukholi: nekotorye voprosy okhrany vykhukholi*. Moscow: Glavnauka, 1928.
Paramonov, I. V., and Korobochkin, N. P. *Nikolai Mikhailovich Fedorovskii*. Moscow: Nauka, 1979.
Pervoe desiatiletie Russkogo obshchestva pokrovitel'stva zhivotnym: Istoricheskii ocherk ego deiatel'nosti v 1865–1875 gg. St. Petersburg, 1875.
Petrov, Fedor Nikolaevich. *Shest'desiat' let v riadakh leninskoi partii. Vospominaniia*. Moscow, 1962.
Plan ustroistva zapovednogo uchastka na ostrove Moritsgolme v Kurliandii. Riga: Rizhskoe obshchestva estestvoispytatelei, 1910.
Pleskov, Vladimir Abramovich. *Oazis v stepi: Chapli—'Askania-Nova'*. Moscow, 1931.
————. *Zveno velikoi perestroiki: Stepnoi institut-zapovednik Chapli—Askania-Nova*. Moscow, 1931.
Pochemu nuzhno zashchishchat' zhivotnykh? N.p. [Khar'kov]: Khar'kovskoe obshchestvo zashchity zhivotnykh i rastenii, n.d. [c. 1926].

Pod"iapol'skii, Nikolai Nikolaevich. *Bozh'ia volia ili agronomicheskaia nauka?* Moscow: Krasnaia nov', 1924.

―――. *Chto daet priroda trudovomu narodu: Ob okhrane prirody v RSFSR.* Moscow: Doloi negramotnost', 1925.

―――. *Kolkhoznik, okhraniaite lesa!* Moscow: Sel'khozgiz, 1926.

―――. *Okhraniaite lesa!* Moscow: Novaia derevnia, 1926.

―――. *Rabochii, okhraniai prirodu!* Moscow: Glavnauka, 1925.

―――. *Rol' shkoly v dele okhrany prirody.* Moscow: Glavnauka, 1925.

―――. *V ustiakh Volgi.* Moscow, 1927.

―――, and Pod"iapol'skaia, A. *Uchastie detei i podrostkov v rabote okhrany prirody, i znachenie etoi raboty dlia sel'skogo khoziaistva.* Moscow, 1933.

Pokrovskii, Sergei Viktorovich. *Izuchai i okhraniai poleznykh zhivotnykh.* Moscow, 1930.

Prezent, Isai Izrailovich. *Biolog-materialist Zhan-Batist Lamark.* Moscow, 1960.

―――, ed. *Khrestomatiia po evoliutsionnomu ucheniiu.* Leningrad, 1935.

Pryde, Philip R. *Conservation in the Soviet Union.* Cambridge: Cambridge University Press, 1972.

Puzanov, Ivan Ivanovich. *Krymskii gosudarstvennyi zapovednik: Opisanie i putevoditel'.* Simferopol', 1928.

―――. *Po nekhozhennomu Krymu.* Moscow, 1960.

Raikov, Boris Evgen'evich. *Russkie biologi-evoliutsionisty do Darvina.* 4 vols. Moscow, 1951–1958.

Ral'tsevich, V., ed. *Materializm i empiriokrititsizm. Sbornik.* Leningrad: Kommunisticheskaia akademiia. Leningradskoe otdelenie, 1935.

Reimers, Nikolai Fedorovich, and Shtil'mark, Feliks Robertovich. *Osobo okhraniaemye prirodnye territorii.* Moscow: Mysl', 1978.

Riadkov, I. *Molodezh', okhraniai prirodu!* Maikop: VLKSM, 1928.

Rossinskii, Dmitrii Mikhailovich. *Okhrana ptits.* Moscow: VOOP, 1927.

RSFSR. Glavnoe upravlenie po zapovednikam pri Sovete narodnykh komissarov. *Polozhenie o gosudarstvennykh zapovednikakh.* Moscow, 1940.

RSFSR. Komitet po zapovednikam pri prezidiume VTsIK'a. *Polozhenie po okhrane gosudarstvennykh zapovednikov.* Moscow, 1936.

RSFSR. Narodnyi komissariat po prosveshcheniiu. *Dekrety, instruktsii i rasporiazheniia Narkomprosa po okhrane prirody.* Moscow-Leningrad: Glavnauka, 1929.

RSFSR. Narodnyi komissariat zemledeliia. *Otchet za 1924–1926 gg.* Moscow, 1926.

Ruzskii, M. *Zubr, kak vymiraiushchii predstavitel' nashei fauny.* Kazan', 1898.

Sabaneev, I. P., compiler. *Ukazatel' knig i statei okhotnich'ego i zoologicheskogo soderzhaniia.* Moscow, 1883.

Salganskii, A. A. *Zoopark "Askania-Nova": Opyt akklimatizatsii dikikh kopynykh i strausov.* Kiev, 1963.

Saushkin, Iu. G. *Velikoe preobrazovanie prirody SSSR.* Moscow, 1953.

Semenov-tian-shanskii, Andrei Petrovich. *Nashi blizhaishie zadachi na Dal'nem Vostoke.* St. Petersburg, 1908.

Semenov-tian-shanskii, Oleg Izmailovich. *Laplandskii zapovednik.* 1st ed. Foreword by German Mikhailovich Kreps. Moscow, 1937.

Severtsov, Sergei Alekseevich. *Problemy ekologii zhivotnykh.* Moscow: Akademiia nauk SSSR, 1951.

Shaposhnikov, Lev Konstantinovich. *Okhrana prirody v SSSR.* Moscow, 1961.

―――. *Primechatel'nye prirodnye landshafty SSSR i ikh okhrana.* Moscow: Nauka, 1967.

―――. *Zapovedniki sovetskogo soiuza.* Moscow, 1969.

Shchadite nashi pamiatniki prirody! Vozzvanie Rizhskogo obshchestva estestvoispytatelei. Riga, 1910. (Also published in German as *Schonet unsere Naturdenkmäler! Ein Aufruf des Naturforscher-Vereins zu Riga.*)

Shcherbakova, A. A., compiler. *Valerii Ivanovich Taliev.* Moscow, 1960.

Shlykov, G. N. *Introduktsiia rastenii.* Moscow-Leningrad, 1936.

Sidorov, S. A. *Vymiraiushchie zhivotnye.* Moscow: Moskovskoe kommunal'noe khoziaist-vo, 1928.
Silant'ev, A. A. *Kak organizovat' v Rossii okhranu poleznykh dlia sel'skogo khoziaistva zhivotnykh.* Petrograd, 1916.
———, compiler. *Okhrana zverei i ptits, poleznykh v sel'skom khoziaistve.* Petrograd, 1915.
Skalon, Vasilii Nikolaevich. *Okhraniaite prirodu!* Irkutsk, 1957.
Smolin, P. P. *Rabochii klass i okhrana prirody.* Moscow: VOOP, 1930.
Sokolov, N. P. *Protiv reaktsionnoi ideologii v sovremennoi ekologii.* Tashkent: Sredne-Aziatskii gosudarstvennyi universitet, 1931.
Sokolov, Viacheslav Davydovich. *Okhrana prirody i povyshenie urozhaia.* Moscow, 1930.
Solov'ev, Dmitrii Konstantinovich. *Okhota v SSSR.* Moscow: Vsekokhotsoiuz, 1926.
———. *Tipy organizatsii, sposobstvuiushiikhsia okhrane prirody.* No. 3 of the Occasional Papers of the Postoiannaia prirodookhranitel'naia komissiia of the Russkoe geografi-cheskoe obshchestvo. Petrograd, 1918.
Spravochnik: Na puti v Askaniiu. Genichesk, 1927.
Spravochnik po goszapovedniku "Chapli." Edited by M. N. Kolod'ko. Mariupol', 1927.
Stalin, I. V. *Sochineniia.* Vols. IX–XII. Moscow, 1949–1951.
Stanchinskii, Vladimir Vladimirovich. *Izmenchivost' organizmov i ee znachenie v evoliutsii.* Smolensk, 1927.
Stanchinskii, Vladimir Vladimirovich, and Kashkarov, Daniil Nikolaevich. *Kurs zoologii pozvonochnykh zhivotnykh.* 2d ed. Moscow, 1940.
Sukachev, Vladimir Nikolaevich. *Rastitel'nye soobshchestva: Vvedenie v fitosotsiologiiu.* Moscow-Leningrad, 1928.
Swanson, James Martin. "The Bolshevization of Scientific Societies in the Soviet Union: An Historical Analysis of the Character, Function and Legal Position of Scientific and Scientific-Technical Societies in the USSR, 1929–1936." Ph.D. dissertation, Indiana University, 1968.
Tolstov, Sergei Pavlovich. *Vvedenie v sovetskoe kraevedenie.* Moscow, 1932.
Trass, Khans Khartmutovich. *Geobotanika: istoriia i sovremennye tendentsii razvitiia.* Leningrad, 1976.
Turov, Sergei Sergeevich. *Zoologicheskii muzei Moskovskogo universiteta.* Moscow, 1956.
Uspekhi biologicheskikh nauk v SSSR za dvadtsat'-piat' let, 1917–1942 gg. Sbornik. Mos-cow, 1945.
Varsanof'eva, V. A., and Gekker, R. F. *Okhrana pamiatnikov nezhivoi prirody.* Moscow: VOOP, 1951.
Vasil'kovskii, Petr Evgen'evich. *Okhrana prirody i kraevedy.* Moscow-Leningrad, 1927.
———. *Promyslovye zhivotnye.* Moscow, 1926.
Voznesenskii, A. N., and Voloshinskii, A. A., eds. *Vneshniaia torgovlia SSSR za pervuiu piatiletku (za period s 1928 goda po 1933 god). Statisticheskii obzor.* Moscow-Leningrad, 1934.
Vserossiiskoe obshchestvo okhrany prirody. *Instruktsiia vsem iacheikam.* Moscow, 1935.
———. *Ustav VOOP.* Moscow, 1925.
———. *Ustav VOOP.* Moscow, 1933.
———. *Ustav VOOP.* Moscow, 1935.
———. Semipalatinskoe otdelenie. *Okhraniai prirodu!* Semipalatinsk, 1930.
Worster, Donald. *Nature's Economy: The Roots of Ecology.* San Francisco: Sierra Club Books, 1977.
Zapovedniki Dal'ne-Vostochnogo kraia. Sbornik. Khabarovsk, 1936.
Zapovedniki SSSR. Sbornik statei. Edited by A. I. Solov'ev. Introduction by V. N. Makarov. 2 vols. Moscow: Gosizdat geograficheskoi literatury, 1951.
Zavadovskii, Boris Mikhailovich. *Zhivaia priroda v rukakh cheloveka: Zapiski okhotnika za gormonami.* Moscow, 1935.
Zavadovskii, Mikhail Mikhailovich, and Fortunatov, Boris Konstantinovich, eds. *Askania-Nova: Stepnoi zapovednik Ukrainy. Sbornik statei.* Moscow: Priroda i kul'tura, 1924.

Zhitkov, Boris Mikhailovich. *Okhrana zhivotnykh i razvedenie pushnykh zverei.* Moscow, 1919.

Zirkle, Conway. *Evolution, Marxian Biology and the Social Scene.* Philadelphia, 1959.

Zlobina, V. I., ed. *Vospitanniki Moskovskogo universiteta—soratniki V. I. Lenina.* Moscow: Izdatel'stvo Moskovskogo universiteta, 1973.

Zykov, K. D., ed. *Geograficheskoe razmeshchenie zapovednikov v RSFSR i organizatsii ikh deiatel'nosti. Sbornik nauchnykh trudov Tsentral'noi nauchno-issledovatel'skoi laboratorii okhotnich'ego khoziaistva i zapovednikov Glavnogo upravleniia okhotnich'ego khoziaistva i zapovednikov pri Sovete ministrov RSFSR.* Moscow: TsNIL Glavokhoty RSFSR, 1981.

V. ARTICLES

Abramov, L. S., and Armand, D. L. "V. I. Lenin i okhrana prirody." *Akademiia nauk SSSR. Izvestiia. Seriia geografii,* 1970, no. 2, pp. 62–74.

"Akklimatizatsiia zhivotnykh." *Vestnik estestvennykh nauk,* 1860, no. 2, p. 42; no. 21, pp. 663–676; and no. 22, pp. 690–708.

Alekhin, Vasilii Vasil'evich. "Istoriia fitotsenologii i ee osobennosti." *Uchenye zapiski Moskovskogo gosudarstvennogo universiteta,* 1946, no. 103, pp. 85–95.

Alferov, L. A. "Krymskie lesa i osnovnoi vopros ikh sokhraneniia." *OPZD,* 1962, no. 7, pp. 25–34.

Alpatov, V. V. "Ekologiia, kak napravlenie kraevedcheskoi raboty v oblasti zoologii." *Kraevedenie,* 1923, no. 1, pp. 26–31.

———. "Ekologicheskaia laboratoriia MGU i ee rabota v 1931–1934 gg." *Uspekhi sovremennoi biolgii,* 1935, vol. 4, no. 6, pp. 533–539.

Anisov, N. V. "Volk i bor'ba s nim v goszapovednikakh." *NMZ,* 1938, no. 1, pp. 60–67.

Arkhipov, S. S. "Instruktsii dlia organizatsii zapovednogo khoziaistva." *NMZ,* 1939, no. 2, pp. 51–90.

Arsen'ev, V. A. "Akklimatizatsionnaia rabota v zapovednikakh." *NMZ,* 1948, no. 10.

Averin, V. G. "Askania-Nova." *Okhota i rybolovstvo,* 1923, no. 5–6, pp. 31–53.

Bega, F. F. "Institut sel'sko-khoziaistvennoi gibridizatsii i stepnoi akklimatizatsii zhivotnykh v Askanii-Nova: kharakter i znachenie ego rabot." *TIGA,* 1933, vol. 1, no. 1.

Belousova, L. S. "Iz istorii okhrany botanicheskikh pamiatnikov prirody v Rossii." *OPZD,* 1960, no. 6, pp. 30–38.

Blagosklonov, K. N. "Iz istorii iunnatskogo dvizheniia." *MOIP,* 1980, vol. 85, no. 1, pp. 123–128.

Bogdanov, Anatolii Petrovich. "Ob akklimatizatsii zhivotnykh." *Zhurnal sel'skogo khoziaistva,* 1856, no. 12, pp. 194–224.

Boguslavskii, G. A. "Iz istorii okhrany prirody v pervye gody sovetskoi vlasti." *Stroitel'stvo sovetskogo gosudarstva. Sbornik k 70-letiiu doktora istoricheskoi nauki professora E. B. Genkinoi,* pp. 258–272. Moscow: Nauka, 1972.

Boitsov, Leontii Vasil'evich. "O biotekhnicheskikh meropriiatiiakh v sviazi s vypuskom piatnistykh olenei v zapovednikakh." *NMZ,* 1939, no. 2, pp. 118–120.

———. "O sostoianii i perspektivnom plane nauchno-issledovatel'skoi raboty goszapovednikov na tret'e piatiletie (1938–1942) po razdelu biotekhniki i akklimatizatsii." *NMZ,* 1938, no. 1.

Borisov, V. A. "K istorii stanovleniia sovetskoi sistemy zapovednikov. Obzor." *Nauchnye osnovy okhrany prirody,* 1971, no. 1.

Borodin, Ivan Parfen'evich. "Khortitskoe obshchestvo okhranitelei prirody." *TBSIIU,* 1912, vol. 13, no. 1, pp. 24–27.

———. "O sokhranenii uchastkov rastitel'nosti, interesnykh v botaniko-geograficheskom otnoshenii." *Dnevnik dvenadtsatogo s"ezda russkikh estestvoispytatelei i vrachei v Moskve, s 28-ogo dekabria 1909 goda po 6-oe ianvaria 1910 goda.* Petrograd, 1915.

———. "Okhrana pamiatnikov prirody." *TBSIIU,* 1910, vol. 11, no. 4, pp. 297–317.

————. "Otchet o komandirovke v Bern na Konferentsii po mezhdunarodnoi okhrane prirody." *Izvestiia Akademii nauk*, Seriia shestaia, 1913, no. 7, no. 2, pp. 1065–1068.

Bugaev, I. I. "Fitosotsiologiia ili fitotsenologiia?" *EM*, 1929, no. 1, pp. 76–92.

Bukovskii, V. "K kritike osnovnykh problem i poniatii biotsenologii." *VEB*, 1935, no. 2.

————. "Puti zoologicheskikh issledovanii v zapovednikakh." *PSKh*, 1931, no. 1, pp. 8–9.

Buturlin, Sergei Aleksandrovich. "Eshche ob osvoenii chuzhezemnykh zhivotnykh." *Okhotnik*, 1928, no. 5.

————. "K faunisticheskoi konferentsii Akademii nauk SSSR." *PSKh*, 1931, no. 4–5, p. 60.

————. "Okhotnich'e delo v SSSR." *PD*, 1925, no. 1, pp. 15–20.

————. "Osvoenie chuzhezemnykh zverei." *Okhotnik*, 1928, no. 2.

Carpenter, John Richard. "Recent Russian Work on Community Ecology." *The Journal of Animal Ecology*, 1939, vol. 8, pp. 354–386.

Daiga, I. E. "Iz rabot Akademika N. F. Kashchenko po akklimatizatsii novykh rastenii." *Trudy Botanicheskogo sada Akademii nauk Ukrainskoi SSR*, 1953, no. 2, pp. 87–96.

Danilov, V. I. "K istorii organizatsii i deiatel'nosti zapovednika 'Galich'ia gora.' " *MOIP*, 1977, no. 6, pp. 151–154.

Dement'ev, G. P. "S. A. Buturlin i ego rabota po okhrane prirody: K desiatiletiiu so dnia smerti." *Okhrana prirody. Sbornik*, 1948, no. 4, pp. 99–107.

————. "V. N. Makarov." *OPZD*, 1958, no. 3, pp. 99–104.

"Den' ptits." *OP*, 1928, no. 1, pp. 16–19.

Ditmar, Boris Petrovich. "Okhrana prirody v Rossii: Istoricheskii ocherk." *OP*, 1928, no. 5, pp. 25–28.

Dolgoshov, V. "O sud'be Tsentral'nogo lesnogo zapovednika." *OP*, 1929, no. 5, pp. 148–149.

Dombrovskaia, E. "Srednerusskii zapovednik." *ITsBK*, 1929, no. 10, pp. 44–45.

Emel'ianov, A. S. "Mirovaia voina i pushnoe delo." *PD*, 1927, no. 1, pp. 3–14.

————. "Sostoianie pushnogo khoziaistva SSSR k desiatoi godovshchine oktiabrskoi revoliutsii." *PD*, 1927, no. 1, pp. 17–18.

Eremina, E. V. "Okhrana pamiatnikov prirody v Rossii i drugikh stranakh." *Priroda*, 1914, no. 7, cols. 907–908.

Fediushin, Anatolii Vladimirovich. "Voprosy okhrany prirody na pervom Vserossiiskom s"ezde po okhrane prirody 1929 g." *Okhrana prirody Sibiri i Dal'nego Vostoka*, 1962, pp. 201–205.

————. "K osnovaniiu Berezinskogo zapovednika." *Berezinskii zapovednik: Issledovaniia*, 1972, no. 2, pt. 1, pp. 3–13.

Filonov, Konstantin Pavlovich. "Dinamika chislennosti kopytnykh zhivotnykh i zapovednost'." [Thesis for degree of Doctor of Science]. *Okhotovedenie*, pp. 1–232. Moscow: TsNIL Glavokhoty RSFSR and Lesnaia promyshlennost', 1977.

————. "O zapovednosti i zapovednom rezhime." *Okhota i okhotnich'e khoziaistvo*, 1975, no. 8, pp. 18–20.

Formozov, Aleksandr Nikolaevich. "Ekologiia za 1917–1937 gg." *ZZh*, 1937, no. 5, pp. 916–949.

Fortunatov, Boris Konstantinovich. "O general'nom plane rekonstruktsii promyslovoi fauny evropeiskoi chasti RSFSR i Ukrainy." *PSKh*, 1933, vol. 6.

Ganeshin, Sergei Sergeevich. "Relikvii nashei rastitel'nosti." *Kraevedenie*, 1929, no. 6, pp. 333–341.

Gekker, R. F. "Akademik A. E. Fersman i ego rabota v VOOP." *Okhrana prirody. Sbornik*, 1948, no. 3, pp. 113–117.

Generozov, Vladimir Iakovlevich. "Ob administrativnoi organizatsii amerikanskikh zapovednikov i ikh ekonomicheskom znachenii." *Nasha okhota*, 1914, no. 14, pp. 4–11; no. 15, pp. 3–8.

Geptner, V. G. "Ob akklimatizatsii i 'rekonstruktsii' okhotnich'ei fauny." *Okhota i okhotnich'e khoziaistvo*, 1963, no. 2, pp. 21–26.

————. "Zoologicheskie izdaniia Glavnogo upravleniia po zapovednikam pri Sovete narodnykh komissarov RSFSR." *ZZh*, 1941, vol. 20, no. 4–5, pp. 659–664.

Gershkovich, N. A.; Razorenova, A. P.; and Maksimov, A. A. "Petr Petrovich Smolin." *MOIP*, 1976, vol. 81, no. 5, p. 120.

Gorokhov, V. A. "Akademik I. P. Borodin–pioner okhrany prirody: K stoletiiu so dnia ego rozhdeniia." *Okhrana prirody. Sbornik*, 1948, no. 2, pp. 42–49.

Grave, Grigorii Leonidovich. "Tsentral'nyi lesnoi zapovednik." *Trudy Tsentral'nogo lesnogo zapovednika*, 1935, no. 1, pp. 4–13.

Greben', L. K. "Askania-Nova." *Sel'sko-khoziaistvennaia entsiklopediia*, 1949, vol. 1, p. 162.

Grossman, I. "Neobkhodimo uskorit' vypusk ondatry." *PD*, 1928, no. 6–7, pp. 22–29.

Il'inskii, A. P. "Naturalizatsiia i okhrana prirody." *ITsBK*, 1929, no. 10, pp. 9–11.

Ioganzen, Bodo Germanovich. "K stoletiiu so dnia rozhdeniia N. F. Kashchenko." *Trudy Tomskogo universiteta*, 1956, vol. 142, pp. 7–22.

————. "N. F. Kashchenko—ego zhizn' i nauchnoe vozzrenie." *MOIP*, 1948, vol. 53, no. 3, pp. 79–87.

Johnson, W. Carter, and French, Norman R. "Soviet Union." Chapter 20 in Edward J. Kormondy and J. Frank McCormick, eds., *Handbook of Contemporary Developments in World Ecology*, pp. 343–383. Westport, Conn.: Greenwood Press, 1981.

"K voprosu o sovremennom polozhenii pervogo Gosudarstvennogo zapovednika imeni Kh. G. Rakovskogo (byvshego Askania-Nova)." *Priroda i okhota na Ukraine*, 1924, no. 1–2, pp. 203–258.

Kabanov, N. E. "Stalinskii plan preobrazovaniia prirody." *MOIP*, 1949, vol. 54, no. 6, pp. 69–76.

Karpov, V. V. Letter to the Editors. *OP*, 1930, no. 8–10, pp. 215–216.

Karpych, V. F. "Bor'ba za marksizm v sovetskom kraevedenii." *Vestnik Kommunisticheskoi akademii*, 1931, no. 8–9, pp. 22–44. Also in *Za marksizm v sovetskom kraevedenii*. Edited by Karpych and I. G. Klaubunovskii. Moscow-Leningrad, 1931.

Karzinkin, G. S. "Popytka prakticheskogo obosnovaniia poniatiia biotsenoza." *ZZh*, 1927, vol. 6, pp. 3–34; vol. 7, pp. 34–75.

Kashchenko, Nikolai Feofanovich. "Razvitie chelovecheskogo gospodstva nad organizovannoi prirodoi." *EG*, 1898, no. 1, pp. 1–24.

————. "Rol' akklimatizatsii v protsesse pod"ema proizvoditel'nykh sil SSSR." *Iugoklimat. Sbornik po voprosam akklimatizatsii rastenii i zhivotnykh*, 1929, pt. 7.

Kashkarov, Daniil Nikolaevich. "Ekologiia na sluzhbe sotsialisticheskogo stroitel'stva." *Trudy Sredne-Aziatskogo universiteta*, 1933, Series 8, no. 1.

————. "Moi put' k bol'shevizmu." *Sovetskaia nauka*, 1939, no. 12, pp. 133–140.

————. "Natsional'nye parki SShA." *Nauchnoe slovo*, 1929, no. 6.

————. "Sovetskaia zoo-ekologiia." *Priroda*, 1937, no. 10, pp. 212–229; 1938, no. 10, pp. 85–88.

Kertselli, S. "K voprosu ob akklimatizatsii v SSSR ondatry." *PD*, 1925, no. 6–7, pp. 9–11.

"Khronika." *IKORGO*, 1913, vol. 22, no. 1, pp. 69–75.

Kir'ianova, E. "Vsesoiuznaia faunisticheskaia konferentsiia." *Priroda*, 1932, no. 5, pp. 453–458.

Knorina, M. V. "Pamiatniki nezhivoi prirody." *OPZD*, 1960, no. 6, pp. 102–110.

"Konferentsiia direktorov nauchnykh uchrezhdenii. Sektsii po okhrane prirody." *Kraevedenie*, 1926, no. 4, p. 101.

"Koordinirovannyi plan rabot VOOP i TsBK." *OP*, 1930, no. 1, pp. 5–6.

Kosenko, I. S. "Protsess vosstanovlenii tseliny po dannym nabliudenii nad 'zakaznikom' Kubanskoi opytnoi stantsii." *Trudy Kubanskogo sel'sko-khoziaistvennogo instituta*, 1925, vol. 3.

Kozhevnikov, Grigorii Aleksandrovich. "A. P. Bogdanov." *EG*, 1896, vol. 1, no. 4.

————. "Kak vesti nauchnuiu rabotu v zapovednikakh." *OP*, 1928, no. 2, pp. 13–16.

————. "Mezhdunarodnoe soveshchanie o vsemirnoi okhrane prirody." *Ornitologicheskii vestnik*, 1913, no. 4. pp. 375–379.

————. "Nekrolog P. Sarazina." *OP*, 1929, no. 4, pp. 111–113.

————. "O neobkhodimosti ustroistva zapovednykh uchastkov dlia okhrany prirody." *TVAS*, pp. 18–27; reprinted in abridged form in *OPZD*, 1960, no. 4, pp. 90–97.

————. "O zapovednykh uchastkakh." *TVSOM*, 17-ogo–25-ogo noiabria 1909g. (Moscow, 1911) pp. 371–378.

————. "Zadachi okhrany prirody v SSSR." *OP*, 1928, no. 1, pp. 6–19.

————. "Znachenie Kosinskogo zapovednika." *Trudy Kosinskogo biologicheskoi stantsii*, 1925, no. 2, pp. i–v.

Kozlov, Petr Kuz'mich. "Askania-Nova v ee proshlom i nastoiashchem." *Russkaia starina*, 1914, vol. 158, pp. 351–371; vol. 159, pp. 19–38.

————. "Gosudarstvennyi zapovednik Askania-Nova." *Nauchnyi rabotnik*, 1928, no. 1, pp. 12–23.

————. "Sovremennoe polozhenie 'Askania-Nova.' " *Priroda*, 1919, no. 10–12, pp. 467–482.

"Kratkii obzor deiatel'nosti Vseukrainskogo obshchestva zashchity zhivotnykh i rastenii (ZhIVRAS) za 1925–1927 gg." *OP*, 1928, no. 5, pp. 28–30.

Kristof, Ladis K. D. "Francis Bacon and the Marxists: Faith in the Glorious Future of Mankind." In *Society and History: Essays in Honor of Karl August Wittfogel*, pp. 233–257. Edited by G. L. Ulmen. The Hague: Mouton, 1978.

Krylenko, N. V. "Polozhenie na kraevednom fronte." *Vestnik Kommunisticheskoi akademii*, 1932, no. 9–10, pp. 96–118.

————. "V. I. Lenin na okhote." *Okhotnich'i prostory*, 1958, no. 9, p. 13.

Kulagin, Nikolai Mikhailovich. "K voprosu o vremennom zaprete dobychi sobolia v predelakh SSSR." *OP*, 1928, no. 5, pp. 11–15.

————. "Sovremennoe polozhenie voprosa ob okhrane prirody v RSFSR." *Nauchnoe slovo*, 1928, no. 2, pp. 108–109.

Kulagin, N. M., and Kozhevnikov, G. A. "K voprosu o vsesoiuznom organe po okhrane prirody." *OP*, 1930, no. 6, pp. 122–123.

Kviatkovskii, K. " 'Nauchnye' bolota." *Varnitso*, 1931, no. 3.

————. "Nauchnye obshchestva pered sudom sovetskoi obshchestvennosti." *Varnitso*, 1931, no. 3.

Lavrenko, E. M. "Razvitie osnovnykh idei sovetskoi geobotaniki (fitotsenologii) za dvadtsat'-piat' let (1917–1942)." *Pochvovedenie*, 1943, no. 3, pp. 15–33.

Lavrov, Nikolai Petrovich. "B. M. Zhitkov i akklimatizatsiia zhivotnykh." *Okhota i okhotnich'e khoziaistvo*, 1973, no. 12, pp. 6–7.

Lavrov, N. P., and Naumov, S. P. "Rekonstruktsiia promyslovykh zverei SSSR v period stalinskikh piatiletok." *MOIP*, 1949, vol. 54, no. 6, pp. 77–93.

Levitskii, V. F. "Sel'skoe khoziaistvo Askania-Nova (Chapli) v sviazi s perspektivami orosheniia doliny Dnepra." *Puti sel'skogo khoziaistva*, 1929, no. 10, pp. 75–92.

Lindeman, Raymond Laurel. "The Trophic-Dynamic Aspect of Ecology." *Ecology*, 1942, vol. 23, no. 4, pp. 388–418.

Luchnik, V. "Bibliograficheskie zametki." *OP*, 1930, no. 9–10, pp. 223–224.

Lysenko, T. D.; Papanin, I. D.; Pozdniakov, E. B.; Varuntsian, I. S.; Prezent, I. I., and others. "P. A. Manteifel'." *Agrobiologiia*, 1960, no. 3, pp. 453–454.

Lysogorov, V. I. "Institut gibridizatsii i akklimatizatsii Askania-Nova imeni akademika M. F. Ivanova." *TIGA*, 1949, vol. 3, pp. 3–9.

Makarov, Vasilii Nikitovich. "Michurinskaia biologiia i nauchno-issledovatel'skaia rabota zapovednikov." *NMZ*, 1949, no. 13.

————. "Nashi zadachi." *PSKh*, 1931, no. 1–3, pp. 2–3.

————. "Zapovedniki." *BSE*, 1st ed., 1931, vol. 26, pp. 238–246.

————. "Zapovedniki." *BSE*, 2d ed., 1952, vol. 16, pp. 439–444.

————. "Zapovedniki SSSR." *FNT*, 1938, no. 6, pp. 63–82.

Manteifel', Petr Aleksandrovich. "Akklimatizatsiia zhivotnykh." *Sel'sko-khoziaistvennaia entsiklopediia*, 1949, vol. 1, pp. 118–120.

———. "Kondo-Sos'vinskii goszapovednik." *SK*, 1935, no. 11, pp. 68–70.

Markevich, A. P. "Sostoianie i zadachi sovetskoi ekologii zhivotnykh" *VEK, Tezisy dokladov*, pt. 3, pp. 12–15.

Markov, E. L. "Ob akklimatizatsii v Zakavkaz'e ussuriiskogo piatnistogo olenia." *PSKh*, 1931, no. 6–8, pp. 121–123.

Martynov, A. V. "Andrei Petrovich Semenov-tian-shanskii." *Priroda*, 1937, no. 4, pp. 139–144.

Medvedev, Sergei Ivanovich. "Kompleksnost' pri ekologo-biotsenologicheskikh issledovaniiakh." *PB*, 1933, vol. 1, no. 1.

Miller, E. E. "Ob okhrane pamiatnikov prirody." *Trudy Bessarabskogo obshchestva estestvoispytatelei i liubitelei estestvoznaniia*, 1911–1912, vol. 3, pp. 181–205.

Minin, N. V. "K voprosu o podrazdelenii areny zhizni." *VEB*, 1936, no. 3, pp. 61–67.

———. "O nekotorykh idealisticheskikh ucheniiakh v ekologii." *Priroda*, 1939, no. 7, pp. 30–43.

Molodchikov, A. I. "K voprosu nauchnoi organizatsii i struktury kompleksnykh zapovednikov." *PSKh*, 1932, vol. 5, pp. 10–24.

———. "Na putiakh k sovetskomu Iellostonu." *PSKh*, 1931, no. 6–8.

Nadezhdin, M. "Obshchestvo bez aktiva." *FNT*, 1933, no. 12, pp. 77–79.

Nalimov, V. P., "Sviashchennye roshchi udmurtov i mari." *OP*, 1928, no. 4, pp. 6–8.

Nasimovich, Andrei Aleksandrovich. "Akklimatizatsiia, naselenie zhivotnykh i zoogeografiia." *Issledovaniia po faune Sovetskogo soiuza. Mlekopitaiushchie. Sbornik trudov Zoologicheskogo muzeia Moskovskogo gosudarstvennogo universiteta*, 1970, vol. 13, pp. 34–50.

———. "Ekologicheskie posledstviia vkliucheniia novogo vida v materikovye biotsenozy (ondatra v Evrope)." *ZZh*, 1966, vol. 45, no. 11, pp. 1593–1598.

Nechaeva, Nina Trofimovna, and Medvedev, Sergei Ivanovich. "Pamiati V. V. Stanchinskogo (k istorii biotsenologii u SSSR)." *MOIP*, 1977, vol. 82, no. 6, pp. 109–117.

Nemilov, A. V. "Zametki uchenogo." *Varnitso*, 1930, no. 6, p. 64.

Novopokrovskii, Ivan Vasil'evich. "O sokhranenii tselinnoi stepi dlia pochvennykh i botanicheskikh nabliudenii i ob organizatsii pri opytnykh poliakh zashchitnykh uchastkov tseliny." *Trudy soveshchaniia po opytnomu delu, s 2-ogo po 5-oe maia 1911 goda v gorode Novocherkasske*. Novocherkassk, 1911.

Nurinov, Aleksandr Ageevich. "Vyshe klassovuiu bditel'nost' v nauke." *TIGA*, 1935, vol. 2.

Ognev, Sergei Ivanovich. "A. P. Semenov-tian-shanskii." *MOIP*, 1946, vol. 51, no. 3, pp. 122–127.

———. "B. M. Zhitkov (20.IX.1872-2.IV.1943)." *MOIP*, 1945, vol. 50, no. 1–2, pp. 114–122.

"Okhrana pamiatnikov prirody na Kavkaze." *IKORGO*, 1914, vol. 22, no. 1.

"Okhrana prirody na Kavkaze." *IKORGO*, 1914, vol. 22, no. 3, pp. 315–317.

"Opyta Izidora Zheffrua-Sant-Ilera nad akklimatizatsiei zhivotnykh." *Otechestvennye zapiski*, n.d., vol. 55, pt. 8, p. 167.

"Ot Postoiannoi prirodookhranitel'noi komissii pri Imperatorskom Russkom geograficheskom obshchestve." *Lesnoi zhurnal*, 1914, no. 4, pp. 725–730.

"Ot Postoiannoi prirodookhranitel'noi komissii pri Russkom geograficheskom obshchestve." *Penzenskoe obshchestvo liubitelei estestvoznaniia i kraevedeniia. Materialy*, 1918, no. 3–4, pp. 274–276.

"P. A. Manteifel'." *Okhota i okhotnich'ego khoziaistvo*, 1982, no. 7, pp. 3–6.

Pachoskii, Iosif Konradovich. "Sotsial'nyi printsip v rastitel'nom tsarstve." *Zhurnal Russkogo botanicheskogo obshchestva*, 1925, vol. 10, no. 1–2, pp. 121–132.

———. "Po povodu stat'i prof. V. V. Alekhina 'Fitosotsiologiia i ee poslednie uspekhi u nas i na Zapade.' " *Zhurnal Russkogo botanicheskogo obshchestva pri Akademii nauk SSSR*, 1926, vol. 11, no. 1–2, pp. 219–224.

Paul, Diane. "Marxism, Darwinism, and the Theory of the Two Sciences." *Marxist Perspectives*, Spring 1979, pp. 116–143.

"Pervyi Vsesoiuznyi s"ezd po okhrane prirody." *FNT*, 1932, no. 7–8, p. 147.

Petrov, Fedor Nikolaevich. [Speech to the Third Kraeved Conference, 12 December 1927.] *ITsBK*, 1928, no. 1, pp. 9–17.

———. "Dumaia o potomkakh." *Ogonek*, 1960, no. 41, pp. 10–11.

———. "K voprosu o planovoi organizatsii nauchno-issledovatel'skoi raboty SSSR." *Nauchnyi rabotnik*, 1927, no. 12, pp. 8–15.

———. "Vsesoiuznaia konferentsiia Glavnauk." *Nauchnyi rabotnik*, 1926, no. 2, pp. 12–16.

Petrov, S. A. "Ob okhrane prirody." *ESS*, 1920, no. 3–5, pp. 29–34.

Pinkevich, A. P. "Predmet sovetskogo kraevedeniia." *SK*, 1930, no. 1–2, pp. 8–21.

Pod"iapol'skii, Nikolai Nikolaevich. "Eshche o znachenii devstvennykh zemel' dlia sel'-skogo khoziaistva." *PSKh*, 1931, no. 9–10, p. 209.

———. "Industrializatsiia sel'skogo khoziaistva i ocherednye zadachi okhrany prirody." *OP*, 1930, no. 3, pp. 49–50.

———. "Vladimir Il'ich i okhrana prirody." *OP*, 1929, no. 2, pp. 35–38.

Poplavskaia, G. I. "Krymskii gosudarstvennyi zapovednik po okhrane prirody." *Priroda*, 1927, no. 2, pp. 110–116.

Potemkin, Mikhail Petrovich. "Fridrikh Engel's ob okhrane prirody." *ITsBK*, 1929, no. 10, pp. 5–6.

———. "Kraevedenie i okhrana prirody." *ITsBK*, 1928, no. 11.

———. "Nado ispravit' politicheskie oshibki." *SK*, 1932, no. 4, pp. 9–10.

———. "Okhrana prirody i sotsialisticheskoe stroitel'stvo." *OP*, 1929, no. 1, pp. 3–5.

———. "Vserossiiskii s"ezd deiatelei po okhrane prirody." *ITsBK*, 1929, no. 10, pp. 1–4.

———. [Speech to the TsBK.] *ITsBK*, 1928, no. 9, pp. 3–5.

"Predstavliaiut li parka dlia zashchity pamiatnikov prirody opasnost' dlia lesovodstva?" *EG*, 1911, no. 6, pp. 85–86.

Prezent, Isai Izrailovich. "O 'chistoi nauke' i vdumchivo-dinamicheskoi ee zashchite." *Iarovizatsiia*, 1936, no. 6 (9), pp. 25–52.

———. "Protiv vredneishei 'filosofii agronomii.' " *PZM*, 1934, no. 3, pp. 198–202.

———. "Uchenie Lenina o krizise estestvoznaniia i krizise burzhuaznoi biologicheskoi nauki." In *Materializm i empiriokrititsizm. Sbornik.* Edited by V. Ral'tsevich. Leningrad, 1935.

———. "Zakon edinstva organizma i uslovii sushchestvovaniia." *VEK*, pt. 3, pp. 21–23.

Puzanov, Ivan Ivanovich. "Okhrana prirody v krymu." *PSKh*, 1932, vol. 5, pp. 25–38.

Reimers, Nikolai Fedorovich, and Shtil'mark, Feliks Robertovich. "Etalony prirody." *Chelovek i priroda*, 1973, no. 3, pp. 7–63.

Rezvoi, P. K. "K opredeleniiu poniatiia 'biotsenoz'." *Russkii gidrobiologicheskii zhurnal*, 1924, vol. 3, no. 8–10.

Ryzhkova, E. V. "Akademik Isai Izrailovich Prezent." *Vestnik Leningradskogo gosudarstvennogo universiteta*, 1948, no. 10, pp. 98–101.

Savich, Vladimir Mikhailovich. "Lesnye zakazniki i ikh gosudarstvennoe znachenie." *Vestnik Tiflisskogo botanicheskogo sada*, 1910, no. 18, pp. 40–44.

Semenov-tian-shanskii, Andrei Petrovich. "Eshche k voprosu o zapovednikakh russkoi prirody." *Novoe vremia*, 24 May (6 June) 1914, no. 13720, p. 13.

———. "K voprosu o zapovednikakh nashei prirody." *Novoe vremia*, 20 April (3 May) 1914, no. 13686, p. 5.

———. "Liubozantel'noe i berezhlivoe otnoshenie k svobodnoi prirode—odna iz vazhneishikh zadach narodnogo vospitaniia. *Sbornik programm shkol'noi nabliudenii nad prirodoi.* Edited by B. F. Glushkov. Petrograd, 1922.

———. "Muzei tsentral'nye i oblastnye i ikh vzaimootnosheniia." *Nauchnye izvestiia Akadtsentra Narkomprosa*, 1922, *Sbornik*, no. 4.

———. "O priiutakh prirody i ikh znachenii v srednei Rossii." *Novoe vremia*, 23 May (5 June) 1911, no. 12641.

———. "Svobodnaia priroda, kak velikii zhivoi muzei, trebuet neotlozhnykh mer ograzhdeniia." *Priroda*, 1919, no. 4–6, cols. 199–216.

Semenov-tian-shanskii, Veniamin Petrovich. "Geograficheskoe izuchenie Sovetskogo soiuza." In *Desiat' let sovetskoi nauki. Sbornik*. Edited by Fedor Nikolaevich Petrov. Moscow-Leningrad, 1927.

———. "Zapovedniki i zakazniki SSSR." *ITsBK*, 1928, no. 3, pp. 5–6.

Sepp, E. K. "Neobkhodimo reorganizovat' nauchnye obshchestva." *Varnitso*, 1930, no. 1 (12).

Serebrennikov, Ippolit. "Okhrana pamiatnikov prirody i Sibir'." *Lesnoi zhurnal*, 1914, no. 6–7, pp. 1076–1081.

Severtsov, Sergei Alekseevich. "Darvinizm i ekologiia." *ZZh*, 1937, vol. 16, no. 4, pp. 591–613.

———. "O deiatel'nosti Goskomiteta po okhrane prirody." *OP*, 1929, no. 1, p. 27.

———. "O mezhduvedomstvennykh komissiiakh po okhrane prirody." *OP*, 1928, no. 1, pp. 24–27.

———. "O repressivnykh merakh, primeniaemykh v nastoiashchee vremia k narushiteliam zakonov ob okhrane prirody i okhoty." *OP*, 1929, no. 5, pp. 150–152.

———. "O zapovednikakh i ob okhrane prirody v RSFSR." *PD*, 1929, no. 7, pp. 35–40.

———. "Ob issledovaniiakh biologii razmnozheniia v zapovednikakh." *PSKh*, 1931, no. 6–8, pp. 142–148.

———. "Okhrana prirody v RSFSR." In *Pervaia otchetnaia vystavka Narkomprosa*, pp. 32–38. Moscow, 1925.

———. "Zapovedniki SSSR." *OP*, 1929, no. 2, pp. 48–52; no. 3, pp. 93–96; and no. 4, pp. 104–107.

Shalyt, Mikhail Solomonovich. "Zakony konstantnosti i minimal'nyi areal v stepiakh SSSR." *SB*, 1935, no. 1, pp. 8–36.

Shapiro, D. S. "Biotsenologiia na sluzhbe sotsialisticheskogo stroitel'stva." *PB*, 1933, vol. 1, no. 1, pp. 12–19.

Shaposhnikov, Kh. G. "Kavkazskii gosudarstvennyi zapovednik." *OP*, 1928, no. 1, pp. 11–15; no. 2, pp. 19–21; and no. 6.

Shaposhnikov, L. K. "Akademiia nauk i okhrana prirody." *OPZD*, 1956, no. 1, pp. 117–128.

———. "Razvitie nauchnykh issledovanii po okhrane prirody za piat'desiat' let obrazovaniia SSSR." *Okhrana prirody i landshaft*, pp. 3–23. Tallinn, 1973.

Shaposhnikov, L. K., and Borisov, V. "Pervye meropriiatiia sovetskogo gosudarstva po okhrane prirody." *OPZD*, 1958, no. 3, pp. 93–98.

Shaposhnikov, L. V. "Akklimatizatsiia pushnykh zverei v sviazi s voprosami sokhraneniia i obogashcheniia fauny SSSR." *OPZD*, 1960, no. 4, pp. 37–51.

———. "Akklimatizatsiia pushnykh zverei v SSSR." *ZZh*, 1933, vol. 17, no. 5, pp. 439–460.

———. "Anatolii Petrovich Bogdanov i akklimatizatsiia zhivotnykh (k istorii voprosa ob akklimatizatsii zhivotnykh v Rossii)." *MOIP*, 1947, vol. 52, pp. 95–103.

———. "K voprosu o vypuske rechnogo bobra v Tsentral'nom lesnom zapovednike." *Trudy Tsentral'nogo lesnogo zapovednika*, 1935, vol. 1, pp. 149–156.

Shaposhnikov, L. V., and Shaposhnikov, F. D. "O sovmestnom obitanii vykhukholi, ondatry i rechnogo bobra." *ZZh*, 1949, vol. 28, no. 4, pp. 373–376.

Sharleman', Nikolai Vasil'evich. "Poslednye dni evropeiskogo zubra." *BKhOLP*, 1917, no. 1, pp. 12–17.

Shillinger, Frants Frantsevich. "Eshche o vsesoiuznom organe po okhrane prirody." *OP*, 1930, no. 8–10, p. 179.

———. "F. Engel's i V. I. Lenin ob okhrane prirody." *OP*, 1930, no. 5, pp. 98–99.

————. "Krymskii poluostrov, ego rol' i znachenie v SSSR." In *Krymskii poluostrov, ego rol' i znachenie v SSSR. Sbornik*, pp. 15–129. Edited by V. N. Makarov. Moscow: Kooperativnoe izdatel'stvo "Zhizn' i znanie", 1935.

————. "Losi i proekt Muromskogo zapovednika." *OP*, 1928, no. 2.

Shitikova, L. K. "*Priroda* ob okhrane prirody." *Priroda*, 1978, no. 8, pp. 69–72.

Shtil'mark, Feliks Robertovich. "Formirovanie seti zapovednikov na territorii RSFSR (istoriia i perspektivy)." *MOIP*, 1974, vol. 79, no. 2, pp. 142–151.

————. "F. F. Shillinger." *Okhota i okhotnich'e khoziaistvo*, 1977, no. 5, pp. 26–27.

————. "Razvitie zapovednogo dela posle Oktiabrskoi revoliutsii." In *Opyt raboty i zadachi zapovednikov SSSR*, pp. 23–37. Edited by A. A. Nasimovich and Iu. A. Isakov. Moscow: Nauka, 1979.

————. "Vasilii Nikitich Makarov i ego rol' v razvitii zapovednogo dela (k dvadtsatiletiiu so dnia smerti)." *MOIP*, 1978, vol. 83, no. 5, pp. 143–146.

Silant'ev, A. A. "Zhivotnye, preimushchestvenno zveri i ptitsy, poleznye v sel'skom khoziaistve." In *Ezhegodnik Departamenta zemledeliia za 1912 god*, pp. 651–675. St. Petersburg, 1913.

Siuzev, Pavel Vasil'evich. "Okhrana pamiatnikov prirody." *Zapiski Ural'skogo obshchestva liubitelei estestvoznaniia*, 1911, vol. 31, no. 1, pp. 82–85.

Skachko, A. N. "Nekrolog P. G. Smidovicha." *Sovetskii sever*, 1935, no. 3–4, pp. 6–25.

Skalon, V. N. "Sushchnost' biotekhniki." *Biologicheskie nauki*, 1971, no. 1, pp. 165–175.

Skoptsov, V. N. "The Desman and the Musk-Rat." *Oryx*, 1967 (April), pp. 54–55.

Smidovich, Petr Germogenovich. [Speech to the Third Kraeved Conference.] *ITsBK*, 1928, no. 1, pp. 3–5.

Solov'ev, Dmitrii Konstantinovich. "Zapovedniki i ikh zadachi." *Nasha okhota*, 1917, bk. 6, pp. 14–24.

Sosnovskii, D. I. "Materialy k voprosu ob okhrane pamiatnikov prirody na Kavkaze." *IKORGO*, 1914, vol. 22, no. 3, pp. 240–255.

Stanchinskii, Vladimir Vladimirovich. "Chapli (Askania-Nova)." *BSE*, 1st ed., vol. 61, pp. 54–60. Moscow, 1934.

————. "Ekologicheskoe napravlenie v izuchenii biotsenozov travianistykh assotsiatsii." *ZhEB*, 1931, vol. 1, no. 1, pp. 133–137.

————. "K ponimaniiu biotsenoza." *PB*, 1933, vol. 1, no. 1.

————. "O nekotorykh osnovnykh poniatiiakh zoologii v svete sovremennoi ekologii." *VSZAG*, pp. 42–43.

————. "O znachenii massy vidovogo veshchestva v dinamicheskom ravnovesii biotsenozov." *ZhEB*, 1931, vol. 1, no. 1, pp. 88–94.

————. "Predislovie." *PB*, 1933, vol. 1, no. 1.

————. "Sukhoputnye soobshchestva zhivotnykh i metody ikh izucheniia." *VSZAG*, pp. 64–66.

————. "Teoreticheskie osnovy akklimatizatsii zhivotnykh: zadachi, puti i metody akklimatizatsii zhivotnykh." *TIGA*, 1933, vol. 1, no. 1, pp. 33–66.

————. "Zadachi, soderzhanie, organizatsiia i metody kompleksnykh issledovanii v gosudarstvennykh zapovednikakh." *NMZ*, 1938, no. 1, pp. 28–50.

Stanchinskii, V. V., and Radionova, T. V. "K ustanovleniiu biotsenoticheskikh poniatii i biotsenogicheskoi terminologii." *PB*, 1933, vol. 1, no. 1.

Sukachev, Vladimir Nikolaevich. "Iz istorii vozniknoveniia i razvitiia sovetskoi fitotsenologii." *Annaly biologii*, 1959, vol. 1, pp. 112–119.

————. "O napravlenii i soderzhanii botanicheskikh rabot v zapovednikakh." *SB*, 1936, no. 3.

————. "Pamiati Valeriia Ivanovicha Talieva (1872–1932)." *SB*, 1933, no. 5, pp. 148–152.

————. "Sorok let sovetskoi geobotaniki." *MOIP*, 1980, vol. 85, no. 3, pp. 13–24.

Sushkin, P. P. "Natsional'nye parki i okhrana prirody v SShA." *Nauchnyi rabotnik*, 1927, no. 4, pp. 70–84; no. 5, pp. 112–124.

Sytin, V. A. "Na dispute ob ondatre." *Severnaia Aziia*, 1928, no. 1, p. 78.

Taliev, Valerii Ivanovich. "Da zdravstvuet novaia, svobodnaia Rossiia!" *BKhOLP*, 1917, no. 1, pp. 65–68.

———. "O dukhe tvorchestva." *BKhOLP*, 1916, no. 1–2, pp. 68–74.

———. "Okhrana mestnoi prirody kak nauchnaia i obshchestvennaia zadacha kraevedeniia." In *Voprosy kraevedeniia. Sbornik dokladov, sdelannykh na Vserossiiskoi konferentsii nauchnykh obshchestv po izucheniiu mestnogo kraia v Moskve v dekabre 1921 goda sozvannoi Akademicheskim tsentrom*. Edited by Vladimir Vladimirovich Bogdanov. Moscow: Tsentral'noe biuro kraevedeniia pri Rossiiskoi Akademii nauk, 1923.

———. "Okhrana prirody." *Priroda*, 1917, no. 11–12, cols. 1161–1164.

———. "Ot Khar'kovskogo obshchestva liubitelei prirody." *Lesnoi zhurnal*, 1917, vol. 47, no. 7–8, pp. 558–561.

———. "Sokhranenie pamiatnikov prirody." *EG*, 1910, vol. 15, no. 5, pp. 1–7.

Teodorovich, Adol'f Adol'fovich. "Problema urozhainosti i okhrana prirody." *OP*, 1930, no. 1, p. 3.

Timonov, Vsevolod Evgen'evich. "Okhrana prirody pri inzhenernykh rabotakh." *Priroda*, 1922, no. 1–2, cols. 72–86.

Tsinzerling, Iu. D. "Pervaia proizvodstvennaia konferentsiia geobotanikov i floristov, 25-ogo fevralia po 2-oe marta 1931 goda." *SB*, 1933, no. 1, p. 72.

Turov, Sergei Sergeevich. "K voprosu o Barguzinskom sobolinnom zapovednike (otchet o poezdke letom 1922 goda)." *IVSORGO*, 1923, vol. 46, no. 2.

———. "V. N. Makarov." *OP. Sbornik*, 1948, no. 2, pp. 5–12.

Uglitskikh, A. N. "Istoricheskii ocherk lesoustroistva v Krymu." In *Akademiia nauk SSSR. Komissiia po izucheniiu estestvennykh proizvoditel'nykh sil soiuza. Materialy*, 1928, no. 2. *Les, ego izuchenie i ispol'zovanie*, pp. 60–88. Edited by A. A. Grigor'ev and S. N. Nedrigailov. Leningrad, 1928.

Vangengeim, Aleksei Feodoseevich. "Kraevedenie i sotsialisticheskoe stroitel'stvo." *Sotsialisticheskoe stroitel'stvo*, 1930, no. 7 (48), pp. 60–68.

Vasil'ev, T., and Karpych, V. "Kraevedenie i turizm—na sluzhbe sotsialisticheskogo stroitel'stva." *Pravda*, 17 September 1931, no. 257 (5062), p. 3.

Vasil'kovskii, A. P. "Literatura po okhrane prirody (obzor)." *ITsBK*, 1929, no. 10, pp. 29–36.

———, compiler. "Perechen' uchastkov i otdel'nykh predmetov prirody zasluzhivaiushchikh okhrany." *Kraevedenie*, 1929, no. 6, pp. 362–378.

Vasil'kovskii, Petr Evgen'evich. "Nazrevshii vopros." *V masterskoi prirody*, 1922, no. 2.

———. "Rol' kraevedov v okhrane prirody i pamiatnikov kul'tury." *Kraevedenie*, 1929, no. 6, pp. 305–310.

Veitsman, Kh. S. "K sozdaniiu akklimatizatsionnogo zapovednika 'Sau-Dombai' v Teberdinskom ushchel'e." *PSKh*, 1934, vol. 7, pp. 107–118.

———. "Za michurinskuiu tematiku v zapovednikakh." *NMZ*, 1940, no. 7, pp. 108–110.

———. "Zapovednik budushchego." *PSKh*, 1934, vol. 7, pp. 105–107.

Vernadskii, Vladimir Ivanovich. "Ocherednaia zadacha v izuchenii proizvoditel'nykh sil." *Nauchnyi rabotnik*, 1926, no. 7–8, pp. 3–4.

Vinberg, G. G. "K izucheniiu produktivnosti vodoemov." *NMZ*, 1939, no. 4, pp. 39–51.

Vorob'ev, Konstantin Aleksandrovich. "Astrakhanskii gosudarstvennyi zapovednik v del'te Volgi." *Priroda*, 1929, no. 6, cols. 551–558.

"Za bol'shevistskuiu bditel'nost' v kraevedenii." *SK*, 1932, no. 1, pp. 7–17.

Zabelin, Konstantin Alekseevich. "Po povodu zapovednikov." *Nasha okhota*, 1917, bk. 7, pp. 17–28.

Zalesskii, K. M. "Zapovednaia step' F. E. Fal'ts-Feina." *BKhOLP*, 1915, no. 5, pp. 1–16.

Zavadovskii, Mikhail Mikhailovich. "Akklimatizatsiia." *BSE*, 1st ed., vol. 1, cols. 807–814. Moscow, 1926.

Zhitkov, Boris Mikhailovich. "Biologicheskie osnovy akklimatizatsii zhivotnykh." *Boets-okhotnik*, 1934, no. 6, pp. 20–26.

———. "Ob itogakh rabot Tsentral'noi biologicheskoi okhotnich'e-promyslovoi stantsii v

Pogono-Losinom ostrove za desiatiletie 1922–1932 gody." *Sovetskii sever*, 1932, no. 4, pp. 41–52.

————. "Ondatra i vozmozhnost' ee rasprostraneniia na Sibirskom severe." *PD*, 1925, no. 3, pp. 29–34.

————. "Raboty Biologicheskoi stantsii TsLOS Narkomzema." *PD*, 1928, no. 6–7, pp. 54–60.

Zibel', V. "Liubov' k prirode i razvitie etogo chuvstva v shkole." *EG*, 1900, no. 7, pp. 51–59.

Zile, Zigurds L. "Lenin's Contribution to Law: The Case of Protection and Preservation of the Natural Environment." In *Lenin and Leninism: State, Law and Society*, pp. 83–100. Edited by Bernard W. Eissenstat. Lexington, Mass.: D.C. Heath, 1971.

INDEX

Academy of Sciences: Lenin, 23; Cultural Revolution, 124–25
Adams, C. C.: published Kashkarov in English, 164
Agriculture, People's Commissariat of. *See* Narkomzem
Alekhin, V. V.: development of Russian ecological theory, 66; on steppe preservation, 91
All-Russian Society for Conservation (VOOP): establishment and goals, 47–50; aesthetic tendency in 1929, 87–88; opposition to Five-Year Plan, 123; TsBK and Goskomitet, 136; Cultural Revolution, 141–46; VSNKh's forest policy, 150; 1933 Congress, 210; after 1933 Congress, 226–27; membership, 274n
Alpatov, V. V.: ecology and university curricula, 66; criticized by Prezent, 222
Anuchin, D. N.: influenced by Sarasin, 18
Arshinov, V. V.: VOOP, 48
Askania-Nova: establishment, 16; threatened during Revolution, 20; conservation efforts of Provisional Government, 22; scientific research, 70–71, 79, 82; history of reserve, 71; conflict over administration, 71–78; liquidation of Scientific Steppe Institute, 189–93; debate at 1933 Congress, 199–203. *See also* Stanchinskii, V. V.; *Zapovednik*
Averin, V. G.: administration of Askania-Nova, 76, 78; on justification of *zapovedniki,* 92

Bakh, A. N.: Varnitso and anti-intellectualism, 134
Balandin, V. N.: local-lore movement and conservation, 137
Bega, F. F.: on research at Askania-Nova, 191, 192, 193; on *zapovedniki* and Askania-Nova at 1933 Congress, 196, 199, 201
Beklemishev, V. N.: development of Russian ecological theory, 66; criticized by Bukovskii, 213, 214
Biocenosis: defined, x
Biotechnics: defined, 262n
Bloshenko, E. G.: VOOP, 47
Bogdanov, M. N.: influence on Lenin, 23
Bolkovitianov, V. D.: supported Prezent, 184
Borodin, I. P.: aesthetic-ethical approach to conservation, 12, 229; supported creation of *zapovedniki,* 16; Permanent Conservation Commission, 16, 17; influenced by Sarasin, 17–18; withdrawal from activism, 38
Brauner, A. A.: administration of Askania-Nova, 72, 73
Brodskii, A. L.: view of nature and *zapovedniki,* 70
Bubnov, A. S.: VOOP and Cultural Revolution, 141
Bugaev, I. I.: on phytosociology, 127–28

Bukovskii, V.: development of Russian ecological theory, 165; modified position in response to political pressure, 213–14; compared to Stanchinskii, 215
Bulankin, I. N.: defended *zapovedniki* at 1933 Congress, 198; utilitarian view and Askania-Nova, 200–201; academic career, 284n
Buturlin, S. A.: VOOP, 47; on acclimatization of muskrat, 173

Catherine the Great: hunting legislation, 7
Central Bureau for the Study of Local Lore (TsBK): support for conservation, 45–46; VOOP, 49, 136, 140; Cultural Revolution, 137–40
Chekhov, A.: on deforestation, 9
Clements, F.: compared to Morozov, 64
Commissariat of Agriculture. *See* Narkomzem
Commissariat of Education. *See* Narkompros
Communist Academy: conflict during Cultural Revolution, 5; debate on dialectical structure of nature, 126, 127, 128–29; local-lore movement, 136; TsBK and Cultural Revolution, 138–39; Mendelian genetics, 175
Conservation: problem of definition, viii–ix
Conwentz, H.: conservation movement in Prussia, 11; influence on Borodin, 230
Cooper, W. S.: on ecological succession, viii

Darwin, C.: cited by Kozhevnikov on predators, 15; cited by Prezent, 220
Demchinskii, B.: attacked by Prezent, 212
Dergunov, N. I.: on acclimatization of exotic fauna, 174
Ditmar, B. P.: VOOP, 47
Dits, V. V.: on predators, 10, 257n
Diunin, A. G.: scientific research and *zapovedniki,* 60; Kozhevnikov on ecological management of *zapovedniki,* 97
Dmitriev, A. M.: endorsed research of Troitskii, 167
Dokuchaev, V. V.: scientific approach to conservation, 12–13; private preservation initiatives, 16

Education, People's Commissariat of. *See* Narkompros
Eitingen, G. R.: Goskomitet, 57; academic career, 264n
Elenkin, A. A.: disputed community ecology, 186, 187; criticized by Bukovskii, 213–14
Elton, C.: Stanchinskii and ecological theory, 80
Engels, F.: Marxian view of nature, 5; Teodorovich, 122; Makarov, 195; Demchinskii, 212; Prezent, 213; Stanchinskii, 215

DATE DUE